"THE RISKIEST THING I DO"

A MEMOIR OF FLYING, FAMILY, AND SELF-DISCOVERY

GOODBYE, PAPA GOLF

CHIP BEARDEN

2023

GREENSMITH HOUSE
PUBLICATIONS

Experts say our brains compress memories to save space, then reconstruct them as needed, often filling in the gaps imperfectly. Recall can also be altered by repression (blocking painful memories), denial (rejecting the intolerable), and rationalization (illogical justification). It's amazing we remember anything more than a few minutes back.

I tried. But I also cross-checked where possible using calendars; datebooks; photos; logbooks; notes; publications; emails; discussions; social media; and a diary my father kept on and off for 40 years that no one knew of until a few months ago. I apologize for any errors that remain.

This is not a "docudrama." The characters are real. There are no "composite" characters, though I changed several names to protect the privacy of friends (and of one pilot who annoyed me).

I don't have recordings of conversations (despite living through the Nixon presidency) so I recreated dialogue to reflect what I think people said.

Unlike my father, I never kept a diary. So my **"Journal Entries"** are my attempt to relate events with the immediacy and voice I would have used then. Speaking of voice, at one point I replaced the occasional profanity in the book with euphemisms. There wasn't much, and I masked most impolite words with asterisks because I didn't want to offend anyone. Then I changed my mind. The revised text just didn't sound like me at different points in my life. A memoir should reflect reality as much as possible.

About swearing, one thing you won't find is careless or disrespectful misuse of God's name. This may seem quaint to some, but I grew up with the Third Commandment. So OMG translates to "oh my gosh" in my world. Does this make sense? With religion, who knows? I'm hypocritical because I've violated other Commandments. I haven't murdered anyone (just to reassure you), but I may have told the occasional harmless lie (though none in this book!) And running most of my marathons on Sundays hardly constitutes resting on the Sabbath. But this is all part of who I am—and it's my memoir.

CHIP BEARDEN

* * * * * *

Cover design by DLab™. Edited glider image on front cover from Condor Soaring Simulator for PC, www.condorsoaring.com. Condor—with state-of-the-art graphics, sounds, and control feedback plus VR capability—provides perhaps the closest experience to flying a glider on the ground. Image of Joseph N. Bearden Jr. on the back cover by Virgil Jones, from his estate courtesy of Lee Jarrard. Photo of author on back cover by Christina Bearden. Interior photos by author or family members unless otherwise credited.

ISBN: 979-8-9872740-0-2

https://chipbearden.com

Email: chip@chipbearden.com

Published by Greensmith House Publishing, Boonton Township, New Jersey

Chapters

INTRODUCTION

G OOD AUTHORS GET INSIDE OUR HEADS. They don't know us, of course. We're just anonymous readers. And we don't really know them, even if we've devoured everything they've written, stalked them on social media, and attended a book signing. We are two people linked solely by the purchase of a book. But it doesn't matter. We are addicted to the way we see through their eyes, what they feel when they write, the sounds they hear in their ears. It's as if we are sitting down with a close friend who is speaking *directly* to us as they share their special insights and understanding of our lives.

That was my reaction reading *Into Thin Air,* Jon Krakauer's gripping account of the 1996 tragedy on Mount Everest, and one of my favorite books.

"I had always known that climbing mountains was a high-risk pursuit. I accepted that danger from a hundred other trifling diversions. It was titillating to brush up against the enigma of mortality, to steal a glimpse across its forbidden frontier. Climbing was a magnificent activity, I firmly believed, not in spite of the inherent perils, but precisely because of them.

"Until I visited the Himalaya, however, I had never actually seen death at close range. Hell, before I went to Everest, I had never even been to a funeral. Mortality had remained a conveniently hypothetical concept, an idea to ponder in the abstract. Sooner or later the divestiture of such a privileged innocence was inevitable, but when it finally happened the shock was magnified by the sheer superfluity of the carnage."[1]

I stopped cold when I read it. "That's it exactly! Jon Krakauer gets it. It's more than these profound words. He *really* understands what it feels like when people you know start to die."

I haven't climbed Everest and never will. What resonated with me was the author's eloquent summation of the seductive appeal of risk in our lives; the casual way we dismiss its danger as too ephemeral to warrant thoughtful consideration; and the anguish that consumes us when life spirals out of control, and we are cast adrift in a world less tempered by idyllic notions of romance.

Apart from climbing, there's one other difference between us. Mr. Krakauer suffered his painful epiphany involving eight friends who died in a single two-day period high on the world's tallest peak in Nepal. Mine encompassed 20 pilots lost over 40 years in the skies halfway around the world.

---

[1] Krakauer, Jon. *Into Thin Air* (New York: Anchor Books, 1997)

PREFACE: RETURN TO THE LAKE

I T'S BEEN THIRTY YEARS since I swerved onto the exit ramp that morning. I'm not sure why I did. It was an impulse. I'd shot by that exit on dozens of trips over the years and never once lifted my foot from the accelerator. The timing was never right. The timing was never right until that day.

Journal Entry: May 14, 1992 (Interstate 71, Southwestern Ohio)

I've been on the road an hour as I make my way northeast, with nine more hours of driving ahead. The landscape outside the car windows is unchanging, receding to the horizon in every direction in the warm morning glow, a flat, endless, orderly expanse of cultivated fields, punctuated here and there by trees, farm buildings, and billboards.

I've made this drive from Cincinnati across Ohio, Pennsylvania, and New Jersey to my home west of New York City myriad times in both directions. It's tedious. But this two-hour stretch between Cincinnati and Columbus is the worst. Whether at night (when there's nothing to see) or in daylight hours (when there's nothing to see), my eyelids are always heavy. This morning, I stifle a yawn, wishing I'd had another cup of tea before I left. Then, sensing the need for heightened awareness, I stiffen in my seat and lean forward, peering through the windshield.

"Did I miss it?"

Sunrise was three hours ago, so the sun is already well above the horizon, splashing into the car at an angle and causing my eyes to tighten despite my aviator sunglasses. No, there it is, the small green sign with four short words in white letters. I slump back in my seat in relief, the air conditioning pushing out cool, dry air from the vents in the dash as we hustle along on Interstate 71 at 70 mph.

"Someday." That's what I say every time I pass by this exit. My mind wanders as I reflect on what lies beyond. It's not fear inhibiting me from making a detour. I'm just not sure what I'll find. It's a trip I should make alone, and my wife is usually with me. Not this time, though.

"Why not?" I ask, rolling my shoulders back. "If not now, when?"

Then the reassuring clincher: "Besides, no one will ever know."

Braking for the exit, I coast up the ramp and pause at the top, the engine ticking over. I have second thoughts. "Do I *really* want to do this?"

Then I turn right on the local road and head across farm country. It's eight miles to the turnoff for Deer Creek State Park. As I motor down Yankeetown Pike along the tree line, I feel a hazy sense of *déjà vu.* This is not an illusion, though. I have traveled this road before—but it's been a long time.

The park office isn't where I recall. Fortunately, we men have an innate sense of direction, so after orienting myself (i.e., I backtrack to the large map at the park entrance), I locate it two miles from the old building.

The office may be new, but the clerk, an older woman, has been around for a while. She remembers the day. The ranger on duty is closer to my age, and he remembers it, too. Both give me odd looks when I explain who I am and why I've come. The ranger hesitates, then walks over to a file cabinet, and returns. Without saying a word, he lays a Polaroid photograph on the counter, watching my face. Then another one. Then more. Seven in all.

I freeze, my mouth open in shock: "Holy s**t!" I nearly blurt, impolite and flustered. I didn't see this coming. I'm not surprised someone took official photos that day. There's a protocol for accident scenes. But I've never seen these before. I didn't even know they existed.

Calming, I arrange them with reverence, touching each one by its yellowed edges. The photographer had circled the site, squeezing off shots from different points of the compass with forensic diligence at a respectful distance. On only one shot did he step in for a closeup.

No one speaks. I stand there, head bowed, face impassive, scrutinizing scenes from 12 years earlier. I'll be 41 in a few weeks, so I was in my late 20s then. I was hardly a kid, but I'm not the same person now.

The prints resemble faded pictures in an old family album from a childhood I vaguely recall. Yet here and there I spot details that, like locked doors springing open, release old memories.

"Why did I put this off for so long?"

The two of them wait politely, watching. At last, I straighten up and smile.

"Thank you. Really, I can't thank you enough. I had no idea these existed. Wow." They smile back, relieved. I'm sure the ranger had reservations about showing them to me.

The clerk warns me the site is overgrown. Driving over, a field looks familiar, half a mile long, recently planted, thin green shoots emerging from the earth just as they did back then. Across the narrow country road, however, is a wild jungle of tall grass, stunted trees, and brambles. It's as if someone drew a line demarcating sanctuary from storm. I park and wade out into it.

It's a letdown. I'm not sure what I expected, but it's not here. For 45 minutes, I struggle, pushing aside prickly thickets and stepping over fallen limbs. I'm triangulating with two trees that look familiar, an improbable technique given the passage of time.

The air is still except for the sounds of insects buzzing and the racket I'm making. A pickup truck clatters by on the main road. But no one bothers me. What I'm doing may be odd, but it's not illegal.

I search the ground for clues, breathing faster, perspiring. More than once, I have this eerie premonition I'm just *one step away* from something momentous, that when I kick aside a fallen branch or leaves, I'll find a familiar object, something connecting me more solidly with the past. But—nothing. Over the years, the earth has swallowed up even the non-biodegradable fragments we left behind, as it does with most things made by humankind. We are not in this world long.

Deer Creek Lake, out of sight down the road, is also man-made, snaking through the gullies for five miles behind an Army Corps of Engineers dam. A few small hills disturb the surrounding terrain. It's not what anyone would call a majestic site. The late spring air is listless, the way I recall it before the storm in 1980.

Whatever I'm looking for no longer exists. But there's no sensation of a brooding, ethereal presence. This spot is neither a shrine nor a memorial. Some might regard my visit as a pilgrimage, a search for enlightenment or new meaning. I wouldn't argue with that, but I don't feel a strong spiritual connection. I have little affinity for this place where my life changed in a few seconds. But there's no sense of dread or unease, either. I'm left with my private thoughts and memories, perhaps a little clearer now.

Still, I bow my head, close my eyes, and say a prayer. I ask God to be with all who were here that day. Then I'm back on the road, headed home.

"I'm finished with that place," I sigh. Another 13 years will pass before I realize my mistake—and begin to make it right.

PART I: FLYING SOLO

CHAPTER ONE

Things I Learned from My Father

I WAS JUST A BOY of 14 when my father taught me how to fly. In most of the U.S. in 1965, I couldn't legally drive a car, drink alcohol, vote, or have sex (not necessarily in that order; priorities are evolving fast at that age). But the Federal Aviation Administration (FAA) allowed student pilots like me to fly solo—*in a glider.*

Despite my early start in flying, I've never quite fit the mold of the stereotypical pilot. No leather flying jacket, no Kawasaki Ninja motorcycle, and (in my opinion) none of the cocky attitude that pilots are thought to have. My flying has usually been more of a quiet admission rather than a boastful declaration. One reason might be that flying wasn't a boyhood dream. I enjoyed reading about it and building model airplanes, but I never felt a burning desire to take to the skies myself. And I guess my father could tell. One of his close friends confided in me recently that my lack of passion for flying had frustrated Dad.

Flying always seemed so far out of reach. I assumed (wrongly) wearing eyeglasses would be a barrier. I also tended to get airsick, which made my first glider flights with my dad stressful. In a later flight in a small Cessna, I was so nauseous that I forced him to land early. As I lay in the grass afterward, so ill I could barely stand, I mused: "Why would I ever want to go flying for *fun?*"

So despite having grown up around aviation my entire life, I never saw myself as a candidate to become a pilot. The very idea seemed presumptuous, like a toddler wanting to drive his father's car. How adorable.

That was the case until my 14th birthday. Then Dad asked me if I wanted to take flying lessons. Suddenly, it was real—and possible.

* * *

Just because it was possible didn't mean it was easy. The weekend after my birthday was the second Saturday in June 1965, Dad's regular volunteer flight instructor day for the Soaring Society of Dayton. SSD's name was misleading. The club drew members from the Southwestern Ohio area, including Cincinnati, 50 miles south of Dayton, where we lived. More confusing, it was located across the state line at the Richmond (Indiana) Municipal Airport.

The weather for my first day as a student pilot was auspicious, the sun casting magical rays of light across the grass, the runways, and hundreds of square miles of flat Midwestern farmland. We strode across the quiet airport, brushing past the "No Unauthorized Personnel Beyond This Point" signs like members of an exclusive club. Dad explained how to avoid aircraft taking off, landing, and taxiing as we approached the hub of SSD's operation, an ancient vehicle with a radio antenna and scheduling board parked in the middle of the airport.

SSD Operations center and L-5 towplane. (photo by Joseph N. Bearden Jr.)

There's a saying in our sport:

"If flying were the language of man, then soaring would be its poetry."

Like so many lovely sentiments, this one isn't always true. I was staring at two exceptions squatting in the grass. Designed at the conclusion of World War II, these Schweizer 2-22 gliders were the embodiment of function over form. With bulbous fuselages; plank-like wings; and harsh dark-blue-and-yellow paint, these were aircraft only their designer could love.

SSD's Schweizer 2-22 landing with student and instructor Joe Bearden.
(photo from estate of Joseph N. Bearden Jr.)

Like an aging NFL placekicker or a favorite rusty hammer, the lowly 2-22 did one thing very well. As a no-frills training glider—i.e., not a high-performance sailplane—its singular virtue was durability, enabling it to shrug off bird droppings when stored in drafty hangars, rain and snow when staked down outside, and rough punishment from clumsy student pilots with equal indifference.

Many SSD students knew today was Dad's monthly instructional rotation and had signed up early to fly with him. He joked easily with the operations crew and students, but he was always in command. In my eyes then, Dad was always in command.

When my turn came, we walked around the 2-22 while he briefed me on the pre-flight inspection of each critical component. Then we helped push it onto the takeoff line. I climbed up into the spartan cockpit. Someone shoved a cushion behind me so I could reach the rudder pedals and the control stick sprouting from the floor. Seat belts were a novelty in 1965—few cars had them—so I needed help with the wide, military-style lap belt and shoulder harness.

Dad vanished behind me into the rear seat. I was still worried about getting airsick. But he had told me not to worry. This was different: an actual lesson!

An SSD towplane, an ex-World War II Stinson L-5, taxied up, dragging a long yellow towrope. Dad kept up a reassuring patter.

"Ok, see that red knob on the left side of the cockpit? The guy with the towrope is going to yell 'Open.' If we're ready to fly, you pull that knob back and hold it until you hear him say 'Close.' Then let it go. That means we're hooked up to the towplane. Don't touch it again until I tell you to."

"Good, here we go. Just rest your hands lightly on the control stick and follow me along to get a feel for what I'm doing." I wiped my sweaty hands on my shorts and reached for the stick.

The L-5 taxied forward with the motor idling to tighten the rope. A volunteer lifted our wingtip to level the wings (with only one main wheel, gliders are tilted with a wingtip on the ground when not flying). The towplane's 190-horsepower engine growled, and the rope tugged at the reluctant 2-22. We were moving!

SSD crew connecting towrope to 2-22 at Richmond, Indiana (Moonbeams, Vol. 28, No. 2/July 1967, Procter & Gamble Company, Cincinnati, Ohio)

The unwieldy glider lurched forward on its single wheel, gathered speed, and bumped along in the grass. The wing runner trotted alongside, steadying the wingtip for a few steps until the glider was moving fast enough for Dad to keep the wings level using the flight controls.

With a lightness belying its heft, the glider's wings bit into the air and the main wheel lifted off. As the aircraft smoothed and quieted, it moved under me like it was floating.

"Ok, keep your eye on the towplane. He'll lift off just after we do."

Seconds later, I watched as the towplane eased off the ground and we rose, bound together by the towrope, passing over the powerlines at the end of the runway. I had to control the urge to giggle! On earlier flights, my focus was on not getting sick. But this, this was *so* different! With my hand resting on the control stick and my feet on the pedals, I could sense Dad's quick, decisive inputs on the back seat controls as we climbed.

Minutes later: "Ok, watch the altimeter, see how the big hand is coming up on zero and the little hand is on 2? Just like a clock. That's 2,000 feet. Now pull that red release knob again. That's good. Pull it again to be sure. See the rope? The glider always turns right after release. See how the towplane turns left? That's to make sure we're clear of each other."

I watched the towplane dive away to the left, trailing the towrope. Dad eased the stick back to where the airspeed indicator (ASI) was showing 40 knots.

"Ok, you're going to do the flying. Keep your hand on the control stick and try to keep the airspeed at about 40 knots. Pull back a little to slow down. Push forward a little to speed up. Keep the wings level. That's right. Your left wing is down a little, so move the stick to the right slightly. That's enough. Now bring it back to the middle. Okay, you're slowing down, so push forward gently."

The glider was better behaved off tow, but I was still spectacularly inept. Still, with Dad's constant guidance, I was able to keep it wallowing in the general direction he commanded. I even managed several turns, banking in the direction I wanted to go and helping it along with a little rudder pedal. We were flying! *I* was flying!

As we glided down, Dad coached me through more turns. In five minutes, we had descended to 800 feet. He took over—still with me following along on the controls—and entered the landing pattern. As we lined up with the runway, I could see the takeoff area ahead as the grass came up to meet us. We leveled out, touched down with a gentle bump, and rolled to a stop where we had started, a wingtip settling to the ground.

I unclenched my sweaty, white-knuckled grip on the stick. The muscles in my hand ached, as if I had been hanging on for dear life. Relief accompanied disappointment the flight was over. I had been nervous, but not afraid. I didn't hesitate when he offered another flight.

These two flights that day triggered a sense of achievement. But the biggest revelation? My much-feared airsickness was a non-issue! From the moment the glider stirred, my full attention was on flying it, not worrying about getting sick. This near-total focus—the way the rest of the world and my life receded into insignificance—is still true today, more than half a century later.

* * *

Not getting airsick didn't translate to being a natural pilot. We took it slow at first, limiting our lessons to his once-a-month instruction days. I assume he wanted to be sure I was serious. I was. The problem was aptitude. Keeping the 2-22 behind the towplane demanded 100% focus, split-second reflexes, and a sure hand on the stick. Everything I did was too much ("overcontrolling" was a constant frustration), too little, or too late. The glider wanted to go virtually anywhere except following obediently behind the towplane, shooting up like a kite on a string in a gusty wind. Landing called for different skills, i.e., a smooth hand on the controls, judgment, and the ability to react to the unexpected. As we neared the ground, we had limited options if something blundered into our path, or the wind increased, or we hit a sharp downdraft, or we misjudged our approach. With no engine, we couldn't go around for another landing. In a glider, there are no time-outs to think things over. And no do-overs when landing.

By August, we were flying more often. Most lessons were "sled rides" gliding down from a 1,000- or 2,000-feet tow: ten or 15 minutes from takeoff to landing. But if student load and weather allowed, we sometimes had longer flights.

Dad was renowned for his skill *gaining* altitude in thermals, bubbles of warm air rising from hot spots on the ground, such as plowed fields, towns, and parking lots. The first time the glider thrust upward was electrifying. At Dad's direction, I made a clumsy circle in this air rising faster than we were sinking through it. The needle on the variometer swung from "sinking" to "climbing" and the altimeter needle reversed to wind around clockwise. We were soaring!

There was so much to learn. When Dad commented favorably, I glowed. His approval meant more than hearing him say "good work" after an upbeat report card. This was his world. I made a lot of mistakes, of course. He allowed me to, including those that taught me important lessons. I never knew how often he intervened to prevent disaster. I couldn't always tell when he touched the controls because he was out of sight behind me. But I had absolute faith and confidence in him.

The culture of aviation is steeped in safety because of the potential for disaster. Dad taught me to respect, but not to fear the risks. We discussed safety often—then and for years after. It instilled confidence and gave me the satisfaction and thrill of mastering skills—and risks—non-pilots could not understand.

That lack of understanding frustrated me. Fear of embarrassing myself had often inhibited me from trying new things. But now, *now* I had stories no one else at school could match! The problem was communicating them. My friends would listen politely, uncomprehending, then change the subject.

"That's nice, Chip. Hey, did you watch *Get Smart* Saturday night?" It wasn't long before I stopped trying to explain soaring to non-pilots.

It also discouraged me that my father's deft, unforced, instinctive touch for flying had skipped a generation. He was a natural pilot. It's the same in other sports. All newcomers must learn the same basic skills, but some are able to absorb these without effort, then leverage them into easy mastery.

I was not one of those people. I would wrestle with the controls of the reluctant 2-22, sawing feverishly at the control stick and booting the rudder pedals with the glider rolling, yawing, and pitching, an aeronautical rowboat tossed in a choppy ocean of air. When I got us so out of position that Dad had to take over (announcing "my airplane"), everything smoothed out, as if flung into the preternaturally calm eye of a hurricane. As I sat defeated, he would urge the controls back into my hands ("your airplane") and off we would go again.

Lesson by lesson, though, my skills improved, as did my confidence. I grew accustomed to new sensations: e.g., the towrope jerking as the towpilot firewalled the throttle; bouncing as we trailed the towplane, fighting to stay in position through turbulence; relief when we were off tow and flying free; higher G-forces pressing me into my seat in steep turns; and making corrections when jostled by a stiff crosswind on landing. Maneuvering the glider filled me with the sense of control, achievement, and pride often lacking in the rest of my life.

By September, I was flying most weekends, sometimes with other instructors. They provided new perspectives, but made me appreciate Dad's chatty, supportive, confidence-inspiring style. Lesson #18 was my first flight from takeoff to landing with no intervention! Could my first solo be far away?

Apparently so. In October: disaster! At Richmond, as elsewhere, all aircraft shared a common rectangular landing pattern. This sequenced us in single file along a three-sided pattern of downwind, base, and final legs to a touchdown point (see diagram) and helped us judge how high we were as we descended.

Typical Airport Landing Pattern

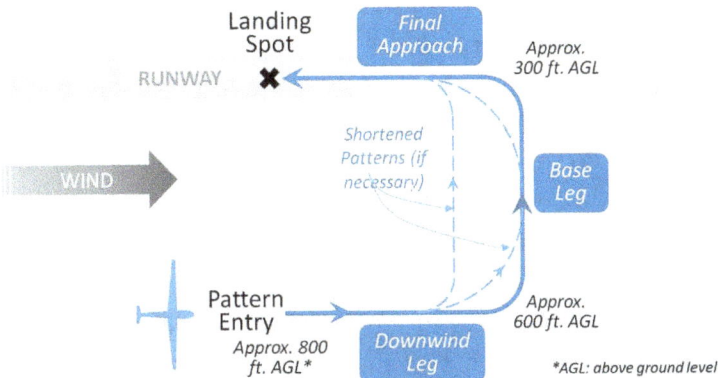

Air can go up ("lift") or down ("sink"). If we encountered sink or stronger-than-expected headwinds, we would tighten the pattern. We saved extra altitude until final, then used the spoilers—small panels that pop up on the wings and add drag—to descend more steeply.

On this flight, I badly misjudged our final approach. We were high, much higher than normal! With my face burning from embarrassment, we were still 100 feet in the air when we floated over the launch/landing point and sailed down the runway, the SSD crew gazing up at us in open-mouthed astonishment.

Dad's voice was calm. "Keep the spoilers out. That's right, just fly the plane. There's plenty of room. Don't worry, keep the wings level and touch down normally." The glider finally rolled to a stop a *quarter mile* beyond the usual landing spot. Dad wasn't fazed. He had seen it coming early but wanted me to learn judgment, not follow orders. For a moment, I wondered if I had "washed out."

The next weekend, another instructor entered "OK" in my logbook. Was this the first of the two SSD-required sign-offs before my first solo?

Journal Entry: October 16, 1965 (Richmond, Indiana)

Late that afternoon, Dad and I bump to a stop on my 33rd lesson. He tells me to stay strapped in while he scrambles out of the rear seat of the 2-22. I know what this means!

"Why don't you fly this one by yourself?" he says casually. I later learned it's normal to send a student straight up for their first solo right after an upbeat lesson. I'm nervous, but unafraid. My father believes I'm ready. The amalgam of stress, excitement, and eagerness to prove myself is the first of hundreds of times I will experience this in a glider. Later in life, I'll experience the same thing before interviews, first dates, and starting new jobs.

I'm sitting upright in the seat, palms damp, focused on what Dad is saying. Then it's quieter in the cockpit. This time, no one is talking to me. No one is talking to me because I'm alone! Dad is snapping away with his camera as I call off the last item on the checklist. The crew hook up the towrope and lift the wingtip. The towplane goes to full power, and the glider surges forward.

Whoa! As my father had cautioned, the glider is lighter without his weight. As soon as the rope tightens, the nose rises faster, it leaps off the ground earlier, and it's more responsive to the controls. I quickly adapt, though, which reassures me. As the landscape recedes beneath me, I'm entering an entirely new realm. Taking flying lessons was a significant leap forward. But flying an aircraft alone is an experience unlike any other. Long afterward, I read successful pilots possess confidence *and* an ego. Today, I have both. I feel special, one of the chosen few.

With the rear seat empty, we rise effortlessly behind the powerful towplane. At 1,000 feet, I release the rope and the L-5 dives away. Being alone in the cockpit is a novel sensation, imbuing me with a sense of freedom and control of which I will never tire. But there's no time to appreciate the luminous light of an October afternoon. I enter the pattern, feeling the aircraft responding to my inputs with one lightweight pilot aboard.

"Don't screw this up."

Launching (l) and climbing out of cockpit after landing (r) on first solo flight, October 16, 1965. (photos by Joseph N. Bearden Jr.)

Everyone is watching as I turn final and aim the glider down the runway. I level out just above the grass, touch lightly, and roll to a stop exactly where I had departed ten minutes earlier: a perfect landing!

Pilots rush up to congratulate me as I climb out. My face is pensive. I'm too inhibited to whoop it up. Inwardly, though, I'm euphoric. I've joined the exclusive club of aviators! I've flown an aircraft alone, fulfilling my hopes, my father's expectations, and—though I don't know it yet—my destiny.

As we drove home that night, I was grinning and animated as we talked nonstop. I had measured up to my father's expectations. It was a proud moment for him, too, and the realization of a dream, one he'd reached later in life himself. Not quite 60 years after this first solo, I found an entry in Dad's diary about his own first solo flight 12 years before mine. It's not lyrical. Dad was more reporter than poet.

> *"Soloing was the result of much wishing over the eight years [since his first lesson]—affords a real sense of satisfaction to pilot the plane alone."*

We didn't say anything when we walked into the house that night, but my mother could tell. She smiled uncertainly, glancing back and forth between Dad's face and mine, sharing in my pride but harboring private concerns. Fifty-plus years later, I learned she was never keen about my father's power flying. She was more accepting of gliding because of no risk of fire and because gliders can land in so many places besides airports.

In *Out of Africa,* Isak Dinesen describes a hierarchy. At the bottom are city dwellers who live in the slavery of one dimension, walking a line as if led by a string. A level above them are those who, liberated from this slavery, wander across the countryside in fields and forests in two dimensions. She reserves her highest echelon for pilots:

> *"But in the air you are taken into the full freedom of the three dimensions; after long ages of exile and dreams the homesick heart throws itself into the arms of space."*[2]

My mother's anxiety about flying's risks made me proud. This shy, insecure boy had thrown himself "into the arms of space," joining those who take up such three-dimensional challenges as flying and mountaineering.

My first solo was transformative. I had done something requiring courage.

---

[2] Dinesen, Isak (Karen Blixen). *Out of Africa* (London: Putnam, 1937)

CHAPTER TWO

Bootstrapping

MY PARENTS HAD IT ALL: intelligence, movie-star good looks, talent, personality, character, ambition—everything, that is, except money. This posed a significant challenge to my father's dream of becoming a pilot. My mother said he had always wanted to fly. It's unclear what ignited Dad's interest. It may have been encountering two barnstorming pilots who landed in a pasture across the road from his family's tin-roof house in Marion, Alabama, when he was 14. He recorded their names in his diary.

The Second World War decimated their 1945 high school senior class, which graduated twenty-five girls and eight boys. Joseph Noah Bearden Jr. and Thelma Louise Pritchett maxed out: academics, sports, and senior superlatives, including Most Likely to Succeed and Ideal Senior Boy and Girl. Dad was the star quarterback. My mother was a cheerleader and editor-in-chief of the school paper. I always thought they were long-term high school sweethearts. But Dad's diary revealed he dated almost every girl in their class (another of his senior superlatives was Biggest Flirt). The paper's gossip columnist broke the story of their engagement before they graduated:

My parents, August 1945. First furlough from U.S. Army Air Forces basic training (photo from estate of Joseph N. Bearden Jr.)

> *"News flash! Look on Thelma's third finger left hand. Congratulations, Noah, 'cept we didn't know it was that serious. You had us wondering if it were going to be Thelma or Linda."*[3]

My father (who went by "Noah" until he entered the military) had a plan. Just before their senior year, with perfect eyesight and top grades, he enlisted in the Army Air Forces at age 17, with the promise of combat air crew training upon graduation when he would be 18. But the war ended halfway through basic

---

[3] *Perri-Winkle,* Perry County High School, Marion, Alabama, May 11, 1945

training at Camp Shelby (Mississippi) and with it the need for more pilots.

Time for a new plan. After discharge, he returned to Marion for two years of junior college, then transferred to the University of Alabama. He graduated in 1950, the first in his family with a college degree. In Air Force ROTC there, he applied for a pilot training slot, again without success. So, with a diploma and a USAF Reserve commission, he went to work in accounting for Procter & Gamble, America's premier consumer products company.

The eldest of four boys, Dad was already mature beyond his years. His talent, focus, voluble confidence, and relaxed charm allowed him to slot easily into the role of loyal corporate soldier. He bought into the collectivist ethic prevalent at large corporations, exemplifying the quintessential Organization Man popularized in the book of the same title by William H. Whyte. His "uniform" comprised starched white shirts (that my mother ironed each day), conservative suits, and a devotion to P&G that would seem quaint today, if not naïve.

Life wasn't easy. My overachieving mother had left college early to support Dad while he was earning his diploma. She talks about window shopping together on Saturdays, dreaming of a life they hoped to build. It sounded poignant but sweet. They were starting at the bottom, a small-town couple in the big city (Jackson, Mississippi) with a college degree and not much else. They needed another responsibility like a dog needs a tuxedo. A year later, though, I arrived.

In the 1950s, the relationship between P&G and an employee was more than a job. It was a tacit contract. My father had grown up poor during the Depression, so job security was imperative then and throughout his career. He would end up being a "lifer," spending his entire 30-year career at P&G.

One aspect of this devotion was relocating whenever ordered: nine postings in as many years. The first move came when I was six weeks old, to the tiny town of Wilson, Arkansas. It was the height of the polio epidemic in this country, anxiety over which my 96-year-old mother still recalls. My siblings, Mark and Diane, were born later in Cincinnati, Ohio (P&G headquarters) and Green Bay, Wisconsin, (P&G's Charmin Paper Products Division).

This uncertain, nomadic life was hardest on my mother. She cried when Boston residents made fun of her Southern accent. But in that less-enlightened era, corporations expected wives to support their husbands faithfully—and quietly. Five years in, my father reflected on his progress with wonder in his diary:

"I feel the Lord has especially blessed us by allowing me to earn $565/month. Eleven years ago, I wouldn't have believed it possible to be earning that much today as this would have seemed like a fabulous salary.

Strangely enough, though, we manage to save very little, but our standard of living is above average, I rather imagine. We accept as normal a lot of wonderful things in this era: plumbing, appliances, autos, entertainment, clothing, and travel."

It's easy to smile at the reference to plumbing. But in *Hoosiers*, the 1986 film about the small-town Indiana basketball team that won a state championship about the time of Dad's diary entry, a high school student is giving a report: *"Progress is electricity, school consolidation, church remodeling, second farm tractors, second farm cars, hay balers, corn-pickers, grain combines, field choppers and indoor plumbing."*[4] I recall seeing lever-action kitchen hand pumps and using chamber pots and outhouses at my grandparents' houses as a kid. So plumbing was wonderful progress for my parents.

By 1959, we had rotated back to P&G's Cincinnati headquarters for the third and final time. We didn't take Dad's job for granted. Fidelity to P&G ranked right up there with love of God, country, and family. One proviso was brand loyalty. To return from the store with a competitor's product would have provoked nearly the same firestorm as if I had been caught shoplifting. It wasn't until I left for college that I dared buy anything except Crest toothpaste, Tide laundry soap, Jif peanut butter, or another of P&G's myriad consumer brands.

My parents at AFROTC formal affair at the Marion Institute in Marion, Alabama, ca. 1948, and Dad with the Aeronca Champ he soloed, near Cohasset, Massachusetts, 1953 (photos from estate of Joseph N. Bearden Jr.)

Somehow (my mother never knew how) Dad had scraped together money for a few flying lessons when stationed in Mississippi in 1945. But his serious training began in 1953 and led to his soloing at 26 (two years after my birth).

---

[4] *Hoosiers*. Directed by David Anspaugh, screenplay by Angelo Pizzo. Orion Pictures, 1986. Film.

Flying was expensive, and we were moving a lot, so it took six years to earn his private pilot's license. By then, his dream of a flying career was over. Dad was 32, on a middle manager's salary, with a wife, three kids, and a mortgage.

Time for a new plan. Enter gliding. Would a young man who grew up dreaming of P-51s be satisfied flying motorless gliders? Would they be a poor substitute for the real thing? Dad's introduction to soaring was a one-hour glider ride in 1954 with SSD. That may have sparked his interest. But he didn't join the club until 1960, when we returned to Cincinnati.

I'm sure the original appeal of gliding/soaring (we use the terms interchangeably) was affordability, i.e., no expensive engines. But Dad became captivated by the challenge of mastering the fine points of airmanship and competing in soaring contests. Soon, soaring was one of the most important parts of his life, right up there with family, church, and job.

Visiting early soaring meet in Chillicothe, Ohio, 1960. A.J. Smith would win the Nationals in this Lo-150 sailplane the next year and feature in our soaring for over 20 years. Author (9) and sister Diane (2). (photo from estate of Joseph N. Bearden Jr.)

He had been dreaming of flying for 20 years, reading, stopping by small airports, and scrounging money for lessons. Now he became one of SSD's most active flight instructors. In a few years, he leveraged his enthusiasm and leadership to get elected club president despite his youth and inexperience. He helped structure training, boost membership, upgrade equipment, and advise groups of pilots how to buy their own gliders. His interest in power flying died.

For many pilots, flying is a secret they keep. Non-pilots often don't "get it" and not all aviators have the ability, the patience, or even the desire (*mea culpa*) to explain. Not my father. He became one of soaring's most passionate evangelists in Southwestern Ohio, eager to extol its virtues to colleagues, church members, neighbors, friends, even strangers.

I learned to dread trying to explain soaring to a non-pilot. Yet he never grew tired of it. He loved giving introductory glider rides. One gambit was to urge the controls into his passenger's hands, then talk them through a few gentle turns. In his slow Alabama drawl, he would set the hook with, "Ah you shuah you've nevah flown a glidah before?" A long-time SSD member estimated he was one of at least a thousand people my father introduced to the sport. He wanted everyone to enjoy soaring. With a warm, welcoming smile, he was the antithesis of the swaggering flying daredevil. And he loved teaching people to fly. I suspect that's why so many told me Dad had been their favorite instructor.

He never passed up the opportunity to promote soaring to the average person. With a flair for self-promotion, he even cajoled P&G into allowing him to display a glider in their corporate headquarters in Cincinnati.

1-26 in P&G lobby with my father in center (l) and with his shared 1-26 (r), 1961.

Retrieving my father's 1-26, 1961. (all photos from estate of Joseph N. Bearden Jr.)

What Dad loved most was flying cross country, in particular in competition. Early on, he bought into a single-place Schweizer 1-26 to earn awards and enter contests. Because of the risk of landing off the airport, few SSD pilots flew cross-country or entered contests. But competition had always been part of Dad's DNA. Moving up, he and a friend bought a neglected Schweizer 1-23B and restored it with the help of a talented club member. Another member, a sympathetic national-caliber pilot, helped him ramp up his cross-country skills.

One notable flight in May 1965 established his reputation in SSD—and tested my mother. The sun was already climbing in the sky, well above the horizon, when he arrived at the airport to find it buzzing with excitement. A cold front had blown through the day before, leaving the rich, dark soil in the surrounding fields moist and filling the air with the scent of earthy freshness. It was a textbook soaring day: cool night air forecast to heat up 30 degrees higher by midafternoon, with a moderate breeze from the west.

"It's a Gold distance day, Joe! Are you going?"

Dad had completed his Silver badge four years earlier with a 50 km (31 miles) flight. The 300 km (186 miles) of the Gold badge was a big step up, possible in the Midwest in his modest 1-23B only on the few perfect days each year.

Dad's 1-23B at an early (Bryan, Ohio, 1963) contest with Chevy station wagon, trailer, and canvas tent. (photo by Joseph N. Bearden Jr.)

He had fallen short at least once before.

"I'm tempted. But my trailer's up here and I rode up with ____, so my car is at my house. And, anyway, my wife has only driven the trailer a few times."

"Get ready to fly, Joe. We'll call Thelma. Someone can drop the trailer at your house this afternoon. You might not see another day this good for years."

That afternoon, a club member telephoned her to say he would deliver the glider trailer to our house. Say *what*? By the time this fellow had hitched the 30-foot trailer to our big Chevy station wagon for her, my father had landed triumphantly at his goal near Akron and telephoned her. Ever the dutiful wife, she loaded us three kids in the car (ages thirteen, eleven, and six), peered back anxiously at the unfamiliar trailer in the rearview mirror, and set off on the four-hour drive. We barely made it out of Cincinnati.

Not 30 minutes in, she missed an exit ramp. Rattled, she pulled off on the shoulder of the busy freeway and tried to back up—at night. As she slowly eased the car in reverse, the rear end of the trailer would swing out. She would stop, pull forward to straighten it, and try again, gaining a few feet each time. In the meantime, traffic boomed by at 70 mph in the next lane, shaking our car.

The situation took on a darker aura of menace as this went on. A sinister-looking motorcyclist stopped under the overpass ahead, parked his bike, and strode back toward us. His leather-jacketed form evoked images of Marlon Brando and *The Wild One*. Closer he came, headed right for us, his helmeted face impassive in the harsh, flickering lights from passing cars.

"Mama, what do we do?" we blurted.

"Lock the doors," she said hurriedly, breathing a little fast.

My anxiety swelled. Who knows what evil this guy intended? He neared the driver's door—then continued right by us without a glance. False alarm.

We reached the deserted Freedom Field Airport in Medina, Ohio, at midnight. Uncertain, we eased to a stop in the circle of illumination in front of the hangar. Was this the right place? Then a shadowy figure strode into the light. My father was grinning proudly.

There was no question of spending money on a motel. Under the lights, we removed the sailplane's wings and loaded them and the fuselage on the trailer. Then we slept while my father drove back in the wee hours of the morning, smiling to himself and savoring his accomplishment.

We got home before dawn. A few hours later, bleary-eyed, we attended church as usual. In the afternoon, Dad gave my mother a lesson on how to maneuver in reverse with the trailer.

Dad's 1-23B/trailer and our early 60s Chevrolet Bel Air station wagon at Richmond Municipal Airport, Indiana, ca. 1964 (photos from estate of Joseph N. Bearden Jr.)

CHAPTER THREE

Rite of Passage

WHY DID I CHANGE MY MIND when Dad asked if I wanted to take flying lessons? Almost 60 years later, I still don't know.

His invitation could have unlocked a latent desire to be a pilot. Sometimes we're not aware of what we really want, even as adults. Flying sounded cool, for sure. I probably hoped it would compensate for what I was missing, e.g., sports, girls, and respect for something other than academic prowess. I may have wanted to impress by doing something daring. I never felt pressured, but I know I craved my father's approval.

Regardless, he made it easy. It would have taken me a long time to work up the nerve to ask for myself. And I knew he was happy when I said yes.

* * *

Flying wasn't the sole reason Dad and I related well, but it helped. We shared something profound and compelling. We were aviators, comrades in the rarefied company of sailplane pilots (cue the music from *Top Gun,* or—acknowledging the period—the theme from *The High and the Mighty*).

Like most young boys who idolize their fathers, I knew mine could do anything: vanquish monsters, excel at any sport, and beat up the neighborhood bully's dad. Over time, this expanded to include business, interacting with people, and—of course—flying sailplanes.

The downside was being intimidated by the gap between my youthful abilities and everything that seemed to come naturally to him. The most glaring hole in my adolescent *curriculum vitae* was sports. My father had been a dual threat in school, an academic standout *and* a three-letter man in football, basketball, and baseball. I had the academic side covered, but my few sporting forays had flopped. My biggest disaster—that haunted me for years—went back to age nine.

At that same age, skier Lindsey Vonn writes in her enlightening memoir: *Rise: My Story,* she informed her father she wanted to be an Olympic champion. What audacity! Alas, I had neither her precociousness nor her ambition.

When I was nine, I didn't think of myself as athletic or non-athletic. So when my friends got excited about Little League Baseball, I asked my parents to sign me up. I had seldom played the game, but I didn't want to be left out. And I assumed I would learn as we went along.

I showed up for the first practice excited but bereft of any real batting or fielding skills, hand-to-eye coordination, or knowledge of the rules. In contrast, my teammates seemed to have been playing baseball since they started walking. The coach sized up my meager talent in seconds. League policy prevented him from excluding anyone with a pulse, so he banished me to the outfield for practice. I was eager but inept.

It wasn't long before a high fly ball came sailing down hard, right between my gamely flailing arms, smashing me full in the face. Somehow, I avoided a broken nose, chipped teeth, or concussion. My bloody nose recovered quickly, but my brief enthusiasm for baseball never did. I plugged away in desultory fashion for two seasons, vacillating between mortification that the coach wouldn't insert me late in a one-sided game and anxiety he would. Mostly, I dreaded baseball as a weekly humiliation.

Years later, I played a little pickup basketball, touch football, and tennis with my equally nerdy buddies. But my humbling Little League experience was the last time I would seek an organized athletic challenge until my late 20s. I could not have been more un-American if I had quit school to join Marxist guerilla fighter Che Guevara in Cuba.

I never admitted these anxieties to Dad. As I grew older and began to excel in academics (and my hand-to-eye coordination improved), I rationalized sports didn't matter, anyway. Some people were good at sports. I was not, and there wasn't much I could do about it. But this experience exacerbated the insecurities of male adolescence and influenced my behavior long after.

* * *

Sports weren't the only shadow my father cast. His ability to interact effortlessly with people also daunted me. Everyone admired Joe Bearden. Affable and poised, he was a natural leader as others thronged around him.

As an introvert, I was the complete opposite. Public speaking was a particular fear. Dad was a master. I saw him in action most often at our church, leading prayers and making announcements to the congregation each week. Every few years, the church elders would prevail upon him to lead the Sunday School program in the hour before the 11:00 AM worship service. Under his leadership, attendance would grow steadily, then decline when he stepped down. He also oversaw the church's finances. I didn't understand then how deep was his commitment. He managed his faith and service to God the way he managed everything else, with an organized, highly structured approach focused on results that elevated his respect in our small church.

Dad was an accountant, but he had a creative streak, one that could cause trouble. I still chuckle about the adult-study course he was teaching one night on Cold War Communist governments harassing missionaries and Christians. At my father's nod, a friend plunged the room into darkness.

"Hey, what's with the lights?" several yelled in alarm.

"Do what you're told, and no one will get hurt," the *intruder* announced in a gruff voice, waving a flashlight, a mask pulled up over his face in the dim light. "Put your Bibles in this box when it comes around and don't talk."

Afterward, embarrassed, a few laughed ruefully. Dad's exercise made the problem real to people, but it could have gone awry. No matter, leadership was just one of many personal assets he possessed that I despaired I never would.

* * *

During the mid-1960s, the media were unrelenting in reporting on a world full of violence, confrontation, and social disorder. This included protests over the Vietnam War and civil rights; the assassinations of the Kennedy brothers and the Reverend Martin Luther King Jr.; and—unfathomable to anyone who didn't grow up in the "duck and cover" Cold War era—existential unease about nuclear Armageddon with the U.S.S.R. Fascinated with how things worked, I collected pamphlets on how to build a home fallout shelter.

One underlying theme in this tableau of disruption pitted proud traditionalists from WWII's Greatest Generation—who had saved the world from tyranny—against an impatient, defiant, youthful counterculture of sex, drugs, rock & roll, and idealism, who demanded radical changes to that same world. At least that's what we read weekly in *Life* magazine, our window on the world.

There was no debate at our house. We lived in Finneytown, a white, middle-class suburb comprising cheek-to-jowl tract houses. There wasn't a lot of diversity, racial or political. Our fourth-grade class held a mock presidential election in 1960, with Republican candidate Richard Nixon receiving all but one or two votes. It dumbfounded me the next morning to learn Kennedy had won.

Life was good. We rode our bikes a mile to school *sans* helmets. We played anywhere in the neighborhood without oversight. At school, the major drama was our football team's won-loss record and the voting for homecoming queen.

Our family had dinner together each night at the same hour after saying the blessing ("saying grace" in Alabama vernacular) with the television news in the background. In our myopic view, the demonstrations we saw in Washington, D.C., Berkeley, and Birmingham seemed as distant as Saigon. Even Vietnam wasn't real yet. I was years from registering for the Selective Service System (draft), and college would provide a four-year exemption after that.

I knew my father's views could be simplistic, e.g., conscientious objector Muhammad Ali was a draft dodger, while Army veteran Elvis Presley was a loyal American. But I hadn't yet begun to question his religious (Southern Baptist) or political (Republican) beliefs. My adolescent attempts to establish a sense of self were muted. Youthful rebellion would have shocked us both. Whether I was a "good son" (true) or just too timid to color outside the lines (also true), we might raise our voices, but we never yelled.

We didn't always agree. I was a teenager and Dad was *old*—38 when I so-loed! Our musical tastes diverged, with The Doors and Perry Como co-existing in uneasy *detente* on our family's Hi-Fi system. But our core values aligned. Notionally, I was a child of the 60s, ostensibly at war with The Establishment. In reality, my father and I navigated my coming of age with little discord.

* * *

Sports are a time-honored way for fathers to bridge the generation gap with their sons.[5] They teach them how to hit, throw, and catch a baseball; how to pass a football with a spiral; and how to shoot free throws and jump shots. Even if they are not athletes themselves, they do it for the sense of pride and accomplishment, and for the unalloyed hero worship returned by their sons.

There wasn't much sporting activity in our backyard. But what was that compared with *flying?* After soloing, I was prepping for the written and flight tests for my FAA private pilot certificate at age 16. This piece of paper would allow me to take my friends for rides.

Dad sent me up to fly two years before I got my driver's license. He helped me buy into a Schweizer 1-26 group, as he had done. The 1-26 performed only modestly better than a 2-22 but was more nimble and lighter on the controls.

I transitioned to this stubby, single-place glider easily. At age 16, I feared many things: embarrassment, talking to girls, bad grades, public speaking, being shown up in gym class by more athletic classmates. But under Dad's supervision, I don't recall ever being afraid as I climbed the aeronautical ladder. Nervous, yes. But I knew he monitored my progress and encouraged me to take each step up only when he judged I was ready. That's not to say I didn't test his judgment from time to time.

---

[5] Clearly, I'm ignoring father-daughter sports experiences, many of which I have been fortunate to share with my own daughters as an adult.

Journal Entry: July 22, 1967 (Richmond, Indiana)

It's a fine summer day in my first season in the 1-26. I'm a *real* pilot, now, no longer relegated to flogging SSD's tired 2-22s around the airport. There are nice-looking cumulus clouds a mile or two away. "Cu" (pronounced "cue") form when air at the top of thermals cools until the moisture condenses. I'm hoping one will reward me with a climb. Not every cu has a thermal below it, though. When the first cloud fails to deliver, I proceed to the next one, which also doesn't have a thermal waiting.

Then, "Where's the airport?" Frowning, I peek over my shoulder. "Uh, oh, this doesn't look right." The airport is farther away than usual. Much farther. I've never seen this view before.

Too late, I reverse course, biting my lip and staring ahead at the Richmond Airport. I know straight away I'm in trouble. The airfield is getting higher on the canopy as I sink lower. The altimeter needle is inexorably unwinding. Soon, I'm down to pattern altitude—and the airport is still too far away. With no choice, I shift my focus to the fields rising around me. There's no way to stop what's happening—or even pause to think. In Eastern Indiana, landable fields are everywhere, so I keep gliding, watching different fields go by. I'm so low I should be on final approach.

"Landing out" is part of soaring. Pilots on cross-country flights can't guarantee they will reach an airport. But that need not be a disaster. Power planes need a smooth place to set down to protect their tall, vulnerable landing gears. Gliders sit much lower to the ground, so they can land in farm fields, pastures, and sometimes even on roads, golf courses, and athletic fields.

I've helped my father evaluate landing spots many times—from the ground. Today, I discover it's much different from *inside* the glider. The cockpit is warm. My hands are sweating. I'm descending over a country road, fields passing by on both sides as I get lower. I spot one ahead. I'm so low I'm viewing it from a shallow angle. I know I've waited way too late to select a place to land—I'm ready to turn final. Other than crop stubble, it looks smooth. No trees or wires on the approach. No ditches or fences. No slope (landing downhill increases the distance to touch down and stop).

"I'm out of time!" Too low for a full pattern, I bank right onto final approach. I pull the handle for the spoilers and descend into an unknown field for the first time. The earth rushes up to meet me as the glider sinks. Then I flare out. I'm moving fast, 40 knots, when we touch down on the bumpy ground. WHUMP-WHUMP-WHUMP-WHUMP!!!!

"Gosh, that's loud!" All my previous landings have been at our airport. This one, with the noise and washboard jarring, is a shock. I clench my teeth, pulling hard on the wheel brake. The 1-26 bumps to a stop as the metal-plated skid under the nose scrapes against the dirt.

It takes a few seconds to breathe normally. "My father is going to kill me!"

There's no damage to glider or field. I radio my status, then wait, face burning, embarrassed over my stupid mistake. I'm sitting in a field a mile from the airport, and *everyone* at the club today knows it. Yet, perversely, I can't deny the secret thrill. No one at school has ever done anything like this!

In less than an hour, my father arrives with the trailer and two carloads of club members. I'm expecting a stern lecture, but he climbs out jocular and upbeat. The entire boisterous crew treats it like an entertaining afternoon adventure. It helps that a magazine photographer is there snapping photos.

Later, I realized my father must have been proud I had managed the non-traditional rite of passage. I could have panicked, or frozen, or chosen a bad field, or simply flown the aircraft into the ground (all of which have happened to other novice pilots). Instead, my performance reflected favorably on him. I had been trained, tested, and proven worthy.

First landout, in a 1-26, Richmond, Indiana, 1967. (photos by Joseph N. Bearden Jr.)

CHAPTER FOUR

Chastened Hero

MY FATHER HAD DONE IT ALL while growing up. Star athlete. Academic standout. Confident, popular, extroverted leader. "Ace pilot" was just one more box to check off.

Joe Bearden emerged on the Midwestern soaring scene in the mid-1960s as a competent, patient competitor who placed respectably in the middle ranks of local tournaments in his 1-23B. But while that glider climbed well in thermals, it couldn't glide as fast or as far as more modern sailplanes.

Dad had lofty ambitions, so in 1966, my conservative, frugal father made a radical departure from his normal behavior. He and his partner sold their 1-23B, kicked in more money (roughly doubling their investment), added a third partner, and ordered a Diamant HBV, a state-of-the-art competition sailplane from Switzerland. This bold step would drop this club-level pilot into the cockpit of a sailplane equal to anything flying at the national level. Dad was going "all in." In early 1967, the Diamant (pronounced DEE-ah-mahnt by Americans) was one of the first generation of fiberglass sailplanes sweeping the gliding world, displacing wood and aluminum gliders.

Andy Warhol inspired the phrase, *"In the future, everyone will be world famous for 15 minutes."* The Diamant facilitated Dad's brush with fame. A Cincinnati publisher was launching an eponymous city lifestyle magazine. The editors wanted a visually striking story for their first issue and dispatched a team headed by a renowned photojournalist. Expecting exotic racing sailplanes, the team were horrified to find SSD's weary Schweizer 2-22s. These maladroit beasts appeared to be relics from the Wright Brothers' era. This was not the stuff of award-winning journalism. Panicked, they huddled to discuss how to salvage this misbegotten project.

As they did, by pure chance, Dad and I wheeled his new Diamant from the hangar into the sun. It glimmered, a pure white, breathtaking piece of techno-Art Déco sculpture. The fuselage was like a missile with a sleek, intricately fitted cockpit and a transparent plastic canopy stretched over the reclining pilot. The glassy smooth, slender wings stretched almost 50 feet from wingtip to wingtip.

Giddy with relief, the film crew hustled over to persuade my unsuspecting father to let them build their story around it—and him. Startled, but with a dazed smile spreading over his face, my father didn't need to be asked twice.

The widely publicized inaugural issue of *Cincinnati* in October 1967 featured spectacular photos of Dad and the Diamant. He tried to play it cool. But decades later, we laughed over how flustered he must have been. One in-cockpit photo series revealed he had forgotten to fasten his seat belt and shoulder harness!

Joe Bearden ready for launch (l) and author running wingtip during launch (r).

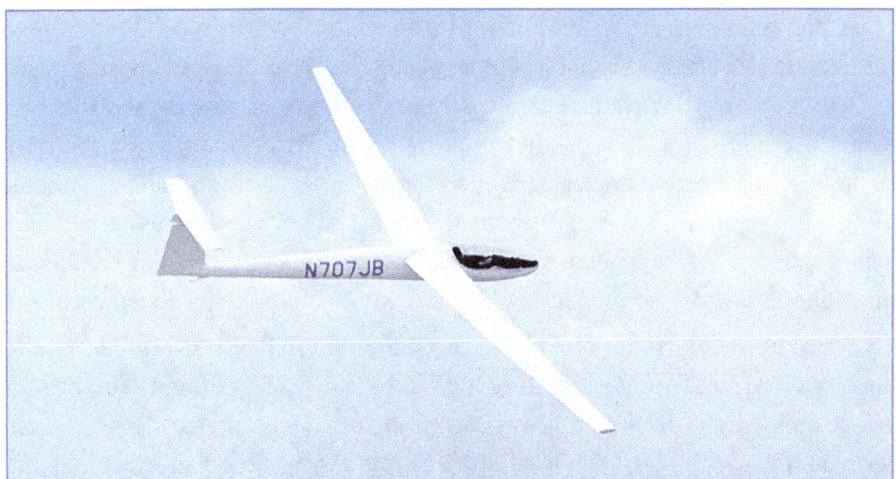

Joe Bearden in Diamant (top), on tow (l) and in cockpit (r). All photos at Richmond Municipal Airport, 1967, by Vernon Merritt III (from estate of Joseph N. Bearden Jr.)

This was also the weekend I outlanded our 1-26. One of the magazine team rode along with the retrieve crew and snapped photos as we loaded it on the trailer. I appeared in the magazine, too, securing my own 15 minutes of renown.

* * *

The exotic Diamant was no magic bullet. Dad and one of his partners entered SSD's spring contest, imagining the glory accruing to pilots of this awesome machine! On the first day, his partner departed the contest site, then glided an ignominious few miles before plopping down in a plowed field, putting deep scratches in the pristine contours of the Diamant's belly. When we arrived with the trailer, he and my father stood side by side, awkward and crestfallen, staring at their no-longer-perfect sailplane.

The rest of that contest was weathered out, which delayed Dad's competitive debut three months, until the Labor Day contest in Adrian, Michigan, against competitors such as A.J. Smith, former U.S. champion.

Dad and his partners kept the Diamant in the big hangar at Richmond, just as we had the 1-23B and 1-26. Both of those gliders had simple flatbed trailers for retrieves and travel to contests. But getting the gliders on and off these trailers was a labor-intensive ordeal involving nuts, bolts, fasteners, and tools. In contrast, new fiberglass sailplanes imported from Europe had begun to arrive in highly engineered enclosed trailers for storage and transport. Assembling/disassembling these gliders using such trailers was so easy that most owners abandoned hangaring altogether. Our partnership couldn't afford a luxury trailer, however, so the factory shipped our Diamant in a wooden crate.

So we needed a trailer for it. Dad owned an old flatbed 1-26 trailer. Under his direction, and with a good bit of loud debate, we hoisted the Diamant's fuselage and wings—draped in heavy canvas covers my mother had sewed—and secured them with bolts; crude wooden fittings; wire cables; shock cords; and duct tape; and padded them with beach towels and carpet squares. It was a ludicrous sight. The wings overhung the trailer at both ends, exposed to damage from vehicles bumping us from behind, and in front from our car making tight turns. Were the Diamant a child instead of a glider, social services would have hauled us into court for irresponsible behavior.

The four-hour drive to the contest in lower Michigan on Friday night exhausted us. We trundled onto the airport long after midnight, in time to grab a few hours of sleep. As usual, we were camping to save money, but it was raining. So we curled up in our car seats. We kids didn't mind, but I'm sure it wasn't restful for our parents.

On Day One, breakfast for our pilot was a cup of coffee as we struggled to unload the pieces of the glider from the trailer without damaging them. Curious pilots and crews strolled by, too polite to comment. Over 50 years later, I still groan at the ridiculous sight. We had piled the most technically advanced sailplane in the Midwest on what resembled an overloaded, third-world donkey cart and set off like Don Quixote for the glider wars.

We worked feverishly for an hour to assemble it. *[The next year, learning the correct procedure slashed our assembly time by 45 minutes]* Too soon, it was time to rush Dad into the cockpit, after which he flew all afternoon attempting to fly around the course, a 300 km (186 miles) triangle: fastest time wins.

The Diamant had dazzling performance—if flown properly. In his 1-23B, Dad would stop to climb in most thermals he found, then glide sedately to the next one. His aim was to complete the task. Average speed was secondary. In contrast, high-level competition involved climbing in the strongest parts of the best thermals—ignoring weaker ones—then gliding on at higher speed.

It was an eye-opening transition for him, like being dropped into an open-wheeled race car and circling the Indianapolis 500 track, giddy and breathless at 80 mph, before looking up, chagrined, as other cars whizzed by twice as fast.

In those days, crews trailed behind their pilots with cars and trailers, exchanging occasional radio messages. We did so as Dad worked his way around the course. On the final leg, creeping shadows warned he was running out of time as the solar-powered thermals expired. Discouraged, exhausted, and with a crushing headache from the sun, coffee, and too little food and sleep, he glided to a halt in a plowed field well short of the finish line.

Minutes before, he had listened on the radio as an obsolete German glider, no better than the 1-23B he had exchanged for the Diamant, floated heroically over the finish line, bringing the number of finishers to 17 of the 25 contestants. Under the harsh scoring system, even this slow finisher would receive far more points than stragglers, like Dad, who landed out. It was a bitter, humiliating public debut for the ambitious 40-year-old aviator.

We flailed at voracious mosquitoes while disassembling the recalcitrant Diamant in the looming darkness, then stumbled through the farmer's yard carrying each delicate piece of the glider, stepping over tractor ruts and cow manure. Sweating profusely in the muggy August evening, we strained to heave them on the trailer and secure them. Then we drove back to Adrian, exhausted, grimy, mosquito bitten—and so late that we totally missed the contest dinner.

I suspect we had all secretly harbored an image of Dad, equipped at last with a glider worthy of his skills, hurling his state-of-the-art fiberglass missile around the course at great speed, helpless competitors trailing behind. The reality was jarring. Dad's shoulders sagged and his eyes were lifeless. The sense of humiliation and failure crushed his usual resolve.

"I'm never flying a glider again."

To my mother, this may have sounded too good to be true! But she wisely withheld comment. I had never seen Dad display weakness, much less fail. We stopped by the motel where Joe Conn, friend and esteemed competitor, sat down to reassure Dad while my mother shooed us out of the room.

Joe's pep talk must have worked, because Dad was ready to fly in the morning. But on Day Two, I learned a lesson I've held onto for over 50 years:

"No matter how bad things may seem, they can always get worse."

As we chased Dad down the first leg, he glided in low over a hayfield where another glider had landed. We watched, anxious, as he circled overhead in a weak thermal, round and round like a vulture, maintaining altitude. Surviving was Dad's *forte*, so when the thermal strengthened, he climbed away. Saved!

He flew on to the turnpoint, then turned back for Adrian, now over 100 miles away. Late in the afternoon, he urged us to catch up, radioing he was low again and approaching the *same* field—this time from the opposite direction! There were countless other places he could have landed, but in his mind, the earlier glider there constituted a *de facto* stamp of approval.

None of us considered that the first glider was an older design. Its high wingtips were well clear of the hay. The Diamant was like a race car, lower and more aerodynamic. Its wingtips were closer to the ground. We arrived in time to see Dad's final approach. The aircraft floated over the wires under perfect control, settled gracefully into the grass, and flared to a gentle touchdown. As we watched in horror, it whirled around, the wingtip slashing angrily across our field of view as it jerked abruptly, the wings flexing and flailing the grass as it thrashed to a stop in mere seconds. Something had gone terribly wrong.

A "ground loop" is the dreaded aeronautical equivalent of spinning out in a car. If the end of a long wing wobbles and touches the ground or snags tall grass or crops during landing, instantly the aircraft pivots on this trapped wingtip and whirls around violently in "crack the whip" fashion. This can put severe side loads on the fuselage and cause considerable damage. I had heard disparaging comments about pilots who ground looped. But I had never seen one.

According to my father, I still hadn't. We were bursting with questions as we arrived in the field next to the glider.

"Wow, what did you do? What happened? Was that a ground loop?"

"No," he fired back, voice rising, shaking his head vigorously. "I didn't ground loop. The glider just made a sharp turn."

We all paused. I looked at him, askance. The "sharp turn" had split the leading edge of one wing a few inches, bent the landing gear, and inflicted other minor damage. Seeing his beautiful Diamant violated like this was traumatic, far worse than the scratches several months earlier. But Dad still wasn't buying into having made a mistake. A ground loop was a minor accident. And he had most definitely *not* had an accident.

My father's refusal to admit the obvious was maddening. It's one of the few times I recall being so infuriated with him that I raised my voice. To me—an obstinate, clueless 16-year-old—it was so clear. If you made a mistake, own up to it. I didn't help with my refusal to acquiesce to his "if I say it didn't happen, then it didn't happen" logic. We never agreed; we just stopped talking about it.

The plane was still flyable, so on the third and final day, we were overjoyed (and relieved) to see Dad finish his first contest task in a modern sailplane. But even that was anticlimactic. The top pilots whistled in at high speed in crowd-pleasing fashion a few feet above the ground before zooming up dramatically in steep climbs to enter the traffic pattern.

My father's finish was sedate, high above the airport. He enjoyed this exciting sport. But as we were learning, he was too conservative to extend himself.

CHAPTER FIVE

My First Time

C ARS, DRUGS, ALCOHOL, AND SEX are traditional "firsts" in the lives of teenagers. I had my driver's license. And I had a vague notion that other milestones lay ahead. But as my high school senior year began, my father announced a different one: my first soaring contest!

Journal Entry: September 21-22, 1968 (Marion, Ohio)

Once again—as when I first soloed three years ago—I am stressed, excited, and eager to do something significant. Flying gives me a sense of freedom, control, and mastery over the aircraft and myself. Nothing else comes close.

This contest is a modest weekend local meet three hours up the road in Marion, Ohio. For two years, I've been flying locally, building hours in our 1-26 but never venturing away from the airport. So I have zero cross-country experience. But I have accumulated a great amount of wisdom from books and magazines. Thus, in my teenage mind, I'm an authority.

My father and I get along well regarding flying. This morning, however, I generously proffer my advice, undiplomatically critiquing what I consider are his competitive weaknesses. As I prattle on, oblivious to his rising ire, I discover his tolerance for this is a world apart from his infinite patience as my flight instructor. Annoyed, he finally cracks and sputters,

"Okay, you think you know so much. Let's see how well you do!" It is a rare and ill-advised lapse of self-control.

It's exciting to be flying after crewing for five years. And I do harbor fantasies. But my realistic ambition as an utter novice is to avoid embarrassment.

Our 1-26 Class has a smallish task. This popular glider is easy to fly, durable, and affordable. It climbs well but doesn't glide much better than the brick-like 2-22. Flying cross-country in a 1-26 is like living paycheck to paycheck; you're never more than minutes away from a crisis (landing) if you miss a thermal. Dad's longer Open Class task should be easy for him in his Diamant.

I circle up as high as I can in a thermal crowded with more gliders than I have ever seen stuffed together. Then I turn my back on the airport and glide deliberately on course toward the next cumulus cloud. I'm surprised how thrilling it is to have the security of the airport receding behind me. As the ground rapidly draws closer, however, the stress increases.

Author, 17, in 1-26 at Richmond, Indiana (l, photo by Joseph N. Bearden) and launching at first contest in Marion, Ohio (r, photo by Thelma Bearden Castleman), both in 1968.

I'm navigating with an aeronautical chart, passing over farmland at 45 knots, looking up ahead at the next cloud. It's a huge boost when I reach it, stumble into another thermal, and begin to climb. This is what it's all about!

One after another, I string together enough climbs and glides to travel 22 miles before missing a thermal. The flight doesn't last long after that. The euphoria of being a real contest pilot evaporates in the overheated cockpit as I descend closer and closer to the terrain. This time, unlike last year's unintended landout in Richmond, I choose a good field from altitude and make a full pattern before landing there. I'm not relaxed, but I'm not terrified, either. Besides, unlike last year's stumble, landing out here is sanctioned: I'm in a real contest.

When the scores post, two 1-26 pilots have flown farther—some of these guys have been competing for years—but no one completes the task.

The weather on Sunday is weaker. I head out again on course but don't make it as far–13 miles—before being forced down in another plowed field. I'm a little subdued, but this is a learning experience. And I'm a veteran now.

My family arrive with cars and trailers to pick me up on the way home. They pile out, laughing.

"You won!" shouts Mark, beaming, his face aglow.

"What do you mean 'I won'?" Are they trying to embarrass me?

Dad explains. "No one else in the 1-26 Class even left the airport. You get first place," handing me the trophy.

My father has a trophy, too. He's taken third in his class. But mine towers over his, a source of enduring hilarity in our family. My brother Mark snaps a photo of Dad and me comparing our hardware in the field where I landed. Later, when the film mysteriously vanishes, my father explains weakly that the photo lab lost it. We, naturally, accuse him of something more nefarious and never let him forget it. Fifty-four years later, I shoot another photo of our two trophies to recreate the moment (below).

First contest outlanding in 1-26, near Marion, Ohio, with trailer. (photo from estate of Joseph N. Bearden Jr.) Recent inset photo of trophies, Dad's 3rd place Open Class (l) and my 1st place 1-26 Class. (r)

According to scientific research, winning triggers the release of serotonin in the body and thus makes us feel good. But until that Sunday afternoon in a farmer's field in rural Ohio, grinning, clutching my first-place trophy, I had never felt the exultation of surpassing my peers. I didn't know it yet, but my life would never be the same. I may not have nursed a boyhood passion to fly, but winning that small contest fed the flame that soloing had sparked. It inspired me to improve my skills and advance in aviation. The desire to taste that sweet euphoria of victory again and again would infuse my contest flying for over 50 years.

It was jarring to return to my high school classes on Monday, however. *I* knew my life was different. Yet in the eyes of my classmates and of nearly everyone I knew, nothing had changed. I was still the same person, with the vulnerabilities, flaws, and narrow palette of skills as I had possessed 72 hours before. This recurring frustration with the invisibility of my successes in the real world would trouble me for many years.

Yes, I was a pilot. But that seemed irrelevant in an environment where sports were such a big deal. I couldn't imagine myself as an athletic star, much less sweeping beautiful girls off their feet. I distinguished myself by making grades and vying for top standardized test scores. I was proud of that, but it didn't count for much. At age 17, I conceded missing out on an important part of the high school social experience. When I thought about the future, which wasn't often, I envisioned being excluded from a rich and exciting existence, one of those men who goes through life solo (and not in an aeronautical sense). For the most part, I accepted my fate with stoic resignation.

I was a different person when I was flying, with the assurance and heightened awareness of mastering an aircraft and my exposure to danger. But this continued to be a secret to most of my classmates, and my social profile remained mired in obscurity. Even for those who learned about my flying, it was imponderable. In those pre-YouTube days, discussing soaring with a non-pilot was the equivalent of trying to describe the exhilaration of skiing to someone who has never seen mountains or snow ("say what?") or to explain the mysteries of sex to someone before they enter puberty ("eww!").

By the time of this contest, I had begun to dodge the subject of flying. The few comments and questions I received were so predictable I could have typed my answers in advance: *Wow, that's cool...aren't you scared? It sounds dangerous. It must be so peaceful up there. How do you fly without an engine?* And the inevitable: *What happens when the wind quits?*

As my senior year progressed in late 1968, I wished I could park them in front of *The Thomas Crown Affair*[6] showing in theaters then. Apart from being a beautifully photographed vehicle for Steve McQueen and Faye Dunaway, the film has a spectacular, three-minute aerobatic sequence by a sailplane similar to my father's 1-23, flown by a pilot we knew, overlaid with the Oscar-winning song, *The Windmills of Your Mind*.

Then, unrelated to anything Hollywood was cranking out, my life changed! Deb, a match-making classmate in the mold of Jane Austen's *Emma,* determined—after consulting with my mother, I learned later—to entice me from my "shell." Deb arranged my awkward first dates. Soon I hit it off with Anna, a very cute "A" student who—it astonished me to learn—seemed to find me interesting. Anna and I attended our senior prom, a tradition I would have scathingly dismissed as impossible for me only six months earlier.

One night, parked in her driveway, I worked up the courage to kiss Anna for the first time. This was mind-blowing, given my lack of confidence with girls a

---

[6] Sailplanes are also beautifully photographed in the remake of *The Thomas Crown Affair* (1999) and in *Fifty Shades of Grey* (2015).

few months earlier. Aside from wavering self-assurance, the principal reason I took so long to plant a kiss on this girl's lips was not that she was unwilling. On the contrary, Anna grew tired of waiting for me to make the first move (not a situation I have often faced since then). I was just woefully unprepared. I had never paid attention to the kissing scenes in movies. Embarrassed and with fatalistic logic, I had reasoned, "Why torture myself studying something I will never get the chance to practice?" She was understanding and persistent, however, and by the end of the evening, I had acquired another skill!

I never knew if my soaring encouraged Deb to consider me a social rescue project. But her "intervention" altered the course of my life, for which I have forever been grateful.

My new interests didn't supplant my fascination with soaring. I still loved flying. But now I had other things, i.e., social life and a girlfriend. I was more complete as a person, more *normal*. Flying no longer had to compensate as much for inadequacies comparing myself to my father. Did I mature as a pilot because I gained confidence as a young man? Or was it the other way around?

* * *

America was in turmoil in 1968, but the anxiety closer to home involved *my* future. Applying to college was simpler then, but I was casual even by those standards. Late in 1968, my high school guidance counselor telephoned my parents to deliver a stern warning:

"I'm not sure if you're aware, but Chip is the only one of the top 20 in his class who hasn't applied to college. He needs to act fast, or he might not be going to college anywhere."

That got their attention. My father cornered me, struggling to remain calm.

"Where do you want to go to college?"

"Uh, I don't know. I haven't thought much about it."

"Well—what do you want to study?"

"I have no idea."

Dad had experience walking people through decision-making processes.

"Well, what do you like in school?"

A sudden, immobilizing tightness in my chest swept over me with the pressure to select a lifelong career. I looked down, not wanting to meet his gaze. Vocational interest and aptitude tests suggested a technical career.

"I'm good with science and math. I dunno, engineering?"

"Engineering is good! [big smile!] What schools are you interested in?"

"I don't know."

[his smile vanished] "With your grades and SAT scores, you can go any-where. [Not helpful; I needed to narrow the choices] You don't have *any* ideas?"

"Uh, I haven't thought about it."

[impatiently] "You must have some names."

I hesitated, not wanting to commit myself (a trait that will plague me for 50 more years). I didn't have a clue. "Well, some friends are going to Purdue."

"Great! [big smile] We'll call Purdue for an application. [Mentioning Joe's Bar & Grill and Institute of Technology would probably have elicited compara-ble enthusiasm from Dad.] Where else?"

"Well [hesitating], Doc Farrar is an engineering professor at Vanderbilt." Dr. Franklin Farrar was a Nashville soaring pilot we knew from the contest circuit.

"Great! We'll call Vanderbilt and get an application."

Now I had two choices, down from thousands. We visited both schools. I had been a pilot for three-plus years, but our short flight to Nashville on American Airlines that spring was my first time on a commercial jetliner.

Purdue was like a small city, spread over four square miles, with buses from dorms to classes. Vanderbilt was far more compact, and I could walk every-where. With my gliding connection at Vanderbilt and my cluelessness regarding the real world, it makes perfect sense I selected it over Purdue.

This is a reminder of how decisions made for trivial reasons can determine the course of our lives. It's the way an executive I knew at investment banking powerhouse Credit Suisse First Boston casually skipped a breakfast conference at Windows on the World in lower Manhattan on September 11, 2001. The sub-sequent post-terrorism economic meltdown in the U.S. cost him his job. To no one's surprise, he concluded he was better off unemployed than dead.

In my case, I suspect I was better off with a degree from a small Southern university when I applied to Harvard Business School four years later than I would have been graduating from a large Midwestern school. And those two years at HBS totally changed the direction of my life.

So without that soaring connection with a Vanderbilt professor-*cum*-soar-ing competitor in the late 1960s, who knows where I might have ended up: as an engineer on the 737 MAX program being laid off by Boeing?

CHAPTER SIX

Whirlwinds

I 'VE SAT THROUGH HURRICANES. But they don't compare to a few seconds riding out a tornado that could have killed us all.

* * *

My dad was a meticulous planner, always mapping the future. In the summer before I headed off to Vanderbilt, his plan for my gliding career included three contests. One of them was a regional event in Adrian, Michigan, where he had experienced such a disastrous outing two years prior. Little did we know that a different type of catastrophe awaited us this time around.

Many experts now emphasize the value of experiences over material possessions. That's a harder sell to those who grew up with little means. My father, who came from humble beginnings, placed great importance on material things, such as our suburban home, our cars, and even our first color television. Our sailplanes also represented a significant investment, of course.

We indulged in experiences, but they were not what most American families would choose. Instead of lavish vacations, we visited our grandparents in Alabama for a week each Christmas and summer. Disney World wouldn't open for two years, but it wouldn't have mattered. We allocated the bulk of our travel and leisure funds to soaring competitions.

Adrian was my first regional contest. Unlike the typical seven-day, Sunday-through-Saturday affairs, this one was scheduled over the last weekend in June plus the three-day July 4th weekend, allowing five total flying days with no need for pilots within easy driving distance to take vacation time.

The weather on Day One was marginal. We struggled to secure the sailplanes on the launch grid in the strong gusts, maps and hats flapping in the wind. There were thermals, but low cumulus clouds scudded overhead, driven by the 30-knot gale howling in from the west. The only viable option was to send us downwind—the path of least resistance—33 miles to an airport on the shore of Lake Erie. The organizers hoped enough of us could then buck the wind on the way back a few miles (and avoid being blown out over Lake Erie) to score the minimum 35 miles required for an official contest day. In this wind, it was a one-way mission, i.e., we would all be returning by trailer.

There were, in fact, zero finishers. But enough of us made it to the turnpoint and part way back to meet the 35-mile minimum. Flying in these conditions was stressful. But it was worth it when I received an ovation—and another boost to my ego—the next morning for my struggle to reach the turnpoint, then turning into the wind for another three miles and a certain outlanding. My hopelessly outclassed 1-26 was the lowest-performing sailplane of 16 there and particularly useless in high winds. The next day, Sunday, was unflyable so we dispersed, and returned four days later for the long July 4th holiday weekend.

That Friday was the no-fly day from hell. Forewarned, we had the gliders secured when the fast-moving storm blew in late that afternoon. Within minutes, the gentle breeze built ominously as dark, foreboding clouds bore down. Almost 50 pilots, crews, and volunteers sought shelter in a fragile wooden clubhouse as the tempest descended.

This violent maelstrom was the leading edge of what would become known as the Ohio Fireworks Derecho. It tore through lower Michigan and Ohio and continued as far as Pennsylvania and West Virginia, killing over 40 people. As the sky blackened unnaturally and the wind rose to a demonic howl, the wooden structure vibrated, shook, and groaned. The noise crescendoed to a deafening shriek. At the climax of the cacophony, with rain stitching the roof like gravel shot from the sky, someone cried out. We rushed to the windows as dark shapes hurtled across the grass and disappeared into the impenetrable downpour. There was a thud like a muffled explosion as lightning struck the airport beacon tower close by and the lights flickered out. It was late afternoon in July, but when the electricity stopped flowing, it cast the room into darkness.

The storm departed as quickly as it had arrived. When the downpour eased, we emerged to assess the damage. A freakish, 100 mph whirlwind had touched down less than 100 yards away. The dark shapes rolling by were our heavy canvas tents. The tornado had torn them loose, wrapped them up with our belongings, and deposited them halfway across the airport in a sodden heap. Then it overturned and destroyed a trailer with a glider stored inside, and snapped the heavy-duty tiedowns of a power plane like twine and flipped it over.

Saturday and Sunday were unflyable, so we departed the Holiday Inn (where we had decamped to dry out our clothes). Still needing two more official days, we all agreed to reconvene two weeks later. The result was the same, i.e., two more nights in the Holiday Inn (our tenting days were over) and no flying.

Conflicts with other contests postponed our last attempt until the long Labor Day weekend, when ten of the original 16 pilots gathered again. Twenty miles along the first leg of Saturday's task, I found myself low, thermaling at 900 feet, barely sustaining altitude. The wind was drifting me inside the landing pattern at Toledo Express airport as the control tower routed power traffic around me.

This was a dangerous rookie mistake, and not just for being close to a major airport. The turbulent thermal was small and weak, and I was circling as slowly as I dared to stay in it. I was hyperalert for the buffeting and sloppy controls that would signal an imminent stall.

In a stall, the aircraft flies so slowly that the wing quits flying and the nose pitches down in an instant. The instinctive reaction is to pull *back* on the control stick to level out. Counterintuitively, the only way to recover is to ease *forward* on the stick to speed up and get the wing flying again. That's difficult to do when you're suddenly staring at the ground. An uncorrected stall usually becomes a spin, a tight, even-more-nose-down, out-of-control spiral at a high rate of descent. Now staring straight at the ground whirling around, the pilot must—again—counterintuitively push *forward* on the stick to unstall the wing, then recover from the dive. The wrong action often leads to a fatal crash. I knew what to do if I stalled, but my 900 feet left little margin for recovery.

There was a lot going on at once. I was watching the airspeed on the ASI, checking below for landable fields, and eyeing the large airplanes sailing by on their way into Toledo Express. Fortunately, the controllers in the tower were accommodating (I suspect they could tell my young, nervous voice). I exhaled a huge sigh of relief when the thermal improved, and at last I climbed away.

That's why I couldn't believe Dad's next order: "You need to land at the airport in Bowling Green just ahead." You've gotta be kidding! I just spent 20 minutes climbing out of a hole and now you want me to *land?*

He had been following below me when a wheel bearing failed, and a wheel fell off the trailer! I met Dad at Bowling Green airport, where he talked the manager into allowing us to stow the glider in a hangar overnight. The next morning, we drove down from Adrian with a borrowed trailer, retrieved the 1-26, then reassembled it at Adrian so I could fly what turned into the last day. Our persistence—four round trips to Michigan plus the overnight retrieve—paid off with sixth place, much better than anyone had expected my outclassed 1-26 to do in what was doubtless the most protracted regional in U.S. history.

That year, 1969, is when I emerged as a pilot. I flew three contests, landed out a dozen times (a dubious personal record that still stands), boosted my best flight time to over six hours (earning my Silver badge at last), and added a Commercial rating to my Private Pilot certificate. I was still a novice contest pilot, but I was moving up and more excited than ever.

CHAPTER SEVEN

The Best Movie in the Whole World

W HEN MY FLYING SUMMER ENDED, it was back to the real world again, this time to Vanderbilt University. The social scene there was dominated by the Greek system. Most freshmen were eager to connect with a fraternity or sorority during the frantic recruiting rite known as "rush week." We donned sports jackets and ties and trooped over to the fraternity houses to relate our life stories in the most intriguing ways possible. With no sports or student government credentials, I could only discuss my soaring.

That wasn't enough. I learned later that when the rush chairman at one house presented my name for consideration, none of the active members I had met could recall anything about me. There was an awkward pause. Then John Colbert—a quiet, laconic, yet popular young man—stirred. He hadn't said a word about anyone the entire week. Now he raised his head and croaked,

"This guy *flies!*"

The room exploded in laughter. No one knew what he meant. He could have said, "This guy battles *space aliens!*" But it sounded good. And it had been a long day. So when the chairman called for a vote, I was in.

My frat brothers included jocks; academic stars; artistic types; pre-med and pre-law students (including a future U.S. Senator); engineers; and those aimlessly seeking to avoid the draft. We had our share of excessive drinkers, although it was tough to differentiate lifelong frontrunners for Alcoholics Anonymous from those merely exhibiting typical college behavior. Drugs were still underground at Vanderbilt, but we had a few stoners. And a handful of carefree perennial students there when I arrived in the fall of 1969 were still making cheerful-but-uneven progress toward a degree when I graduated in 1972.

This was the South, so we had a few overt, unapologetic racists. One of our few Jewish active members was allegedly voted in because the brother who was most zealous about maintaining a white Christian membership had stepped out of the room. Like most fraternities, ours had the "blackball" system, i.e., one nay vote sufficed to deny membership. The rationale was being able to assure each new member of his unanimous approval. The effect was to preserve a stultifying *status quo*. Another hale fellow was equally outspoken about defending the racial purity of our chapter—whenever he bothered to show up.

This jovial "good ole boy" discrimination was new to me. At my mostly white high school, I had naively envisioned racism as something displayed by sinister, red-necked oafs in the movies. And while our fraternity was more enlightened than some others, condescending, sexist attitudes toward women were common. That said, the fraternity helped me continue the personal growth I had begun in high school, building on the self-confidence flying had given me. And I needed that because in college, as in high school, my lack of athletic experience nagged at me. I boosted my fraternity's grade-point average. I dated attractive women, which helped. But my lack of sports credentials never seemed far away.

* * *

Adding to this was my rising unease over Vanderbilt engineering. It was a respected program. But the buildings and even the professors seemed tired and fusty. I had expected something glitzier, more evocative of a glowing future. I knew little about the alternatives. I was flourishing academically, so staying in engineering made sense. Then, in two hours and twenty-two minutes, my world turned upside down.

On Her Majesty's Secret Service—the sixth cinematic installment in the James Bond series—had opened during Christmas break with spies, villains, pursuits, and explosions. I exited the theater in Cincinnati, deeply troubled. This spy thriller crystallized my growing anxiety. I had made a dreadful error!

As I watched secret agent James Bond reconnoitering amazing European locales, driving exotic automobiles, and cavorting with beautiful women, a sense of gloom swept over me. I knew this was a movie. But I despaired that, as an engineer, I would never get to experience *any* of that excitement or glamor.

In melancholy moments, I envisioned being chained to a drafting board, condemned to a life designing boilers and machinery in what was then an almost exclusively male profession. Against this grim prospect, I imagined the splendid post-graduation lives of my College of Arts & Science classmates.

I couldn't stop obsessing about that damned movie! Maybe I was overreacting. Back at Vanderbilt, I walked a mile and a quarter into downtown Nashville to sit through it again—twice. I returned the next night for two more viewings. By the fifth sitting, I had memorized most of the dialog and spotted several video editing errors *[watch the helicopters hovering overhead near the end]*.

I knew actor George Lazenby's James Bond and I had almost nothing in common, but the silver screen was a window into a more fabulous life than what I believed Vanderbilt's engineering degree offered. The solution was obvious. I must transfer to Vanderbilt's College of Arts & Science as soon as possible!

My father reacted to my solution with less enthusiasm, especially when I couldn't articulate my reasons. I could hardly admit a James Bond movie had inspired me. Somehow, we got past that, but I faltered at his next question.

"What do you want to do instead?"

"Something in business, I guess." I had absolutely no idea what that meant.

"Business? Alright, what specifically are you interested in?"

"I don't know. [awkward pause—I was still struggling to answer] But it seems like a better career path for me than engineering."

[sigh] "Okay. If you really want to go into business, why don't you stay in engineering and get your degree? Then go to business school. An engineering degree with an MBA is the coming thing."

[long pause as I debated revealing my ignorance] "What's an MBA?"

The rest of our conversation is hazy, but in ten minutes in January of my freshman year, we mapped out a much different strategy for my life.

Freed from the prospect of ever using my engineering degree, my goal became earning the grades to gain entry to a top business school. I was a speed reader with strong conceptual skills and a near-photographic memory. This enabled me to rip through a textbook, take the exam, and set the curve in the small mechanical engineering classes—while retaining distressingly little afterward.

I was so open about my plan that the faculty awarded another senior with somewhat lower academic standing the honor of best mechanical engineering graduate. She deserved it. She was focused on her future in professional engineering. I was intent on winning acceptance to a leading business school.

I can't say where that young woman ended up in life, but *my* plan worked. During my first week at Harvard Business School, I strolled around the campus on a perfect fall evening. Head up, shoulders back, I took a deep breath.

"For the first time, I'm where I belong. *This* is where I will learn how to build a life for myself."

My two years at HBS led to investment banking, the first of nine different careers—none of which involved designing boilers and machinery.

I haven't seen that many other Bond films. I'm still a little discomforted that a spy movie was the catalyst for the extraordinary change in my life. College students switch their majors all the time. But if Ian Fleming's work ever had the same influence on others as it did on me, they're probably working for the CIA.

CHAPTER EIGHT

Freshman Disorientation

NON-PILOTS DON'T REALIZE HOW EASY IT IS TO GET LOST. The world looks different from the air. You know this if you've ever peered out the window of an airliner when there are no skyscrapers, sports stadiums, or large bodies of water. And sailplanes rarely fly over skyscrapers, sports stadiums, or large bodies of water. Too often, the landscape below is a patchwork quilt of fields, forests, unmarked roads, and anonymous towns. Until GPS, certain pilots reliably got lost at least once every contest or two. In 1970, I learned it could happen to me, too.

My freshman year Spring Break coincided with the regional soaring contest in Chester, South Carolina. This storied event was the season opener for serious pilots in the East. I was not one of those pilots. Neither I nor our little 1-26 belonged there. Every other sailplane entered had vastly greater performance. I didn't have to be an expert to predict this contest would be humiliating.

Coach Dad disagreed; he thought it would be valuable experience. He might also have been motivated to spend quality time with the family after his oldest child had left the nest. And what better quality time than at a soaring contest?

Growing up, I had been closer to my mother. She was the stay-at-home mom who cared for us. She supervised schoolwork, arranged music lessons, and scheduled us. It was she to whom I confided insecurities about my appearance. She enrolled me in a ballroom dancing class to help me through my painful shyness with girls. She was also the disciplinarian.

That said, Dad was in charge. He wasn't domineering. But when we went astray, his forehead would furrow, his voice would deepen, and he would "guide" us in the right path. He seldom shouted or threatened. When reason failed, his fallback technique was guilt. Head shaking with regret, he would refer to our "obligation," (which often existed only in his mind) adding:

"You wouldn't want to disappoint so-and-so, would you?"

"Sure; why not?" was not an acceptable answer.

So my relationship with my father was strongest in gliding. He continued to instruct at SSD and fly for fun. But for eight years he subordinated his love of competition—and his ambition—to manage my contest "career."

That's not to say he sat quietly on the sidelines. He assumed the responsibilities of coach with enthusiasm. The rest of my family still relate how, cowering in the backseat of our big Chevy station wagon, they pleaded with him to slow down as he barreled along Carolina roads at 70+ mph with the glider trailer bouncing and swaying behind. Gazing skyward with one hand casually draped over the steering wheel and the other hand cradling a microphone, he would occasionally glance back to the highway to adjust his track. His aim was to stay directly beneath my 1-26 as I struggled around the course.

The backwoods array of odd-shaped fields and unruly roads was disorienting to someone accustomed to the neat squares-and-section-lines grid of the Midwest. One incident took a comic turn, although it wasn't funny then.

Journal Entry: March 27, 1970 (Chester, South Carolina)

I knew this was a mistake. I have been toiling all afternoon to grind my way around the task, climbing in every decent thermal I can find, then gliding at a sluggish pace toward where I hoped the next one will be. Completing the long task is hopeless. The organizers set it so the high-performance crowd could play. All I want to do is avoid landing out in the dirt somewhere.

Many pilots grow lyrical about landing out. Adventure! The drama of the unknown! Meeting colorful people! Heroic tales of narrow lanes, locked gates, farm animals, and lifting the pieces of the glider over a fence.

They can have all that. I *hate* landouts. I crewed for my father for years, helping disassemble and carry his glider out of fields in the dark, heat, humidity, rain, mud, and mosquitoes. Last year, I added a dozen of my own. They're stressful. Hazards lurk in the fields: hidden rocks, woodchuck holes, wire fences, tall crops or grass, fenceposts, power lines, etc. And in these pre-mobile-phone days, the pilot must hike to the closest farmhouse; awkwardly explain why he landed his glider there; get driving directions for the retrieve crew; and use their telephone to call contest headquarters.

Most landowners are happy to help. But waiting hours for your crew can be tedious, answering repeated questions, preventing bystanders from trampling crops, and hoping the police don't screech to a halt looking for the "airplane crash." That sounds amusing but can trigger bureaucratic officiousness as rural law officers freeze the scene until they resolve what laws you broke or which federal agencies they must notify (none, in both cases).

And capping all other hassles, landing out usually means lower points unless there are few or no finishers. I'm not worried about points. Pageland Airport may be a landout for scoring purposes, but at least it's an airport. And it's a sure thing, less than 20 miles down the main road southeast from Monroe. The big four-lane highway is unmistakable, slashing a bare streak across the rural countryside.

Then, with no warning, my compass malfunctions. Crap! It says I'm flying due east, not southeast, 45 degrees off course. Not possible. I can see Pageland appearing ahead. I choose to believe my eyes rather than my lying compass. Soon, my father and I are announcing our imminent arrivals at Pageland Airport. Curiously, his radio transmissions are getting weaker.

I grab the mike: "Just go to Pageland Airport and I'll meet you there."

"Roger, (scratchy) at the Pageland Airport in (garbled) minutes."

Soon I'm overhead at Pageland but can't find the airport. Three miles beyond the town with a paved runway, it should be easy to spot.

Dad is waiting: "Okay, (garbled) the airport. How far (garbled) you?"

"I'm over town. I just can't find the airport." Where the hell is it?

"(garbled) outside of town."

My unease is growing and my voice is unsteady: "I know, I know. I just can't find it."

Something's not right. Airports don't vanish. I'm biting my lower lip. I glide over and around town, scanning the ground with increasing desperation. No airport. Which way is southeast? The stupid compass is no help. Where's the sun in the sky?

Now I'm lower. A lot lower. I need a thermal. I've been fixated on finding this worthless airport and in minutes, I've let my situation deteriorate severely. This can't be happening! Crap!

Frustrated, defeated, and at pattern altitude, I'm forced to land in a plowed field outside of town. As I descend on final approach, I spot a water tower in town and turn my head. I am stunned to read the name: "Marshville."

No-o-o-o-o-o-o-o-o-o-o-o!

The big highway I had followed was brand new, not yet on the aeronautical charts. I hadn't even noticed the smaller "main" road to Pageland. My compass is perfectly functional. Now I'm sitting in a field 15 miles from the airport where my father and brother are expecting me to arrive any second.

When we drag into contest headquarters that evening, pilots and organizers who had listened to our frantic/comic exchange on the radio subject me to merciless kidding. Already embarrassed to be flying here, I'm mortified by my inept performance.

When Dad was growing up with little money, he relished the status of being an athletic and academic standout. So, no surprise, as an adult, he was shameless in chasing minor celebrity by promoting our accomplishments.

Our neighborhood free weekly newspaper was hungry for content. They would happily print virtually anything residents submitted. My father obliged, typing up and mailing little stories much as people post on social media today. He reported on our family reunions, academic honors, college acceptances, and, of course, our flying. Dad embarrassed me by making a fuss over my achievements, which began to include winning the 1-26 Class at local contests. Yet, hypocritically, I was quietly pleased when these flying photos appeared in the local newspaper for my friends to see.

These vanity press releases evidenced my father's fascination with the accoutrements of success: awards, trophies, badges, certificates, diplomas, etc. He pushed me to apply for state soaring records. Since few junior records existed, the Soaring Society of America (SSA), the national membership organization, ratified anything I bothered to submit. Somewhere I have a box of framed state record certificates from various states certifying what were, even by the standards of the day, uninspiring flights.

Dad's early public relations, in The Hilltop News, *Cincinnati, Ohio, July 24, 1969, pp1.*

CHAPTER NINE

Breakthrough

G ANGS HAVE COLORS. Fighter pilots have call signs. Soaring pilots have contest numbers. Most modern racing sailplanes look alike. They aren't NASCAR race cars with garish color schemes (in fact, they're all white) and sponsors' decals the size of bedsheets. So, like NASCAR cars, sailplanes carry a prominent identifier, a "contest number" (e.g., 44, A8, XX).

A contest number is a personal, almost totemic alter ego, displayed on the glider's tail, under the wing, and on the trailer and tow vehicle. Contest numbers identify pilots on launch grid lists, radio communications, and scoresheets. Start/finish gate crews use contest numbers to identify planes and record their times. Pilots use them to call out who is close to them in the air. Contest numbers often subsume real names, with pilots referring to each other that way.

Dad hadn't needed a contest number for his 1-23B in local contests. But that changed with his Diamant and higher aspirations. His dream was "JB," his initials *[and mine; legally I'm Joseph Noah Bearden III though I've been "Chip" since birth]*. But JB had long been assigned to a Mr. John Baird out West.

We also needed a Federal "N" number required on U.S. aircraft. In another creative stroke, Dad envisioned JB standing for James Bond. He inquired of the FAA if N007JB were available. To Mark and me, that was cool—our father as James Bond! "Sorry," the FAA responded, registrations cannot begin with zero.

"What about N707JB?" my father wrote back.

A decade earlier, Boeing had reserved blocks of 707 numbers for their dominant commercial airliner. But N707JB was available. When Dad learned John Baird was selling his glider, he wrote to explain our Diamant and N707JB. He asked John to keep us in mind if he ever gave up the number. John, whom we had never met, shocked us by graciously responding he had planned to move JB to a new glider, but Dad deserved it by reason of better planning!

In 1970, we replaced the Diamant with a beautiful Glasflügel Standard Libelle 201 from West Germany (with the optional trailer this time) and transferred JB and the federal N707JB registration to it. These were the "colors" I would campaign for over 50 years.

Flying gliders was a progression. The 2-22s were like trucks: slow, ponderous, noisy, and unresponsive. Our 1-26 was like driving our Volkswagen Beetle:

sitting upright in the bathtub-like interior, bouncing on the stiff suspension, one hand jabbing at the tall gear shifter and the other sawing away on the big steering wheel while flogging it down the slow lane of the freeway.

Our Libelle was like a sophisticated, lissome sports car. I squeezed my lanky frame into its sleek reclining cockpit, adapting to its sensitive controls, retractable landing wheel, high performance, and less forgiving landing characteristics.

Our new Libelle and factory trailer, 1970 (photo by Joseph N. Bearden Jr.)

I had won a handful of local 1-26 Class contests before the Libelle arrived. Besides the fleeting exhilaration of each victory, I was inwardly joying that when my name appeared on an entry list, I was one of those favored to win. But I knew luck played an outsized role. Staying aloft in a 1-26 was so much work that improving my cross-country average speed was secondary. In the 1-26, I was never more than minutes—or one minor tactical error—from landing.

In the Libelle, it was easy to stay aloft on a decent soaring day. The focus was on flying farther and faster. I was more at one with an aircraft than ever before, my hand on the stubby control stick, my wrist moving easily as I translated thoughts into inputs so subtle, it often seemed I was *wishing* the responsive glider to follow my direction. When I pulled up and flung the Libelle into a tight spiral to enter a strong thermal, the G-forces pressed me into the reclining seat, supporting me from my knees all the way to my shoulders. The lift surged and pushed the glider from below, one wing dipping and the other rising as I rolled into the turn and centered the thermal. In the Libelle, I first experienced true oneness with an aircraft high above the humdrum custodies and minutiae of life, in command of a sophisticated machine soaring rapturously through the air as a member of an inner sanctum. It was heady stuff for a 19-year-old.

I couldn't deny that one draw was gliding's uncontrived danger. It didn't loom over us so much as hover quietly in the background, always there, real, unlike the manufactured hazards of traditional team sports. Before I ever tasted alcohol, I was intoxicated with wonder that I could control my fate, mastering soaring's risks through the exercise of my free will and skill.

How many people experience the same emotions, the same sensory perceptions? I was too young to realize how rare this was. Add this to the list of things I didn't appreciate then.

Mark, Diane, author, and parents with the Libelle, 1971.
(photo from estate of Joseph N. Bearden Jr.)

* * *

Cordele, Georgia, population 10,000, is a tired settlement in the peanut and watermelon country 125 miles south of Atlanta and 35 miles east of Plains, home of future President Jimmy Carter. In August 1971, Cordele was hosting the large SSA-sanctioned regional contest Dad had chosen for my competitive debut in a high-performance sailplane.

I thought I was prepared for America's Deep South climate based on our annual trips to Alabama. But Cordele in August was worse. Seconds after exiting our car or air-conditioned indoor space, the thick, steaming, oppressive heat left us gasping. Sweat poured down our faces and necks, drenching our clothes in minutes, like being bundled in a blanket in a steam room. The slightest exertion left us drained and exhausted, with sweat trickling down our backs.

Adding to the misery, clouds of gnats swarmed into our ears, noses, mouths, and eyes. By wretched luck, Cordele lies below the Gnat Line, a 20-mile-wide border separating North Georgia's red-clay-like dirt from South Georgia's gnat-friendly sandy soil. Insect repellant provided brief respite, but frequent use prompted concerns about the consequences of exposures to chemicals.

And speaking of exposure to chemicals, the bitter, acrid, pungent odor of pesticides and herbicides was pervasive at the big ex-World War II airport on the north side of town. That's because the airfield—spread across thin, parched grass, the three mile-long runways shimmering in waves of blistering August heat—was a hub for crop-dusting airplanes that operated there from dawn to dusk during certain seasons spreading chemicals on fields.

Cordele is where I received my first "attaboy" from a top-tier pilot. On Day One, I had been in a trickle of nervous competitors creeping up the first leg under low cloudbases, never getting much higher than tow release altitude. To-day, a competition director (CD) would never dream of sending us out that low, but this was a different era. It was a rude initiation to departing on a task in weather so iffy we wouldn't have bothered going to the local gliderport to fly.

Each time we climbed into the low, murky tendrils of the cloud capping a thermal and headed for the next one, it was potentially our last glide. At one point, I was the high man as we topped out. I knew—by some unspoken but clearly understood protocol—it was my turn to lead out, to take the risk of find-ing the next thermal while other pilots opportunistically trailed behind watch-ing to see what happened to me. Nervous, I leveled the wings and aimed for the next cloud a few miles away. Later, one of the big names in the Southeast, a Delta Air Lines captain who lived in Atlanta, smiled at me with my father stand-ing there.

"JB, nice job today. You led out when it was your turn. That's the mark of a champion."

Hearing this was a thrill, but not as much as the first time I drove a sailplane down to ground level for a high-speed pass across the finish line.

Journal Entry: August 19, 1971 (Cordele, Georgia)

I'm about 15 miles out on final glide. The Cordele airport is out there some-where. Because our 1-26 couldn't glide very far, I could always see where I was going to land: right *there* just ahead. But the glide angle of the Libelle is so flat that the landing spot is often out of sight in the distance.

My glide calculator says 3,500 feet should be enough. But I've never glided in from this far out. That light-colored blotch on the horizon *could* be the big airport. Or it could also be a hay field. If I'm wrong, I may not find out until I'm too low to find a thermal. It's like overspending your retirement savings; by the time you realize your mistake, it's too late to replenish them.

I push on, descending 200 feet every mile, the familiar stress, excitement, and eagerness mounting. It's warmer at lower altitude, but that's not the reason my right hand is sweating on the control stick or that I'm breathing a little faster.

"Jake Baker Ground, switch to Three," I instruct my crew to change to the primary contest frequency of 123.3 MHz (from 123.5 MHz), alerting them to my final glide. Jake Baker (for JB) is the informal call sign we have used since Dad first heard it in the '60s. Officially, I use the ICAO phonetic Juliet Bravo. But with family and flying buddies, it's Jake Baker. Aside from the note of nostalgia, it seems to punch through radio static better.

I'm concerned about doing something stupid on final glide, especially after three and a half stressful hours in the cockpit. I'm almost there. Then I spot a sailplane ahead, flying fast, bobbing up and down like a porpoise under the clouds. I'm higher, so I push over to speed up and close the distance. As I draw closer, I'm relieved to see it is BY (Bravo Yankee), senior Eastern Airlines captain Ed Sessions. If this glide is okay with Ed, it's okay with me!

We're speeding under a line of cu. Flying into a strong thermal, we "bump" it—zooming up sharply, nose high as the G-force increases; slowing to 40 or 50 knots as we fly through the core to gain energy; then pushing over without stopping, briefly weightless as we go over the top, then nosing down to 70 or 80 knots—and gain several hundred feet without pausing to circle.

I'm checking off the landmarks passing below: a road, a lake, the big state park just west of town. Now I can see runways materializing in the hazy ground clutter ahead. Five miles from the finish line, we're still gaining on glide path each time we bump a thermal. Stretches of sink between thermals are unsettling, but they're brief.

Now it's time to burn off the safety altitude. The last few miles go by fast at 100 knots, two miles a minute. Slamming through low-altitude thermals at high speed knocks us around. With my left hand, I tighten the belt and harnesses to avoid punching my head into the canopy a half inch above it.

Ed announces, "Bravo Yankee, one mile," and I echo, "Juliet Bravo, one mile." I've crossed finish lines in our 1-26, but it's different at this speed.

Charlie Spratt at the finish gate acknowledges: "Bravo Yankee, Juliet Bravo, winds are light and variable."

Diving down to drop in the last mile, we come sweeping across the airport boundary in close formation like two fighter jets buzzing the tower a few hundred feet above the ground, smoking along at over 100 knots.

I follow rules in life. I don't take chances. I don't seek thrills. I've never displayed a compulsive need for excitement or adventure. Whether I secretly crave the neurophysiological effects of high-risk activities is irrelevant because my natural caution always kicks in to squelch any impulses.

Today, however, my true personality is out. I'm an adrenaline junkie, too! And a fast final glide headed for the finish line of an SSA-sanctioned contest trailing a professional pilot with thousands of hours gives me leave to do things other people might label irresponsible, e.g., hurl my sailplane down over a hard, unyielding runway at 120 knots, faster than I've ever flown.

It's electrifying to return to the airport where we launched earlier that afternoon. I have tunnel vision with BY in my sights. Cars, glider trailers, and spectators are blurring by off my right wing as we level off less than ten feet above the centerline of the wide, east-west runway shimmering in the heat. The wind noise is louder. The controls are ultrasensitive in the low-level turbulence. I brace my forearm against my thigh to steady the control stick with a sweat-soaked hand. Were I to twitch, the glider would leap into the air or slam into the unforgiving asphalt below in an instant.

I've watched hundreds of high-speed passes but never done one. Is this the right time? Will my father approve? He's too conservative to try it himself. But on this big regional stage, I am young and eager to impress. Without ever knowing, I've been waiting for this my entire life. I want it. I *need* it. Down on the deck, heart thudding in my chest, I'm right on BY's tail, a few hundred feet behind him. We streak down the runway, the immovable surface unfurling below, seconds from the finish line, each glider emitting that wondrous, whistling exhalation of a fast, clean sailplane traveling at speed.

"Mark! [pause] Mark!" barks Charlie Spratt on the radio as we cross the line in succession. "Bravo Yankee and Juliet Bravo, good finish."

What a rush! We're hurtling down the runway, aimed *away* from our trailers and tiedowns. We need to get turned around. My airspeed has decayed to 100+ knots. We're two of the first finishers, so every eye is on us.

"Stay on his tail and you'll be okay," I reassure myself, ignoring the warning to pilots and teenagers that just because someone else does something doesn't mean you should, too. BY pulls back hard on the stick and soars into the air in a steep, graceful, climbing turn to the right, gaining several hundred feet. I follow, momentarily pressed into the seat by the G-forces of the pullup. Nose high, I'm staring at the sky until I level out and hold the turn for 270 degrees, then reverse, rolling smoothly into a 90-degree left turn *[fellow New Jersey drivers will recognize this as the aerial equivalent of a jug-handle U-turn]*. My heart is pounding in my chest.

"Keep the speed up!" I caution myself, leveling out, knowing that stalling and spinning from 200 feet would be fatal. We're still in trail, headed back down the same runway, now in the opposite direction. I switch hands on the control stick and slap the landing gear lever down, hearing the wheel drop into position, then switch back to get my right hand on the stick. That little-used landing gear lever is tucked away on the right side of the cockpit.

As we level off, BY extends the dive brakes on his wings to descend and settle onto the runway. I don't want to risk overrunning him, so I pull the lever on the left side of the cockpit to open my dive brakes, too.

WHEEEEEEEE!!! Damn! The shrill electronic tone is jolting. Somewhere in the recesses of my brain, it occurs to me this is the landing gear warning.

"That can't be right. I know I put the wheel down." With the noise blaring, I keep the dive brakes out and sink into the runway. Almost but not quite certain, I wait for a bump as the tire touches, chirps, and spins up to speed.

Rolling ahead of me, BY rudders hard left at the intersection to steer onto the glider runway, headed for the trailer tiedowns. I'm too close behind, so I continue straight on the main runway, then coast off to the side in the grass. As I roll to a stop, the left wing settles gently and CLUNK, the perfect, pure white wingtip knocks over a runway light on a short steel post.

My euphoria turns to horror! I can't see if there's damage, and before I can climb out to check, Dad and Mark skid to a halt in our car in the grass, grinning like madmen. They are as excited as I am about my electrifying finish. Stricken, I call out to Dad and point at the left wingtip as I fold the landing gear handle securely against the cockpit wall (silencing the gear warning horn). As I unbuckle my harnesses, the glider shudders from another noise.

BONK!!!

What the—? Bent over, Mark staggers from under the right wing, holding his head and grimacing.

"Owwww! What'd you do that for?" he asks, his face twisted in pain.

He had ducked under the raised right wing to reach the cockpit at the exact moment my father, obsessed over the smallest scratch, had grabbed the left wing and yanked it up to inspect for damage (happily none). The right wing came down on Mark's head like a seesaw, almost knocking him out!

These early Cordele flights exposed a latent thrill-seeking aspect of my personality. They also signaled soaring's primary appeal was now competing against my peers and being perceived as a contender. I still appreciated the beauty of flight in all its splendor, more in the Libelle than ever before. My life was richer for being connected to things non-pilots couldn't imagine. But even back home when friends and I landed in the evening, what I remembered was not the visual spectacle but the pilots I had bested in our informal game of "last man down."

I played that game on the final contest day. Thunderstorms were a daily occurrence in August, dumping rain, lightning, wind, and turbulence before blowing out. But they were usually isolated, unlike in the Midwest. We could deviate around or fly under them to reach the sunlight beyond.

Not this time. Storm cells coalesced into a contiguous squall line across the course line, blocking the way. By the time I came along, there were gaps. Nervous, I slipped through one and glided to the last turnpoint at Tifton, then glided back toward Cordele under a gray, lifeless sky.

My father had returned home for business, so Mark trailed me and advised on landing sites. I had never flown a contest without Dad's presence. So with this first-time freedom came pressure. Jumpy, eyeing other landing sites that *might* be better than the one I had chosen, I set down in a plowed field, five and a half hours after takeoff. The two of us removed the wings and carried them through the soft dirt to the trailer, then rolled the fuselage to it through the furrows. I was exhausted. Rivulets of sweat etched creases in the thick layer of dust on my skin. And I was subdued, unsure how costly my landout would be.

We returned to the airfield that evening to learn no one had completed the task (relief!). Few pilots had gone farther (yay!). And several above me in the standings had landed early because of the thunderstorms (even better!).

A small crowd poured out of the air-conditioned office in welcome. I assumed they were happy to see "the kids" had made it back safely. But before I could climb from the car, one of the organizers bounded up with a big grin on his face and an outstretched hand.

"Congratulations, Number Two!"

CHAPTER TEN

Wire and Rain

T HERE IS NO SAFETY NET IN COMPETITIVE SOARING. Traditional sports have coaches, officials, and medical personnel to provide order, direction, and aid when things go wrong—in full view of cheering spectators on the sidelines. Soaring pilots compete alone, thousands of feet above vast expanses of sparsely populated farmland, forests, mountains, and deserts. A crash during a competition—infrequent, but possible—might go unnoticed. Before the growing popularity of emergency locator transmitters (ELTs) in the late 1980s and satellite trackers (e.g., SPOT) 30 years later, pilots could go missing for hours or even days before anyone discovered their fate.

It's a high-stakes, high-drama world, where even the slightest mistake can lead to disaster, with no one to assist. Once the start gate opens, there are no timeouts, rain delays, or yellow caution flags. Whatever happens, the pilot's mandate is always the same: *fly the aircraft* until it is safely on the ground.

My father knew soaring's risks. He diligently taught his students how to manage them. When addressing safety, he always offered the same reassurance.

"The most dangerous part of soaring is driving to and from the airport."

I'll never forget those words or the way I repeated them reflexively whenever someone asked about safety. And non-pilots *always* asked. It was a wonderfully soothing phrase coming from a man as risk averse as Joe Bearden. I was untroubled by having no evidence to support or refute it. I hadn't known anyone killed in an automobile *or* a glider. So, just as I had adopted my parents' religious and political beliefs, I echoed Dad's safety declaration like a mantra:

"The most dangerous part of soaring is driving to and from the airport."

* * *

In 1972, I ventured closer to the edge than ever before—three times.

I've heard countless stories involving pilots who landed in prison yards, military facilities, highways, athletic fields, tiny clearings, rock-strewn desert landscapes, and other unlikely places. I once landed our 1-26 across the fence from a Nike Missile site near Oxford, Ohio, attracting the interest of armed soldiers. Years later, I squeezed into a golf course near Covington, Virginia. Unimpressed golfers continued to play through, forcing me to push the glider off the fairway. But my most outrageous landout occurred at the Chester Regional in 1972.

"Watch this" is the aeronautical equivalent of "hold my beer," often a precursor to an ill-advised, ego-stoked antic in an aircraft. One particularly dangerous gambit is attempting to fly *under* things, e.g., bridges and electrical wires. Such craziness never tempted me—until it seemed like a good idea.

Journal Entry. April 1, 1972 (Chester, South Carolina)

Of *course* I'm missing out! College males during the peak of the sexual revolution should be dedicating their Spring Breaks to endless days of beach parties in Fort Lauderdale, reveling in alcohol and chasing girls. But for the third consecutive year, I'm flying gliders instead.

My freshman year Spring Break featured my "lost in Marshville" debacle. I spent my sophomore year Spring Break with Dad at a small gliderport in the mountains in Lexington, Virginia. My college roommates came back tan and hungover, boasting of their debauchery. I returned with a flight to 13,000 feet in my logbook and the memory of soaring above the ghostly, lens-shaped lenticular clouds in the mountain wave, shivering in the cold as I pointed the nose of the glider straight into the wind in utterly smooth lift, so different from the turbulence of thermal flying, and peering down through gaps in the clouds at the mountains far below, hoping these holes didn't close and trap me "on top."

Back at Vanderbilt, I didn't bother regaling anyone with that story. They would never understand. In college—as I had in high school and would in my career—I mostly deflected questions about my vacations. Skiing in Jackson Hole sparks head nods and respect. Days in the stifling heat of an obscure town they've never heard of to fly gliders draw blank looks—and a quick change of subject.

So in 1972, for my junior year Spring Break, we are back at the Chester Regional. This time I'm flying our Libelle, so I can't blame the sailplane for my poor showing. It's a real letdown after my success at Cordele last summer.

I've been fighting a strong headwind on the last leg of the task. Each time I stop to circle in a thermal, the wind drifts me backward, *away* from the finish. I top out and buck the wind again, retracing the path I already traveled plus some. Then, when I stop to climb, the wind drifts me part way back.

I can't keep this up forever. The sun is declining and with it, the thermals. But I have a more urgent need. It's colder than I expected at altitude late in the day. That has triggered my kidneys into producing more urine than usual. As the back pressure rises, it's difficult to focus on anything else.

"I can't believe this! Am I gonna have to land just so I can pee?" I can't hold it much longer. And there's nothing in the cockpit I can use as a container. Someone who's never been strapped into a narrow, confined cockpit several thousand feet in the air can't appreciate the sense of helplessness, desperation, and near panic in this situation.

Then, eureka! The daily task sheet is on cheap copy paper. Frantic, I fold it twice to form a small paper cup like a schoolboy. I loosen my harness and leather belt, unzip my jeans, and awkwardly push them down a few inches so I can pee into the makeshift cup. It's difficult, but I'm *very* motivated. The relief is so immediate, it's tough to stop when the cup fills in seconds. Balancing the leaky paper vessel, I slow the glider, open the vent window on the left side of the canopy, and toss the contents into the slipstream.

Bad idea! The liquid explodes in the 40-knot breeze, though most of it stays outside the canopy. With one hand on the [glider's] control stick, I hurriedly refill and empty the sodden paper cup twice more before it disintegrates.

Flying at 60 knots seems to blow most of the mess off the clear acrylic plastic canopy over the cockpit and the white gel coat on the fuselage and wing. I've bought time, but the day is dying. I'm low and need a place to land.

Just ahead and below, I watch another pilot flitting back and forth over trees, checking out a questionable field. It would be okay if not for a creek snaking across the middle, dividing it in half. Worse, a row of power poles runs along this creek supporting a single electrical wire. The section of the field before the creek isn't long enough. The section after it would be, but the power line blocks the approach.

"What the hell is he doing?"

I watch as he turns final and skims over the first half of the field headed straight for the creek and the wire. At the last second, he floats over the creek, squeezes *under* the wire, touches down, and brakes to a stop in the grass just beyond it. Unbelievable!

Glider pilots fear wires because they are often invisible from the air. Stories abound of crashes and deaths associated with flying into them. Ordinarily, I would never consider flying under wires. But this guy has shown the way!

As I turn final, this pilot comes on the radio calmly talking me into his field like an LSO directing a Navy jet approaching an aircraft carrier. Here, though, there will be no wave off (or "eject, eject" command). I don't have a big jet engine to try again if I misjudge. Too fast and I won't touch down and get stopped in time. Too high and I'll snag the wire with the tail or wing-tip—disastrous. A few inches too low and I'll clobber the far side of the raised creek embankment and wipe out the landing gear.

With his voice in my ear, I level out, aiming for the narrow "mail slot" bounded by the embankment jutting above the creek, two power poles 200 feet apart, and the wire strung between the poles 20 feet above. There's no margin for error as the wind buffets me. My hands are sweaty in the cold.

The obstacles at mid-field are approaching fast. I slip beneath the wire, then plant the main wheel on the far side of the creek with a bump. Then I'm on the wheel brake furiously to stop before the pasture turns swampy. What a rush! It takes a few minutes to calm down, after which I'm absurdly pleased with my precision airmanship. Dad isn't so happy when he arrives, but a dialog with the other pilot reassures him.

My father remained my coach and greatest supporter, but I was becoming more proficient, aggressive, and successful than he had ever been. We would sit at night planning the next big contest and discussing what it would be like if—or, as he would say, *when*—I would make it to the U.S. Team going to the World Gliding Championships (WGC). I feared he would embarrass me by discussing it with our flying friends, but it still thrilled me to imagine such a thing. Later I wondered if Dad had adjusted his expectations, redirecting his focus from reaching the top himself to doing so vicariously through me.

These discussions played a crucial role in maintaining my motivation. Soaring can be fulfilling, elevating us to a level of bliss so intense it is unseemly. But it can also invoke exceedingly low moments, whether from faulty judgment or bad luck. Ironically, one of those moments vouched for my father's reassuring:

"The most dangerous part of soaring is driving to and from the airport."

Journal Entry: July 2, 1972 (Interstate 74 near Andersonville, Indiana)

Late Sunday night, we're headed southeast on Interstate 74 from Indianap-olis to Cincinnati. The torrential downpour, reminiscent of a hurricane, mer-cilessly assails the windshield with torrents of water, rendering the wipers' high-speed thrashing nearly useless. They flog the glass, carving brief slivers of sight through the deluge. Beneath the car, the tires churn up vast quantities of water, which scour the chassis like a noisy sandblaster. Ahead of us is an inky black sea, the taillights of vehicles ahead barely visible through the dangerous rooster tails of spray they are spewing. We're hauling the Libelle trailer, still an hour from home, returning from a weathered-out contest in the Chicago area over the Fourth of July weekend.

I had slowed when it was my turn to drive. Something didn't feel right. Now Dad is at the wheel, barreling along grimly, his jaw set, at 70 mph, ignoring the conditions. I'm tired, dozing, and dreading the alarm the next morning.

With no warning, I am jolted into wakefulness. Our full-size Chevrolet station wagon feints and slithers sideways like it is on ice, first to one side, then the other. When I look over, Dad is gripping the steering wheel fiercely, his face tight, not daring to take his eyes off the road.

"I can't hold it," he blurts, the fear thick in his voice.

To say Dad is thrifty is analogous to saying the U.S. government has a little spending problem. Extracting the last miles from his tires is yet another manifestation. The rubber on our station wagon is devoid of tread. At high speed, with the highway awash in rain, the tires have aquaplaned, lost their grip on the pavement, and climbed up on top of the water layer.

With 1,500 pounds of loaded trailer nudging us from behind, the car fishtails once more, still moving with appalling velocity. Out of control, it skates left off the freeway. With a sickening thump, it drops into the swampy depression of the grassy median strip, skidding broadside in a shower of spray. The tires are shuddering in a grassy liquid plume and the car is bumping and shaking as it spins counterclockwise, plowing a furrow, scrubbing off speed as headlights from oncoming traffic bloom in the darkness in my window.

In slow motion, I wonder, with analytical detachment, if the grassy median will guide us down into its dished-out center as intended or fling us up into the westbound lanes for an 80,000-pound oncoming truck to obliterate. Somehow, the car stays upright as it spins. In a few interminable seconds, it slides abruptly to a halt aimed over 90 degrees from our intended path. The true danger crystallizes in the next instant.

"Get out of the car!" I yell. In the dark with the rain-spattered windows, I can't tell if we've slid up into the oncoming lanes. We unbuckle, throw open the doors, and scramble out.

Safe! We're still in the grass, unharmed, a few yards from the freeway lanes headed back to Indianapolis. By a miracle, the car seems undamaged.

Shaken, but giddy to have escaped, we stumble through wet grass alongside the vehicle, hoping to find the glider trailer also unharmed.

The next blow is cruel. Our elation over escaping a catastrophe turns to despair. In the flickering light of passing vehicles, we see our sleek German trailer, as elegant as the sophisticated sailplane nestled within, had jack-knifed hard—crushing the rear corner of the car and severing the fuel line—before toppling over onto its side. Like a hard-boiled egg, the trailer had fractured on impact. The uneven grass had flexed, cracked, and partially stripped away the fiberglass shell. Wings and fuselage are twisted, split and piled together loosely inside, visible through wide fissures, streaked with mud, and mottled by wrinkles warning of hidden damage.

The rain pours down as we stare dully at this ghastly scene. Looking southeast, I realize the trailer had sacrificed itself, dragging us to a halt seconds short of the enormous prow of a reinforced concrete bridge support that would otherwise have crushed the passenger side of the car where I sat.

My father is like a child gazing forlornly at a broken toy. "Look at our little sailplane," he murmurs, devastated by the unfathomable enormity of the damage and sense of loss. Instinctively, I fling my arm around his shoulder. I know the glider and trailer are insured and repairable. We need to expunge what happened—and what *could* have happened—from our memories. Something passes between us then as, for a moment, we swap roles, united in our shared experience of escaping a potentially fatal catastrophe.

We rent a U-Haul box truck from an all-night gasoline station. Indiana State Troopers help load the glider's wings, fuselage, and tail, plus our equipment and luggage. The roll-down door is useless. The glider's wings protrude from the back like skis hurriedly tossed into the trunk of a small car.

I clamber up into the back while Dad takes the wheel (at a more sedate speed). Drained, I stare back at cars following us in the heavy rain. The shock of the accident settles in and my eyelids flutter, drift down, and close. I'm awakened by the truck coasting to a stop on the hill in front of our house at daybreak. I shake my head in fatigue, then sit up wildly and turn to look for the fuselage. Before I fell asleep, it had been resting in its wheeled cradle from the trailer. My job was to guard against losing anything. Has it rolled out the back door and fallen onto the roadway? No! My last waking act had been to rope it to steel rings on the front wall of the truck! Relief!

My parents embrace, both understanding how close we came to disaster. Then we unload and carry the wings and fuselage piece by piece through the narrow gap between the houses. We angle them through the sliding glass patio door and into the big TV room. There we set them down gently, laying down beach towels and throw rugs to shield carpets and furniture and protect the Libelle's formerly perfect skin. We treat these fractured pieces like the body of a soldier who died in battle, as if by avoiding further injuries, we can somehow make amends for wounds already inflicted.

Then, because it is Monday morning, we shower and head to our jobs, where, bleary-eyed, I relate our latest story to incredulous co-workers.

The Libelle's damaged trailer after the accident. (photos by Joseph N. Bearden Jr.)

Fortunately, by then we owned shares in two Libelles, so I still had something to fly. Inconceivably, weeks later, I almost wrote off *that* glider in another incident involving wires, this one at a weekend contest in Cynthiana, Kentucky. The irony was that I was trying to play it safe to protect the glider for the Cordele Regional coming up in less than a month.

Journal Entry: July 30, 1972 (Cynthiana, Kentucky)

I coast in low over the last turnpoint, the small airport at Georgetown, Kentucky, late in the afternoon under the cloudy steam of low overcast. A weak thermal allows me to stay airborne, not climbing but not sinking. I stall for time, circling endlessly. Then, 30 minutes later, the sky breaks open, the sun reappears, the thermals cook off again, and I climb back up to altitude. Saved! The family catch up to me there and wait while I consider. The finish line is only 12 miles away, but there are few landing options on the way.

"Take no chances. Call it quits and land, Chip. Cordele is coming up soon." But one more thermal will do it. No one else has gotten this far. It would be really cool to be the sole finisher. Ego prevails.

"Go for it!"

Ten minutes later, I'm halfway back, needing a final climb—when it clouds over again and the thermals die. S**t! Do I have enough altitude to glide in from here? Probably. Maybe. I'm not sure. It depends on how far out I am. I made a marginal final glide into Cynthiana once before, arriving with only enough altitude to make a 90-degree turn and land. But that was approaching from the south when I had it in sight the entire time. This time, I'll be approaching over the hills, hoping the airport will appear in the haze in the last valley. If I'm wrong, I could find myself squeaking over a hill low, staring at tobacco fields instead. Ignoring the risk of damaging the glider, tobacco is an expensive crop in Kentucky, along with thoroughbred racehorses.

"Take no chances."

I select the last decent field, on top of a gentle hill. Tall high-voltage towers are marching across it, but the wires are well above the ground. There's plenty of room to touch down early and roll under them.

"I did it once; I can do it again."

I've been studying the power lines so closely that I haven't paid attention to the field itself. Turning final, it's like I'm staring head-on at a ski slope rising in front of me. The uphill slant is much worse than I assessed. It's also pitched from right to left. Worst of all, the grass is much higher. Oh, crap!

There's nowhere else to go. I dive to pick up speed, then flare to land uphill, aligning the wings and fuselage parallel with the slope. The touch down is graceful, but I know I am going to ground loop in the tall grass. So I push the nose over to keep the tail off the ground. As I feared, the grass catches the right wingtip and snatches the Libelle around violently, just like my father's Diamant five years earlier, scrubbing off speed as it slides sideways.

Once a ground loop starts, the pilot is just along for the ride. After the glider is jerked to the right, I wait for the abrupt crunch of the tail hitting sideways and breaking off. The rear fuselage is a known weakness in Libelles. It often snaps in ground loops less dramatic than this one.

The aircraft shudders to a halt, the wings bouncing, aimed off to one side. Shaken, I hesitate for a second. I'm an utter idiot. I fling off my harness, lift the canopy, lean forward, then lunge around to look behind me. I'm expecting to see the rear fuselage broken off just ahead of the tail.

I'm shocked. The glider is intact. It's freakish luck. The tail stayed in the air as the glider whirled around and didn't hit the ground until it had come to a stop. The only mark is grass stain under the right wingtip.

And the wires? My rollout after I touched down was so short because of the upslope, tall grass, and ground loop, that I stopped well before the high-voltage towers. They weren't even a factor.

It didn't help my mood when I learned I could have reached the airport in a dead glide if I had known my position more accurately in those pre-GPS days.

My family arrived too late to see my landing and ground loop. But they received a jolt of adrenaline when I radioed I saw the wires and would "go under them." I neglected to mention I intended to *roll* under them after touching down. My mother said Dad almost bit off the microphone trying to respond.

I've never seriously considered flying under wires again.

Libelle and trailer at landout in 1973, both extensively repaired after highway accident the previous year. (photo by Joseph N. Bearden Jr.)

Our freeway-mangled Libelle was the most extensive repair the shop in Erie, Pennsylvania had ever undertaken, with myriad holes, fractures, and internal damage. In my father's calls with the shop, he refused to mention a suspicious shadow I had seen that night in the rear fuselage.

"They'll tell us if they find anything. I don't want to create problems where there aren't any."

I exploded. WTF? This was a variation of his "if I say it didn't happen, then it didn't happen" philosophy. Would he risk flying a glider with a compromised structure rather than investigate potential damage? Grumbling, he passed along my warning. The shop found a cracked bulkhead, which they repaired.

I also rolled my eyes when he came home excited a few nights after the accident. An office colleague had diagnosed the cause as "planing."

"Yes, yes, yes!" I exploded. I had told him the tires had hydroplaned due to too much water and speed and too little (read: no) tire tread. But Dad didn't want to listen. I suppose I could have been less confrontational. Somehow, his colleague had contrived to ascribe the blame to something arcane and outside my father's control. Ergo, it wasn't his fault.

At 21, I had zero patience with this. Decades later, I gained some insight into how my father may have dealt with such situations. Two-time world soaring champion George Moffat talks a lot about the psychology of winning. He recommended *Learned Optimism,* by psychologist Dr. Martin Seligman. The fascinating thesis, backed up by clinical evidence, is that optimism has a disproportionate causative effect on one's success, health, and mental wellbeing. Call it a winner's attitude or the placebo effect: if you *believe* you're better—at a job, in a sport, even recovering from illness—there's a good chance you *will* be.

Dr. Seligman maintains you can learn this to manage the psychology of winning. It requires developing your "explanatory style," so you do not view setbacks as personal failures. It's better to regard them as temporary impediments—owing to external factors—that you can surmount. To paraphrase Dr. Seligman, successful individuals are those whose normal response to failure is: "it's somebody else's fault!" This simplistic and upbeat (some might say delusional) outlook is part of the complex profile of a great many successful people.

The best glider pilots *are* supremely confident. Whether displaying fighter pilot swagger or quiet assurance, they seem to possess the certain conviction they *will* find and exploit better soaring conditions if they push on, no matter how low they glide in pursuit.

In contrast, I have spent too much time reproaching myself for past mistakes and hesitating in new situations. Playing amateur psychologist is dangerous, but I've speculated that my father may have subconsciously had a better explanatory style than I did. It didn't give him a competitive edge in soaring, but it seemed to work well for him elsewhere in life.

I finally made it down to Fort Lauderdale for a beaches-booze-and-girls Spring Break during my second year at business school. It was great fun and yielded a few outrageous tales. But to be honest, the Spring Break stories I remember most fondly now involve flying. Maybe my father was right all along.

CHAPTER ELEVEN

National Debut

I T WOULD HAVE BEEN *REALLY* COOL if my second place at Cordele in 1971 had triggered a dazzling rise to the top. In fact, I did win occasional days and even outright at local meets. But to my frustration, I was inconsistent, doing well for a few days before stumbling.

Still, the Cordele regionals of the early to mid-1970s helped shape my competition style and my reputation. It was there I learned there were often key decision points where, by taking a different route or electing to climb higher or leave the thermal earlier, I could sometimes get away from the gaggles. Some of these sallies proved embarrassing, but enough of them paid off, sometimes dramatically so, that my confidence in flying alone flourished. Several times I worked my way around storms and finished the task late in the day, long after other pilots had given up or been forced to land.

My speed in these heroic struggles wasn't impressive. Deviating from the course line to go around storms or to get to the last clouds in the sky or making a slow, painful climb in the last thermal of the day to get altitude for a final glide costs time. But completing the task when others landed out compensated for the slow speed. I became known for scrambling when things turned sour, with a "never say die" attitude.

Journal Entry: August 18, 1973 (Cordele, Georgia)

Four of us are topping out in a thermal on the last leg of the task, closely spaced, with that delightful floating sensation of flying at speed with other gliders in buoyant air. Despite cu in every other direction, however, the last 20 miles is a giant blue hole stretching all the way beyond the finish line at Cordele. When the other three pilots roll wings level on course, I trail them, reluctant, unconvinced this is the smart move.

Blue holes can be treacherous. Sometimes there's lift out there, sometimes not. If the latter, you may not know until you're well out into the blue, often too low to escape to the clouds. We don't have quite enough altitude to make it to Cordele. These guys are betting they will find one more thermal.

To me, it's not worth the risk. I do a 180 behind them and return to the clouds. The other three are already out of sight when I contact a thermal and begin to climb back up to cloudbase again. I'm breaking two basic rules.

First, stay with the gaggles when it's blue. They have a better chance of finding that invisible, isolated thermal than one pilot alone.

Second, never, ever reverse course and go back. Covering even a short distance not once but three times is a costly time penalty.

Wondering if I've blundered, I climb up to cloudbase again. This time, the wind drifts me a few miles closer to the finish line. As I approach Cordele after a long final glide through still air, I pass over the last landable field before a forested area bordering the airport. In the dirt, a quarter mile short of the finish, are all three of my erstwhile fellow pilots. My gamble has paid off!

That decision earned me another second place overall when the contest ended, this one an oh-so-close 1% behind the winner. Not all such bets paid off. I needed to be more consistent. Even so, I soon eclipsed my father's record.

When I was young, I just assumed Dad was a "player" on the local soaring circuit. Yet he never won a day or scored an SSA finisher's medallion at a regional contest. Part of growing up is accepting one's father for who he is—a man, like any other man, with strengths and weaknesses. I can't say whether that realization came earlier for me because of flying, but it was less equivocal given the unremittingly quantifiable scoring systems at soaring tournaments.

He and I had seldom competed head-to-head. Then, in May 1975, we both wanted to fly our club's Wright Memorial Glider Meet. I just assumed he would defer to me, as usual. I was a little taken aback when he insisted he wanted to play, too. He proposed a compromise: "Let's team fly. I'll take the first day. You take the second. Whoever has the higher score gets to fly the third day."

Fair enough. My father did okay on Day One. I did better on a challenging Day Two and then won Day Three for the overall win. This put our names on the club's perpetual trophy as a team, my first appearance on it. It was the only time my father's name appeared at the top of a competitive event of any consequence. Club members joked about the kid vanquishing the old man. I didn't want to humiliate Dad. But part of me gloried in publicly besting him.

* * *

We were now competitors, but still flying partners. That summer, I commuted five hours on good weather weekends to Cincinnati from Chicago, where I had taken my first job out of graduate school.

The following spring, we drove to North Carolina where I completed my Gold badge with a flight to over 14,000 feet over Mount Mitchell, the highest peak in the Eastern United States.

Author in Libelle over Mount Mitchell, North Carolina, on the way to 14,000 feet, 1976. (photo by Joseph N. Bearden Jr.).

Two months later, I relocated to New Jersey for a new job. This complicated my weekend trips to Cincinnati but was too good to turn down. Not long after, I flew back for my first Nationals, the 15 Meter Class in Bryan, Ohio. Our Libelle was not fully competitive under this new class's less restrictive rules, but Bryan was a few hours up the road. Like the new job, it was too good to turn down.

I had never flown with so many gliders (53) or famous names. For years, Dad had dreamed of flying the Nationals. It's a *big deal*, the pinnacle of American competitive soaring. There *is* something different. It's the Major Leagues, the Masters, the Super Bowl. Top pilots driving in from around the country are serious, not there to have fun and socialize. But one of Dad's SSD buddies had floundered in 1965, placing near the bottom. Add Dad's unhappy experiences with the Diamant and I'm not surprised he deferred. Now my rise in the ranks provided an alternate path for him.

Journal Entry: June 29, 1976 (Bryan, Ohio)

It's Contest Day One. I've been here before many times—just never at a nationals. As always, I'm stressed but excited and eager to step up. I know the routine, but there's more at stake this time.

Wheeling over the airport, I peer down through an awesome, slowly rotating gaggle of what looks like half the planes in the contest—more than I have ever seen at one time. I cross the start line just after some of the big names. Around the second turn, I'm flying aggressively, keen to show I am worthy to be here. Alone, pushing hard to get to the finish line 20 miles ahead, I pass up a moderate thermal and drive out into a blue hole, hoping to find something better. Of course, I don't. This is a problem I'll have for a long time, i.e., no backup strategy.

Damn! I could continue in the blue. It's high risk, but I'm trying to be aggressive. Yet this is Day One. A landout today will kill my chances of doing well overall. Cursing, I play it safe. Once again, I ignore conventional wisdom and retreat a few miles to the thermal I rejected. It's still there and I climb up, then cross the blue hole to the clouds on the other side. I'm relieved to finish but dreading the hit I'll take on my score.

As the numbers begin to pop up on the digital display, I can't believe it. Pilots are still out on the course, though more than a third of the field lands out. But as the scorer posts their speeds, the results stand. Dazed, I'm in second place! This time, my whole family are there to share it.

Life is full of "if onlys." Forty-six years later, I made some assumptions about the extra distance and the altitude consumed flying into the blue and backtracking, and the average climb rate. I compared that to the gap between my speed and first place. I can't say for sure. But if I hadn't botched my initial sortie into the blue, I might have kicked off my first national appearance with a win. This is not my only "I coulda been a contender"[7] story, but it was special.

That was the opener in a string of top-ten days. I grew more confident, flying with the gaggles when it made sense and independently when I judged I had a better idea. I had a secret hope old guard pilots were watching me. Midway through the contest, one of them commented: "You sure are flying that Libelle well." I realized finishing at the top was a means to an end. It was hard to separate my need for the respect of my peers from my desire to beat them. The downside was I imagined every mistake I made was also being scrutinized.

I had arrived as the nervous new kid at the Nationals. Now I was getting cocky. The Greeks call it "hubris." The next day, I was miles down the first leg when I looked down at the variometer, disgruntled with my first few thermals. I told myself, "I can do better," and reversed course, heading back for another

---

[7] *On the Waterfront,* Directed by Elia Kazan, screenplay by Budd Schulberg, Horizon Pictures, 1954. Film.

start. In regionals, I'd been flying aggressively, often being one of the last to start and pushing hard all the way around. This day, I ignored that 50+ pilots of all abilities were already on course. I returned, climbed up, and crossed the start line a second time. I knew it was a mistake even before I went through the gate. The Bryan area was empty. I was the last pilot to start.

"This is really stupid," I reproached myself. Once out on course, I flew aggressively, but there was not a single glider in sight ahead of me to mark thermals. At last, after hours alone, going into the last turn, I was relieved to spot a few gliders ahead. I finally caught them and came home with their gaggle.

My 27th for the day dropped me from third to sixth overall. It was harder to stand up straight that evening at the cookout hosted by the contest. It could have been worse. But it punctured the balloon I'd been riding for almost a week. Dispirited, I vowed to do better. Unfortunately, no matter how bad things seem, they can always get worse.

Journal Entry: July 6, 1976 (Bryan, Ohio)

Day Seven: we race to get home, knowing all of us started too late to beat the enormous storm blowing up ahead. It's frightening, towering tens of thousands of feet over the course line, white peaks thrusting up and crowning a bulwark of angry, boiling clouds. A dark curtain obscures the way, a malevolent, faceless mass of slate gray hardening to near black. Flashes of lightning precede muted rumblings of thunder. The horizon has disappeared behind a wall of water. I've never felt so insignificant in a sailplane.

The contest radio frequency—normally quiet—erupts with alarmed cries of pilots being forced down, many declaring they can barely see in the heavy rain. I listen, incredulous and envious, as three pilots penetrate the downpour, lightning, and strong sink to finish the task in near-zero visibility.

I started late, behind the pack, so I retreat from the threatening overhang of the thunderstorm into the sunlight where the thermals are still working and climb up. I'll wait for the storm to blow out, then try to glide in behind it. I have played the waiting game many times before. It's what I do.

WHAM!

S**t! I gasp when something pounces on my Libelle like a big predatory cat springing onto the shoulders of its prey, teeth buried in the neck for a quick kill. I glance out to both sides, uselessly. There's nothing to see. The plane shudders violently in turbulence. Banging the stick left, right, forward, or aft has little effect. That predacious cat has seized the glider and shaken it a few times. I've never experienced anything like it.

Then, seconds later, whatever captured the aircraft releases it and I am flying normally. I'm in disbelief. What the hell was that?

I'm gathering myself, exhaling the breath I didn't realize I'd taken and starting to breathe normally again when, WHAM, the clear air turbulence snatches up my Libelle like a toy again. The glider shudders and shakes, loose items in the cockpit—including me—momentarily flung weightless. And then it's over.

After the third shock, I am so unnerved and spooked, pulse racing, that I simply give up. This is my first time tangling with anything like this. I turn tail, glide away from the storm and the finish line, find an airport on the chart, throw away my altitude, and land. It is a total, abject, humiliating capitulation.

I try to rationalize doing the prudent thing. This kind of rough air is totally outside of my experience. But it's in my father's face. He knows. The turbulence ahead of the storm would have subsided. I should have remained aloft waiting for the storm to exhaust itself and glided in behind it, as I have done so many times before and as a fourth finisher later proves was possible today. Instead, I finish 49th of 54. The small number of finishers devalues the maximum score and, thus, the penalty for not finishing, but I still drop one place, to seventh.

I give up trying to justify my decision based on safety. I know I let fear control me. In classic vernacular, I choked. Sagging, staring down at my feet in the car, I'm more depressed than I have been in a long time.

My humiliation was so overwhelming that the only way I could put it behind me was by vowing it would never happen again. I flew the last few days strongly to hold on to seventh. That helped put a positive spin on the contest.

We flew nine of ten days, my most ever. When it was over, I knew I had arrived. My better days and high finish gave me the confidence to say, "I want to be national champion" with a straight face, at least to myself. I had been embarrassed to discuss it with my father, but it no longer seemed so outrageous.

CHAPTER TWELVE

Self-Inflicted Wound

THE 1976 NATIONALS WERE JUST THE BEGINNING. I knew I was improving. The following spring, using business trips and cheap tickets, I commuted from New Jersey to Cincinnati to fly with Dad on weekends. We practiced hard and both entered the Standard Class Nationals in Ionia, Michigan, in June. This would be my second nationals, at age 26. At age 50, Dad would be flying his first. He never mentioned it explicitly, but I suspect both of us viewed this as his long-overdue reward for his years as coach.

Dad's Libelle (WE) and author's (JB) on the grid at 1977 Nationals in Ionia, Michigan.

Ionia was 100 miles north of Bryan, so I was still flying in my backyard, this time against other Standard Class gliders, not the slightly superior 15 Meter gliders I'd flown against in 1976. I was ideally positioned for success.

Journal Entry: June 22, 1977 (Ionia, Michigan)

On Day Three, I'm asking, "Why am I chilled?" It's not cold, even at altitude. When I reach under me to check the thin seat pad, I know what's happened. It's soaked in cold water. Damn! The water ballast system is leaking.

Lightweight gliders like our Libelles are great for the slow, tight circles needed to climb in gentle thermal updrafts on weak days. But when the thermals are stronger, we need to be heavier to cruise faster. So we load up to 200 pounds of water into ballast tanks in the wings. We can't climb quite as fast but we more than make it up by cruising faster, with a higher overall average speed. If the weather weakens or we get low and need to climb out in a desperation thermal, we can dump the ballast in minutes and be flying a weak-weather sailplane again.

The first two days, we've carried the ballast around the course, dumping it on final glide as we approach Ionia. A modern sailplane hammering across the finish line at well over 100 knots at treetop level, a heavy plume of water vapor exploding out the back of the aircraft like smoke, is a spectacular show for spectators (and ego-enhancing for pilots)[8].

The minor water leak is more annoying than disastrous. So far, my parachute isn't wet, and the instruments and the glider are undamaged.

But I am fuming as I streak across the finish at high speed, pull up, and land. I'm still furious when, after a delay, we finally get towed back to the main hangar. Straight away, we begin working to find and fix the leak in full view of officials and spectators. I totally forget the time. An hour later, my crew asks if I have turned in my turnpoint film.

"Oh, s**t!" I can't breathe. I can't even answer. Unlike in sailboat racing, soaring has no observers positioned at the turnpoints to verify competitors go around them. Instead, each glider carries two Kodak Instamatic cameras aimed out the left wingtip. The pilot flies over a turnpoint, aims the wingtip at the ground, and snaps a photo. The rules require handing in these films within one hour after landing to minimize the chance of tampering.

I'm five minutes over the one-hour limit.

Panicky, I hustle over to the scorer's office, hoping fervently I can skate by. I have a genuine excuse: the delay being towed to the hangar and the problem with the ballast system. And I've been in full view of officials the entire time; there's no question of cheating. It's a technicality. To my knowledge, no CD has ever levied this Draconian penalty. This CD notes the problem. After I explain, he smiles reassuringly, winks, and says they'll look into it.

My family are subdued as we drive back to the cabin on the lake where we're staying. I'm suffering a private hell. No one knows what's going to happen, but we're afraid to discuss it. After dinner, I go out on the lake and row furiously back and forth in an old rowboat for an hour. Exhausted and

---

[8] See examples of high-speed passes at https://www.youtube.com/watch?v=UK5XVGV8eM8

with blisters on my hands, I feel a little better and am able to fall asleep.

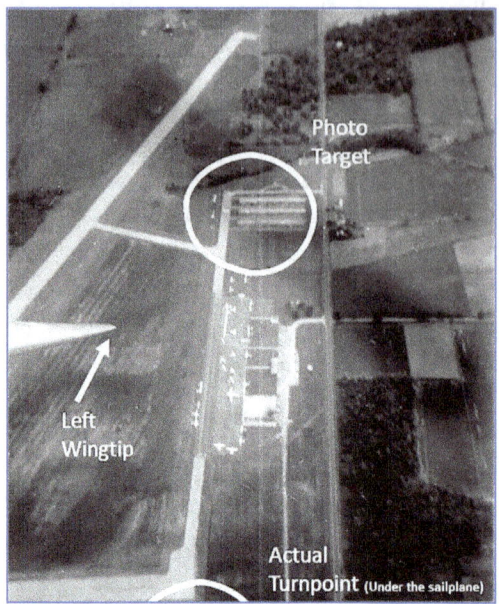

Typical turnpoint photo. The pilot banks and aims the left wingtip (peeking out of the left side) at the photo target, (the far end of the airport taxiway) while flying over the turnpoint itself (the other end of the taxiway, half hidden under the glider).

We're all still subdued in the morning. As we near the scorer's office, I grow apprehensive. I was always a good student, so I've never approached "grades" taped up on a professor's office door with such anxiety.

I peer at the scoresheet. Where's my name? S**t! It's near the bottom. My minor infraction has knocked me from seventh to 43rd for the day. With the penalty, I lost 550 of my 950 points (vs. a normal daily maximum points of 1,000). Two days into a ten-day contest, I'm finished. I could win every remaining day (not freakin' likely!) and not make the top ten. For once, Dad doesn't know what to say.

I learn later the CD intended to grant me an exemption based on my problem with the glider. But a contest volunteer—incomprehensibly, a fellow club member "helping out" at the contest, but incorrigibly self-important and officious—butted in to warn him he couldn't. WTF?

I appeal to the CD, citing the extenuating circumstances. He says his hands are tied. I'll never understand why, but at the pilots' meeting a few minutes later, he makes a mystifying, faltering announcement about the penalty, with no details or context, adding the only way he can remove it is by "unanimous consent of the pilots." He just makes that up; it isn't in the rules.

My chest is tight. The room is abuzz. Most pilots know nothing about the situation. But this is asking too much. I will never forget one highly placed fellow—I'll call him "Dan," an Atlanta pilot from my Cordele days sitting nearby—leaning forward, red faced, and shouting over the chatter of puzzled pilots.

"If you do it for him now, you'll have to do it for everyone else *for the rest of the contest!*"

"You a**hole!" I mumble under my breath. That's total BS. CDs make case-by-case rulings all the time. But I'm too stunned and embarrassed to push back. It wouldn't make any difference. As the babble continues, the CD, with magisterial unease, senses he is losing control. He takes command again and cuts off discussion, looking over apologetically.

"Sorry, Chip." With that, any chance I had evaporates, as does the contest for which I've been preparing for a year.[9]

That was Thursday. My best strategy to salvage what remained of my season was to stay through Sunday, then jet home and save my precious second vacation week for the Cordele Regional in August. I hadn't planned on flying there, but it was a better consolation prize than finishing a now meaningless contest.

The weather cooperated, and we flew three of the four days. With nothing to lose, I flew aggressively and closed out my contest with a second on the last task, by one minute, to a many-time national champion and U.S. Team member.

My misery wasn't over when I showed up awkwardly at my office on Monday. I had to endure the senior executives kidding me about "cheating." It was good-natured, but they couldn't know how this tortured me.

It's a cliché that "when one door closes, another opens." My desperate search for relief after the lowest moment in my soaring career helped open a new chapter in my life, one that is still unfolding 46 years later, one that would change my life as meaningfully as soaring had. I just didn't know it yet.

Journal Entry: June 30, 1977 (North Bergen, New Jersey)

I returned home from Ionia four days ago. They say true champions leave

---

[9] I did file an official protest with the national organization, pointing out the disparity between the infraction and the penalty, the near impossibility of my having cheated, and the extenuating circumstances—with no more success. In the spirit of "don't just complain, make it better," I then submitted proposed rules changes for my infraction and one other rule with equally disproportionate and devastating results. I had to pursue it with three different rules committee heads but years later, my language was adopted almost verbatim, albeit many years too late to help me.

their mistakes behind them and move on. I must be a real loser, because I can't let five minutes go by without castigating myself. For more than a decade, soaring has made me feel better about myself. Now it's the opposite.

I need to manage stress. Alcohol tempts, but I'm not trying to drown my sorrows after being rejected by a girl who says, "I don't want you anymore." I just want to obliterate my stupidity from my past. Rowing around the lake helped in Ionia. Could exercise do it now? I tried running for a month at Vanderbilt after a breakup (speaking of a girl who said "I don't want you anymore"). I'm still insecure about my athletic creds, but I need *something*.

Marathoner Jim Fixx's *The Complete Book of Running* had helped kick off the popular movement in the U.S. Many friends—including pilots—have taken up the challenge. So before work, I lace up my ancient leather tennis shoes and drive over to the scruffy county park next to my high-rise condominium on the Hudson River cliffs overlooking New York City. The neglected asphalt track looks to be a relic from the 1930s. One light pole at each end of the field is functional, the rest having succumbed to age or gunshots. Uncut grass is knee high everywhere except on the sorry playing field itself. The gravel parking lot is muddy and treacherous after heavy rains.

No one else is there. That's good. I set off jogging at a slow pace. I just want to keep moving as long as possible. I'm surprised to make it four circuits of the track, one mile, without stopping. And it works! For a few minutes, I've ceased to obsess about one of the most frustrating experiences of my life.

I started setting my alarm and driving to the decaying track to run a mile or two or (sometimes) three, slowly at first, then faster. I logged each workout—as I still do 46 years later—just as I've logged every soaring flight for the past 58 years. I still have these running logs, beginning with the last day of June 1977.

From a baseline of not much more than youthful exuberance, my time for one mile plunged. Soon, I reveled in the sensation of distinguishing myself from the average person in an *athletic* sense. I was relishing the same reassurance and boost in self-esteem that soaring had provided for over a decade.

I wasn't sure how long I could stick with it. But I already knew running was different in one noteworthy way. Soaring was an arcane activity no one understood. Running was a mainstream sport anyone could appreciate.

CHAPTER THIRTEEN

Deep Season

P ARENTS EMBARRASS THEIR TEENAGED CHILDREN. It's inevitable, like a circle of life. Birth. Embarrassment. Death. It can be the stodgy clothes they wear, or the dated music they listen to, or the corny jokes they blurt in front of friends. Whatever, children close their eyes, hang their heads, and plead silently, "please stop, just stop," cringing over how parents' oblivious behavior might blemish their youthful reputations.

I suffered less than some, which was fortunate given my uneven self-confidence. Dad got points for flying gliders and even more for his Corvette. That car manifested another aspect of his personality. In my father's Alabama hometown, there were two car dealers, Chevrolet and Ford. You were either a Chevy guy—like my father—or a Ford guy, for those who didn't know any better.

This was a serious issue, with no room for debate. My father was like a partisan voter whose support for a revered politician is unshaken by the revelation of scandalous affairs. Dad held an absolute, unshakeable conviction that General Motors' products were indisputably superior. When a soaring friend had a problem with his big Ford station wagon, my father shook his head sadly behind his friend's back.

"It's so predictable. Everyone who knows anything about cars knows FORD stands for Fix Or Repair Daily. They just aren't as good." Dad was an accountant, not a car expert. But to him, this was objective fact, though it ignored the reality of our new Chevy station wagon: an oil-guzzling, problem-ridden lemon.

The original Ford Mustang intrigued Dad, but he couldn't bring himself to buy one when it debuted in 1964. Instead, he shocked us by purchasing a Corvette—a beautiful silver-blue 1963 Sting Ray convertible. I was too young to drive it and he sold it before I got my license.

Dad had yearned for a sports car, but the Corvette wasn't a good fit. One big reason was it was pre-owned. For years, I avoided buying used cars because— in another of Dad's confident assertions—to do so was "buying someone else's problems." He couldn't fathom how someone would part with their car for any reason other than hidden malfunctions. The other reason for disgruntlement was it had been an impulse buy. This ran counter to his accountant's mindset. In Dad's world, major life decisions like this were not to be made on a whim.

Author with Dad's 1963 Corvette Sting Ray. In 1965, I could fly a glider but was two years away from driving a car! (photo by Joseph N. Bearden Jr.)

Joe Bearden's disciplined approach was perfect for his job overseeing conservative retirement programs for Procter & Gamble employees. At home, he would sit up at night updating ledgers of income and expenses, flying logbooks, detailed car expenses, investments in sailplanes, church budgets, Sunday School attendance records, and anything else where he could collect data. We joked he had a record of every dime he'd ever made and where it had gone.

Flying gliders and driving a Corvette didn't prevent Dad from mortifying me. At a crowded, controversial PTA meeting my senior year, the agenda was how to foster high moral standards among students, focusing on alcohol, sex, and drugs. One female classmate stood and declared her "inciteful" philosophy: *"if it feels good, do it; and whatever turns you on."* This elicited wild applause from students and gasps from horrified parents.

Sitting with friends, I flinched when my father rose to propose the School Board engage respected public figures as role models to speak to the students. The idea had merit. But the example he used was Bart Starr, quarterback for the Green Bay Packers and, previously, of Dad's beloved University of Alabama. Mr. Starr, one of his heroes, had led the Packers to victory as MVP in the first two Super Bowls in 1967 and 1968. A Christian, he had been married to his high school sweetheart since college. After Dad sat down, one of my friends stood in counterpoint and smiled tolerantly.

"The school's budget for things like this is roughly $65. I seriously doubt whether we can get Bart Starr to appear for $65," he amiably explained.

Few students knew the speaker was my father. And I wasn't eager to claim him. He never forgot the condescending rebuke, though. And I never admitted the young man who dispensed it was a friend.

* * *

I escaped further embarrassment until I was 26, when we were competing at the 1977 Ionia Nationals. The first few days confirmed I was the better pilot. Then Dad's name popped up in fifth place for the day, well above mine. What the hell? As he eagerly explained how he'd done it, I realized he hadn't vaulted into the ranks of top pilots. He had morphed into a "leech."

In other sports, success depends on strength, endurance, reflexes, tactics, hand-to-eye coordination, etc. Not so in soaring. An undistinguished pilot flying a sailplane that performs equally well as those of the leaders (commonplace with the advent of affordable mass-produced sailplanes from West Germany around 1970) can start seconds behind one of them, then follow their every turn and glide to post the identical time. I don't know of another sport where a less-talented competitor can blindly shadow a more accomplished one.

Expert and aspiring pilots alike disdained leeches for never taking a turn out ahead to find thermals. On course, we winced whenever a leading pilot curled into our thermal, knowing he would be trailed by leeches emulating his every move and oblivious to anyone else. There were even stories of clueless leeches following an expert off the course when he became temporarily disoriented.

No one would admit to being a leech, though we referred to the more notorious behind their backs. Thus, I listened in growing alarm as my father proudly described his strategy of latching onto expert pilots and following them. I struggled to contain myself.

"Dad, that's leeching! You can't do that."

"No, it's not," he protested, appearing to be puzzled. "I'm just using other pilots to fly faster."

"Yes, it *is* leeching," I hissed. "And you'll get a reputation for being a leech if you keep doing it."

As in the past, his "if I say it didn't happen, then it didn't happen" denial infuriated me. Later, I realized my real anxiety was fear of being embarrassed to have my father branded as a leech. I should have been mature enough to let him enjoy contests the way he wanted so long as he was safe.

That said, I was fine with Dad following *me* around a task. I led out in practice. The few times he had tried it at contests, though, I had gotten away from him or he had given up because I scared him going low after a better thermal.

Journal Entry: August 17, 1977 (Cordele, Georgia)

At most August Cordele contests, there's one crucial decision each day: i.e., when to cross the start line. Choose correctly and you can win the day. Start too early and you'll fly much of the course in weaker weather compared to someone who starts later and catches the stronger mid-afternoon lift. But start too late and the thermals may dissipate before you can finish or, worse, overdevelop into thunderstorms, forcing an outlanding.

This Cordele Regional is my "redemption" contest. Others may not see it that way, but I do. I'm still obsessed with my failure at the Ionia Nationals months earlier. On Day Two, we're sweating in our cockpits, circling over Cordele in the heat and humidity, waiting to start, anticipating the thermals will improve. Many pilots have already gone through the start gate, wary of waiting too late. In second place, I'm keen to finish high so I can move up. But as the minutes go by, I'm growing nervous about afternoon thunderstorms. The other top pilots are all hanging back. Why is no one going? I decide it's time. I radio the start gate to alert them and dive through it, headed for the turnpoint.

"Mark! Juliet Bravo, good start." That starts my clock.

I'm about 25 miles down the course, more than halfway to the turn, when I roll into a thermal. To my glee, and then horror, it's much stronger than anything I've seen so far. The next thermal confirms it. The weather forecast was spot on (who knew?). I left too early. *Now* I hear my top competitors, most of whom held back, radioing as they cross the start line.

I'm f**ked! They're going to kill me over the first 25 miles—almost one-third of the task. So far, there's no sign of thunderstorms. I could turn around, fly back to Cordele, and take another start myself. But I'd be at least half an hour behind the leading group. And if thunderstorms actually do blow up, I could end up with the worst of all worlds: an early start…followed by a late start…followed by a landout. No, my best alternative is to ignore what's done and fly out the rest of the task, knowing I'll fall in the standings rather than move up.

Over Tifton, I drop my left wing in a steep bank to photograph the turnpoint, then head back up I-75 toward Cordele, still berating myself. Today's task is an out-and-back. On the way north, I pass over the southbound gaggle of fast movers who started late and have been enjoying the stronger lift for the entire first leg. We're so close, I can imagine their gleeful smiles.

As I approach Cordele, I'm on final glide, storming toward the finish line only minutes away, still angry. Like many other bad decisions I've made, I wish I could do it over and re-fly the day.

Then it hits me: I can! As I near Cordele, the early finishers are radioing in, spewing contrails of water ballast like skywriting smoke, swooping across the finish line, zooming up in big, joyous, arcing turns, then landing on the glider runway to the southwest and coasting to a stop near the trailers. The tarmac is wet with water draining from ballast tanks as sweaty pilots hoist themselves from their cockpits, exulting. It's like a winning locker room after a game: wide grins; boisterous pilots and crews; and relaxed excitement.

I maintain radio silence until I'm minutes from the finish gate. I don't want to give anyone else the same idea.

"Cordele Operations, Juliet Bravo will land on the glider runway to the northeast. I need another tow, please. Can you have a crew ready? Please confirm." My request triggers a panic to pull together a launch crew, who had escaped to the shade after takeoffs concluded hours earlier. My plan is simple. The course is only 85 miles. Under the rules, I can land, relaunch, and fly it again. If my second lap is worse, I'll still get credit for my first flight.

I finish low and fast, then pull up hard, sweep around, and land downwind *over* the tangle of gliders that have just landed on the same runway but in the opposite direction. I ease the wheel onto the runway with care because I'm still carrying 200 pounds of water ballast. A launch team are waiting for me when I coast to a stop (the wheel brake doesn't work well at this higher weight). Like an Indy car pit crew, they pick up the tail and pivot the Libelle 180 degrees on its main wheel to aim me back into the wind. I don't even unbuckle my straps.

I groan at the sight. The far end of the runway resembles a giant car wreck on the freeway, littered with gliders, vehicles, and people. And the fast guys who started behind me are on the way in now, too, adding to the mix. I'll be stuck here for half an hour waiting for the runway to clear off!

A towplane taxies up loudly alongside. The towpilot signals to ask if I'm ready. I point at the tangle of gliders clustered at the far end, less than 3,000 feet away, and gesture with my hands helplessly. He shrugs his shoulders, as if to say:

"It's your call."

We shouldn't launch over them. If something goes wrong—the rope breaks or the towplane's engine falters—we won't have the rest of the runway available for an aborted takeoff. But the towpilot is Ed Sessions, the senior Eastern Airlines captain with thousands of hours who won the contest my first year here and led me through my first high-speed finishing pass. Just as I said then: "If it's okay with Ed, it's okay with me."

With an angry outburst, the towpilot gives it full throttle. The glider stirs, reluctant to budge. This Super Cub towplane isn't the strongest and Georgia heat has sapped its power. And I'm heavy, still full of water ballast.

On and on we roll. We're glued to the runway as heat waves shimmer, the airspeed creeping up. At last, the glider seems to take a deep breath and I coax it off the ground. The towplane struggles off the runway and we both hang there in ground effect—bound together by the towrope—gathering speed, the engine snarling full out, still not climbing. We're approaching the critical point, the tangle of sailplanes and cars straight ahead of us.

"Come on, Ed! I hope you know what the hell you're doing. Come ON!"

I'm seconds away from releasing when, at last, the towplane eases up into a slow climb and I follow him. We clear the crowded assembly by less than 200 feet. Looking down, I see faces peering up to see who is relaunching.

I release at 2,000 feet and glide from cloud to cloud over the airport, searching for lift. The minutes are ticking away. If this is gonna work, I have to leave *now*. But it's taking forever in these weak thermals to get high enough to dive through the start gate at high speed. I hear Dad, inspired by my action, relaunching behind me. Am I too late? Is the day dying already? Finally, I connect with solid lift and gain the altitude I need. I alert the start gate, then nose over to 120+ knots and dive across just under the 3,300-feet top of the gate. I'm already pulling back sharply to zoom up, regaining altitude when the gate responds, "Juliet Bravo, good start." Dad hasn't been able to climb all the way up, but he goes through the gate right behind me, albeit lower and slower. Then it gets quiet. Unlike in other sports, there will be no race officials or referees to observe us until we return to cross the finish line. The course is empty. All other competitors have finished or landed out.

Back down the course line, it's a different sky. Thermals and the cumulus clouds they feed are always cycling, lasting anywhere from a few minutes up to 20+ minutes, drifted by the wind. Very little of my first lap is relevant.

The fat, spread-out cumulus clouds promise great thermals. But there's only one spot under each of these white masses with a strong core, which can be hard to locate. Today, it's as if I have a map. Time after time, I drive under a massive cu straight for where I think the core is and bang! Up I zoom, wrapping the sailplane in a steep turn, pointing the wingtip at the ground while easing the stick back. When I center the thermal, it thrusts us up, the G-force pinning me in the seat, the audio vario singing a sweet song as it celebrates my mastery. As in other sports, sometimes you're just "on."

I hammer down the course at high speed, my rising confidence inspiring me. Each time I stop to climb, though, Dad is a little lower when he pulls in under me. He probably dumped his ballast when he landed, so he's losing on the glides. At last, not long before the turnpoint, he's too low to leave when I do. When I look back, he's gone, like an injured animal who falls off the pack and slips from sight behind. Guilt flickers only for a few seconds. The whole *raison d'être* for a second lap is to fly without restraint, to take chances, to win. That's what he would tell me—if we were discussing this academically and not at 3,000 feet over South Georgia as the soaring day winds down.

For the second time today, I pivot over the Tifton turnpoint, snap the required photos, and head north. A few miles later, I fly over Dad, still on his way south. Perversely, it gives me a boost that I'm now so far ahead.

Halfway back, I'm below final glide altitude, hoping the sky will keep working to get me home. The sun is declining, but I drive on, rejecting weaker lift, waiting for my go-home thermal. Is it out there, or am I too late?

Finally, I connect, but it doesn't go quite high enough. When the climb rate falls off, I head north again, still too low. I could keep climbing in the weaker lift, but I want to win, not just finish. A line of clouds has formed ahead (a "cloud street") and I work the street aggressively, zooming up in the weak lift and floating along without circling, then accelerating to the next cloud, in a long, tense final glide all the way into another high-speed finish.

As the air cools and the thermals wane, I blast through the finish gate at ground level with water ballast exploding from the tanks—with a speed 8 mph faster than my first trip. When I land and roll to a stop, Diane meets me, all smiles, to catch my wingtip—and to tell me Dad landed out.

My encore lap was good enough for second place. After Dad fell off my lead, he couldn't keep moving fast and ran out of time. My mother left with the trailer to retrieve him while Diane and I put my Libelle away. Later, Dad congratulated me quietly. I commiserated over his landout. It never occurred to me to wonder if he might have had mixed emotions. For so long, he had taken such obvious pride in my soaring achievements that I hadn't worried about anything else.

* * *

When Dad and I started flying contests together, we needed two crews in case we both landed out. Mark's summer jobs soon conflicted. Diane had been crewing for years. Now, almost 19, she could do it all, with one exception, i.e., reversing the trailer. To make a U-turn, she needed a large parking lot or a circular drive or going around the block. That doesn't always work in the countryside where reluctant gliders typically come to earth.

So before this contest, I taught her how to back up the long trailer with the car, including which way to turn the steering wheel to move the back end of the trailer the correct direction. I assured her she would be fine while privately hoping she wouldn't have to prove it.

Family on launch grid at the Cordele Regional, 1977. A different look than our similar pose six years earlier. (photo from estate of Joseph N. Bearden Jr.)

On the last contest day, driven by demons unloosed by my stumble in Ionia, I didn't just want to do well. I wanted to win. As the thermals weakened and died, I overflew an airport, gliding slowly over fields recently harvested of cotton and peanuts, crossing narrow roads and tree lines, wringing the remaining few miles from my altitude under a gray, quiet sky.

I waited, passing up one choice landing spot after another, gliding resolutely with growing nervousness until, at a few hundred feet, in the final moment, I turned into a field and landed to maximize my points, hoping no one would complete the task. They didn't. As I was to learn in a few hours, I won the day and my first regional contest when I slid to a stop in an empty peanut field nine miles short of the finish. I walked to a nearby farmhouse and explained.

"Yes, sir—the wind quit." It's the question I most often get after landing out. Sometimes it's easier just to go with it. I used the farmer's telephone to call contest HQ. My father had landed behind me. My mother was retrieving him.

Less than an hour later, I spotted our car and trailer approaching on the deserted country road. Diane stopped and rolled down the window, the cool air spilling out into the South Georgia heat. I explained we had to get turned around and head back in the opposite direction to reach the glider.

"You want me to drive?" I finished.

She didn't hesitate. "No, I'll do it!"

How would we ever know? "Okay, you know what to do."

She pulled the rig past the gravel farmhouse drive, then spun the wheel and backed the trailer smoothly into it on her first attempt, in perfect position to pull out in the opposite direction. She let fly a delighted whoop of triumph and pumped her fists! From that moment on, Diane had my absolute trust.

* * *

My win at Cordele allowed me to lay to rest my Ionia debacle. A month later, we returned to Marion, Ohio, for the weekend contest where I had first flown in competition nine years earlier. On Saturday, I flew for a while in a pack that included A.J. Smith, ex-U.S.-and-world champion.

There was pressure to do everything right, thermaling precisely and aggressively, not stopping for weaker thermals. Something worked; I was fastest in Standard Class. Afterward, my father and I stood talking to A.J. He was usually spare with his remarks, so he surprised me by commenting to my father:

"The first team looked good today," glancing at me, smiling conspiratorially.

Swelling with pride, I wanted to laugh gleefully and celebrate. A.J. Smith, one of the best pilots in the world, was acknowledging me! We chatted about the field at the 15 Meter Nationals the previous year at Bryan, where some of the big names had gone missing. Then he continued.

"Wait till you get to the Worlds. That's a whole different level."

It was an awesome finish to my most tumultuous year in gliding. At 26, in four months, I had gone from believing I was a future contender to flaming out of the biggest contest of the year, then rebounding with my first win at a major regional. And now one of America's finest pilots had implied I had what it took to make the U.S. Team. As events would remind me many times, the highs and lows in soaring are fierce, profound, and mercurial.

CHAPTER FOURTEEN

The Sweet Ride

O UR NEW SAILPLANE WAS TRAPPED on the Philadelphia docks. It had arrived via ship from Germany days earlier, but now there was no way to drive it away before the waterfront shut down for the weekend. Oh, and a major blizzard was descending on the East Coast.

All our talk of my qualifying for the U.S. Team was just noise without a competitive glider. And our Libelle was obsolete. Not by much—a few percent less than newer models—but we needed a new ride. We had decided to switch to the nascent 15 Meter Class that had debuted at Bryan the year before. The only difference with 15 Meter was flaps: moveable control surfaces on the trailing edges of the wings that provide lower thermaling speeds (when they flex down) *and* higher cruise speeds (when they flex up). It was the class of the future.

Early in 1978, our new LS3 arrived at the port in Philadelphia. Dad had business on the East Coast and drove from Cincinnati to take delivery on Friday.

Acquiring a new glider wasn't like dropping by the local Chevy dealer to buy a car off the lot. We ordered it through the U.S. dealer and waited six months for the German factory to build it using precise molds and skilled workers hand-layering fiberglass, epoxy resin, and polyester gel coat. The final product was a highly polished aircraft with critical pieces assembled to precise tolerances in a custom-fitted trailer. After we transferred Deutschmarks, the factory loaded it on a freighter headed to the U.S. It was the most expensive thing my father had ever purchased. Even our house had cost less 20 years earlier.

The day before Dad arrived in Philadelphia, I received a troubling telephone call from Dan, the Atlanta pilot who had so pugnaciously objected to granting me an exemption from the penalty at Ionia months earlier. He was in Philly to pick up his own LS3, which was being delivered on the same ship.

In future years, shipping companies would switch to the roll-on, roll-off model (RORO) used for automobiles. But in 1978, gliders arrived on the freighter in their trailers with the wheels, axle, fenders, and tongue removed and stowed inside. A crane lifted the trailer from the hold of the ship and set it down on the dock. The new owner bolted everything on and towed the trailer away. Dan was calling to warn me the dockworkers had stolen all the wheels from our trailer. It was an awkward conversation.

"So, Dan, let me make sure I understand. They stole both of our loose wheels *and* the spare bolted down inside, but they took only *one* of your loose wheels and left the second one sitting right next to it, plus the spare?"

"Uh, yeah. That's what they did."

I thanked him for calling and hung up. I confess I assumed the dockworkers had opened the front doors of both trailers and snatched the two loose wheels resting conveniently in each, leaving each trailer with a spare wheel bolted firmly down inside. If true, then Dan had combined the two spare wheels to drive his trailer away, leaving us with none. At least we had some warning.

The next day, my father could process the customs paperwork, but he wouldn't be able to move the wheelless trailer before the docks shut down for the weekend. And he had to be back in Cincinnati on Monday.

After hours of frantic phone calls, I learned the trailer's wheels were from GM's Adam Opel brand, imported from Germany by Buick. Armed with this, on Friday morning, Dad hustled over to a Philadelphia Buick dealer to have tires mounted on two new wheels. I'll never forget the wonder in his voice when, at my urging, he slipped the service manager $20 to get his work order moved up in the queue and watched the rubber-clad rims appear not long after.

Growing up poor—and now—my father was mindful of every expense. My mother jokes he was attracted to her in high school because she was a cheerleader, which meant he didn't have to pay to get her in to watch him at games where he was playing. The idea of his picking up a restaurant bill and generously offering to pay for a friend ("I've got this; you get the next one") was unfathomable. To him, paying meant precisely allocating the check and adding a miniscule (if any) gratuity. The concept of tipping for improved service was a newfound experience for him, as if he had entered an alternate reality.

He raced back to the docks to complete the paperwork as light snow fell. In the last vestiges of daylight, a helpful longshoreman raised the trailer with a forklift truck so Dad could bolt on the axle, wheels, and tongue. Five minutes before the port locked the gates for the weekend, he triumphantly drove away with the trailer—and straight into a blizzard.

The New Jersey Turnpike had closed to trucks and trailers, so Dad crept north on secondary roads in the deepening snow, updating me via payphone. The usual two-hour trip took three times that.

We needed a place to stash the car and 30-foot trailer overnight. The indoor parking spot at my condominium was useless. It was a full-on snow emergency, plows rumbling up and down the Palisades.

I wracked my brain. "Where's the logical place to park a glider trailer during a blizzard? Of course, at an airport!" Teterboro Airport—a major business and general aviation airport—was seven miles away. I drove out into the storm to meet Dad there late that night. The winds had abated, but snow was still falling. We begged/bribed a security guard to let us leave Dad's car and trailer in the lee of a hangar, then drove back on the snow-packed streets to my condo.

The next morning, we woke up to brilliant sunshine bathing New York City in front of my terrace from 29 floors up. Dad seemed dazed at the life I had established. I was thriving two years into my second job after business school. My family used to joke that if my mother weren't around, my father would be helpless coping with the normal chores of living—e.g., meals, housekeeping, and laundry. He had never lived on his own.

Back at Teterboro, we extracted Dad's car and trailer from the snow. In the bitter cold, we rolled the LS3 fuselage from the trailer and gawked. We swapped places in the cockpit, grinning at each other like goofy kids on Christmas morning while we gazed at the most sophisticated flying machine we had ever owned. When I closed the canopy, the aroma of cured epoxy resin—the sailplane version of that new car smell—penetrated my icy nasal passages. Then we packed it up again and Dad left for Cincinnati.

New LS3, Teterboro Airport, New Jersey, 1978. (photos by Joseph N. Bearden Jr.)

Over the next few months, I stopped by Cincinnati on business trips to install instruments and radio, since those tasks were beyond Dad's abilities. A few years before, SSD—now known as the Caesar Creek Soaring Club (CCSC)—had purchased a farm in Waynesville, Ohio, and converted it into a gliderport. We had to wait until the grass runway there dried out.

I jumped when Dad offered me the first flight. I was cautious about the takeoff. This was the costliest vehicle of any kind I had ever operated. But from the moment the wheel broke ground and the graceful wings lofted me gently into the air behind the towplane, the LS3 flew like a dream with what seemed like electrifying performance compared with our Libelle. I was at home in it within seconds and eagerly anticipating the first contest.

LS3 first flight with author, Caesar Creek Soaring Club, Ohio, 1978 (photo from estate of Joseph N. Bearden Jr.), and piloted by Mark Bearden, Chilhowee Gliderport, Tennessee, 1980. (author in chase plane; photo by Kathleen Jerolmon)

But where? To me, the logical place was the 1978 15 Meter Nationals—2,200 miles away in Ephrata, Washington. But Dad wasn't excited about driving west for four days, so I could tilt with the big boys. He would want to fly, too. That would involve a long haul with two gliders and crew vehicles.

Dad had ambitious plans for my soaring future. But he also had a day job with a June 30 fiscal-year end at Procter & Gamble that conflicted with a Western trip. I wasn't happy, but we compromised, agreeing to fly three local/regional contests, he in the Libelle we still co-owned and me in the new LS3.

I won the opener and placed in the next two, winning a day at each. It was a satisfying season with many compliments about the new glider and the way I was flying it. But skipping a nationals for the first time in three years inspired me to embark on one of my most remarkable—and unlikely—personal journeys, one that would eventually have as much impact on my life as soaring had.

CHAPTER FIFTEEN

The Planes of Marathon

I N MY FIRST YEAR AT HBS, a book appeared provocatively titled *The Gospel According to the Harvard Business School,* written by a former student. The book was an over-the-top indictment of the single-minded pursuit of wealth and power, the primary motivations, we joked, for any self-respecting Harvard MBA. We sneered, then read it anyway.

After entering the workforce, I discovered wealth and power were not what drove me. The work was challenging, and I was well paid. But my job was not my passion. As a young executive, I analyzed investments, solved problems, and authored reports. The biggest downside was political conflicts.

In a sailplane, however, I was already a seasoned competitor going up against the country's best pilots risking defeat, a damaged glider, and (improbably) injury. My desk job couldn't provide the same highs and visceral thrills.

After my first two exhilarating national contests, passing up the 1978 nationals was like being sent back to the minor leagues after pitching my first game in Yankee Stadium. Regional contests were fun—especially giving winner's speeches at each one. But something was missing. Subconsciously, I needed a new challenge, one that would give me the same thrill and validation.

At a party in Manhattan, a young couple were proudly showing off their bib numbers for a 10K race in Central Park, twice as far as I had ever run. Suddenly, my one-to-three-mile workouts seemed insignificant. I had gotten faster in the year I had been running, but progress had plateaued. Each second I shaved from my mile time was painful. Running was no longer fun. Then I had a brilliant flash of insight. Instead of faster, perhaps I could run farther, possibly even ten kilometers. That evening at the track, I held myself back at a slower pace in the inside lane. The laps kept adding up: 8, 12, 16, then 20! Five miles.

Exciting stuff! A few nights later, I slowed even more and circled the track 40 times—ten miles! I was grinning, almost laughing out loud with amazement. Running had new meaning. I saw myself in a new light.

My HBS roommate and I often joked about what we referred to as the classic American credo: "if some is good, more is better." Or as John Updike said about sex and money: *"Only too much is enough."*[10] Ten miles was thrilling. But was

---

[10] Updike, John, *Couples* (New York: Alfred A Knopf, 1968)

it enough? Could I do more, a lot more? I had found I could learn almost anything from the right book: business, soaring, auto repair, weightlifting, antenna construction, and even sex. Many books in my growing running library highlighted the marathon, the legendary 26-mile-and-385-yards test of endurance.

The 1978 New York City Marathon beckoned. Three years earlier, it had comprised a gaunt pack of skeletal devotees lapping Central Park four times in obscurity. In 1976, it exploded into a five-borough festival. I wasn't that athletic, but my books said a marathon was within my reach—with the right training.

Fitness was but one obstacle. The New York Road Runners Club (NYRRC) required entrants to be members of the Amateur Athletic Union (AAU), doubtless to differentiate real runners from wannabees with delusions of grandeur—like me. I nervously called the AAU for information. Would they pick up on my inexperience? I waited in their undistinguished Manhattan offices, glancing around furtively as they processed my application. I was a rookie runner, not an ex-collegiate athlete or a member of a running team. Luckily, all they wanted were my personal data and money. I fled to New Jersey with my new AAU card and mailed in my marathon entry. In those days, there was no complex lottery to winnow 100,000 applicants down to a select 50,000. Like the AAU, the NYRRC's main interest seemed to be my personal data and money, in this case a check for $5.00 (vs. today's registration fee of $295). A month later, I was in!

I told no one about my outrageous plan, not even my flight attendant girlfriend. I had met Kathy on a TWA flight several years earlier when she was living near JFK Airport. When TWA opened a base in Boston—her dream—she moved up there. We began what would become a four-year long-distance relationship. There were problems. It suggested an answer to that classic (and crude) question, "How far would you travel for sex?" In our case: 245 miles. But years later, I admitted selfishly that in some ways I *liked* having a committed girlfriend who was there for me but not around all the time to make demands.

I hung a popular 13-week training program from *Runner's World* magazine on the wall. I had subscribed to *RW* because picking up the magazine at the newsstand was only slightly less awkward than buying *Playboy*. At least I'd *had* sex; I was just self-conscious acknowledging my lustful interests to a magazine seller. In contrast, I had never run a single race, much less a marathon. I imagined most people would snicker at me as a presumptuous imposter.

Gradually, I extended my weekly long run to 18 miles. After finishing my nine-to-five job, I would drive home, change into my workout gear, and head to the track. Cuban and Dominican immigrants dominated the informal soccer games there every evening, so I rarely heard English. As the summer ended and the days grew shorter, it was eerie when the park emptied out. As night fell, I continued running, passing through small circles of illumination cast by the surviving lights at each end. Most problems involved wildlife. I startled a skunk several times and almost tripped over a rat the size of a small dog.

Unlike the way novice marathoners train today, I worked out alone: no advisors, coaches, clubs, or group runs. Nearly all of my training—up to 50 miles/week—took place as I wore a groove in that quarter-mile track.

Journal Entry: October 22, 1978 (New York City Marathon)

On the big day—the New York City Marathon—I almost break my ankle before the gun goes off.

I confessed my plan to Kathy—now a runner—so she drops me off in pre-dawn Manhattan to board one of the first race buses headed for the staging area on Staten Island. The bus brakes to a halt three hours before the start. Trailing other runners, clutching my bag in the dim light, I step off the bus—straight into a ditch. I go down hard, rolling but not injuring my ankle.

Walking around Fort Wadsworth, I'm as nervous about being revealed as a phony as I am about running 26.2 miles. What will happen if the organizers of this world-class event discover I'm a novice? As the sun comes up, I try to blend in like the newest prisoner in the yard, head down, never looking anyone in the eyes, confident without confrontational. I can pass, even though I'm wearing white cotton gym shorts instead of the featherweight, pastel-colored nylon shorts favored by the lean, serious-looking types. At least my Brooks Vantage running shoes are the real thing. Spotting other runners wearing T-shirts reassures me, although mine is the only one emblazoned with *"1976 15 Meter National Soaring Championships."* At least I know to pin my race number on the front, not the back, of my shirt. I had read it in one of my books.

As the sky lightens, race morning resembles recent NYC Marathons—on a smaller scale. With *only* 8,000 runners, it's still a huge crowd scene with announcements and music and more portable toilets than I have ever seen. The world's longest urinal is an impressive-albeit-revolting plastic-lined trough descending gradually along 100 yards of the hedgerows. As an hour slips by, I take deep breaths and will myself to relax. No one seems to have the slightest idea who I am, or to care. Then, I'm jolted to hear my name.

"Chip? Chip Bearden?"

Disaster! Will they heckle me with derisive laughter, or just eject me quietly? Wait, I'm an official entrant. Maybe I can talk my way out of this.

I don't have to. My "accuser" is a guy my age from my soaring club in Ohio. An ex-P&G marketing manager and former student of my father, he's a marathon rookie, too, with similar anxieties. My soaring T-shirt gave me away! We chat for several hours. It's my first chance to discuss marathon training. It's also the first time I feel I have as much right as anyone to be here.

Just before 10:00, crowd-control marshals release the mobs of runners to swarm onto the approach to the Verrazzano-Narrows Bridge *[spelled "Verrazano" then]* looming above us. Formations of helicopters are beating sound waves against the bridge towers. I've never been part of such a lavish, exhilarating, noisy sporting spectacle. When the cannon booms to start the race, my breath catches for a second. I've made it. I'm really here!

Per my books' advice, I start slowly. Staten Island lasts minutes until we crest the bridge. Brooklyn takes forever. Queens is over quickly. Coming off the Queensboro Bridge into Manhattan, we trot down the bridge's steep, spiral ramp and turn north up First Avenue through the scream tunnel of spectators cheering in front of the singles bars there, including Maxwell's Plum and the original TGI Fridays. I allow myself a wide smile and a disbelieving look around. Nothing I have ever done compares.

The cheering gives me a surge, but by 18 my pace is sagging when I exhaust my energy reserves and "hit the wall." I keep plodding, determined to run every mile without walking. We cross the Harlem River and are in the Bronx for less than a mile before returning to Manhattan. I'm slowing through Harlem, then plodding up 102nd Street into Central Park from Fifth Avenue. With three miles to go, my body aches in places I didn't even know I had.

Kathy had cheered me on First Avenue. Past 25, I exit the Park and turn onto Central Park South in front of the Plaza Hotel. She pops up again there and thrusts a can of Coke into my hands. Grateful, I yank the aluminum pull tab and take a deep swig. In the next second, I pitch forward, coughing and spewing foam and bubbles. "Defizzed" Coke is the insiders' sports drink of choice. Now I understand why they let the carbonation bubble out.

At Columbus Circle on the southwest corner of Central Park, I know I'm going to finish as we turn back into the Park. I trot up the last rise with a pulse beating in my head and breath burning in my chest. It's mystical. My body opens to absorb the sounds of the finish area: screams and cheering, loudspeakers blaring the theme from *Rocky* (which had premiered to wild acclaim two years earlier), and hundreds of running shoes slapping the pavement like slow applause. There's a harmony, a wholeness, an order I've never known that encompasses New York and the littered roadway below and the untainted sky above and the lavish pre-war apartments overlooking Central Park West and the thousands of cheering spectators, separated from the racecourse by snow fencing. Euphoria breaks through pain as, for the first time, incredulous, I am one of the athletes *on* the field, no longer relegated to watching from the sidelines, envious and intimidated.

Author finishing first marathon, October 1978. (photo by Kathleen Jerolmon)

Then, yards from the finish banner at Tavern on the Green restaurant, I almost fall when my calves knot up in painful cramps. Grimacing, I hobble stiff-legged along the grandstands into the finish chute, which I have read about but never seen. I stagger across the line and stumble to a halt, clutching my calves. It is one of the most moving and exhilarating moments of my life, yet I can barely walk as finish line workers swarm around.

Pain is cool—because this pain is from an athletic accomplishment! Me, an athlete! I have done something involving physical strength and endurance. Two volunteers knead my calves until I can stand and Kathy shows up. At that point, the pain stops being cool. None of my books mentioned this.

In 1978, marathoning was still relatively uncommon. Running 26.2 miles elevated you to near-mythic status. It was exhilarating to see astonishment and deference for an *athletic* accomplishment. Overnight, being an athlete was as integral to my identity as being a pilot. My slow time (4:45) didn't matter, nor did the fact that many of my colleagues could have done the same thing if willing to endure the training. Running the New York City Marathon dispatched insecurities I had carried with me for most of my life. That may seem foolish, even pathetic for a 27-year-old man today. But it was *very* real to me then.

Soloing a glider at age 14 had changed my life, infusing me with confidence and a new sense of identity. Thirteen years later, completing my first marathon had a similar effect. But unlike flying, I accomplished New York entirely on my own. Thus, I came to believe, for the first time, I could do almost anything with courage, the will to commit—and the right book.

It was addictive. Six months after New York, armed with the assurance conferred by what had eluded me for close to 20 years—i.e., pride and satisfaction over an athletic achievement—I doubled down on my training and slashed my time by a full hour in the 1979 Long Island Marathon.

A month later, I opened the soaring season by winning my second regional, hosted by our home club, CCSC. A few weeks later, my father and I competed in the 1979 15 Meter Nationals at Adrian, a site where we both had some history. After waiting two years to atone for my lapse in Ionia, I notched a fifth and a third on the first two days, dropped as low as 18th mid-contest, then fought back to finish eighth against my toughest field ever.

It wasn't a bravura performance, but it enabled me to put the embarrassment of Ionia behind me. I was still inconsistent. But I had reaffirmed I could go up against the country's best pilots on any day. When JB appeared on the grid, I imagined I might be viewed as a contender, not just as a promising kid.

In October, I ran the New York City Marathon again. The news of my first marathon had stunned my father, especially when I explained how far a marathon was. By then, Mark had resumed the running he had done in high school cross-country. My mother reminded me not long ago that Dad began to accompany my sister to the local track when she started running. I didn't know what motivated him, his health—always excellent—or rising to some unspoken competitive family challenge.

PART II: FLYING WITH SUPERHEROES

CHAPTER SIXTEEN

Where Were You When You Heard the News?

C OULD LIFE GET ANY BETTER? In 1980, my life was on rails. I was flourishing professionally, at the peak of my flying career, a marathon runner, and in a strong long-distance relationship with Kathy. And the SSA had awarded the 15 Meter Nationals to our own Caesar Creek Soaring Club.

Our CCSC gliderport was too small to accommodate 67 aircraft, so we planned to use the decommissioned Clinton County Air Force Base 15 miles east. It was perfect: huge concrete ramps, little traffic, a two-mile-long runway, and removed from the population centers and heavy powered aircraft traffic of Cincinnati, Dayton, and Columbus. CCSC had hosted a proof-of-concept regional contest in 1979—which I had won in my debut in the LS3 (cough, cough).

But weeks before pilots would converge on CCSC from around the U.S., we discovered no one had officially requested use of the former airbase. Now it was unavailable, putting the entire national contest in jeopardy. In the scramble, the club found the Springfield (Ohio) Municipal Airport as a replacement. Far from ideal, it was much busier, and was situated only 20 miles from Dayton's big commercial jetport and just 11 miles from Wright-Patterson Air Force Base.

Unlike Clinton County AFB, Wright-Patt was still very active, though the last of its B-52 long-range bombers had departed five years earlier. It hosted logistics, communications, support, medical, research, flight, and other operations, and was a frequent stop for Air Force officers on the way up, some of whom joined CCSC to fly with us while stationed there.

Wright-Patt was also notable for being the site of the National Museum of the U.S. Air Force. This was a popular tourist destination, in particular for glider pilots on weathered-out days at local soaring meets. Years ago, I had dragged a college girlfriend there, although I'm sure she, as an impressionable freshman, was less intrigued by aviation than by my status as a recent graduate. That visit was my first exposure to a phenomenon I would encounter many times, i.e., a woman assuring me she *really* enjoyed sharing my flying—until she realized that could mean being trapped at an airport (and not in New York, Los Angeles, or Paris) for hours, days, or even weeks.

The Air Force Museum holds one of the world's largest collections of military aircraft and spacecraft. One notable item is the heavily modified Boeing 707 formerly designated Air Force One. It was used by several U.S. presidents, including President and Mrs. John F. Kennedy for their trip to Dallas the day Lee Harvey Oswald shot and killed JFK from his sniper's perch.

"JFK's assassination" is my answer to the trivia question: what was your first "where were you when you heard the news?" moment? These are the events so seared into our collective memories as Americans that most of us who lived through them can recall precisely where we were when the news broke. These are communal memories, not *your* memorable firsts—e.g., your first cigarette, your first beer, your first kiss, or your first home run (athletic or sexual).

For my parent's generation, it may have been the Japanese attack on Pearl Harbor with President Franklin Roosevelt's "a date which will live in infamy" speech, heard live on the radio or read about the next day in the newspaper for those, like my parents, who didn't have radios. Young adults of my daughters' age (29 as I write this) might cite the 9/11/2001 terrorist attacks, which they learned about from their second-grade teacher as the school raced to determine which students had parents working in the City. Alerted by a telephone call while I was home preparing for a meeting in downtown Manhattan that afternoon, I switched on the television just in time to see UA 175 hit the South Tower of the World Trade Center. Needless to say, that meeting was postponed.

Some moments are cultural, e.g., the U.S. Men's Olympic Hockey Team's "Miracle on Ice" victory over the Soviet Union in 1980, Princess Diana's death in 1997, and Mark McGwire breaking Roger Maris's home run record in 1999. I remember exactly where I was when I learned of each. Some might say Kanye West's rude interruption of Taylor Swift's acceptance speech at the 2009 MTV Video Music Awards "rises" to this standard, but I draw a blank on that one.

The first "where were you?" moment for those coming of age during the 1960s' Space Race might be Neil Armstrong exiting the Apollo 11 Lunar Module on the moon. On July 20, 1969, we—like 50+ million other American families—watched, mesmerized, on our first color television, purchased for the occasion.

Years later, I had the privilege of meeting the man. My small-town-boy-made-good father was star-struck by celebrity and not bashful about chasing it. When he learned Armstrong, a glider pilot, was friends with the Air Force captain who had been a partner in Dad's Diamant while stationed at Wright-Patt, he finagled an introduction.

We were excited to meet him at his farm, purchased when he left NASA to teach at the University of Cincinnati. He walked us around for a tour and introduced us to his wife, Jan. I had expected the stereotypically cocky, larger-than-life personality of a combat naval aviator, test pilot, and astronaut. He was quiet and unassuming as we chatted, meeting our eyes when he answered and then looking down. Years later, it surprised me to learn he was 5'11". Memories are imperfect, but I would have said he was at least as tall as I was (at 6'3").

His farm wasn't far from the CCSC gliderport, so he offered one of his empty farm sheds to shelter our glider trailer from the weather. Dad invited him to fly the Libelle during the week whenever he liked. I still have a copy of the insurance form he filled out to be added to our policy. I had fun pondering how he logged his days of time in space until I learned this was a genuine issue for astronauts. For years, we would arrive at his farm on Saturday mornings, hitch up the trailer and tow it over to CCSC to fly, then return it that night, occasionally exchanging greetings with the First Man on the Moon. When I read now that Armstrong turned into a "recluse" when he moved to his farm (a contention he laughed away), I consider myself fortunate to have caught a glimpse of this humble "reluctant American hero."

This was one of multiple experiences comparing my perception of interacting with famous people vs. reading media accounts. I shared a classroom with former President George W. Bush three times daily during our first year at HBS. Future U.S. Senator John Kennedy of Louisiana was a Vanderbilt fraternity brother. I spent time with the late "Superman" actor Christopher Reeve, a soaring pilot. And as a veteran of 24 Philadelphia Marathons, I chatted with four-time NYC and Boston Marathon winner Bill Rodgers at press conferences.

But JFK's assassination was my first "where were you when you heard the news?" moment. On November 22, 1963, I was 12 years old in seventh-grade Language Arts class. The intercom speaker above the blackboard hummed to life, then broke in with the shocking announcement. We watched through classroom windows, more curious than comprehending (it was a simpler, less acculturated era), as someone lowered the U.S. flag to half-staff, then—in a moment of dark comedy—ran it back up again in confusion. Soon after, with the uncertainty horrifically resolved, they brought the flag down again to stay.

For much of the country, this was one of the most traumatic events of that era. Yet I was too young to react emotionally. Death was an unfamiliar, abstract concept. I had never lost a relative or friend. Much later, the wife of an office colleague passed away. When I entered the church for her funeral—my first—it was like visiting a foreign country. Everyone dressed differently and seemed to be communicating in a language only I could not understand. I wasn't uncomfortable with the concept of death. But I didn't understand the protocols. What should I do? What should I say—and not say?

Like many young children, I had expressed anxiety to my parents about their dying. They had admitted solemnly that everyone died eventually. Disturbing! But they assured me they didn't plan on doing so soon. I vaguely recall asking them to promise me they wouldn't die. To my immense relief, they responded in a way that satisfied us all.

* * *

Not long before I turned 30, I summoned the courage to ask my father another Very Important Question that had always troubled me. We were driving up to CCSC on Saturday morning just weeks before the 1980 Nationals.

"Hey, Dad, did it ever bother you when I was growing up that I didn't get involved in all the athletic things you did when you were a kid?"

My question startled him. I was 28 years old. When he realized I was serious, he thought for a moment, then spoke carefully and confidently.

"Of course not." He told me he was far happier I had pursued academic and musical interests, the latter an area where he had always felt inadequate. And he told me how proud he was of what I had achieved flying sailplanes competitively, which he viewed as the most demanding thing he had ever tackled.

The exchange was brief. Later, I wondered: had he been forthright? How carefully had he selected his words? But I didn't waste time overthinking it.

Growing up, we strive to gain our parents' approval. Despite having a happy childhood with supportive parents, I struggled with self-doubt and inadequacies. I compared myself unfavorably to my father, who was athletic, confident, charismatic, and well-spoken, qualities I believed I lacked. I obsessed about my inadequacies the way I assumed others did, rather than being happy with who I was. Is it possible to overcome this on our own? Or must someone tap us on the shoulder with the flat of a sword and proclaim, "go now and fear no more?" That's a rhetorical question; it's clear *I* still needed assurance—at age 28.

Hearing my father dismiss my anxieties eased my life. It wasn't like the wind calmed, the rain ceased, dark clouds lifted, and the sun broke through with birds chirping brightly. I'd had a happy childhood and a good life. My parents had lavished attention and love on us. I had achieved much success and respect. Most people would opine I had led a charmed life. But from that moment, I no

longer worried there was a shameful secret lurking in my past, waiting, like ma-
lignant cancer cells, to explode, multiply, and vanquish me.

At my 20th high school reunion, I learned my classmates had held me in
higher esteem than I had thought, in part because of my flying. Over time, I
came to appreciate that their view—viz., I was involved with a demanding and
risky endeavor—might have been more perceptive and prophetic than mine.

*Author and father, Chilhowee Gliderport, Benton, Tennessee, October 1979. One of his
few LS3 flights. (photo by Virgil Jones, from his estate, courtesy of Lee Jarrard)*

CHAPTER SEVENTEEN

The Competition

T HIS WAS MY TIME! Most pilots expected the 1980 U.S. 15 Meter Nationals to be the most fiercely contested soaring event in the country. With youthful exuberance fueled by my recent record, I ambitiously hoped to vault onto the podium, and perhaps—with luck—even win outright.

How likely was that? Some people thought it was possible (and not just Dad). At 29, I had been gliding since I was 14. I had won regionals. I had come second in daily tasks at the nationals with top-ten finishes. There were few leading pilots in the Eastern U.S. I hadn't bested multiple times on a day-to-day basis. I believed that if I could fly consistently—the big "if"—it *could* happen.

One factor was we were swimming in an exceedingly small pond. If soaring is obscure, then competitive soaring is almost invisible. Only 600 U.S. glider pilots compete, and far fewer in the classes in which I was flying at the national level. Few possess the requisite skills to win. That said, while the competition isn't deep, it is intense. Aficionados comprise amateurs like us but also professional pilots, many of whom chafe under the constraints of the regulated, automated world of commercial aviation. For ex-military pilots, especially, racing some of the highest-performing sailplanes ever built is an antidote to a tamer, more pedestrian existence as civilians. That Dad and I could measure ourselves against this kind of talent was unimaginable, akin to amateur drivers appearing on the grid at the Indianapolis 500—albeit with a chance to win.

Competitive soaring might be more popular if it were conducive to instant gratification. A newcomer can solo a glider in a week via an intensive course at a commercial flight school. Afterward, pilots can progress much faster than I did. But it still takes years to become competitive—with demands on your personal life. You can stop by the driving range after work to hit a bucket of golf balls or tee off early for 18 holes and be home by noon. You can schedule tennis lessons and matches whenever it's convenient (and, if indoors, in all weather).

But waiting until that morning to know the weather, then motoring an hour or more to a remote gliderport, assembling the glider, getting a launch, then flying a practice task—knowing an outlanding will torpedo any evening plans— mandates soaring be an all-day activity. Airports are not particularly family friendly. And the cost—while less than for power flying—is also a factor.

Too, contest flying doesn't appeal to everyone. Most recreational soaring pilots enjoy the flying and camaraderie yet can't relate to the sense of purpose—and stress—associated with pursuing regional or national championships or a spot on the U.S. Team. In their view, it's mad to set off cross-country at low altitude in marginal weather over difficult terrain just to score points.

In contrast, competition pilots would consider this an exhilarating mission, the dearth of which often seems to render our lives distressingly tame. They might grumble that a task was too difficult in dodgy weather. Yet when the start gate opens, few abandon the course and return to the airport for zero points. Peer pressure is a factor, but so is the satisfaction that accrues from being in a community of remarkable individuals who take up extraordinary challenges.

And, without analyzing it too deeply, for some pilots, it's all about the thrill.

Regardless, competitive soaring is enthralling for the few it captivates while remaining unfathomable to those who are indifferent to its charms.

* * *

I had never been more ready for a major contest. I knew the arena better than anyone, including sharing a secret with my father that could give us an edge. We had made careful and thorough preparations. What could go wrong?

The first crisis involved our equipment, which had worked flawlessly all spring. Now both gliders' radios had become erratic. This jeopardized communications with crews; other pilots; air traffic control; and the officials who timed our starts and finishes. Mine was working again, but Dad's was still flaky.

Another frustration was a minor leak in my LS3's water ballast system. This was more worrisome than the loose hose clamp that caused the leak at Ionia in 1977. Most manufacturers used rubberized life raft fabric to assemble ballast bags, with heat and/or adhesive to secure seams that could be 15 to 20 feet long. We could ignore this tiny leak if not for the possibility it presaged a catastrophic failure of one of those seams. Last year at a nationals, an LS3's tank ruptured, releasing a torrent of water that poured from the wing and flooded the cockpit. On final approach, the water sloshed into the forward fuselage, making it impossible to level out before slamming belly first into the runway.

Allegedly, our LS3 ballast tanks were of a newer, stronger design than those first-generation ballast bags (now disparagingly referred to as "shower curtain" bags, for their flimsy construction). But we needed a replacement.

And then there was my physical problem, which struck early.

Journal Entry: June 17, 1980 (Springfield, Ohio)

On Day One, I am cruising on course with a group of top pilots at 75 to 80 knots. It's "blue," referring to the lack of cumulus clouds to mark the thermal updrafts, not to our moods. We've spread out abreast, hurrying across the landscape toward the next turnpoint, porpoising up and down and darting left and right, assessing subtleties in the ocean of air, hoping we will encounter an invisible thermal before we hit the ground.

I fly into turbulence. This could be the edge of a thermal, so I ease back on the stick for a few seconds, slowing, uncertain, waiting for the upwelling, watching the instruments for indications this is not just choppy air and a waste of time. Then a surge, and something pushes the glider up powerfully beneath me. I know it's real even before the needles on both variometers swing over to indicate strong lift.

I haul back on the control stick, directing the nose of the glider into the air in a steep zoom. If a thermal is worth stopping for, the pilot must slow down—*right now*—or fly through it in seconds. My body sags under the higher G loading. The wings flex up at the tips. Nose high, the glider sweeps into the air like a close air support aircraft pulling up sharply after a strafing run. This feels great when done right. With the nose up, I'm no longer looking at the ground ahead; the canopy is full of sky. The zoom converts excess airspeed into hundreds of feet of altitude.

Near the top of the climb, the airspeed drops below 50 knots. I push the stick to level out, becoming partially weightless in the cockpit. I had felt the surge push the left wing up more than the right, so I resist it, banking in that direction to turn into the core, pushing the left rudder pedal with my toe to coordinate the turn. We do so dozens of times each flight. This time:

"Y-E-O-W-W-W-W!" With no warning, my left calf knots up in an agonizing cramp! The pain is excruciating, like someone plunging a knife into my leg.

I lunge forward, helpless, tightly strapped into a reclining cockpit with my feet tucked snugly into the tapered forward fuselage, knees bent and unable to straighten my legs or pull them from under the instrument panel to massage the painful knot. As a distance runner, I'm sometimes awakened by a similar agonizing cramp in the middle of the night. But now I can't stumble out of bed and lean against the wall to stretch the seized-up muscle.

S**t! Will I have to land? Despite the agonizing pain, I know the first rule in any aviation crisis, i.e., fly the airplane. I'm cursing loudly and my eyes are watering from the pain. But training has drilled into me that too many accidents result from pilots distracted by an unlatched canopy or a bee in the cockpit or a buzzing noise from loose tape. They lose focus on the critical tasks of maintaining adequate airspeed and control.

Desperate to stop the pain, I pull my toes toward me to draw out the calf muscle. No luck. Stabbing blindly with my feet in the forward fuselage, I touch a small ledge. I plant my toes and push my heels down hard.

Relief! As I draw out the calf muscles in my lower legs, the spasm releases and the pain subsides. For the rest of the flight, a calf muscle threatens to knot up every time I shove a rudder pedal with one foot or the other. Since most competition flights involve circling to gain altitude at least 25% to 30% of the time, this is a serious complication.

My subsequent progress through the air was erratic, but I made it to the finish line (even scoring a seventh-place speed) using the rudder as little as possible. I suspended my daily early morning fitness run. I don't know if that helped, but the problem didn't recur on Day Two.

Last night, Dad and I worked late on his glider. This was his second year in the ASW 20 that we and two partners had bought from another pilot. Made by a different manufacturer, it had the identical performance to my LS3.

Late in the evening, we concluded the radio problem was lurking somewhere in the wiring. We gave up and just bypassed it, splicing in temporary wiring and a speaker box from an earlier installation laid along the cockpit wall, then wedging a spare battery into the luggage space behind his head to power it. It was vintage Dad: crude but functional. After the contest, I would rip it all out and do it right.

We finished dinner at 10:30 pm feeling a little sorry for ourselves and wondering, tempting fate, what else could go wrong?

Journal Entry: 8:30 AM, June 19, 1980 (Springfield, Ohio)

Day Three, Thursday, is a beautiful morning, bright and clear in the low 50s F. The sun is up before we are, but there's still a golden glow on the eastern horizon. Has our luck changed? Like most competitors, we are staying at the Holiday Inn on U.S. Highway 40, once known as the Main Street of America. After breakfast, we drive our crew cars to the airport.

The U.S. dealer for LS sailplanes has loaned me a more robust water ballast bag. Last year, the LS3 was one of the "hot this minute" ships. This year, most pilots have switched to the ASW 20 like the one Dad is flying. I was the best-placing LS pilot in last year's nationals at Adrian. It's not like being the #1 driver on a NASCAR team, but it's nice to get semi-official support.

My father's first launch in his ASW 20, Caesar Creek Soaring Club, Ohio, 1979 (PG contest number not yet applied).

In auto racing, being able to afford a faster ride is a significant advantage. Soaring used to be that way. The best sailplanes often ended up in the hands of a favored few in the upper firmament of well-to-do pilots. Now the availability of more affordable fiberglass sailplanes from Europe means more pilots can campaign the identical glider flown by a national champion.

"Affordable" is relative. Some pilots compete in the less-expensive 1-26 Class, where a complete kit might cost $7,000 to $10,000. Investments in our two gliders total $18,000 to $20,000 each, including trailers and avionics[11]. Many pilots slash their investment by owning in partnership (we have two partners in our ASW 20). We rationalize our investment in sailplanes is comparable to boats or motorhomes. Of course, boats and RVs are more family friendly than single-seat gliders.

In a few minutes, I yank the leaky ballast tank from the LS3's left wing and install the new one. I'm ready for the new day! On to the Pilots' Meeting.

---

[11] Today, comparable figures for a Standard Class or 15 Meter glider would start at $40,000 used and be well north of $100,000 new. The larger classes (18M and 20M two-seater) would edge up into quarter-of-a-million-dollar territory, including the sustainer or self-launch motor that is increasingly popular.

CHAPTER EIGHTEEN

Pre-Game

Journal Entry: 9:00 AM, June 19, 1980 (Springfield, Ohio)

On Day Three, the briefing hall fills quickly at 9:00 AM. There's a pecking order. Officials and volunteers stand or sit at the front tables. Pilots plop down in rows of folding chairs. Crews scramble for any remaining spots.

Competition soaring has tribal distinctions. Some take part for pure enjoyment. Others are more competitive, with the top ranks vying for a spot on the U.S. Team. Many find pleasure in the camaraderie and the chance to rub shoulders with the best pilots in the country. Others relish the chance to serve as crew members or as part of the organizing team. It's a small, close-knit meritocracy that transcends conventional class and demographic lines, recognizing piloting skill and attitude over social standing or net worth. Although some recreational pilots perceive it as elitist, I believe the community welcomes anyone with a genuine passion for the sport.

After some administrative notes, the Contest Manager calls on yesterday's winner to discuss his/her flight. Many pilots are more at ease in the cockpit than in front of a crowd. Some daily winners mumble a few words and sit down to polite applause. Others cover the high points and toss in a few self-deprecating comments as we chuckle. A few stride eagerly to the front and drone on and on in exhaustive detail, inviting the sarcastic joke that the winner's speech must not consume more time than did the winning flight itself. I've delivered winner's speeches at local and regional contests, so I know how meticulously prepared these "extemporaneous" orations can be. They are occasionally entertaining but rarely enlightening.

Then the mood turns serious as the CD announces the task *du jour*: a 152-mile speed triangle. Springfield is at the top of the triangle with a short first leg 34 miles southwest, bucking the headwind to Lebanon's Warren County Airport. The second leg turns straight east with a quartering tailwind for 68 miles, overflying our home CCSC gliderport and the ex-Air Force base where CCSC had planned to hold the contest, on the way to the second turnpoint at Pickaway County Airport near Circleville. My father and I exchange looks and smirk at each other. We know a secret about Pickaway County. The last leg returns 50 miles northwest across the wind to finish at Springfield.

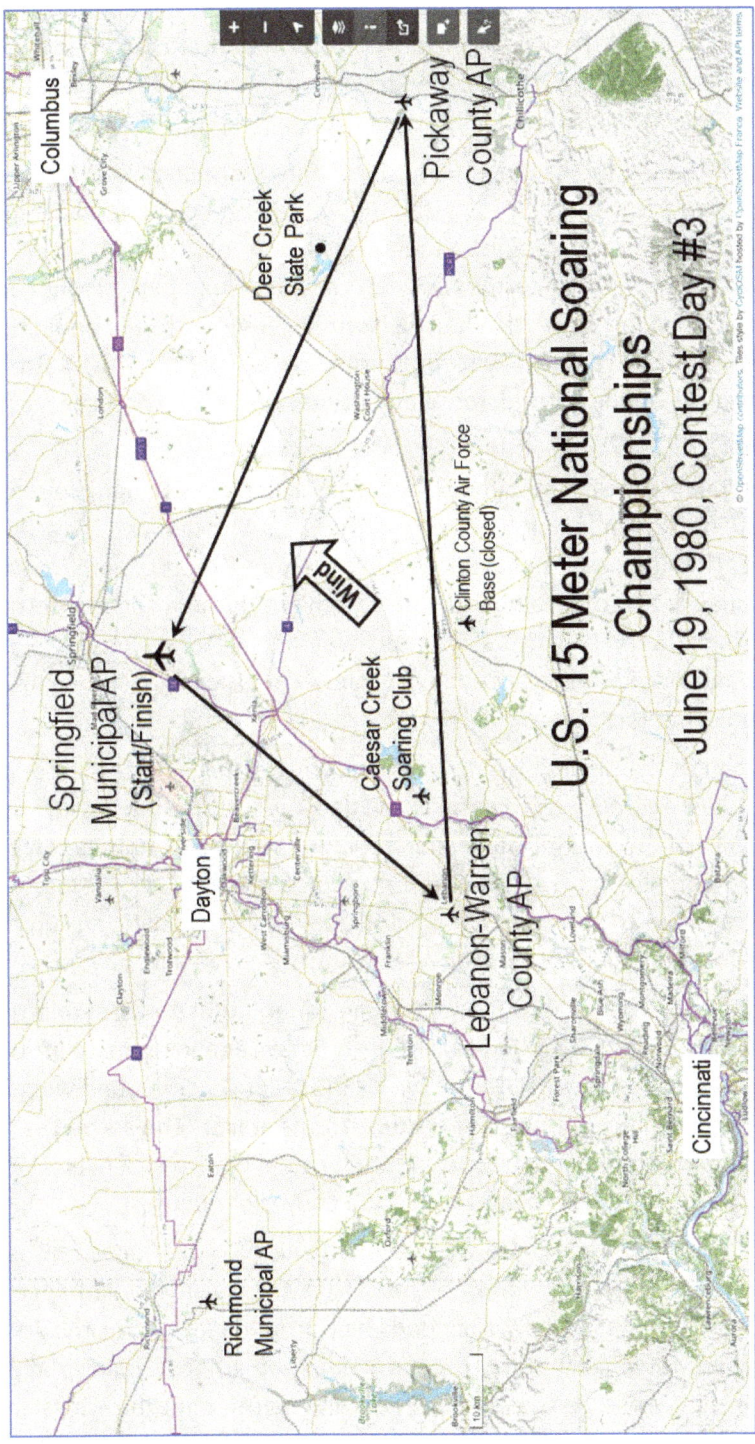

U.S. 15 Meter National Soaring Championships
June 19, 1980, Contest Day #3

Best guess: three hours elapsed time, 50 mph or better. It's an ambitious course given the cold front swinging down from the Great Lakes this evening. Laid out to the south, it's designed to keep us away from that weather and major population centers while still challenging the top-ranked talent.

Weather—including forecasting it—is critical. Pilots complain loudly about the accuracy of contest meteorologists. But we're eager to hear what they have to say even if we don't believe them. This guy drones through his briefing using as many technical terms and charts as possible to buttress his conclusions and provide excuses if/when he is wrong. Temperatures should rise into the low 80s, which bodes well for thermals. The wind could be bothersome: ten knots on the ground, more at altitude. Too much wind can shred the thermals down low.

The pilots cheer when he announces that today's air holds enough moisture to generate fluffy cumulus clouds atop the thermals. The first two days have been blue. That increases the chances a pilot could—like a soldier strolling blissfully unaware through a minefield—fly straight through an area dotted with invisible thermal updrafts without ever encountering one and be forced to land. Days with cu are still uncertain—clouds can linger long after the thermals that form them expire—but are less stressful.

The cold front is marching down toward us from 150 miles north. Although high clouds will encroach by the end of the day, the weatherman assures us the front will not arrive until late evening. I joke a politician knows he's lying whenever he moves his lips. A weatherman actually believes the useless things he says. But this guy has a good story, so—as when politicians promise lower taxes *and* higher spending—we want to believe him, anyway.

Back at our tiedown, it takes Diane and me ten minutes to assemble the LS3. The wings weigh 175 pounds each—but the trailer allows me to lift the heavy inboard end of the first wing while Diane holds the 50-pound wingtip so we can plug it into the fuselage resting on the trailer. The second wing goes on the same way. Then I insert two hefty steel pins to lock everything together. Installing the horizontal tail adds a couple of minutes.

I monitor Dad and my mother as they assemble his ASW 20. I'm astonished to see the wings go on with no problems. That's the way it should happen. It never does, though. Dad always needs help from one of us for the ASW 20. Otherwise, my mother gets trapped holding up a heavy wingtip at an awkward height while he tries to decipher why he can't get the wings and fuselage to align.

He has some unfortunate history. Fifteen years ago, we had struggled to support the wingtips of his 1-23B, shifting our weight from one leg to the other, our feet sinking into a muddy field, chilly rain pouring down, shivering, beach towels draped over our heads and shoulders in a futile effort to stay dry, lifting and yanking trying to separate the wings from the fuselage while he shouted orders and peered in to study the problem, puzzled. Twenty minutes later, facing a mutiny, he discovered he had forgotten to disconnect the aileron control rods, and they were still holding fast.

My father has many talents, but mechanical aptitude is not among them. I joke he is challenged by anything more daunting than squeezing toothpaste from a tube. Much later in life, my mother explained. When Dad and his three brothers were growing up, their father took care of the house and vehicle maintenance. Dad never worked much with tools as a young man.

He can handle a flat tire. He can even change the oil in his cars. But more ambitious tasks—i.e., anything requiring more than duct tape, shock cords, a large screwdriver, or a small hammer—are beyond him.

I've always attributed my aptitude for technology—which was invaluable as I pursued a degree in mechanical engineering—to my mother. An attractive, soft-spoken Southern woman with the enterprise, quiet confidence, and self-effacing determination of a fleet admiral's wife, she—not my father— was the do-it-yourselfer of the house. Her father and brother were mechanically adept, so she was the one who refinished antiques; built furniture; repaired the washing machine; and helped us kids with our projects.

* * *

Back at Springfield, our checklists confirm all our equipment is functioning properly—including the radios. It's going to be a great day!

I'm six inches taller than Dad. The LS3 fits me better and I like the way it flies. He prefers the ASW 20, which now carries his new contest number, PG. He needed a new one because I appropriated his original JB contest number years ago. He's only flown it a few times.

At our first nationals together, in 1977, he flew a Libelle displaying the previous owner's contest number, WE, officially "Whiskey Echo." We tortured him by suggesting it stood for "War Eagle," the motto of Auburn University, the hated rival of his cherished University of Alabama. He was not amused.

By last year's 15 Meter Nationals in Adrian, however, he was flying the ASW 20 with contest number PG and an FAA registration number of N707PG, corresponding to the N707JB on my LS3.

Military pilots receive their [often-unflattering] call signs from their squadrons. In contrast, glider pilots select their own from what's available. Many try to secure their initials as their contest number (e.g., JB). Some buy a used glider and accept the ID already on it. Others try for something clever or memorable, e.g., 7U (7Up instead of Seven Uniform) and DQ (Dairy Queen in lieu of Delta Quebec). George Moffat, who—on his teacher's salary—often flies borrowed gliders to access the latest technology, snatched up XX because it is easy to apply with strips of tape. I know of only one other pilot besides Dad (an Eastern Airlines pilot from the Southeast flying EA) who leverages his long-term employer into his soaring identity.

Family with author's LS3 (JB) and father's ASW 20 (PG).
(photo from estate of Joseph N. Bearden Jr.)

I load batteries and other gear and check off the myriad items on my written checklist. As soaring has become more complex, my checklist and the rigor with which I enforce its use have grown. Later in life, I will know a pilot who failed to confirm the attachment of the horizontal tail to the fuselage and died when it departed during takeoff.

Diane remains the compleat crew. A bright, well-spoken, 21-year-old young woman with dark hair down to the middle of her back, she is slender and attractive. It's comical to watch younger male pilots and crews perk up a day or two into a contest when they discover she is my sister and not my wife or girlfriend.

Loading water ballast is one of the last items. She holds a funnel connected to a hose into the wings while I empty two five-gallon plastic jugs of water into each wing. It's straightforward, but there are hazards. A few years ago in Cordele, I landed with one wing empty and the other full of water, dragging the heavy wing and grinding off part of the wingtip skid. The valve in that wing—which had been a slow fill in the morning—failed completely in the closed position. I'm more careful now to monitor the filling process.

Using a rope behind our car, we tow the LS3 to my assigned grid number, with Diane walking the wingtip. Our number changes each day with a formula that rotates each pilot from near the front (where PG is today), to the middle, to near the rear (where JB is). The start gate won't open until everyone launches and has time to climb up, so it works reasonably well.

Springfield launch grid: crews pull each glider down the taxiway to its grid number, then push it into the grass to leave room. The last step is moving the gliders to the taxiway in single file. (photo by Harry Dunn, from Soaring *magazine, October 1980, used with permission).*

Springfield Municipal is a busy public-use airport near a major city available to power planes and business jets. With 9,000 feet of runway (twice the usual), it even hosts a wing of Ohio Air National Guard fighter jets. We can't block the runway with our takeoff grid, but the airport agreed to close the main taxiway a few hours each day so we can stage and launch from there.

The nationals might be a big deal for us, but the outside world hardly notices. Unlike major sporting events that attract tens of thousands, our contest is more likely to overwhelm a budget motel with a swimming pool and functioning air conditioning than an entire town. Total headcount comprises, at most, several hundred pilots, crews, and contest personnel.

Besides motels, primary beneficiaries include gas stations, the local hardware store, laundromats, and nearby restaurants. After a long contest day, pilots and crews often pack into a few eateries, the primary criteria for which are passable food, low prices, and the ability to push enough tables together to seat 15 or 20 people.

These regular gatherings spawn unusual friendships sparked by a singular common interest. They are sustained by periodic but brief encounters at contests around the country and are sometimes based more on shared tribulations of hot weather, insects, and rain than on common convictions or intimate personal disclosures.

Though fiercely competitive, pilots most often enjoy amicable relationships with those who challenge them on the scoresheet. Is it the absence of prize money? Or is it just the nature of those who share this obsession?

My father discussed this in an article he wrote for *Soaring* magazine early in his soaring career. He used a term—fellowship—familiar to him from church and alluded to soaring's mystical appeal:

"Contests such as the [SSD] Wright Memorial and the [Bryan, Ohio group's] Midwest Meet contribute a great deal to the soaring movement by bringing together so many who enjoy competition and fellowship with each other. One of the big rewards of soaring is getting to know the pilots, families and sailplanes around the country."[12]

Because of soaring's dependence on the weather, there's often more fellowshipping than flying. Even when rain isn't falling, many days we sit on the grid for hours waiting for the overcast to burn off and the sun to warm the ground. If the weather improves, we launch and fly a task. If not, it's back into the trailers, hoping for better weather the next day.

The wait can be maddening. Today, however, I'm certain we will fly.

---

[12] Bearden, J.N., Jr., "Club News: Soaring Society of Dayton." *Soaring*, October 1963, pp 18-19. Used with permission.

CHAPTER NINETEEN

Priorities

Journal Entry: 11:45 AM, June 19, 1980 (Springfield, Ohio)

"I think everything is finally coming together!" My father had been ebullient when I congratulated him for assembling the ASW 20. It was a minor, but auspicious, turn at a contest that hasn't been going his way.

Just before noon, I stroll the quarter mile to the front of the grid, where Dad will be one of the first ones up. He is an excellent pilot. But he is as risk-averse in the cockpit as he is on the ground, overly so in my view. I'm not reckless; he has taught me well. But compared to my 53-year-old father, I fly with less restraint, suffused with confidence; the conviction of unlimited promise and invulnerability; and desire to make my mark that are so often appropriated by the young. So whether practicing or competing, I tend to pull away from the man who has been my teacher, my mentor, my coach. His 34th and 40th on the first two days have deposited him in 36th overall, halfway down the score sheet. That's consistent with his placing 34th of 58 in last year's nationals.

A few months ago, we celebrated Dad's 53rd birthday. He is still handsome, a fully grown Alabama boy with a wide smile whose face can express humor and *gravitas* equally well. Even after 30 years up North, his voice still betrays his Southern roots. He is of medium height with blue eyes and a thick mane he has been coloring to hide the gray for ten years since he lost 25 pounds and regained his athlete's build. That was also when he swapped his drab suits and white shirts for more stylish alternatives, though still compliant with the informal-but-inflexible Procter & Gamble HQ dress code, e.g., no short-sleeve dress shirts unless wearing a jacket. We applauded these changes. No one wants to admit loving their parents less because of superficialities. But it was great that Dad proactively improved his health and appearance. He presents as being much younger than he did ten years ago.

I'm aware the 50s can be a challenging time for men, though it will be years before I understand the full import. Dad has exhibited signs of the stresses of middle age, both personally and professionally. He may be struggling to come to terms with aging and with the responsibility he has always felt—as the eldest son—to look out for his sedentary parents in Alabama. Added to this, all three of us kids have moved out of the family home after 30 years of bustling family life. He is grappling with many changes.

I've never seen him in action at P&G, but I suspect management view him as a competent, responsible middle manager well suited for his sensitive position overseeing employee benefit plans, which brings him into frequent contact with senior executives. But he has reached a plateau in his career. Recently, he confided his frustration that the regular promotions and stock option grants he formerly received have ceased. Although his job is secure, there is little room for advancement. He will probably remain in his current position until he retires, which is still ten years away. It's no surprise Dad is no longer the unequivocal P&G cheerleader he used to be, especially since his 30th work anniversary passed with little fanfare only days before.

I'm sure Dad holds onto the old-school notion of wanting his kids to lead a better life. But the rapid advancement of my brother's and my careers and compensation packages facilitated by our MBAs may have contributed to his frustration. In a startling concession, not long ago he confessed he might make different choices if he were starting over. It's too late for that, though. Given his age and temperament, he has too many responsibilities and has invested too much in his career at P&G. In a not entirely unpleasant way, he is trapped. And soaring is, for a few hours at a time, his temporary escape.

When I arrive today, whatever midlife anxieties are overshadowing his life are on hold. Dad seems relaxed and eager to fly. To confirmed soaring addicts, even a bad contest day beats a good day almost anywhere else.

We stand side by side, surveying the 67 gliders on the launch grid. Over the 12 years since my first contest, Dad has continued to be a competent, middle-of-the-pack pilot. During the same time, I've risen unevenly through the ranks to become a contender. But at every contest, we chat, psyching each other up, the way we did at that first weekend meet in 1968. I stand tall next to him, smiling, watching his expression.

"This is our day, Dad. You're flying better than ever before! We both have a built-in advantage with navigation. And we've been waiting for a task to Pickaway County for a year. If ever there were a day made to order for both of us, this is it. Let's both make up some ground!"

He grins broadly, almost boyishly. It helps my confidence to boost his. And confidence is crucial. Like inveterate gamblers, soaring pilots cling to hope— no matter how far down the score sheet they are—that today will be The Day, the come-from-behind performance that will make everything better.

It can happen. Even a pilot who is out of contention could step into the spotlight with a daily win. Top pilots stumble. And occasionally, mid-pack pilots break through in the daily standings. I suspect most of us, regardless of our abilities, launch each day thinking, "Today, it could be me!"

One reason for our optimism is home-field advantage. Navigation is easier for us in this pre-GPS era of maps and compasses. Soaring flights involve a lot of tight, repetitive circles a few thousand feet above the ground in hazy weather. It's easy to get disoriented and lose track of one's position. My father and I had grinned when a few pilots had complained yesterday about locating a turnpoint in a confusing tangle of highways and populated areas. This was our backyard, and we had scarcely consulted our maps.

A more significant factor is knowing reliable sources of lift and sink. This is more common at mountainous sites with predictable air flows but can also apply to flatland sites where dead air lurks downwind of large bodies of water. None of that exists here. Our task is ordinary farmland: thousands of square miles of dark, freshly plowed fields disturbed only by traceries of roads, rail lines, and small towns.

But—there is one exception. Pickaway County Airport, the second turnpoint, is just another community airstrip to everyone else, officials included. Dad and I, however, have been waiting a year for it to be part of a task. A virtual black hole of soaring, the Pickaway County "Sinkhole" often sucks unwary sailplanes into nearby pastures and plowed fields.

It's not the Bermuda Triangle of Southwestern Ohio. Gliders don't vanish inexplicably; they just land out there more often than expected. The mystery might have remained a local legend, like a reputedly haunted house. Then, a year ago, an analytical club member offered an explanation. The last 15 miles headed east into Pickaway County fall off almost imperceptibly into a glacial basin carved thousands of years ago by the movement of ice. It is indistinguishable from the air but is some two hundred feet lower. This basin retains rainwater like a sponge and diminishes the strength of the thermals when the ground is damp, as it so often is in the spring.

Like inside information on Wall Street, local knowledge is worthless if everyone has it. So my father and I have told no one about the Pickaway County Sinkhole, hoping at least one task would take us there. Today is that day. We grin like conspirators as we envision eager competitors pursuing beautiful, puffy cumulus, only to discover they should have "shifted gears" and slowed down to stay high ten miles earlier.

As we prepare to part, we pause for Dad to interrogate me about my competition primacies. It's a tradition we began at my first contest 12 years ago.

"So, what are your priorities today?"

I respond in formal fashion, like a schoolboy reciting his lessons:

"First priority is personal safety."

"Second priority is the glider."

"Third priority is contest points."

Then, as I turn to walk away, Dad hesitates, looks up with a serious face, and tosses something at me he's never said before.

"You know, we haven't really flown together much this contest. Why don't we try to go around together today? We hardly ever get to do that."

I am ashamed to admit my first, unkind reaction is, "Sure, if you can keep up." But I swallow those words and concur, smiling, adding a last remark:

"Okay, I'll look for you at the start gate."

That's like saying, "See you later," but it's my way of agreeing to fly with him—*if he takes the initiative to find me.*

Soaring is a selfish sport. We fly alone, driven by personal motivations and obsessions. There are no monetary rewards. There are no screaming fans or fawning groupies. Whatever glory there may be in victory, we seek it for ourselves as individuals. So, frankly, my focus is on *my* flying today and on the opportunity to move up in the scores. Flying with my father would be nice. But the thrust of my ambition is leveraging Pickaway County Airport into my best chance ever to win a day at the national level—and move up.

* * *

The quality of the 65 other pilots we face varies. In my early days in the 1960s, the gap between the handful of top pilots and everyone else seemed enormous. Parity in aircraft performance and expanding knowledge of how to fly fast has helped level the playing field and increased the number of serious contenders. The star-studded entry list reads like a *Who's Who* of contemporary U.S. soaring with nine former national champions and a few up-and-comers vying for the national title and a spot on the U.S. team at the world championships next year in West Germany.

Karl Striedieck, two-time national champion and second in the world in this class two years ago in France, sits atop the heap after winning yesterday's task. Tall, lean, hard-eyed, and plainspoken, he is the epitome of the military fighter pilot he once was. Already one of America's most successful pilots, Karl will be a fixture in my soaring career for many decades.

Soaring is a game primarily for middle-aged and older men, in part because of the time and money needed to excel. But there are exceptions. I turned 29 a few days ago, so I am one of them. I like to think I've developed a reputation as a solid young pilot who can scramble when conditions sour. Yet my youth is deceptive. Because of our family's years in soaring, my memories go back as far as many older competitors' do.

Other young pilots have similar backgrounds. Slender, preppyish-looking Tigger Hall won Day One and lies second. USAir pilot Tom Beltz (third place) seems laid back like a good-time frat boy but exhibits a dangerous will to win in the air. Promising Westerner and recent film school graduate Chris Woods could pass for a blond, California surfer but has a fine touch on the controls of sailplanes, powered aircraft, and cameras.

I've known Eric Mozer the longest. He's a former national champion and U.S. Team member who, like Tommy Beltz, is disarmingly charming on the ground with a disingenuous killer instinct in the cockpit. Eric and I both grew up in the Midwest as junior pilots. He appeared at the Cordele Regional one year in the early '70s, with a cherubic face framed by shoulder-length hair, a full beard, and a T-shirt with "MICHIGAN" emblazoned across the chest, provoking considerable controversy in backwoods South Georgia.

Local police stopped him one night, speeding down a back road in his father's refrigerator-white Ford Torino with Michigan license plates. Eric ascended into the realm of soaring mythology by talking his way out of a traffic ticket, "mistakenly" handing the officer his pilot's license and pleading earnestly that he and his younger brother were trying to reach their campground before it closed. Awesome! In the cockpit, he was streaky, brilliant for a few days before tumbling from contention. Then, overnight, he settled down and vaulted into the top ranks.

It's no accident we five are engrossed in soaring. Eric Mozer's father Rudy, Chris Woods' father Woody, and my dad are veteran pilots competing here. Pilot Richard Hall is crewing for his son, Tigger. And Tom Beltz's father, Dave, a retired airline pilot, owns a farm/gliderport in Pennsylvania, where their family has flown for years. The pursuit of excellence in soaring is as intrinsic to our families as politics and ambition are to the Kennedys.

Five other former U.S. Team pilots trail the leaders by varying amounts, including two of America's three world champions, A.J. Smith and George

Moffat, plus several world record holders. As in other obscure sports, perhaps two-thirds of the pilots here are an unremarkable supporting cast who fill the entry field for ten days of adventure travel. That's a harsh commentary, but I'm less intent on rubbing shoulders with top pilots than I am in joining their ranks.

Eric Mozer and father Rudy Mozer. (photo by Richard Devilbiss, from Soaring *magazine, September 1977, used with permission).*

This desire drove me to work tirelessly on sailplane preparation and practice all spring, even though it meant commuting to Ohio from New Jersey each weekend. My girlfriend, Kathy, is not happy with these absences. But I rationalize it is only for two months before the Nationals.

I am unapologetic that the national contest is the most important event of the year for me. My priorities are already a source of friction in my romantic relationships. Later, I will realize I am emulating my father, who structured his life, then presumed his wife and family would fall happily into line and support him. My mother is a strong, smart, resourceful woman. But she grew up with the traditional notion that women should support their husbands unconditionally.

In my life, I will learn what worked for Dad won't always work for me. The girls I've dated have been no stronger or smarter or more resourceful than my mother. But they are from a more independent generation playing by different rules and with different expectations of their partners. My inability to discern this fundamental distinction will be an irritant in my personal relationships, including throughout my marriage. But this insight will come later, after considerable turmoil, as does so much essential knowledge of how to achieve balance in our lives.

CHAPTER TWENTY

"Gentlemen, Start Your Engines"

Journal Entry: 12:00 PM, June 19, 1980 (Springfield, Ohio)

It's possible we could assemble and stage 67 gliders and never launch a single one. Weather is a factor in outdoor sports, but never more so than in soaring. Rain is an obvious disqualifier. But other days may look great yet be unflyable if thermals don't develop. The weatherman promised cu marking the thermals. But as pilots, crews, and officials circulate quietly up and down the grid, waiting for the launch, I'm annoyed that an inhospitable bowl of azure sky arches from horizon to horizon laced only by a few feathery bands of high-altitude cirrus clouds. I wish this weatherman were consistently wrong so we could assume the opposite of what he predicts.

Cumulus clouds aren't mandatory. Blue days can be soarable, as the previous two proved. But the luck factor is higher. And bad luck is the biggest threat to my ambitious goal for this contest, or so I imagine.

The gusty wind buffets the gliders sitting ready to fly, waiting for the uncertainties to resolve. Will the thermals develop as forecast? Is the task too long or too short for the conditions? Then, before 12:30, the "sniffer" pilot already aloft reports sustainable lift. With that, the CD comes on the radio:

"Listen up, pilots. Launch will begin in 15 minutes!"

And with that, the tone changes. People stand up straighter. Pilots stride back to their planes with purpose. The early launches slide into their cockpits and strap in. Crews rush back to their tow vehicles to put away the folding chairs, coolers, and beach towels they've had sitting on the grid while waiting. Operations team members tug on their high-visibility vests and review launch and safety procedures one last time. It's real.

In five more minutes, towplane engines cough to life and props spin. One by one, towpilots advance throttles and trundle into an almost military echelon alongside the taxiway, noise adding to the tension. The first towplane taxies in and pivots in front of the grid, wingtip sweeping around, coming to rest facing up the taxiway, the engine muttering at idle. Watching the first takeoff is a custom for me. It makes it official.

On the narrow taxiway here at Springfield, we're staged in single file, not in the rows of two, three, or even four gliders abreast we see on wider runways. That's a long queue, roughly 1,800 feet from the first glider to the last. That's how much less runway the lead gliders will have compared with the last gliders if something goes wrong on takeoff and they need to abort the launch and land straight ahead.

The taxiway here should be long enough to accommodate that, but stuff happens. People make mistakes. Mechanical things break. Aviation is a culture of attention to detail, of anticipating what could go wrong, and pre-planning for contingencies rather than improvising. Mechanics secure bolts with locking nuts that can't vibrate loose or render them immobile with stainless steel safety wire. Designers build in safety margins for the never-exceed limits on the airframes. Gliders have checklists, operating handbooks, and annual inspections. Pilots have training and licensing requirements, written and flight tests, and recurrent training and reviews.

The noise rises to a peak, drowning out everything else as the towplane and glider begin to roll. As they gain speed down the runway, lift off, and climb out, another towplane taxis into position. It doesn't stop. The first tows claw their way to altitude and the gliders release and begin to search. The early thermals are low and weak. Today, like the first two, is developing slowly. Dad is one of the first to launch today, so Diane had hurried up to the front of the grid to wish him luck and run his wing. Now, at 12:50, I watch him being pulled aloft, his PG contest number emblazoned on the tail and on the underside of the wing for easy visibility.

Staring at the sky, we watch the gaggles, crowded and disconcertingly low, gliders wheeling in tight formations like birds, desperately searching for lift, climbing little or not at all. The brisk wind drifts them downwind, i.e., away from the first turn. This is not sustainable. Unless the thermals strengthen, the wind will carry them away before they can gain much altitude. The lowest ones will have to break off and glide back here to avoid landing out.

It's already started. "Alpha Hotel turning final for a relight." Respected veteran and Pan Am airline captain Jim Smiley (AH) radios he's being forced to land and will need to tow off again. Ugh. Conditions are tough. I'm happy to sit on the grid and let my competitors thrash as the weather improves.

It takes over an hour to launch 67 gliders. The first pilots, like Dad, must work harder to stay up in the weak early thermals until the rest of us are airborne and the start gate opens. Offsetting this, they will have more time to evaluate the weather. Those of us at the back of the grid will have to climb up as fast as possible with less time to assess the day.

As the launch progresses, the advancing high clouds and freshening wind provoke new anxiety about the cold front. To our surprise, the meteorologist strides up, waving the latest weather map. We remaining pilots pounce on him like children clamoring for a baseball hero's autograph.

"The cold front is in Southern Michigan [still 150 miles north]," he asserts with confidence, gesturing at the map while reiterating this disruptive air mass will not arrive before evening. He dismisses some worrisome thunderstorms depicted in Eastern Indiana—well south of the front and less than 100 miles upstream—as an isolated build up.

"No," he shakes his head, annoyed at our fixation. The incoming cold front will *not* be a factor in our southerly task. We want to believe, but we watch the gaggles orbiting at low altitude downwind of us, stragglers exiting the bottom of the stack for a low glide and landing back into the relight area.

The line of gliders ahead shrinks as they're towed up one by one. I shrug on the emergency backpack parachute required for competition, snapping buckles over my thighs and chest, and tightening straps. It's an insurance policy. I don't expect to use it. But I know half a dozen pilots who have when their gliders broke up in flight or they collided with another glider.

I lower my body into the cockpit and position it to join myself with my aircraft for what could be up to six hours. Unlike in the office or even in a car, there's no way to stretch or ease sore spots. I cinch the thick lap belts and shoulder harnesses down tight in case something goes wrong on takeoff. The steeply reclining seat, minimal padding, stark panel of gauges, and utilitarian interior bear a passing resemblance to the functional, no-pretense cockpit of a purpose-built race car.

I pencil off the remaining items on my checklist. I've installed the turnpoint cameras; marked the course on the aeronautical chart; tucked away the daily task sheet and turnpoint photo booklet; zipped my wallet into the side pocket so I don't sit on it for six hours; and tossed in a sandwich and water bottle. I use the master switch to select the primary battery, switch on the radio and two electronic variometers, and adjust the altimeter.

With another full-throttle takeoff, the big T-shaped tail of the glider ahead rolls up the runway behind its towplane. The prop wash arrives, rattling dust and shaking my uplifted Plexiglas canopy. I'm next. Over the roar of the tug engines, I remind my sister Diane: "Stay with the wingtip as long as you can."

CHAPTER TWENTY-ONE

Launch

Journal Entry: 2:00 PM, June 19, 1980 (Springfield, Ohio)

This takeoff is riskier. Not dangerous. There's just more that can go wrong. Diane wishes me luck, then I pull the canopy down. My previous top-ten finishes have left me with a sense of entitlement. Tenth place is not where I want to be, especially in front of CCSC. I call off my final checklist items:

A: altimeter (set)
B: belts and harness (checked)
C: canopy (locked)
C: controls (checked)
C: cable (operations will be connecting it in seconds)
D: dive brakes (closed and locked).

It's quiet again, as it was 15 years ago before my first solo. Aviation author Ernest K. Gann candidly described this moment in his book, *Island in the Sky*.

"Before takeoff, a professional pilot is keen, anxious, but lest someone read his true feelings, he is elaborately casual."[13]

I don't have the thousands of hours over decades my older competitors do. But I aspire to *be* them. So I'm alert, but mindful that my peers should perceive my effort to execute an uneventful takeoff as nonchalantly adept. Like NASA's Mercury astronauts, as recorded by author Tom Wolfe in *"The Right Stuff,"* my aim is to:

"Maintain an even strain."[14]

At my signal, Diane crouches and—using both hands—heaves the heavy left wingtip off the tarmac. It lightens as she holds the wings level and the water ballast gurgles and settles evenly in the tanks. In ten to fifteen seconds, they balance, the sailplane poised for takeoff on its main landing wheel and the small steel tailskid.

When my towplane taxis up, the line boy grabs the yellow towrope and inserts the hardened steel ring into the tow release in the belly of the LS3. The towplane also has a release, but the towpilot won't "feed me the rope"

---

[13] Gann, Ernest K. *Island in the Sky* (New York: The Viking Press, 1942)
[14] Wolfe, Tom. *The Right Stuff* (New York: Farrar, Straus and Giroux, 1979)

unless something goes wrong. The slack comes out as the towplane idles forward and pauses. At my thumbs-up signal, the operations chief gives the okay. The towpilot firewalls the throttle, the engine snarls loudly, and the acceleration presses me back into the seat. It is 2:00 PM.

The LS3 surges forward and Diane's legs churn furiously to stay with it, fighting gusts that threaten to upset the wings. She's been running wings for years. Trying to keep up, others might hold back on the wingtip without realizing it and curl me off track into the steel post of a taxiway light. The wingtip slips seamlessly from Diane's hand just as the rush of air across the wing enables me to keep the wings level myself. The rudder is also responding as we follow in the towplane's turbulent wake.

When I sense life infusing the glider, I pull the flap lever back to +10 degrees. The curved airfoil bites into the air and the heavy LS3 breaks free of the ground, ballooning up softly behind the towplane. Seconds later, that aircraft also lifts off, engine growling, fighting to gain airspeed, the rope sagging over its 200-foot length. The needle on the ASI rotates through 60 knots as we pass over the end of the taxiway, the airport recedes, the hangars and taxiways spread out and disappear behind us, and the farms and houses surrounding the airport slide by as we labor to climb.

Accident investigators publish statistics about the most dangerous times for a glider pilot. One of them is *right now* during the first minute of flight, when the towplane and glider are low, slow, and struggling to gain altitude and airspeed. Both aircraft have limited options should the engine falter, the towrope break, or either pilot botch what is, for all intents and purposes, formation flying. Water ballast increases the risk. It takes longer to get the heavier glider up to the higher speed required, and it's less maneuverable.

The airspeed stabilizes at 70 knots. I call out "200 feet" aloud as the altimeter needle swings past that mark and I relax a little. If something goes wrong, that's enough altitude to make a 180-degree turn and glide back to the airport, rather than having a few seconds to select an emergency landing field.

This is the moment when life changes, when the waiting and talking cease and I am transported, literally and figuratively, to a more exalted state that transcends my earthly distresses. Whatever might be troubling me in life, towing off in my sailplane begins an interlude—sometimes of only minutes but more often hours—when everything else dwindles to irrelevance.

When I awaken, I know my competitors and I will share a common purpose:

to fly around the course as fast as possible. Throughout the day, that will be our foremost thought, displacing other cares and apprehensions.

Soaring infuses me with a euphoria and enchantment that escape most people. Part of the appeal arises from engaging the country's best pilots in a complex sport. I enjoy the sense of self-reliance. Much later, *Into Thin Air* author Jon Krakauer will write that Everest teammate, John Taske, a commander in the Australian Special Air Service, began climbing to provide what he missed on retiring from the military: viz., *"[T]he challenge, the camaraderie, the sense of mission."*[15] When I read this, I will smile in understanding.

I never served in the military, so nowhere else have I experienced the collective sense of resolve, the missions through marginal weather over hazardous terrain in an arena where each pilot is relentlessly pushing and being measured by and against others. In the cockpit, I alone am responsible for everything that happens. Part of the allure is pushing myself to my perceived limits, a sensation few seek, much less experience, in their sensibly ordered lives on the ground. I wonder how many people know, *really* know their limits. Caught up in what author and pilot Richard Bach referred to (in his book, *Stranger to the Ground*) as a *"droning adventureless existence,"* most have never really tested themselves, be it in combat or climbing Mount Everest—or in flying or marathon running.

Soaring's unique challenges cannot be described. How do you communicate the way unpowered aircraft weighing more than half a ton can fly 1,000 miles at upwards of 100 knots without turning, surfing the wind flowing over the Appalachian ridges? Or how they are able to fly 500 miles averaging 100 mph over the deserts and mountains of the American West, ascending 1,000 feet every minute in thermals—faster than most high-rise elevators—and cruising between climbs at speeds that would outpace a small Cessna? Or how they can climb, using only the power of the wind of the mountain wave, to 50,000 feet?

How do you convey what it's like in the last few miles of a long final glide, with the airport comfortably in sight, when you push over to near redline speed, the controls stiffen and grow heavy with the air loads, and you open the ballast tank valves to jettison hundreds of pounds of water into the slipstream, leaving a contrail like heavy white smoke?

Up ahead, the terrain is unreeling swiftly, the sailplane drawing closer to the ground, threatening to merge with its shadow. The trees are flashing by in a green blur. The aircraft is shuddering and bouncing. Your body is jarring as the wings flex to absorb the impact of gusts and low-level turbulence. You are but a flick of the control stick—an almost imperceptible hesitation or misjudgment—away from slamming into the trees at 140 knots or over-stressing the wings. Leveling out above the runway, gunsighting the white line, you hurl your aircraft through the finish gate with that lovely, explosive moan of a modern sailplane being driven hard, then bring the stick back smoothly and soar 500 feet in a steep, spectacular climbing turn that re-leases the pressure in one long sigh of exhalation. Your body sags and the wings bow with the G-forces. The canopy fills with sky. The last tendrils of water vapor mark your path in an effortless, breathtaking curve like a sky-writing plane. Then, as the airspeed falls off dangerously, you push the stick forward to level out, inhale, deeply satisfied, drop the landing gear, and en-ter the pattern to real or imagined applause.

Author dumping water ballast crossing finish line. (photo by Guerry Howard)

How do you express this to others?

You can't. It's ineffable. The vocabulary doesn't exist. The most lyrical, mov-ing, and emotional poetry cannot fully convey the concept of love. Likewise, the richest, most eloquent, evocative erotica can never truly communicate the luxuriant essence of emotional and physical intimacy. The same is true for the myriad sensations that comprise soaring. You must experience these things to know them. And most people—even most pilots—never will.

CHAPTER TWENTY-TWO

Redline

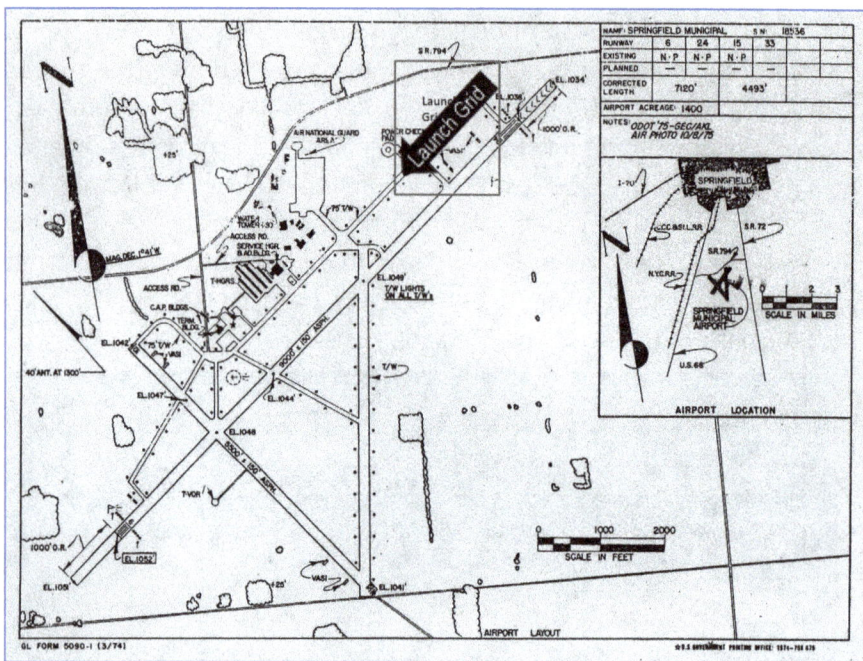

Springfield Municipal Airport, with launch grid on June 19, 1980, shown. Original map from U.S. Government Printing Office for Federal Aviation Administration.

Journal Entry: 2:10 PM, June 19, 1980 (Springfield, Ohio)

Our airspeed stabilizes at 70 knots and our climb rate improves. I focus on tracking behind the towplane while stealing glances above to spot the gaggles. It's easy to lose 500 feet or more searching for the first thermal and be in trouble—even forced to relight—before the flight is 20 minutes old.

A few minutes later, at 2,000 feet, I release the towrope. As the towplane dives away to the left, I pull up to the right and retract the landing gear, hearing the doors snap into place to cover the wheel. I turn into the bottom of a gaggle and sigh in relief when the heavy LS3 trembles and then begins to climb. The choppy air pushes the glider up and down roughly, but the net effect is positive as I complete the first circle. This early updraft bubbling up from an overheated spot on the ground is disorganized, making it difficult to control the airspeed precisely. Carving circle after circle, three per minute, the lift smooths out and soon I'm going up continuously.

I'm not the low man anymore. The last gliders behind me on the launch grid have joined the thermal below. A dozen of us are circling in the same direction at different altitudes. It looks, from the ground, like a flock of vultures wheeling patiently above a dying animal on the sunbaked plains of Africa.

Fifteen minutes after takeoff, I leave the thermal at 3,000 feet and glide upwind, then carve into a stronger, more heavily trafficked thermal, scanning contest numbers for PG. It's like merging into a three-dimensional traffic circle. Three and four gliders are circulating at slow speeds at the same altitude, with more gliders just above and below. Unlike traffic circles, however, gliders enter a pre-start thermal in quick succession from all directions—but they don't necessarily exit right away. Another complication is gliders move in three dimensions, floating up and down as they change airspeeds. Last year at the Nationals, one pilot came busting into a thermal and zoomed up sharply, not seeing the glider directly overhead.

BANG! The collision damaged his glider's tail and crushed the other plane's belly. Both pilots had earned reputations for aggressive thermaling, so the fault was unclear. After the "Mayday" call, I listened as a third pilot calmly advised the other two about their gliders' conditions. Both landed, shaken.

Entering a thermal without drama is just the first step. Thermals are where soaring pilots' independence, self-reliance, and opportunism come to the fore. Each pilot has their ideas regarding the location of the best lift, how steep and fast to fly, and when to leave. And they're not shy about shifting their circle to seek advantage. Let one pilot open up his circle and ease out to one side, then tighten up, rising a little faster and it's like a radio call saying, "Over here, it's better over here!" Within seconds, every nearby pilot has moved over. Add the varying skill levels and it's common for gliders' paths in a thermal to intersect and potentially conflict.

If someone cuts me off, I can take evasive action by banking more steeply to turn inside, though that might put me in someone else's path. I can roll level to go around on the outside, with the same hazards. If I have speed, I can zoom up and coast over them, praying they don't pull up. I can even dive away, calling on the radio "[contest number __], did you see me?" Translation: "You stupid idiot, you almost hit me!" If a repeat offender scares someone multiple times, the comments are harsher, e.g., "[contest number __], that's the third time you've made me flinch!"

Today, sailplanes crowd into the two thermals closest to the inbound side of the start gate. They climb up, then loiter at the top, creating even worse traffic. Savvy experts are waiting for the gate to open. Leeches are milling around, hoping to hitch a ride with one of them. I still don't see PG but there are 66 men and one woman up here and I have eyes only on a handful. If I spot Dad, great. But I'm not going looking for him.

The CD has radioed to open the start gate, so we listen to non-stop radio chatter as sailplanes make their starts. We're all looking for a perfect start. Some pilots prefer a conservative strategy. One many-time national champion used to joke, "Start early and pray for rain," hoping storms would trap later starters while they were still on course.

Others (and I'm solidly in this camp) wait for most competitors to depart, then use earlier starters (referred to as "markers") to spot thermals. Like cheating on one's income taxes, starting late is often successful, but the downside can be severe. When the weather turns sour or a pilot gets low and loses time, they can fall behind or even land out. Too often I've found myself alone in the afternoon searching for one last thermal for an achingly slow last climb as the sky grows calm, from which to launch a desperate, maximum-performance final glide, creeping in embarrassingly slow swearing I'll never do it again. Contrast this with my father, Mr. Belt-and-Suspenders, who invariably starts early and, overtaken by the leaders, trails the ubiquitous gaggles around the course.

I have all but forgotten my promise to look for Papa Golf as I climb through 4,000 feet. Welcomed cumulus clouds are, at last, sprouting at the tops of smoother and stronger thermals. I guess I owe the weatherman an apology. I hope he's right about the cold front, too.

This is not a day for "start gate roulette," gambling on a late start. I haven't heard a word from Papa Golf since he launched, but it's not his style to hang around. I can't worry about him, though. Time to start. The high clouds are moving in from the north. I glance out to check traffic going into the gate.

Whoa! To my surprise, Dad's ASW 20 pulls up strongly into the thermal right below, bearing the familiar German high-visibility red checkerboard pattern on its rudder. Good for him! It's another sign our fortunes have turned. After a few more circles, I exit the thermal headed straight for the Initial Point (IP), my excitement building.

I wheel in the prescribed 90-degree left turn over the Initial Point (a spot on the ground that helps start gate observers with binoculars know where to look for incoming sailplanes) and key the microphone button on the stick:

"Juliet Bravo, left turn IP." Then I level the wings, headed for an invisible window in the sky one mile away and over 1,000 feet below.

I hear gatekeeper Charlie Spratt's calm voice: "Juliet Bravo, proceed."

I give the control stick a firm push, lowering the nose to build speed. As if falling from a high precipice, the LS3 plummets and I am briefly light in the cockpit when the aircraft seems to drop away from me, gathering speed. As the ASI needle wraps around from 60 to 80 to 100 knots, I relax the forward pressure on the stick. It would be easy to exceed the redline speed.

As I sight along the runway leading into the gate, the airspeed is passing through 120 knots. The controls stiffen and the wind noise increases as the dive stabilizes. Turbulence that was merely annoying at thermaling speed hammers at the glider, shaking and tossing me in the cockpit. The LS3 bounces and shudders; it sounds like someone is heaving clods of earth at the fuselage behind me. I have my right hand in a tight hold on the control stick, forearm braced on my thigh. If we hit a strong thermal at this speed and my grip loosens or my arm twitches in response, it could overstress the glider and pull the wings off.

Starting at the right time is key. So is diving steeply to duck under the top limit of the gate (1,000 meters, or 3,300 feet high) traveling as fast as possible, then converting that excess velocity into altitude in an abrupt pull up while slowing to normal cruise speed. Being called back for being too high is costly. It involves detouring several miles back around behind the gate, climbing up again, and then restarting. That can take 10 to 15 minutes. By then, the fast gaggle could be miles ahead.

Being too far below the height limit is also costly. It guarantees you a start time. But you give away the free altitude you *could* have had if you'd done it right. Being just a hundred feet low—only two wingspans—could put you 30 seconds behind the pack before flying the first mile of the task.

Even from 4,000 feet, the visual and audible sensations of streaking along at high speed are obvious. As the airspeed mounts and the turbulence worsens, I reassure myself I've done this many times before. My LS3 is built like a tank. The airspeed creeps up to 130 knots, then 140 knots. My ears and hands on the controls are alert for the high-frequency buzz that would signal the onset of "flutter," the rapid vibration of a movable control surface on the tail or wings that can precede its disintegration by seconds. Later, when I'm older and wiser, I will shake my head that I got away with it so many times. But now, I assume because it's never happened, it won't.

I steal a quick glance out to each side. The runway is an arrow guiding me into the gate. But I can't see directly below—the cockpit is in the way—so I can't tell how far away the line is. I'm watching ground features I had selected on either side of the runway directly aligned with the start line: a tree line, a road, a silo. The altimeter is unwinding, the hands spinning around in reverse. I am still too high, so—knowing I'm pushing it closer to the edge—I ease the control stick forward to trade altitude for more speed.

In a few years, the SSA will replace high-speed starts with a GPS-based tracking system that records each pilot's start at a more sedate speed. But in 1980, these few seconds at redline are the second-most exciting moment of a contest flight, trailing only the high-speed finish pass at ground level in pure adrenaline-fueled intensity. With youthful exuberance, I relish each plunge across the start line the way a downhill ski racer embraces each timed run down an icy course, i.e., with dread and eager nervousness.

One pilot I know bailed out when his glider came apart explosively while starting. The pieces rained down on the airport and narrowly missed pilots and crews on the ground. Later in my career, two other pilots I know will have similar scares. One bailed out successfully when he lost control. The other landed in a dangerously compromised glider. So my views will change, as they often do with age and experience. But today I'm young and heedless, confident my glider and I can withstand anything we encounter.

Somewhere near the never-exceed redline at 146 knots on the ASI, I judge I will just squeak under the top of the invisible gate I am streaking toward. The wind noise peaks. The turbulence shakes and tosses the glider, rocking me in my straps, threatening to knock my head against the canopy.

It happens fast. My pre-selected landmarks come up on either side below me as we explode across the line a fraction under 3,300 feet high. I'm already hauling back on the stick smoothly when I hear Charlie Spratt's calm voice saying, "Mark!" Everything gets heavy as the G-forces press my body down into the reclining seat and the glider soars back into the air, nose high, converting excess speed into altitude. Safe! The thumping in my chest subsides and I stabilize at 75 knots headed southwest. I hear Charlie intone "Juliet Bravo, good start," punctuated with another "Mark," a few seconds behind me, and Papa Golf receives his confirmation.

It is 2:32 and the clock—the task clock, the only one that counts—is ticking.

CHAPTER TWENTY-THREE

On Course

Journal Entry: 2:35 PM, June 19, 1980 (Springfield, Ohio)

The first thermal after the start gate is like the first impression in a job interview: disproportionately unfair. It can be the foundation for subsequent success. But mishandle it or simply encounter bad luck and you can spend the rest of your flight (career) fighting to recover.

The start gate radio has quieted, now. Most pilots started just before I did. Good, that will put more markers ahead of me. Getting to the last turn at Pickaway County a little later could be a problem if the front arrives early and cuts us off from the north. But I'm hoping that won't happen, or, if it does, that we'll all face the same problem.

But that first thermal is critical. Even after zooming up hundreds of feet in a perfect high-speed start, we're still headed out on the task less than 4,000 feet above the ground. That's often lower (sometimes thousands of feet lower) than where we might usually leave on a cross-country flight.

I aggressively push this first glide a little faster. My sense (okay, my gamble) is the thermals are still improving and I'll find stronger lift ahead if I keep going. Stronger thermals call for higher cruising speeds. The risk, of course, is spurning too many weak thermals and getting low, then thrashing around in weak survival lift, or—horrors—landing out.

That's the nightmare scenario: landing early a few miles away and scoring almost no points. Until a few years ago, a pilot who did so (referred to as "lawn darting") could—if his/her crew arrived straight away—hastily throw the glider into the trailer, then race back to the airfield at high speed with the trailer swaying, then hurriedly reassemble, relaunch, and start again.

Dad and I have done that several times. But the rules no longer allow it, in a nod to the risks not only of high-speed driving but also of hasty disassembly/reassembly of the glider. So a pilot who lands out a few miles from the start gate—like an Indy 500 driver who spins out on the first lap and taps the wall—is finished for the day and, as a practical matter, for the contest.

Three or four miles down the course line, I slide under a promising cumulus cloud after bumping and rejecting several gaggles working unimpressive thermals. I'm nervous as my altitude dwindles, but there are sailplanes climbing out ahead so there must be stronger lift here somewhere. As I fly under the edge of the cloud, the air gets choppy and the sink increases. I'm going down even faster than before!

I cringe. I'm already lower than I want, but this sink *should* be a good sign. It often surrounds strong thermals. All that rising air must go somewhere. So I push on. Several anxious seconds later, my patience and nerve are rewarded when I fly into a surge, turbulent and uncertain at first, then strong. The thermal thrusts the plane upward and I'm pressed into the seat. Yes!

The needles on the two electronic variometers in the LS3 sweep around the dials past the zero mark, from "sink" to "lift" and the audio output sings urgently—WHEEEEEE!—signaling good lift. Relieved, I haul back on the stick to convert speed into altitude, the increased G loading pressing me down into the reclining cockpit. Near the top of the zoom, I level out and, with the flick of a wing, bend the sailplane into a steeply banked turn, the upper wingtip gracefully tracing an arc against the cloud overhead. Less than one complete circle into it and I know I have hit the best thermal yet today, a climb rate of 3 to 4 knots (300 feet to 400 feet per minute)!

Too bad about Dad; he'll be dropping behind, well below me, when I finish my first circle. I'm sure he didn't follow me through the start gate at the same airspeed, inhibited by the mysterious, self-destructive flutter in the wing flaps that plagues early ASW 20s. Dad's ship is of that vintage but has never hinted at flutter. Still, I doubt he's ever taken it all the way to redline.

Here at the 1980 U.S. Nationals, two weeks after my 29th birthday, four days after Father's Day, and a few minutes beyond the start gate, I have some of the same concern for my father's performance he doubtless had for mine back in 1965 when I soloed.

"Be safe, but don't embarrass me either, Dad," I breathe to myself.

As I complete my first circle, I glance back toward Springfield to assess how far he's trailing. I am astonished, with a sudden breath, when Dad hauls the '20 up and enters the thermal easily just below me, the big PG on the tail!

"How'd he do that?" I grumble, chastened. "I guess we're flying together."

We follow each other around the circle, climbing, the thermal lifting us 100 to 150 feet with each orbit. In a dozen circles, we've regained the altitude we lost in the first glide. Then, as the lift weakens, I level my wings, drop the nose to aim down the course line, and accelerate to 75 knots.

Papa Golf stays in trail as we work down the first leg, picking up a few stragglers and gradually gaining on a large group ahead of us, pushing through the turbulence, bumping but spurning weaker thermals, driving into the wind down to 2,000 feet for the strong thermal that seems always to be waiting, climbing rapidly and impatiently, then leaving it well below the wispy cloudbases when the rate-of-climb declines. It's tempting to stay in the thermal as long as it's going up, but the weaker lift at higher altitudes translates to being slow. Three to four minutes of circling per climb, then five to seven minutes of straight flight. Boom, boom, boom.

A gaggle of sailplanes is relaxing and stately and peaceful to view from the ground, like watching soaring birds cavorting lazily in the summer heat in slow motion. But from a seat nearby in the same thermal, the urgency and decisiveness speak of tension. Unlike in the pre-start gaggles, there is no wasted motion. The better pilots are forceful and ruthless, constantly making decisions, shallowing their bank angle to move into a stronger part of the lift, then slashing into a steeper turn to stay in the best air. Then, when the climb rate subsides, they abruptly roll wings level on course.

It is textbook stuff. And today it is working for me as we pass over Xenia, Ohio, and keep pushing, the town of Lebanon in sight ahead. I'm eager to round the turnpoint there and put the wind at my back on the second leg.

It turns out I'm *too* eager.

CHAPTER TWENTY-FOUR

Near Miss

Journal Entry: 3:20 PM, June 19, 1980 (Lebanon, Ohio)

On my way into the turn—Lebanon-Warren County Airport, a small airfield outside of the town—I commit my most egregious error of the day.

We've collected a whole gaggle. I want markers ahead, not a bunch of gliders thrashing around in my thermal, forcing me to dodge and weave. So, impatient, I leave the thermal early and drive out alone. My plan is to glide into the turnpoint low and snap the photos there, then stop to thermal on the way out with the wind at my back drifting me on course rather than the wrong direction. This well-known tactic could help me jump to the next gaggle, which I have been eyeing ahead of us most of the first leg of the task.

The risk is not being able to find a strong thermal after I round the turn. There's an old saying: "low is slow." I might have to take weak thermals to survive until I can reach a better one. Worst case, I might even have to land. In a perfect world, there would be a gaggle thermaling short of the turn, allowing me to hit the turnpoint low and shoot my photos, then glide back out to connect with the bottom of that stack of gliders for a fast climb to altitude. But not this time. I'm the one leading from the front.

I gambled that I'd find the core of a strong thermal under wispy clouds before the turn. Instead, I hit sink. I've bet everything on these wisps—with no backup. Now I can't glide to the turnpoint without flying almost into the ground. And I can't reach any other clouds unless I retreat.

Down, down through 1,500 feet, I push on toward the turn, maintaining speed through the bad air, still sinking, features on the ground suddenly larger. Within a few minutes, I have gone from being high, fast, and confident to low, fraught with anxiety, and cursing aloud. Forget flying fast; I may not even be able to remain airborne. My palms are sweaty again.

"Jake Baker, Code Two," I key the mike to alert Diane I am in trouble. This warning does nothing except reassure me that if I am forced down, Diane will know to hook up the trailer and wait at the retrieve office for me to telephone with instructions. I'm radioing her now because our line-of-sight aircraft radios are useless when both parties are on the ground.

Finally, the sink abates, and I arrive low in an area of turbulent, disorganized lift. Improvising, I crank the glider into an exploratory circle at 1,200 feet—up a few feet on one side of the circle, down the same amount on the other—the rough air tossing and teasing and frustrating me. After a few circles, I'm relieved to have arrested my descent. But I'm not going up! This was okay when I released from tow, when I had time to kill, when there were other gliders around to mark thermals—before the task clock started.

None of that is true now. I work these choppy scraps, the glider being shoved up and down in the rough air. I'm swiveling my head, wishing I had another set of eyes, searching in vain for another sailplane, a hawk, any sign of the better thermal I know *must* be nearby. I'm still airborne, but I'm trapped at low altitude with the wind drifting me backward, *away* from the turnpoint ahead, at the rate of a quarter of a mile every minute. I can envision the gliders I so foolishly left in my wake overtaking me up high. Idiot!

This low, even strong thermals will be narrow. The wind has shredded this one so the tiny center that is going up keeps churning and boiling over itself. My only chance to stay in it is slowing the glider while banking steeply on one wingtip and easing back on the stick to make small circles. But if I'm *too* slow, a mistake or a gust could stall the wing and lead to a spin. Recovering would use up much of my precious altitude and almost guarantee a landing.

I'm still clinging to my water ballast because I'll need the 10-knot higher cruise speed after I climb out. *If* I climb out. But being heavy makes climbing out less likely. I'm really tempted to pull the plug and start dumping. Damn!

I can't wait too long. It takes three minutes to empty the wing tanks. From 1,200 feet, if this poor excuse for a thermal quits, I could be too low to thermal safely by then. I hate landing out more than anything else in soaring. If it happens this time, it would be the end of yet another national contest. Should I open the dump valves, or not? Should I shift my circle a few hundred yards one way or the other in search of better lift, or stay where I am? I'm not sinking, but neither am I climbing. I might as well be parked by the side of the road. Meanwhile, my competitors are overtaking me.

Decisions, decisions. And, always, I need to fly the airplane, one circle after another, no two of which are identical, each consuming 20 precious seconds. I'm nudging the stick and rudder pedals constantly to maintain the correct bank angle and speed. I'm trying desperately to edge into the invisible bubbles of lift and avoid the areas of sink. The latter is always a fear; a half turn in sink could cost me several hundred feet.

If I were a few thousand feet higher, I would have a picturesque view: a lush collage of fertile fields interspersed with occasional forests, towns, and lakes, a postcard of Middle America. From low altitude, however, the scene is harsher: straggly trees; uneven fences; thin spots in the crops; bumps and rocks in the pastures; shabby paint on impoverished farm outbuildings, and stains on the drive and barnyard areas.

Then, straight ahead, I spy the horror of what could happen. Another sailplane is *on the runway* at Lebanon-Warren County Airport, testimony to the treacherous micrometeorology into which I have blundered. Later I will learn that no less a personage than former world champion A.J. Smith, one of our country's most brilliant and intense pilots, followed the same strategy. He drove into the turn low, was trapped between convective cycles, and, after thrashing around in broken up bits of thermals not far above the ground in the wind (just like I am), ultimately had to land there.

A.J.'s day is over. His national contest is over. The former world champion's quest for another trip to the world championships on the U.S. Team might be over. I don't have as much at stake as he does, but if the same thing happens to me, I'm finished, too. An hour ago, being stuck in tenth place was frustrating. But in five minutes I could be in 50th place. I'm not far away from a landout and a devastatingly low score, watching the turnpoint receding in this blasted wind like a tiring swimmer being carried out by the tide. I can envision my year-long preparation leading up to the Nationals evaporating like those wispy clouds that promised so much minutes ago.

I'm still at 1,200 feet, so I continue to circle, opening it when there's a surge, then tightening, moving around in a search pattern in the scraps of lift and sink, hoping the feeble bits will coalesce. I'm like a Navy destroyer seeking a submarine running quietly, invisibly beneath the water, emitting only occasional confusing signals that provide hints of where it is and which way it is traveling. There *must* be lift nearby, but I can't nail its precise position.

Finally, I gain a few hundred feet. I'm going mad watching the turnpoint recede in the wind. Though it makes little sense, I roll the dice, straighten out, and make a run for the turn. It takes a l-o-o-o-o-ng few minutes to glide there. Sliding in low, I point my left wing at the runway number that appears terrifyingly large from this altitude. I switch hands on the stick and use my right hand to fire both camera shutters in quick succession as I continue a 180-degree turn overhead, then switch back. I can't afford to miss the shot and make another full circle over the turnpoint to repeat it.

With nowhere else to go, I glide back to where I think I was circling. It's difficult to judge my precise position over the ground 1,000 feet below. I find the same broken-up scraps of turbulence I've been mining for the past few minutes. I'm still not climbing, but at least the wind is at my back, drifting me on course.

Earlier in my contest flying, I would occasionally resort to praying for help as I sank relentlessly closer to the ground.

"Please, God, let me find a thermal."

Intellectually, I knew this wasn't right. Why would God care how well I scored? Emotionally, I wasn't above asking for help. But now I know it's up to me. I need to make the most of what I'm given.

Way up high, I spot my erstwhile gaggle gliding in for their photo runs. Maddening! My palms are still sweating. I'm so low I can't afford to follow them. I must wait, helpless and frustrated. Will I ever learn? Why, why, why did I bet everything on this one decision? I continue, one circle every 20 seconds, barely hanging on, still in survival mode, holding altitude as a steady stream of gliders overtakes me, passes overhead, pivots over the turnpoint to snap their photos, and departs on the second leg, leaving me far below. I can't follow them blindly. At my low altitude, I'll be in a landing pattern unless I find another thermal in the next mile or two.

Then—hope surges wildly! Not long after they leave the turn, I see them pull up sharply and, one after the other, enter a thermal. It's the real thing; the entry zooms seem to lift them powerfully and each circle takes them higher and higher. There's no guarantee their thermal extends down to my low altitude, but the odds seem better than staying here. I roll out and use up the last of my altitude reserve at best-glide speed, aiming at where I imagine the bottom of their invisible thermal is bubbling up from the north edge of Lebanon, a mile away, tilted by the wind. I slide in far below them, less than 1,000 feet above the town, still with full water ballast in the wings. If this doesn't work, I'll have to start dumping and glide away from town to a landable field. I've drifted enough in the wind that the airport is already beyond gliding range. I'm betting the day and the contest on this.

There's a moment of dread when I hit sink! But I am through it in seconds. Then, the heavy LS3 shudders and, at last, I feel rising air pushing the plane up forcefully, as if a rocket booster has kicked in. With an audible sigh of relief, I watch the variometer needles kick over gleefully to indicate a fast rate of climb. I throw the LS3 up on one wingtip in a steep bank to make the smallest possible circle in the strong, narrow core, ease back on the stick, and begin—at last—to climb joyfully, the audio tone singing enthusiastically from the variometers like a chorus.

WHEEEEEEEEE!

The near-60-degree bank presses me into my seat, not quite doubling my body weight. But the tiny thermal and the steep lift gradient at low altitude call for it. It's fantastic to be climbing up fast again in this bubble, watching the altimeter needles rotating clockwise. The glider is giggling on the edge of stall in the turbulence, as relieved and exultant to be carried aloft as I am.

As the thermal widens, I shallow the bank to 45 degrees and slow down a few knots. I realize with glee I am gaining on the competitors above. The thermal is not as strong at their higher altitudes. And there are so many of them, dodging each other, that they are reduced to the lowest common denominator of the least-aggressive pilot. These clueless types will waft around lazily in a thermal as if they're flying airliners, reluctant to disturb their passengers with anything but the shallowest bank angles. An aggressive pilot can sometimes creep up behind, then bank steeply in the strong core of the lift and suck the stick back to turn inside, climbing right through them like a race car taking the inside line on a turn. Other times, as is the case here, competitors are trapped, as if behind a slow motorist on a two-lane highway while I close on them, relentless, from below.

As I approach the lowest glider, concentrating fiercely, another gaggle comes swarming in at my altitude, the gliders spreading out and sliding in ahead and behind to maintain separation. My momentary start turns to jubilation when Papa Golf materializes right below. Then it hits me: these gliders are from our old gaggle. The wings just above us must be the ones we chased down the first leg. We've caught them!

The euphoria of escaping from a close call intensifies the satisfaction of flying well, flooding away anxiety, anger, and depression in seconds! As world champion George Moffat so aptly put it:

"Gliding is a manic-depressive sport."[16]

I have no perspective, no sense of balance. The governor has signed a stay of execution. I've won the lottery. I'm in love! Everything is wonderful! My despair of five minutes ago is a distant, fading memory.

The only blot on this perfect moment is chagrin that Papa Golf had the good sense not to follow me. I suspect he remembers the day at the Adrian

---

[16] Moffat, George B. *Winning on the Wind* (Los Altos, California: The Soaring Press, 1974)

Nationals last year. There he trailed me trustingly as I passed up thermal after thermal until we were down to 800 feet, waiting for the big one that never came. We circled there for a long time in survival mode like chastened children before climbing out, then separating. It is maddening to repeat the same mistake, even more so when someone—especially my father—witnesses it. If I had landed back there at the turnpoint, I would never have heard the end of it.

But I banish those thoughts. I escaped a humiliating disaster, but that's history. Now I need to focus: what can I do right? I was 55 minutes to the first turn, about 37 mph. Even allowing for ten knots of wind (i.e., meaning I averaged about 48 mph through the air), that's slow. Getting low cost me time. We've been averaging 50 mph to 60 mph the first two days.

I am moving aggressively again, as each sailplane dives off the top of the thermal, one after the other in a long procession, headed east on the extended second leg, with a quartering tailwind. A quick "Jake Baker, Code One" on the radio tells Diane I'm out of trouble. Then it's run and climb, run and climb again. Every pilot is doing the same thing, so logically we should stay together in a gaggle. But somehow three of us are saving a few seconds through more efficient or more aggressive flying, and those seconds add up. For whatever reason, we are easing ahead of them, dropping the other ships in our wake. Maybe they got low and dumped their ballast, or they don't want to cruise as fast.

Soon it is only Papa Golf, two-time world champion George Moffat, and I out ahead, on the way to the second turnpoint. My hopes for a high-scoring day rebound as I view the next gaggle so tantalizingly ahead.

CHAPTER TWENTY-FIVE

Double X

Journal Entry: 3:40 PM, June 19, 1980 (Southwestern Ohio)

Having one of the world's best pilots across the thermal from me stokes the pressure. Moffat is banked up steeply 200 feet away on the opposite side of the circle, the sunlight glimmering on his transparent canopy facing mine. The famous XX is emblazoned on the vertical tail (officially "X-ray X-ray," but "Double X" informally). As I stare into his cockpit, I wonder what he is thinking. I realize, with a rush of disbelief: "I'm flying with George Moffat! Twice world champion! Not as part of a big gaggle, but directly with him!"

It is the culmination of a boyhood dream, like having your father watching from the stands while you pitch your first Major League game. It is a reward for years of practice, setbacks, and learning. At 29, I'm too old for adolescent hero worship. But I still bask in the satisfaction of flying straight up against one of the worlds' best pilots.

It's also stressful. Making an error or flying inefficiently in view of this man would be the ultimate mortification. There's even more at stake today than flying against A.J. Smith a few years ago. That was a local fun contest. This is the Nationals. XX is trying everything he can to get away from us. So I am vigilant as we match him turn for turn.

We don't know George—aka The Speed King and Mr. Calculator for his analytical approach to competitive soaring. He and his triple-threat wife, Suzanne (bright, beautiful, and a pilot) seem to keep to themselves, chatting quietly with the few elite pilots who are intimidated neither by their intellects nor his contest record. Nevertheless, we know a lot about his flying.

I was a pre-solo pilot when Dad drove us up to Adrian, Michigan, to spectate at the 1965 nationals, where George was in contention. He's the chairman of the English department at New Jersey's Pingry School (where Suzanne teaches French): tall, slim, white-haired, with an intellectual's precision of reason and cultured speech. A successful competitive sailor before coming to soaring, George is one of the finest pilots this country has ever produced. Yet our community has never entirely warmed up to him, possibly related to his candid, tell-it-like-it-is writings in the SSA's monthly journal, *Soaring*.

I can't recall how my father came to be a fan. I doubt it was a factor, but it's interesting that Dad and George are exactly the same age, having been born a month apart in 1927. Regardless, I followed suit in Dad's fandom, as I did in so many other ways. We began to cheer for George starting in 1965 as his climb to the top gathered speed. He missed winning several U.S. championships by narrow margins (including in 1967 flying a Diamant similar to my father's) before nailing fourth at the World Championships in Poland in 1968, not far behind winner A.J. Smith. He won his first U.S. national title the following year before taking it all in 1970 to become World Champion in Marfa, Texas, then repeating in lopsided fashion in Australia in 1974.

In those pre-Internet days, my father would telephone the national contest each day (there was only one U.S. championship then compared with three in 1980 and seven at this writing). Using P&G's long-distance telephone lines, he would interrogate whomever he could find in contest headquarters during the day, scribbling down information about the task, speeds, and scores.

Suzanne and George Moffat. (photo by Larry Sengbush from Soaring *magazine, November 1982, used with permission).*

We took vicarious pleasure in each of Moffat's myriad daily wins, like cheering for a favorite sports team. The high point was his first world championship, captured on U.S. soil in 1970. The nadir was his omission from the U.S. Team at the 1976 Worlds in Finland, denying him the chance to defend the second title he had won in the previous Worlds. To us, outside the tight community of top-ranked pilots, such an inconceivable injustice was literally the subject of dinner table debate. A few years later, I met George and found him to be personable and no larger than life than most other skillful pilots.

At each thermal, we climb to 3,000 feet, sometimes 3,500 feet if the lift stays strong. George never relaxes. He's aggressive without making us nervous. With no wasted motion, he wrings every foot of altitude from a thermal until it slackens, then dives through the soft air around it, and heads for the next one. Lose concentration for a second and he's by you in the thermal. Take your eye off him for a circle and he's gone, receding in the distance. He is *always* competing.

Then it's nose down to get back to cruising speed and run the course line in five- and ten-mile chunks until we're down to 2,500 or 2,000 feet, ruthlessly rejecting the weaker lift. We pull up into the next strong thermal marked briefly by a departing gaggle that stays maddeningly ahead. Each time we reach the bottom of the stack where they're pirouetting, they are exiting above us on course. We're flying well. But so are they.

Cruising farther east, we turn our backs on the populated areas outside Dayton and Cincinnati and embark upon a vast expanse of bountiful farmland and quaint towns. XX is leading most of the time, although I break away once or twice to take my turn. If this were a blue day, we would spread out abreast to sample more airspace and increase our chances of encountering a strong thermal. However, on this occasion, we all have our sights set on the same clouds up ahead, following closely behind one another, rising and falling as we ascend and decelerate, evaluating the air before descending again, rejecting any thermals that don't meet our standards. The tailwind propels us forward, and we cover ground rapidly.

Dad stays with us, matching every turn and glide. I have never seen him fly this hard and consistently well! Even in leech mode, I might expect Dad to fall behind, hesitating, overly cautious, slowing up a little as we drive lower, wanting to play it safe, then coming in below us as we hit the stronger lift and climb away from him. It only takes one or two such hesitations to lose contact with an expert pilot flying well. But here he is, matching us turn for turn, glide for glide. Amazing!

My insensitive worry a few hours ago that he would somehow embarrass me gives way to pride as he hurries the ASW 20 deftly along, the thin wings bowing and flexing to absorb the turbulence at our 80-knot cruising speed. Part of my reaction is surprise. Frankly, I didn't know he could do it.

I look out my left wing to the north. Damn! The high clouds are thickening toward Springfield. The shelf of overcast is encroaching. To get home, we *must* get around the Pickaway County turnpoint and hook hard left to turn under the worst of this gray clag. A sense of unease takes form. This is what we feared—the early arrival of the cold front. It's what the meteorologist assured us wouldn't happen.

As we approach the town of Washington Court House, 20 miles short of the Pickaway County turnpoint, we zoom up into a thermal to circle and climb again. The milky, high overcast so dramatically evident to the north is spilling across the course line ahead of us. Our best hope—our *only* hope, actually—is to turn the corner at Pickaway County and get high enough on the last leg to glide home under the overcast.

Without the warmth of the sun, the thermals will disappear. And without thermals, here in the flatlands of Ohio, our flights will end in the dirt. We all started too late, not because we delayed but because of the late launch. That's another way of saying this task was an overcall. It happens. There's nothing we can do now except keep flying.

Decision time! We're one cloud away from the Pickaway County Sinkhole. Even without the encroaching overcast, we should expect the lift to decline. This is the moment I have waited for since we learned last year our club was bidding to host the Nationals. This is my best chance—perhaps the only chance I'll have for a long time, maybe ever—to leverage unique local knowledge of a national competition site to my advantage.

As we approach 3,500 feet, the lift is weakening, as usual. We're still 1,000 feet below cloudbase, but I know XX is only a circle or two from departing on course. Should we follow his lead? Or, let him break away while we keep climbing in the weaker part of the thermal?

In some sports, competitors make critical decisions in a fraction of a second. A baseball batter sees the spin on the ball and reacts to a pitch. A skier senses a patch of ice and edges more aggressively to turn. A Formula One driver spots a fleeting opportunity and dives inside another car to pass. Certain soaring decisions are comparable to these, e.g., which way to turn when pulling up in a thermal, tucking inside another glider in a steep turn to outclimb it, and recovering from an inadvertent stall.

Other sports decisions offer more time to deliberate. A baseball pitcher shakes off a catcher's sign for the next pitch, waiting for the one he wants to throw. A golfer contemplates a putt on a tricky green. An auto racing crew chief signals his driver to pit for fuel and tires. Likewise, certain soaring decisions are more measured. Before the start, there's time to assess the day. When tacking back and forth in the wind blowing up the face of a steep ridge, a pilot can consider whether to glide across the next gap or stay put, hoping a thermal will bubble up to make the crossing less risky.

Today's decision is in the latter category. We have one or two more circles—20 to 40 seconds—to decide whether to keep climbing or to push on with XX. What to do?

I make the call and hold my circle. As expected, XX becomes impatient with the weaker lift and strikes out alone for the last good cloud to the east. He has led us on a rapid passage, but I am allowing him to get away.

"Are you sure you know what you're doing? What if you're wrong? Why would you have a better idea than a two-time world champion?" I watch his glider disappear in the haze. Is this stupid? Will I end up kicking myself?

No. Climbing up as high as we can in this thermal is the smart move. I believe—maybe not with 100% certainty, but close enough—that this time, just this once, I know more than George Moffat does. Dad stays with me. Does he trust my judgment? Or has he arrived at the same conclusion?

From 3,500 feet—where we've been leaving with XX—it has been easy to see the next cloud ahead. But now we top out at cloudbase, in the mist at 4,500 feet, and the ground almost disappears. It's like flying down a smoke-filled tunnel with a low ceiling. There's a small bright area visible ahead as we dive and duck under the dank, sinister tendrils of cloud reaching down for us as we speed up before squirting like watermelon seeds into the sunlight, instantly warmed in the cooler temperatures at this higher altitude.

We glide in undisturbed air away from the cloud into the long, blue gap toward the next cu. The air is disconcertingly smooth, so I ease back and trim for 70 knots as we whisper down through 3,500 feet, the LS3 sighing with the more languid pace after being pushed harder for most of the flight. The long glide seems to go on forever, in slow motion. I haven't seen PG in almost ten minutes, but I know he's at my six (i.e., trailing directly behind me). After an eternity watching the lone cumulus ahead, at last we approach it.

Damn! It is decaying. For the past hour, we have watched the crisp white edges of cumulus clouds in sharp relief against the blue. Now everything is desaturating into shades of gray, as if all the color has bleached from the sky. The bleak, ever-thickening cloud cover invading ahead blends into the deepening gauze of lifeless overcast and obscures the view of the horizon and of the distant finish line far to the north.

The bases of the few remaining convective clouds are also significantly lower now that we're in the Pickaway County Sinkhole. We have crossed into another world, one of slower climb rates and cruising speeds, higher uncertainty, and lower expectations.

It takes forever to reach the dissipating cloud. This is by far the longest glide of the day, over 15 miles. After more than ten minutes of flying straight with nary a bump, we approach the cloud, listening for the chirp of the audio to announce lift, waiting for the surge of the updraft or the flick of the variometer needle. Nothing.

Visibility is also worse. Through the dull haze, I see a sailplane circling under the far side of the cloud, sunlight glinting off the wings occasionally as it makes slow turns. It's not going up very fast. We glide toward it, craning our necks to glance overhead at the gray mass above us in frustration. At last, we reach his thermal and roll into weak lift several hundred feet above him.

Anticlimactically, I spy XX on the tail. Damn! This is what our much-vaunted local knowledge—the secret information we have been hoarding for a year to exploit—is worth today, a few hundred feet?

This time, XX holds back. The three of us climb all the way together and top out in the last gasp of this thermal. We want every foot of altitude. Dad and I maintain the margin over XX and our three-ship formation moves toward the last turn under the high, thickening shelf. We're more conservative now, flying not much over best glide speed at 70 knots. With conditions deteriorating by the minute, I have a wild urge to speed up and drive into the turn before the high cover clamps down. But this would only hasten our demise. The new game is to conserve altitude while continuing to make progress.

There are few convective clouds now in the graying sky. Perversely, there is no worse place to be when things turn soft than the Pickaway County Sinkhole. Thermals are born of the sun's radiation on the ground. The lethal combination of overcast above and soggy terrain below is suppressing whatever feeble updrafts might otherwise remain. The elation of escaping the first turn and flying well since then is now a memory.

I chastise myself for not starting earlier. The gaggle ahead has the advantage. We've gained on them throughout the flight, but that will be irrelevant if their small lead spells the difference between enjoying a beer after completing the course and slapping at mosquitoes in a muddy field. I curse to myself and wonder, idly, if the top pilots' flights are as full of recriminations as mine. I'll bet George Moffat isn't wasting any time on this stuff.

CHAPTER TWENTY-SIX

Pickaway County Sinkhole

Journal Entry: 4:30 PM, June 19, 1980 (Pickaway County, Ohio)

The air is ominously smooth as we approach Pickaway County Airport, visible ahead in the hazy light. CCSC tasks often incorporate this turnpoint because it's the last available airport in the flatlands headed east, before reaching the rolling hills of Southeastern Ohio, where landing fields are as scarce as in New England. The sun has vanished behind the high clouds. The horizon is a soft vista. I imagine, though I can't yet hear, a low rumble of thunder to the north as the front bears down on us.

Twenty miles back, strong thermals rocked us as we drove through them at speed. Now there's only a gentle nudge. We've left a churning ocean of air and are easing into a tranquil bay—but that's the opposite of what we need.

Without warning, I blunder into a weak thermal in the gray and make a few circles, waiting for other gliders suddenly all around us to mark it. The unfamiliar contest numbers on the nearby wings tell me we have finally caught the early starters. We've all piled up, easing our way into the same murky airmass, like commuters milling around a subway train door looking for the best way to enter. With the tailwind, I am drifting past the airport. I should duck in for my photos. But I don't want to abandon the thermal—which isn't well marked by a cu—without knowing I can find it when I return. So I orbit, circling, waiting, climbing. Finally, a glider exiting the turnpoint joins below, releasing me to glide cautiously into the turn to take my pictures, followed dutifully by Papa Golf.

It's taken us 1:12 to cover the 68 miles of the second leg, about 57 mph. But allowing for the tailwind, our speed through the air was no better than on the first leg, reflecting the time I lost climbing out of the hole at the first turn and our slow progress since coming into range of Pickaway County. But forget speed. What matters now is finishing, or—failing that—getting as far as we can toward Springfield.

I open the dump valves. The water spews from the wings behind me, as if I were trailing smoke from a damaged aircraft. I no longer need to cruise fast. Climbing in weak thermals will be more critical. And I need to get rid of it before the next climb. Dumping on competitors in a thermal gets their wings wet and hurts their climb rate and is rude and unsportsmanlike. It is 4:40.

The thermal I found is still working, now with a gaggle, when we rejoin it at 2,500 feet. The many gliders winding around with me are reassuring. They will help find the remaining scraps of lift in this deteriorating sky. Papa Golf and XX are below and several of the leaders are above as we struggle to extract the last few feet. *Sans* water ballast, my LS3 is unbeatable in climb, and I gradually gain on other competitors.

One by one, drifting in the wind, we top out in the thermal and dribble northwest toward home in a long string of gliders. A few miles on, someone finds another weak thermal and we all rush to join, circling gently. Given the bleak weather ahead, this could be our last climb.

Were this a fun flight or a local contest, many pilots would have seen the deteriorating sky an hour ago and abandoned the task, cutting the corner early to turn north and slink back to Springfield for a DNF. Others might be giving up and turning back now for a safe landing at Pickaway County Airport. Few pilots would head unswervingly into the gray leading edge of the front to a certain outlanding in the dirt, possibly in rain.

But this is the Nationals. The leaders don't hesitate. When the thermal expires, they roll out on course straight into the gloom. This is not group think, with people coercing each other into a collective decision they would never reach as individuals. Each pilot is acting independently for the same reason: they want to win. Today, that may not mean finishing the task, just getting closer to Springfield than anyone else.

To those with a fear of heights, low is good. But for sailplane pilots, higher is better. Altitude is the aeronautical equivalent of money in the bank, a currency we can hoard, then dole out parsimoniously as needed. When circumstances conspire against the careful pilot in some combination of unexpected downdrafts, headwinds, or scarcity of thermals, we can convert altitude into distance. Altitude offers a reprieve from the intense concentration needed to fly one of these exotic racing machines to study the weather and the landing prospects and to consider the next decision.

Now, as the end of our day looms, we are consuming our altitude reserve, converting each foot of altitude lost into roughly 40 feet of forward glide, five to seven miles per 1,000 feet depending on the wind. Lay a yardstick flat on a table and pick up one end a little less than an inch. That's how unbelievably flat the best glide angle of a modern 15 Meter sailplane is.

Again, the lead planes turn northwest under gray skies. The map says we're still 40 miles from the finish line. Best case, we're 3,000+ feet short of enough altitude to complete the task. That means two or three more thermals, which is doubtful bordering on hopeless.

There *is* one alternative. The cold front is sliding over us from the north. But it is still lighter out to the west whence we came. Clouds are glinting in the diffused sunlight there, beckoning me on an uncertain path to the finish and one of the most glorious moments in soaring, i.e., being the sole pilot to muster the skill, audacity, and perseverance to complete an arduous task.

Over the years, I have earned many contest points and some notoriety by taking circuitous routes to stay in soarable air to get home. This can be chancy if the deviation is large and I waste precious altitude only to find no lift, but I've often been right. Analyzing these decisions is not a precise undertaking. In soaring, as in life, sometimes intuition is better.

On impulse, I alter course 45 degrees toward the big cloud buildups out west. It's a gamble whether this will lead to glory or ignominy. I hope none of the early starters complete the task, devaluing the scores of those of us who fall short. When there are many finishers, landing short of the finish is an unrecoverable disaster. But if there are few or no completions, the maximum daily score is far less and the penalty for landing a few miles behind the leader is small. If there are no finishers today, I should be well up.

The radio has been gratifyingly quiet since we all poured through the start gate two-plus hours ago. Radio chatter varies in inverse proportion with experience. Experts talk little. Newer pilots jabber away as if on a therapist's couch, babbling every detail of their flights and thought processes. Now the airwaves come to life as pilots descend on their last glides. Dad and I have made brief radio reports to my mother and Diane during the flight, but we have not spoken to each other since before takeoff. This contrasts with the bantering exchanges we enjoy on the weekends. Formal team flying—i.e., pilots exchanging information via the radio for their mutual benefit—is a necessary skill at the world championships when the honor of one's country is at stake. But it is against the rules in the U.S.

"Jake Baker, Code Four," alerts Diane to my final glide into the dirt ahead. I don't elaborate. No sense tipping off other pilots I am about to land.

"Papa Golf, Code Four," Dad echoes my call. He doesn't believe we'll finish either. Translation: hook up the trailer and stand by the telephone. That should be no surprise to Diane and my mother. Springfield is upstream, so the overcast first slid over them hours ago. They might already be ready with the trailers to head out once we call in.

Under the gray, I stumble into a feeble, unexpected thermal. I circle slowly, gingerly, in a shallow bank. Seven minutes later, I have gained 500 feet. That's an abysmal climb rate, but this gift will deliver me three miles farther.

There are no gliders nearby. Where the hell are Papa Golf and XX? I haven't seen them, or anyone, in a while. There's a solitary white shape circling low, off to the west—where I would like to be—and a few shadowy wings to the northwest, but apparently no one followed me. If I were XX, there'd be a dozen gliders trailing in my wake like minnows, emulating my every move.

But I'm not XX. I'm flying alone, as I often do. Now I realize I can't reach the clouds to the west. So when this thermal gives up at 2,500 feet, I reluctantly turn northwest toward Springfield. My fate is certain. I will land somewhere ahead in the sprawling farmland, miles from the nearest airport.

I've abandoned all pretense of speed. The strategy is simple: squeeze the maximum distance from the altitude I have left. After running all day at 70 to 80 knots in a ballasted glider, my 60-knot dry best glide speed seems to take forever skimming down through 2,000 feet. Years ago, George Moffat mused about the challenges of soaring's final glides:

"At such moments, there should be something to do. In other sports, one can run faster, try harder, concentrate more. In soaring, one sits quietly and waits to see what happens. The sailplane is doing all it can do. I am only the curious passenger."[17]

My course will take me right into the approaching cold front. There's still no sign of rain, lightning, or towering storm clouds, just the high overcast deepening to the somber color of tarnished silver farther on, where the flat Midwestern plain vanishes into an indistinct horizon.

A stone quarry emerges from the haze ahead with the enticing possibility of a thermal rising from warm rocks giving up their residual heat late in the day. But nothing. Down to 1,500 feet, still descending, I coast along the shore of an irregularly shaped lake, hoping the temperature differential will kick off a last bubble. At 1,100 feet, the audio variometer chirps, and I curve into a weak thermal. It's only zero sink this time—just sustaining altitude—but for the moment it is better than landing. I'm a half-mile from the lake as I turn in gentle circles, drifting away from it on the wind. Nearby fields are landable, so I continue circling, drifting, preparing to glide it out.

---

[17] Moffat, ibid.

I can squeeze out another five miles from this altitude. Ohio is one big landing field because crops are just peeking up from the tapestry of immaculately disced soil. It's an aggressive tactic. I'll overfly a landable field, inspecting it as it slides underneath, then continue toward the next field ahead. If that field is okay, I'll push on. At some point, I will either land in the field below or, if it's unlandable, reverse course and glide back to the last acceptable field behind. It's nerve-wracking as the altitude shrinks or the fields are far apart and the safety margin evaporates. And it ignores the rule about a full landing pattern. But I've gotten away with it before.

"[Contest number] ground, I'm landing near ___." It's like airline flight boarding announcements at LaGuardia Airport during rush hour: one after another, each one about a different pilot but with the same message: "I'm landing out." I've gotta admit, that's great news—from my selfish perspective! No one has yet stretched their final glide to the finish line. If that holds, there won't be any speed points today. But every mile still matters. It's time to leave my tenuous perch for that last, slow, tension-filled glide into a field that, from 1,100 feet, is not yet in sight ahead in the gray light.

Critical junctures in our lives can turn on trivial events. A shoelace left untied triggers a disastrous fall. A chance meeting of two strangers sparks a lasting marriage. A letter lost in the mail changes the course of a relationship.

For reasons that will forever be a mystery to me—a flicker of movement in my peripheral vision, chance, destiny?—I turn away from the varios, altimeter, ASI, chart, and the terrain to the northwest where I will land and look straight down.

Another sailplane is passing below. Wow, he's low; half my altitude! He must be in a landing pattern, headed south over 90 degrees off course. I carve a few more circles in the glassy smooth air, mulling it over. That makes no sense. He's headed straight for the unlandable lakeshore area.

Where did he come from? Better yet, *where the hell is he going?* Could he be in the pattern to land in that beautiful field behind him? No, that would mean landing downwind, adding the speed of the wind to the glider's airspeed for a much faster, rougher touchdown in the dirt.

What's he doing? As I complete a circle and peer out and down, I spot him right away. My eyes flare behind my aviator sunglasses as I watch.

CHAPTER TWENTY-SEVEN

The Most Important Decision of My Life

Journal Entry: 5:25 PM, June 19, 1980 (Pickaway County, Ohio)

The sailplane is low, roughly 300 to 400 feet above the rough ground, too low for anything except a landing pattern. It is drifting along in that graceful, imperturbable way of high-performance sailplanes gliding slowly. In that moment, the aircraft seems to float, poised, suspended by a thread, still flying straight and level on a southerly course. It's a snapshot, a still picture, the pure white cross of the fuselage and wings framed against the lush green terrain below in the soft light of a benign sky with the slate-gray waters of the lake as a backdrop. It is a serene photograph-to-be-taken at the conclusion of a long, stressful day.

As my LS3 continues to sweep around in a circle, however, something disturbs this quiet vista. Without warning, the other glider's right wing drops hard. The left wing flicks up to match it as the aircraft rolls violently into a vertical bank. The nose falls through until it points almost straight down. The aircraft picks up speed, falling unbearably fast. I can sense the pilot struggling to pull it out, the wings bowing impossibly upward with the G-force as the velocity peaks. For a fraction of a second, as the arc of the dive curls and comes up close to level, as if approaching the bottom of a loop, it seems the aircraft will merge gracefully with the earth, kissing onto it in a perfect tangent. As the ground rises to meet the falling glider, it appears the pilot has executed the maneuver intentionally.

But no. SLAM!!! The glider, still sinking, pancakes brutally into the terrain. I feel its weight and velocity as it whomps into the ground, still plowing ahead. Despite the vertical component of its path, it is still hurtling forward at high speed when it hits, slewing across the ground, the wingtips bouncing once, twice, thrashing the grass. Then it skids between two low trees and strikes their trunks, which arrest it, stopping it partially hidden from view beneath the foliage.

It is over so fast, gone in the partial circle my LS3 painted in the gray sky while I watched. A few seconds earlier or later and I would have missed seeing any of it. I would have flown on, never knowing. The plane is hard to spot from the air. If I hadn't seen it go down, I wouldn't know it was there.

What the hell kind of landing was that?

The human mind works in mysterious ways to protect us from things we do not wish to accept. It takes a few seconds for me to acknowledge the obvious. This was not deliberate. This was not a landing. It was a crash.

Years later, I will watch a movie where a blissful, happily married man arrives home early to find his wife in bed with another man. At first, the reality is totally incongruous with what he thinks possible. His eyes say "yes, yes, I see it," but his mind says "no, no, it's a trick, it's not happening"—until his mind can no longer deny it.

My denial doesn't last long. I orbit mechanically atop the remains of my thermal, no longer focusing on the task. This was a crash. The pilot must have been inexperienced. The entry requirements for a nationals are not rigorous. There's no rookie test. A pilot only needs to have flown in an earlier contest at the regional level and scored high enough to be seeded one of the 67 accepted for entry. I know plenty of pilots here who, were this a more popular sport, wouldn't have the requisite standing to compete. Losing control of the aircraft like this is something only a novice would do. He wasn't even turning. The air is silky smooth. And the wind, while noticeable, is not hazardous, though after seeing the last few seconds of this flight, I sure as hell will land facing into it.

I didn't see the contest number. Nor did I notice if it had a red checkerboard tail. I'm not even sure of the sailplane type. But I dismiss the idea it could be Papa Golf. Dad has been flying sailplanes for twenty years, most of those as an instructor, close to 2,000 hours, 3,000 flights, a decade and a half in high-performance ships, much of it cross-country with a lot of competition experience.

I recall our "three priorities" interrogation hours earlier. Dad observes the same rules, sometimes to my frustration. Ten years ago, at our club's Wright Memorial Glider Meet, I pulled off the highway with the trailer, watching as he circled low over a field in a small thermal. He was stuck, not going up or down, flying too fast in big circles. Stymied, it wasn't long before he landed.

I was mildly critical. "Why didn't you slow it down? You looked like you were really flying fast." He might have climbed away, I said, if he had been a little more aggressive.

Dad pushed back. He didn't want to risk stalling and spinning. I couldn't argue. Safety is paramount. But his overly cautious style was the reason he landed out that day, which comes with its own hazards.

Still, just to dismiss the impossible scenario, I key the mike:

"Papa Golf, Jake Baker."

No answer. I broadcast the same message a second time with the same result. Later I will learn Diane, listening intently with the static noise suppression feature switched off temporarily, hears me faintly 40 miles away in Springfield but is not alarmed. Nor am I. Our radio problems could have recurred. Or perhaps Dad landed and left the sailplane to find a local telephone to report in.

Still, I grow uneasy when the idea something might be wrong takes form. I always thought his anxieties about my more flamboyant landings were amusing. They fed my ego. Now, however, I understand what anxiety can induce, how the initial unease coalesces, like the first doubts about a cancer growing in one's body, into something more disturbing. I haven't always had the greatest confidence in my father's competitive prowess. But until now, I have never worried about his safety. I sneak peeks at the crash site on each circle, drifting a little farther from it in the wind. Finally, a car stops along the narrow road and several people strike out through the brush toward the plane.

"Okay, back to the contest, Chip. You'll have to get the news tonight, like everyone else."

The bystanders should have an ambulance on the way. With no medical training, I couldn't help if I tried. I doubt I even know the guy if he's a newcomer. I consider calling for help on the radio, but what am I going to say? That I saw someone crash, but I don't know who it was or exactly where it was or whether he's injured? Brilliant! That's a terrific way to panic everybody at Springfield, most of whom are pilots' families.

To be honest, I don't *want* to do anything. This is the Nationals. Every mile will count, especially if no one finishes. Given the way we sliced through the pack, I might move up a few notches. My LS3 can take me three or perhaps five more miles.

"Why land if I can't help?" I reason, "This is no time for melodramatic gestures." It's an easy call. I came here to win. Landing now would be a symbolic effort—and would throw away points. And for what? *I would be useless at an accident scene.*

Then I remember the horrific accident involving Joe Conn, my father's friend who talked him off the ledge at Adrian in 1967, when Dad swore never to fly gliders again after his debacle in the Diamant. Joe, now retired from competition, was landing out seven years ago in the Chester, South Carolina regional contest. Something in a hostile field—tall grass, weeds, a bush—snagged the wingtip of his ASW 17 seconds before it touched down. This was worse than a ground loop; the aircraft was *still flying*. The trapped wingtip wrenched the heavy, long-winged Open Class machine around 180 degrees. The other wing swept around and rose, lifting the aircraft into a grotesque near-vertical bank. Then, with the glider poised in an impossible position, one wingtip resting on the earth and the other one high in the air, the aerodynamic forces ceased. The heavy ASW 17 dropped in nose first, crushing the forward cockpit. Joe survived the harrowing crash, but with severe injuries. Friends of this popular pilot were more upset when they learned several competitors might have witnessed the accident but—with their focus on competitive placing—had flown on without landing to help.

This memory and our anger over the allegedly callous behavior cuts off my internal debate. My responsibility is clear, and points be damned. I doubt I can help, but I cannot fly on after seeing someone crash like this.

For it to matter, I need to put the LS3 down as close to the crash site as possible. With a firm movement of the stick, I roll out, headed right where the other aircraft hit, now over a mile away. The plowed field just north of the wreckage is the best choice; it's into wind and just across the road.

I'm doing a full by-the-book pattern this time. After I turn onto the downwind leg, I lower the flaps, extend the landing gear, and pull the rudder pedals back so I can use the heel brakes for the main wheel. I won't need the brake—I'm going into a plowed field. But it's part of the LS3 landing checklist. I set full nose-down trim and unlock the dive brakes, then bank into a 90-degree left turn onto base leg, perpendicular to my intended landing direction. The wind is drifting me to the right, too strong to ignore. I look left, upwind, and glance sideways at the field. It's my last peek before I turn final. It looks smooth. No wires. No fences. No odd discolorations or vegetation or patterns in the furrows that might warn of a watercourse or a ditch or other hazards.

I make the last 90-degree left turn onto final into the wind. Still holding 60 knots, I extend the dive brakes to descend steeply in front of the trees, then ease them back in when I am over the furrows and let the airplane float along. I know from experience the far end of the field appears to be alarmingly closer than it is. But it's tough to skim along above the soft dirt, bringing the control stick back to bleed off the speed a few knots at a time while watching the ditch approaching. I hold off as long as I dare while the airspeed decays, reaching for the ground with the main wheel, like my toes stretching for the bottom of a lake in neck-deep water. I let the LS3 settle, holding the stick back to keep the nose up. The main wheel touches softly. Then, as the weight of the glider comes on, it digs into the earth, spreading a furrow and decelerating us with a scrape of soil under the belly, as if I had slammed on the brakes in a car. In seconds, we're down with room to spare, undamaged. The flying sounds have ceased, and the glider is still after three and a half hours of constant motion. A blink, and I'm back in the real world.

I have a checklist for everything in flying, including landing out: switches off; remove the delicate external instrument probe from the tail and tape over all the instrument ports that invite ignorant bystanders to blow into them; photograph the glider from all four quadrants and pocket the film; retrieve my wallet from the side pocket; and grab the task sheet with the retrieve telephone info. It's a ritual I have performed many times. But today is different. I climb out and drop the parachute in the cockpit in haste, lowering the canopy but not bothering to lock it down. Filled with urgency, I trot down a furrow until I reach the end of the field. I jump the ditch, turn, and jog down the narrow country road toward the accident site somewhere up ahead. I'm trying to stay calm, but this is like a scene from a "B" movie.

A farmer in a pickup truck pulls alongside as I approach the intersection. "They already called the ambulance."

"Anybody hurt?" I yell back. He doesn't know. There's an unexpected edge in my voice. I had fancied myself to be calm and collected. Then I'm past him, breathing hard. I slow as I turn onto the side road and jog the remaining 50 yards on the asphalt to where cars have pulled over, hurdle the ditch, then cut diagonally through the tall grass, still unable to see the glider.

Where the hell is it? Do I have the right place? Finally, I come around several spindly trees and the wreckage comes into view. Out of breath, I join a crowd standing, huddled quietly, helplessly around it. The Plexiglas canopy disintegrated in the impact, so I have an unobstructed view of the cockpit interior. I can't see much of the pilot because the first responders have covered him with a blanket and are holding his head up.

It's selfish and uncaring. But I'm so relieved it's not someone I know. The pilot's face is unfamiliar, with closed eyes, slack features, and unnatural pallor, strapped in the mostly intact forward fuselage. There are trickles of blood from his mouth and ears. I don't recognize him. He has some of Dad's features and coloring, but the facial expression is all wrong. I must have run harder than I thought because I'm still breathing too fast. I can't recall what he was wearing this morning, but it doesn't matter because the blanket covers his body. It doesn't look like Dad, and that's the most important thing. But I must be certain.

There's one sure way, the thing that uniquely identifies every glider in the contest. I tear my eyes away from the inanimate figure, then turn and scan back along the white, once beautiful, now horribly distorted curves of an ASW 20. It is a shattered wreck. My initial impression of the cockpit was inaccurate. Now I see the impact partially crushed it. The two trees split the wings at half span on each side, leaving the branches splintered and spearing through the gaping, fractured fiberglass cavities in the once-pristine contours. The force of the crash broke the rear fuselage, then twisted the tail off, leaving it aimed at an awkward angle. Everywhere I look on the structure there's severe damage.

I *need* to know who the pilot is. Finally, looking past everything else, I can see the vertical tail. It would be a lie to say I'll never forget the sensation because I did—within days, if not hours (the human mind's marvelous powers of self-preservation in action again). But I remember being shaken, momentarily unsteady, not dizzy so much as frozen in place, as if I had locked my knees standing on the deck of a sailboat rocking in gentle waves, unable to reach out for something to fix my balance. For the contest number on the unscratched vertical fin, leaning over precariously and half-hidden by the horizontal tail, is Papa Golf.

CHAPTER TWENTY-EIGHT

Aircraft Down

Journal Entry: 5:30 PM, June 19, 1980 (Deer Creek State Park, Ohio)

For a long moment, I do nothing. My mind is racing, but no thoughts are coming out. When I turn back to the cockpit, I am powerless—with no sense of purpose, watching the world in slow motion—when the pilot's head moves almost imperceptibly. Shouldn't we, shouldn't I, be doing something? CPR? Or would that make things worse, given his obvious internal injuries? The people propping up Dad's head turn and tell me he has a pulse. I don't know if they're offering hope, reassurance, or information. I squat down by the cockpit to verify it. But then it ceases. A husband-wife EMS team appear on the scene to confirm what I know: my father is gone.

Those first on the scene comment Dad had struggled for a few seconds to sit up and seemed to be choking. But he never regained consciousness. I estimate not much over ten minutes elapsed between the crash and the moment I arrived, but getting there sooner wouldn't have mattered. He was never able to look up, to ask where he was or what had happened, to gasp goodbye, to say or do anything except quietly wheeze his last breaths.

I'm numb. What I'm seeing is impossible. I stand there, shoulders slumped, speechless, trying to square the scene with something, anything, in my experience that would make sense—without success.

Afterward, a few people would ask me if I felt panicky. And the answer, self-serving though it may sound, is no, with one later exception. Doubtless I am in shock. Irrationally, I am overly concerned with how people will judge me, and how I should act in what has turned into a scene from a movie, one I have viewed many times growing up. The hero is dead.

But in my attempt to maintain an impassive expression, my face must look grim because one of the EMTs switches her attention to me when she discovers who I am. After being on the move all day flying, and capping that with the one-two punch of an adrenaline-fueled outlanding and finding my father lifeless in the cockpit, I rouse myself. I cannot just be a spectator. I need to *do* something. We Americans are men of action.

That proves frustrating. I have landed my LS3 on private land, but the crash site just across the road is inside Deer Creek State Park. The Park Office is only a quarter mile away, but someone directs me to the Dam Shack, a convenience store-*cum*-fishing shop down the road.

The small shop is full of the folksy, down-home characters you would expect to find. When I enter, it's obvious they've heard about the crash. The chatter quiets when they learn who I am. Someone gives me directions for the crews to drive out from Springfield, then points me at the pay telephone mounted on the wall. That's the easy part.

As I had surmised, 60+ pilots have landed out and are trying to call in simultaneously, overwhelming the two telephone lines installed for the contest. These aren't short conversations. It can take five to ten minutes for a pilot to report his/her position and status plus the turn-by-turn directions for the retrieve crew—and for the contest retrieve desk to read it back to confirm.

The number is busy. I hang up and redial, reciting my telephone credit card again. It's busy again. And again and again. The unceasing, recurring busy signals are intolerably unfair. This is the only time in these bleak hours when the tide of panic rises like floodwaters. I'm the bearer of unspeakably sad news with a compulsion to get the word out, to share it, to unburden myself of its pressing weight with someone in my world of family and friends and gliding. The dial on my inner pressure gauge is climbing into the red zone.

I don't last 10 minutes, gripping the heavy, old-style Ma Bell handset tightly, before anger and frustration boil over. I take a deep breath to settle myself, then dial the local operator and ask for an emergency interrupt. At first, she refuses. Everyone thinks their situation is an emergency. But I push back and the words "airplane crash" get her attention. I hear her break into a call in progress—I'm pretty sure it's another pilot and I feel a twinge of guilt— and ask the parties to hang up so she can put my call through.

"Contest headquarters."

"Hi, this is Chip Bearden. Juliet Bravo. I landed out. But before the details, I have some bad news. I should probably speak with the CD if he's there."

"Chip, your brother Mark is standing here. Would you like to talk to him?"

"Yes! Please, that would be great." I didn't expect Mark to be at the airport today. But for all my urgent need to share the terrible news, I realize this is not a message I want to convey to a stranger. After a pause, he comes on.

I lean into the wall, head down, my elbow resting on the telephone to prop me up. I'm quiet but clear: "Mark, I have some really bad news. *[searching for the right words]* Dad was in an accident. *[longer pause; I still don't know how best to say this]* He's dead."

My normally unflappable brother is stunned. I'm sure that word is utterly inadequate to describe his reaction.

"Are, are you sure?" he asks, his voice weak and pleading, the strain clear. But he recovers quickly as I explain what I know. Then we agree on a plan. He will deliver the news to my mother and Diane. There's more guilt but also relief. I cannot envision having that conversation over the telephone.

I urge him to get both trailers on the road as soon as possible. I need familiar people around me. "My LS3 is fine," I tell him, "But Dad's ASW 20 is pretty banged up and we're going to need help to get the pieces out of the crash site and into the trailer. So bring some extra people."

Back at the crash, I find Pete Mozer pulled over, searching for his pilot, older brother Eric. It's like walking into a huge room packed with strangers, then spotting a familiar face. I exhale in relief and hasten over.

The approaching frontal system has brought down a dozen sailplanes within a few miles, prompting a commotion in this quiet farming community that has citizens and police equally agitated. Under the glowering overcast, residents are calling in airplane crashes as often as the panicked townsfolk of Grover's Mill, New Jersey reported alien spaceships the night of Orson Welles's 1938 *War of the Worlds* radio broadcast. It doesn't help that the gliders look the same except for the contest numbers on the tails. And those aren't always visible from the road.

"Pete." He looks up when I call out, but I don't have to explain. He has already assessed the situation. He's an experienced competition pilot. His brother and their soaring patriarch, Rudy, are both flying in the contest. Pete says all the right things men say to each other in times of tragedy and loss, flings his arm around my shoulders at the appropriate moment, and stays as long as he can before driving off to retrieve Eric, assuring me they will return. As his rig disappears down the road, a wave of despair sweeps over me.

"Please, Pete, please come back after you find Eric," I whisper to myself.

The nervous energy and need to take action that have sustained me since the crash dissipate. The air seems to grow heavier, as if a depression is building in the sky with the approaching front. This is my lowest moment, following the temporary boost of Pete's arrival, with a crowd of strangers, none of them pilots, none of them able to understand what I have experienced today. One or two well-meaning bystanders attempt to make conversation, but I politely respond only with head nods and impassive, one-word answers. They're deferential, and their intentions are good. But none of them has any insight or understanding of how this day unreeled for Dad and me following our flight together in our ethereal aircraft.

I wait, in silence, next to the body of the man who knew me best as a pilot and who would be proudest of me for the flight I'd put together, including my decision to abort and land at the crash site. Instead of receiving his blessing, however, I can do nothing but stand there alone, not knowing how long it will be before I glimpse a familiar face.

At an emotional level, the impact is staggering. Rationally, though, I know it is not the end of my life. I will recover, as anyone who loses a parent does. What is unclear is my continuing existence as a pilot. That night, it never crosses my mind that I will not fly again. But I do wonder "how?"

As the cold front looms and the overcast thickens, obscuring the sun dropping to the horizon, I'm focused on my father's death and on the crushing emotional blackness. I recognize I can never again share my triumphs with him or be reassured and encouraged by his support. And as much as I have chafed under his conservative advice and our occasional disagreements, I accept he will never again be there to offer his opinion or direction.

* * *

Mark, in Richmond, Virginia, and his fiancée, in Dayton, have been interviewing in each other's cities to allow them to live in the same place. Today, the company Mark has been pursuing offers him the job in Dayton. They decide to share the good news. It's sunny, so on impulse they drive the half hour to Springfield to watch the finishers, with Mark still in his business suit. By the time they get organized and arrive, however, the leading edge of the front has slid over Springfield and the weather has turned ominous. My mother reports she has been listening on the radio to what sounds like the entire fleet landing out on the last leg before the gathering storm.

Mark walks over to check the retrieve office. There's no news on Dad or me, so he hangs around, expecting we will call in soon. When I telephone, the woman on the retrieve desk recognizes him and offers him the phone.

After our demoralizing call, Mark walks outside and spots Diane standing nearby. When he delivers the news, he reaches forward to hug her. She draws her hands up to fend him off and steps back, stiff, her face impassive and her body rigid. This is not the way it should happen, the way it always has in the past. One of the family should be returning with directions from the retrieve office, hoping for a quick retrieve with the trailer so they can attend the social event the organizers have planned for the evening.

The two of them return to my mother, sitting in the car. She asks if he has heard anything about either of us. He hesitates. I suspect, unlike me, he has rehearsed what he's going to say on the walk from the retrieve office.

"Chip landed. (pause) But Dad crashed."

At first, she doesn't understand. "But he's okay. He can land anywhere." Being able to set a glider down safely in a variety of terrain was one tenet of my mother's tacit support of Dad's soaring.

Mark tries again. "He crashed."

She doesn't understand—or doesn't want to. "But he's okay."

Mark has issues of his own, and her denial isn't helping. "No, Mama. He *crashed*. He's not okay."

Mark and Diane describe her response as a loud, anguished, chilling wail of total despair. Forty years later, when we discussed it for the first time, she referred to it simply as "The Scream." But she catches herself in seconds.

"No, I can't do this. I have to take care of the kids." This is her maternal instinct. We "kids" are 29, 26, and 21 years old. Until she gave up her driver's license in her 80s, my mother sometimes treated us to another endearing maternal reaction. Whenever she stepped on the brakes for a hard stop, she would thrust out her right arm. This was to prevent anyone on the front seat from pitching forward. It goes back to the days before car seats and seat belts when, as a toddler, I would ride along standing on the front seat. She was still forearming me in the chest in my 50s.

As word spreads among the stunned crowd at the airport, many club members offer to help. Mark is careful whom he selects. He knows this situation could bring out the best—and worst—from the quirky personalities in soaring. He doesn't want take-charge types, or those who might speculate or criticize or offer banalities. Tonight we need solid, supportive colleagues who can be there to help, whether by lifting a broken glider or standing quietly in the rain waiting for us to imagine what comes next in our lives.

Then he hitches up both trailers and leads a solemn procession of cars out of town on local roads, driving to an Ohio State Park he's never heard of.

CHAPTER TWENTY-NINE

Recovery

Journal Entry: 7:00 PM, June 19, 1980 (Deer Creek State Park, Ohio)

My head falls back and I exhale a huge sigh of relief when Pete returns with his brother. Eric greets me and offers condolences. The crash has spun me into an alternate world. Everything looks the same, but I can feel the ground unsteady beneath me—and Pete and Eric are my lifelines.

A chill comes over me. It could be shock—I know little about that—but the air temperature is falling as the cold front continues to slide over us. The wind is shifting and rising. The cold soaks in. Pete offers me his jacket, which I wear most of the night, even with sleeves that are too short.

People speak of near-death experiences. I was never in danger today. I was, however, standing next to my father when death stepped in to claim him. It will be years before I acknowledge it, but this near-death experience will alter the course of my life in ways I can't imagine.

* * *

I've speculated (but never asked) what the conversation must have been when Pete rolled up to his brother's landing site with the news, and they pulled Eric's ASW 20 apart, stuffed it into the trailer, then raced back to my location. A recent U.S. national champion, Eric is close to my age. He knew my father well from many contests. Our families go back to the mid-1960s.

The three of us speculate a lot that night. As darkness falls, we stand uneasily, one on either side of me, hands gesturing to illustrate various aeronautical maneuvers, discussing what might have happened. I was an eyewitness, yet I can't explain what I saw. We explore different theories and talk in dispassionate voices about low-altitude turns, departures, straight-ahead stalls, sharp-edged gusts, wind shears, downwind landings, spins, and spin recoveries. As I recall, our entire extended conversation is one of veteran pilots discussing an anonymous crash in unemotional, impersonal terms.

It helps to have two savvy pilots with whom to discuss what I saw and try to fit it into an explanation for something inexplicable. In all of this, we talk about the crash—but not about death. As pilots, we deal with the accident the way I imagine fighter pilots might deal with air combat victories or losses, viz., in an abstract sense, avoiding the subject of death itself. I skirt delicately around the fact that Eric's and Pete's father, Rudy, is flying here. He landed safely and other family members are retrieving him.

Most of all, we wait. I'll never forget both of them standing there for what seemed like hours, helping me keep myself together. As the sky darkens, our moods, as if reflecting this, grow gloomier. It's 40 miles to Springfield via car, less than an hour. But I know it will take time to get both rigs ready and organize the group I had asked Mark to bring.

When our colloquy wanes, I retrace my steps and trudge down the road and into the field to the LS3, pocket the turnpoint films, verify the switches are off, and secure the glider. My faithful sailplane rests silently in the soft earth, undisturbed, uncomplaining, incongruously pale and clean in the murk above and below, as if nothing untoward occurred a few hours earlier.

It's nearly dark when the cars from Springfield show up. My memories after that are less distinct. Rather than a sequence of events, they comprise short video clips. In one, my mother is sobbing helplessly in her seat in the car, her face contorted in grief. Like my father's empty face in the cockpit, her visage is unrecognizable as she gazes up in disbelief. This is not a character in a movie wailing about loss. It's something far more terrible, the helplessness and despair overwhelming every sentient response.

"Chip, are you sure?" she sobs. How could this be true? How is it possible? She, too, is hoping desperately that somehow there's been a terrible mistake and Joe Bearden is only injured, and not dead.

In another clip, Mark insists on hiking out to the crash in long, deliberate strides with a flashlight, high-stepping through the grass and brambles in his suit, with that same disbelief in a grim, detached, analytical mode. He's gone only long enough to talk his way past the suspicious law officer guarding the site, walk to the fuselage, pull aside the blanket covering Dad's body to reveal his face, inspect the wreckage, then return.

He has to see it for himself. How could this have occurred to one of the safest pilots around? There must be a mistake. It's a common reaction that night. A few hours earlier, I had sailed through the "denial" stage of grief in a matter of seconds. But my family and our soaring club members arrive hoping I have somehow misreported the accident.

Diane is holding it together by sheer force of will. Her face still impassive, she had refused all offers to ride with her in the car pulling the ASW 20 trailer. At last, after repeated entreaties, she agreed to allow a club member to ride along—if he didn't attempt to talk. Two other video clips are of Eric diverting her attention from the surrealistic nightmare scene, then—with Pete—leading shell-shocked club members to de-rig my LS3, carry the pieces from the field, and stow it in the trailer.

One of them is venerated senior club member Bruce Helvie. "Senior" is an understatement. One of the Wright brothers signed his first pilot's license! He nods respectfully and offers a quiet remark.

"I understand you behaved in very cool fashion landing like you did."

I was flattered. Later, I will realize gaining the approval of others was still too important to me. Yes, I behaved calmly, but I liked hearing it acknowledged. It's another cliché: I had been tested under fire and proven worthy.

While we wait, the rain arrives, as if in sympathy with this tableau of misery. It is a quiet, desultory drizzle, not a violent thunderstorm. Eric and Pete leave. Tomorrow will probably be a flying day and they need to sleep.

We expect the National Transportation Safety Board (NTSB) to send a team to investigate the crash. But the FAA are standing in for them and communicate through local law enforcement that we are to leave my father's body in the sailplane until they arrive, which could be hours. We are all gathered near the road, but there are slashes of light in the undergrowth where the broken glider and my father lie as flashlights bounce their beams here and there. I have no desire to revisit the crash site. As the rain continues, I know everything is getting soaked.

After what seems like an interminable wait, the coroner gets the okay to remove my father's body. That is the impetus we need to leave. Members of the local chapter of the Civil Air Patrol (CAP) are now on site and promise to guard the wreckage—which the FAA investigators have still not arrived to inspect and release—against the souvenir hunters and vile scavengers who seem to crawl out of the ground after publicized tragedies.

Unable to face my devastated mother, I drive back to Springfield towing the LS3 trailer with Diane, leaving Mark to stash the empty ASW 20 trailer nearby and chauffeur my mother. The journey back to the contest site on narrow, pitch-black roads illuminated only by the headlights of our vehicles trailing one another takes on the look of a dreamlike late-evening funeral procession. My sole memory of that drive is of reassuring Diane—who, unlike my mother, is suffering in silence—that her life will go on, including her education. She followed me to Vanderbilt and will soon begin her master's degree at Miami University in Oxford, Ohio. I know little of my father's financial situation. But I have a good job and assure Diane she can continue her studies. In the face of the devastating blow we have suffered, it seems important for us to cling to things we can rely on for constancy and support.

Our arrival late that night at the airport is off the third reel of the "B" movie playing intermittently in my head. By chance, my girlfriend Kathy had planned to fly into Columbus, Ohio, from Boston late that afternoon. A year earlier, she had joined us at a regional in Cordele for a few days. But I wanted her to experience a national contest this time, hoping she would understand better why soaring was so important to me. It's a colossal understatement to say my timing could have been better.

Before leaving for the crash site, Mark had dispatched his fiancée to meet Kathy at Port Columbus Airport an hour away in a borrowed pickup truck. I'm told it was an awkward first encounter.

Back at Springfield, I bring the LS3 into our tiedown spot in the grass, the trailer bumping gently on the hitch behind the car. As we stop, I see Kathy in the darkness, running on the uneven turf, stumbling toward us, her face streaked with tears in the headlights. She had met my father only once, in Cordele, but they had taken an immediate liking to each other.

No one gets much sleep. My mother is lying on one bed sobbing quietly. Diane leaves with Chris Woods, a friend and young pilot whose father, Woody, is also competing here. Mark and his fiancée return to Dayton.

Incapable of sleep and unable to bear the oppressive air of total hopelessness in the room, I duck out with Kathy and find an outdoor stairwell. It's shielded from the parking lot and out of earshot of other rooms. There, under the harsh light of the Midwestern motel where most of the contestants are staying, I hug her fiercely. When she pulls me into her arms, I lose it. For the first time since I arrived at the crash site, I succumb to my grief. No one is there to impress, or about whose opinion I worry. So, Kathy, more than a foot shorter than I am, holds and comforts me like the mother who—incapacitated by her loss—cannot. I weep briefly and powerfully, emotionally crushed and struggling to deal with the calamity that has befallen us a few hours earlier, sobs wracking my body, until relief coalesces with embarrassment, and I cling to her, breathing deeply.

My body recoils physically from the sharp, unexpected demise of my father. My soul grieves for the bewildering upset to my sheltered, sensibly ordered life, which, until that afternoon, had been untouched by tragedy or even by a loss more serious than breaking up with a girl. And underneath it all, I sit there railing, almost anesthetized, against the abject unfairness.

"Why me? Why us? Why now—and this way?"

Compared to those who lose entire families in accidents or wars, my selfish complaint is uncaring and churlish. But for 15 years I have smugly taken satisfaction in the aura of danger that envelops soaring while simultaneously feeling guilty around my non-flying acquaintances because the risks are over-hyped. For I know, with the secret and absolute certainty of a religious zealot embarked on a holy mission, that the only pilots who get hurt, much less killed, are those who don't have *the right stuff,* the term chronicled by Tom Wolfe in his 1979 book about test pilots and astronauts[18].

And I believe, with that same conviction, that my father and I have those attributes in abundance. It is fun and ego enhancing to envision ourselves as aerial daredevils. But the truth for properly trained pilots like us is:

"The most dangerous part of soaring is driving to and from the airport."

Flying a glider is no more dangerous than driving a car. Or so I had thought and said many times reflexively, like a child echoing a parent's religious or political views without question.

Now my world has shifted on its axis. How could we have blithely mouthed that stupid, f**king platitude for so many years and not seen the reality? And how unfair is it we should have to face it so abruptly? Unlike any other loss or defeat in my life until that day, my father's death offers no hope— not on this earth, anyway—of any reversal, reunification, or rematch.

With my tears, the stress and tension that have been building since the crash drain away like enthusiasm in the explosive decompression of a losing political campaign on election night. I gather my composure, and we return to the motel room. My mother has finally succumbed to exhaustion and is sleeping uneasily. Diane is still out.

I switch on the lamp over the small Formica-topped table by the curtained window of the Holiday Inn room. In the hours before dawn, I record all the details I can remember, knowing some are already fading as my defense mechanisms kick in to help me through this shattering experience.

In a college psychology course, I had researched a lengthy paper on defense mechanisms. I know these marvelous subconscious coping devices will help me deal with this tragedy. But they will also cloud or obliterate my memories. I can't sleep, anyway, and documenting the details in words and

---

[18] Wolfe, ibid. I use the phrase "the right stuff" multiple times in referring to the amalgam of courage, skill, and demeanor held in high regard by test pilots and astronauts in the early days of the U.S. space program. Although popularized by Mr. Wolfe's book, the phrase pre-dated it.

sketches is the only record I will ever have. It keeps me busy, keeps me diverted. In later years, chatting with witnesses to other accidents, I would offer the same advice: "Write it down." In times of great stress, our minds play tricks. What we saw today will not always be what we recall tomorrow.

Then, exhausted, after I commit to paper all I can remember, I lie down on the other bed—still wearing the clothes I wore in the cockpit—and drift off for the remaining hour or two before morning.

In subsequent weeks and months, I would log more details of the day itself, which form the basis of this account. Though I could recall a surprising number, there was one sequence that defied my every attempt to retrieve it.

After Dad's pre-launch request that we fly together, I said goodbye, turned, and walked away. It is difficult to comprehend, even 40+ years later, that this final, casual parting was such a turning point in our lives. This wasn't a Hollywood movie scene. There was no stirring music, no portentous pull back shot with the camera rising or arcing around the figure standing alone. I have struggled in vain to remember what our last words were or what he looked like as I departed, full of my own thoughts.

We shared other moments of consequence that day. Some, like seeing my father roll into the thermal below me when I was sure I had left him behind in my high-speed dive through the start gate, I would remember for the rest of my days. Others, like the crash itself and my arrival at the cockpit, my mind moved swiftly to squirrel away in obscure corners of my brain to protect me from the consequences of their lasting pain.

The images would return late at night, fading as the weeks went by. I didn't want to feel. I didn't want to hurt. But I did want to remember what Dad was like, how he flew, the experiences we shared, and the times I saw the world from his perspective. Most of all, I wanted to remember his last words to me.

But that moment is missing. It's a gap in the tape. Of our final parting, I would recall few specifics, not because it was intolerable—though it has occurred to me my subconscious might be repressing the memory to protect me from pain—but because it passed, as do so many events in our lives, on a commonplace occasion, unnoticed, unrecorded, and in this case unremembered.

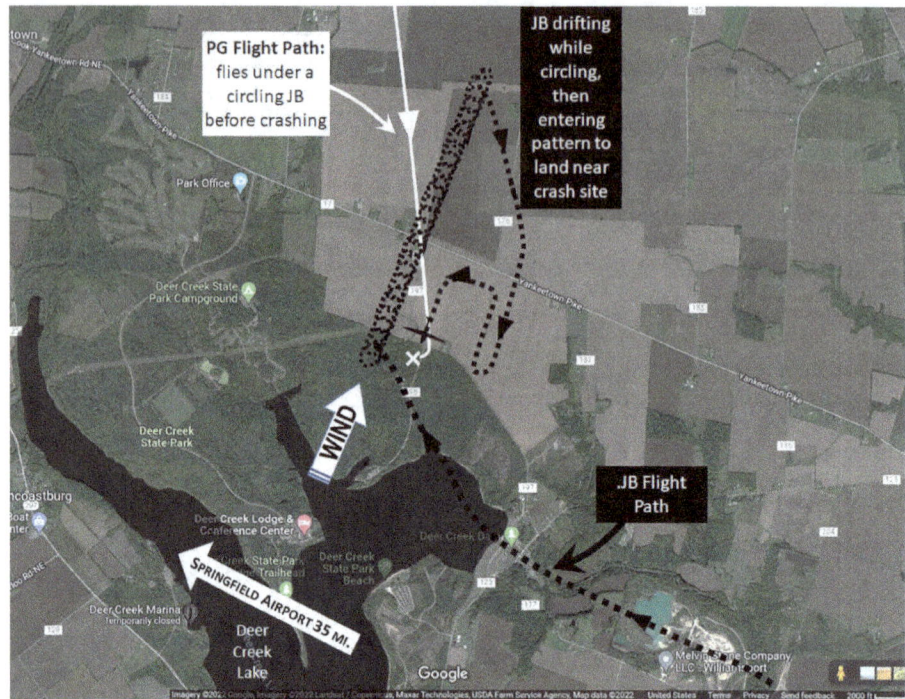

Deer Creek State Park, Ohio, 2022, details added (Imagery ©2022 Google, Im-agery©2022 Landsat/Copernicus, Maxar Technologies, USDA Farm Service Agency, Map data ©2022 United States)

CHAPTER THIRTY

The Morning After

Journal Entry: June 20, 1980 (Springfield, Ohio)

The morning after the crash is a beautiful, classic post-frontal soaring day, ideal for what will be the longest task of the contest. There is only one thing that could pluck me from the surreal nightmare that began at 5:30 PM the previous day, viz., to keep flying the contest, to lose myself once again preparing for the daily task, to focus on getting the LS3 ready, tow off into the sky, climb up, and fling myself through the start gate with controlled abandon with the rest of my competitors, knowing that completing the day's mission will be my only focus for a few hours.

That's what I want. That's what I need.

But I can't have it. Even if I were to turn my back on my family, I doubt anyone would allow me to fly. While my father can no longer advise me, someone else would: a contest official, or a fellow competitor who is a doctor, or a trusted friend. They would pull me aside to say what I would grudgingly admit. This time I can't throw myself into soaring to escape the real world.

Instead, my eyes heavy and puffy from lack of sleep, morose, and uncomfortable, I shuffle my feet outside the motel in the parking lot with my family in an impromptu receiving line, accepting condolences from pilots and crews who gather instinctively around our room as the brotherhood of fliers come together over a fallen aviator.

The uneasy pilots all have the same question: what happened? They want to know. And, frankly, many of them are uncomfortable talking about anything except flying in situations like this. I wish I had the answer. Beryl Markham, in her perceptive memoir, *West with the Night,* commented that professional aviators of the 1930s shared a *"camaraderie sans sentiment of the kind that men who once sailed uncharted seas in wooden ships must have known and lived by."*[19] That is an apt description of pilots uneasy expressing their feelings about the horror conceivably awaiting them at the conclusion of a flight.

By comparison, the pilots' wives are more like spouses in wartime or at an active airbase following the loss of a pilot. They hug my mother, listen to

---

[19] Markham, Beryl, *West with the Night* (Boston: Houghton Mifflin Company, 1942)

her cry, and reassure her she will get through this. I suspect each one is praying, as they seldom are brave enough to do, that they will never be the one left alone, shattered, weeping, and struggling for meaning.

I'm struggling for meaning myself. So, after everyone else leaves, Kathy and I drive back to Deer Creek State Park on another mission. We find the trailer Mark stashed and load the pieces of the ASW 20 into it with the help of a competitor's young son we've brought with us and the CAP who stood guard all night. After a thorough search of the tall grass ahead of the impact zone [Are we being diligent or am I looking for reasons to delay my return to Springfield?], we find the two turnpoint cameras that had ripped off their mountings and been flung 20 feet in front of the cockpit. We also locate both wristwatches Dad had been wearing: his dress watch and an inexpensive running watch. The shock of the impact had ripped the straps from his wrists, a sobering reminder of the brutality inflicted on his body in a few milliseconds less than 24 hours before. We remove the ruined wings from the fuselage and—together with all the broken glider parts and scraps we can find—pour everything into the trailer to deal with later. Then we drive back to Springfield, pick up the LS3 and trailer, say our goodbyes at the contest (staring wistfully up at competitors wheeling overhead under a gorgeous sky), and head for what is now my mother's house in Cincinnati.

A few days later, we three kids accompany her to the funeral home to make the arrangements for a memorial service at our church in Cincinnati. The funeral director has a "showroom" (there's no other word for it) full of gleaming, hermetically sealed metal caskets tricked out with every conceivable option—all available at substantial cost. I'm half surprised I don't see scantily clad models beckoning us to the latest in burial accoutrements.

My mother is still in shock, so we three seize the initiative, inspecting the ostentatious sarcophagi, peering in and under them cynically:

Me: "For the price, this thing ought to have a motor."

Mark: "Yeah, and four-wheel drive. Who knows where it's going?"

Diane: "This upholstery doesn't look very durable. And no radio."

Our dark, gallows humor shakes our church's pastor, escorting my mother. But it is our way of getting through the pain. To the funeral director's ill-disguised disappointment, we select a simple, well-finished oak casket.

The contest organizers call a rest day for Sunday to coincide with the memorial service for my dad. The timing is appropriate; competitors have flown five days in a row, which suggests a rest day per the rules. And the weather for the remaining contest cooperates, with flying on three out of four days, bringing the total to eight of ten scheduled contest days, exceptional for the Midwest. Still, we are appreciative, for today is another perfect soaring day. Looking up at the sky as I stand outside the funeral home before the memorial service, I reflect on memories and thoughts of what might have—and, in fact, should have—been.

Mark picks up a picture frame and a large sheet of photo mat board. The night before the service, he labors for hours, expertly cutting it to feature myriad wallet-size photos of my father in different contexts: as a pilot, a husband, and a father. That same night, one of Dad's P&G soaring colleagues slips into their headquarters to retrieve a framed flying photo of him from Joe Bearden's office wall and delivers it to our house.

At the funeral home the next day before the viewing, our anger flares when we discover the expression arranged on my father's face by the undertaker is nothing like his actual appearance (the second time I'd experienced this in a few days). It's too late to do anything, so before anyone arrives, we say goodbye the last time and close the casket lid. Then we stand up the two photo frames for people to see as they pay their respects. This causes many to speculate, wrongly, that the violence of the crash had been disfiguring.

I'm astonished when visitation begins. Where are all these people coming from? The line of mourners waiting patiently outside the funeral home builds and doesn't collapse down until the end. I lose track of how many, but when I check the guest book, it's virtually full, with 450 names.

Many people express condolences, with the usual platitudes. One of the most moving things is the number who take the time to say how much my father had meant to them and what a force he had been in their lives.

I know the soaring crowd, of course, although not all of Dad's many students who show up. Procter & Gamble and our church are well represented. And there are neighbors and others my father knew over the years.

We shift to our church nearby for a brief service. To conclude it, Mark, Diane, and I stand at the front of the church my father served for so long and where we grew up. We take turns reading the lines from John Gillespie Magee Jr.'s "High Flight."

I had listened to this poem hundreds of times as a kid. One of the local television channels signed off each night (in the days when TV stations didn't operate 24/7) by running a short video of an F-104 Air Force fighter jet soaring through the heavens with a voice-over of the poem and stirring music.

"High Flight" was, I had imagined in moments of maudlin teen melodrama, what I would want to have read if I ever crashed. I've wondered if viewing it repeatedly helped lay the groundwork for my latent interest in aviation. Many nights in that pre-YouTube era, I stayed up late just to watch it.[20]

I don't trust myself to remember the words exactly, but the night before, we find them in a poetry anthology. Mark, Diane, and I divide up the lines among the three of us, retype them into complete sentences to avoid awkward pauses, and agree on a system of hand signals to each other in case— at the lectern—one of us cannot continue [we all make it through]. Like my father, we don't want to leave anything to chance.

High Flight

By John Gillespie Magee Jr.

Oh! I have slipped the surly bonds of Earth
And danced the skies on laughter-silvered wings;
Sunward I've climbed, and joined the tumbling mirth
Of sun-split clouds—and done a hundred things
You have not dreamed of—wheeled and soared and swung
High in the sunlit silence. Hov'ring there,
I've chased the shouting wind along, and flung
My eager craft through footless halls of air....
Up, up the long, delirious, burning blue
I've topped the wind-swept heights with easy grace
Where never lark nor even eagle flew—
And, while with silent lifting mind I've trod
The high untrespassed sanctity of space,
Put out my hand, and touched the face of God.

---

[20] See low-resolution version at https://www.youtube.com/watch?v=EzQYd_INSOg or https://www.youtube.com/watch?v=xTlWC7kfpDE

CHAPTER THIRTY-ONE

Post-Game Wrap Up

A FTER THE CONTEST, I reconsidered the "trick play" my father, and I called going into the Pickaway County Sinkhole. It didn't get us home to Springfield. But did we gain an advantage? We had picked up a few hundred feet on XX. I still had that margin the last time I saw him near Pickaway County Airport. After that—who knows? I scored two miles more than XX, but there were roughly 45 minutes of decisions we made in the interim, any of which could have had an impact. But it's a good story. Those two miles equated to a five-point margin—a 1.4% advantage—on a day where the winning score, because no one finished, was only 358 points.

The margin should have been larger. If I had glided out my altitude as I intended rather than landing at the crash, I could have gone another three to five miles, boosting me into the top six, or even the top three that day. That would have broken what turned out to be my eighth-place tie in cumulative results with Eric Mozer when I stopped flying. As George Moffat says, it's a game of seconds or, in this case, miles. But I've never lost any sleep over my decision.

Papa Golf scored zero for the day. We didn't recover his cameras until the next morning, and it didn't occur to us to turn in the film. If we had, Dad would have leaped almost ten places overall.

When the contest concluded a few days later, Karl Striedieck had retaken the lead. Of the younger pilots, Tommy Beltz placed third; Tigger Hall was fifth; and Eric Mozer—the previous winner—finished just behind his father in 11th. World champions George Moffat and A.J. Smith were seventh and 12th, reflecting the latter's disastrous landing at the first turn where I nearly came unstuck.

Chris Woods and his father, Woody, finished 16th and 17th. I always thought that was a coincidence. They seemed evenly matched as pilots, but I knew Chris had said they never pair flew, *per se*. Then, while researching this book, I discovered that three days after my father's crash, the two of them scored the identical daily distance, apparently landing at a popular airport with half a dozen other competitors. Two days later—the last contest day—they finished with close to the same elapsed times (1+ minutes difference) over a 2 ½ hour task. Were these coincidences, as can occur so often in large contests with big gaggles? Or was it possible Woody and Chris were subconsciously drawn together for a few days after another father-son duo suffered an almost unimaginable tragedy, perhaps acknowledging the menace of their endeavors?

Experts speak of how memories can be fluid and unreliable even among smart, strong, self-aware people. The truth of that was never more apparent than after I began researching this book. I consulted my logbooks, pored through boxes of photographs and long-ago-saved papers, and looked up the results of ancient contests in *Soaring* magazine to refresh my memory. Sometimes these facts forced me to correct those memories. And it wasn't just me. More than once, pilots I contacted recalled events differently than I had—often in conflict with the published score sheets for long-ago contests. We all do it. But because it operates at a subconscious level, we are seldom aware when it happens.

Some sources of information disappeared straight away. The night after the crash, Cincinnati's leading news station, WCPO-TV, featured a story about it during their nightly broadcast. I was fielding a telephone call from sympathetic soaring friends and missed it.

Dad preparing to give first glider ride to Cincinnati WCPO-TV anchorman Al Schottelkotte in SSD 2-22, 1963. (photo from estate of Joseph N. Bearden Jr.)

A few nights later, Mark and I drove to the studio. The station graciously allowed us to view the tape of the broadcast. In it, anchorman Al Schottelkotte had inserted a few seconds of film from 17 years earlier when he had come up to Richmond, Indiana, and taken a glider ride with my father. Rather than succumbing to sensationalism (e.g., "How I narrowly escaped death with doomed pilot!"), the admired Mr. Schottelkotte simply stated he had flown with my father. We couldn't talk the station into giving us a copy of the tape, per their policy. This was before mobile phone cameras, of course.

My father's close friend, Edward P. "Ted" Williams, glider pilot, former P&G executive, and respected soaring author, penned a moving *In Memoriam* for *Soaring* magazine. It honored my father, provided reassurance to our family that he was admired and would be remembered, and reiterated the theme that he died doing what he loved.[21] Already in his grave, Joe Bearden couldn't have cared less. But for us, getting it right was important.

We buried my father in a family plot in an unassuming little graveyard overlooking a pond in his hometown of Marion, Alabama. The small-town boy had returned 30+ years after leaving to chase the American dream. His parents were still alive there, bitter—no surprise—over what they always thought was his dangerous flirtation with flying. It was a reminder of how powerful my father's desire was to fly that he pursued his dream for so long with no parental support.

A few days after the funeral, our energy waning, we drove back to Cincinnati. This trip had always been interminable to me (12 to 14 hours before the Interstate Highway system and still ten hours today) so we trudged into my parents' house that night exhausted. It was our longest trip ever without my father doing most of the driving. My mother had had the entire day to reflect and rehearse what she wanted to say. She gathered herself and looked at each of us with fatigue in her eyes. She spoke in measured fashion, looking down as she began, then up to look directly at each of us, choosing each word with care.

"This past week, we've done everything according to the way we think your dad would have wanted us to do it. But that's over. From now on, we must live our lives. So do what you need to do for you, what's best for you, not because of what you think your father would have wanted. I don't want to burden any of you with that, or with me."

It was a remarkable speech from a woman who had lost her first love, her husband of 34 years, her best friend and confidant in a violent death. I wish I could believe each of us—including her—listened to those words and moved on. But it was more complicated than that.

---

[21] Mr. Williams' *In Memoriam* is appended to this book.

CHAPTER THIRTY-TWO

Revelations

T HE PRELIMINARY NTSB REPORT (and the final report that followed) revealed little I didn't know. There was no suggestion of any mechanical failure. Dad had put the wheel down in preparation for landing. An eyewitness account of the spin from a park ranger on the ground matched mine. Both of us agreed the pilot appeared to have regained control of the glider quickly and nearly recovered a normal attitude when it hit. The coroner's autopsy concluded Dad had been in superlative health for his age, with no evidence of a heart attack or other obvious medical problem. The cause of the crash remained a mystery.

I knew investigators often blamed accidents on pilot error. I was certain the final NTSB report would read this way. But Dad's case didn't fit the profile: he was not making a low turn at slow speed when he stalled and spun. The wheel being down and the near recovery from the spin strongly suggested he wasn't unconscious.

Then—shortly after the crash—a bombshell! I was kneeling in the back of the ASW 20 trailer, sweat pouring off me in the mid-summer heat, sorting through the wreckage before turning it over to the insurance company. I must have noticed something odd, because I took the unusual step of removing the rudder. That's how I discovered a hefty chunk of lead ballast secured in the tail.

This didn't look like a factory install. I wasn't aware if the seller had mentioned it to Dad. The center of gravity (CG) of the glider—the balance point—is critical. It affects flight characteristics, control, and performance. Adding weight in the tail was a standard performance tweak for competition sailplanes to shift the CG back to the aft limit allowed in the handbook. I had done the same thing with our LS3 based on my weight in the cockpit. I believed our ASW 20's previous owner was somewhat heavier than Dad. I also knew this pilot favored flying with an aft CG. That meant Dad might have been flying it for over a year with the CG behind the rearmost limit based on his weight.

Like many things in life, CG isn't binary. Being one percent too far aft wouldn't cause the glider to fall from the sky. Both of us had flown it without incident. The risk was the glider could have been less resistant to stalling, more susceptible to entering a spin when stalled, and/or more difficult to recover from a spin. I had never stalled or spun our ASW 20 to assess it, and I doubted

Dad had—at least intentionally.

I stared at the lead weight bolted into the aft fuselage. Could this have contributed to the crash? I wasn't looking to blame anyone. As the new owners, it had been our responsibility to weigh the glider and ensure the CG was in the correct range. Rushing to get it in the air, we had installed our instruments and, skipping that step, flown it.

I didn't tell anyone except Mark about my discovery. I never raised it with the former owner (now deceased). I've never brooded about it. It could have been a contributing factor. The glider appeared to be recovering from the spin when it hit the ground, so who knows?

I had already played mind games by ignoring my role in helping secure the temporary battery behind Dad's head to get his radio working the night before. We both knew better, but we were in a hurry then, too. When Dad's aircraft hit the ground, that battery came loose and struck the back of his skull. A doctor friend who reviewed Dad's autopsy opined his other injuries were sufficient to have killed him. Maybe this MD wanted to be sure I didn't carry that burden with me forever. I don't think consciously about the role I played or if I should have talked Dad out of it. The past is the past. Who knows what might be lurking in my subconscious? I could be rationalizing like a pro. I've never done anything like it again and have spoken out often against the practice in my safety talks.

* * *

We worked to support our mother as she put her life back together. Diane was living at home with her. Mark was moving to Dayton nearby. I flew back often and telephoned her an average of five times a week that first year to check up, answer questions she had about everything from investments to car repairs, and listen as she poured out her frustration, anger, anxiety, and grief.

Condolences and tributes to my father continued to roll in as word spread. He had touched many lives. These heartfelt expressions of support supplied emotional therapy. But they didn't answer the question: *why* had he stalled the aircraft, triggering the crash?

This wasn't a television mystery where a search party stumbles across the crash site, but no one knows what happened. I knew what happened. I watched the accident unfold, then dissected it with Eric and Pete when the details were fresh and unfiltered. What I didn't know was the cause. If Dad had been making a low turn, I might be willing to believe he had gotten careless. But no one stalls and spins from straight-and-level flight in smooth air.

A few weeks after the crash, wanting to consult with experts and longing for the emotional therapy of chatting with fellow pilots, I drove up to Elmira, New York, for the Standard Class Nationals with Kathy. While she went to mass in the city (she never missed a weekend mass), I wandered along the grid before launch. I came upon A.J. Smith fettling with his glider.

My family and I had known A.J. for almost 20 years. He had stayed at our house. We had competed and chatted with him many times. An urbane, award-winning architect and ex-World War II Navy pilot, he showed up each year at our club's Memorial Day weekend contest with a state-of-the-art, immaculately prepared glider and a luxurious new car. He always dressed in khakis and a perfectly fitting white shirt. This compares to the typical airport dress code then (and now) of weekend hardware-store casual.

Like George Moffat, A.J. was a former world soaring champion with superb skills. He was equally renowned, however, for his passionate competitive drive that could transform this quiet, thoughtful, brilliant, and successful man into a brooding, manipulative, quick-tempered jerk. We had never observed this Jekyll-and-Hyde transformation. But we had heard enough accounts over the years from people we trusted to know they must be true.

Oblivious, I strolled up to A.J. and began asking questions about what might have happened that day at Deer Creek State Park.

Danger, danger! To say I was playing with fire was an understatement of epic proportions. A.J. was preparing his sailplane for battle in less than two hours. He once admitted during a lecture this was precisely the time during which he often withdrew, distancing himself from the world around him and seeking irritants to ignite his combustible spirit with a burst of anger he could channel into a competitive fire.

Even more provocatively, the day my father crashed was the same day A.J. had been "shot down" at the first turn where I came so close to landing. That outlanding ruined the entire contest for a man most still considered a contender for the national championship and U.S. Team.

A.J. probably wanted to reflect on that day about as much as Brooklyn Dodgers pitcher Ralph Branca wished to reminisce about his infamous "Shot Heard Round the World" home run pitch to Bobby Thompson of the New York Giants to lose the National League pennant the year I was born. A.J. didn't need an irritant to ignite his anger. I was handing him a lighted stick of dynamite!

But there was no explosion. A.J. was the perfect gentleman. He couldn't pause his pre-flight work as the launch approached. But as he walked around the glider attending to last-minute details, he listened closely to my account of the crash and to my queries. He questioned me about the flight and about the autopsy. After some discussion, he opined dehydration could have been a factor, that medical experts often overlooked it if they weren't looking for it.

This man of few words was a lifelong bachelor who returned to our contest each year with a succession of attractive women as his crews. With rare candor, he shared with me his own personal loss, of a woman he had known closely, who clearly meant something to him, who had been an innocent victim in a fatal car accident. He spoke of the difficulty he had accepting what had happened so randomly and, yes, unfairly. I recalled seeing her with him at our contest.

A.J. Smith accepting trophy at SSD contest, ca. 1960s.
(photo from SSD archives)

A.J. Smith was smart, analytical, and insightful. He was not, however, what anyone would ever describe as a "warm and fuzzy" type. Yet that morning, in his characteristic spare, careful, detached pattern of speech, he provided not only expert opinion on what might have killed my father but also a kind of desperately needed therapy for my wounded spirit.

Many pilots were scathing in their jokes that the shortest list of soaring enthusiasts comprised those who had crewed for A.J. Smith twice, a sardonic commentary on his volatile and occasionally abusive demeanor. Yet that morning I spent close to an hour with the man and not once, as the clock ticked down and pre-launch tension built, did he express the slightest impatience.

In later years, as I listened to pilots criticize and mock him behind his back for his moody and sometimes boorish behavior, I held my temper and offered a simple rebuttal: I didn't dispute the veracity of these tales. But A.J. Smith had always treated my family and me with the utmost respect and consideration—and never more so than on that day.

The NTSB report didn't mention dehydration. As expected, they blamed the crash on "FAILED TO OBTAIN/MAINTAIN FLYING SPEED."

I disagreed. Judgment degraded by dehydration was consistent with the facts. My father still had most of his drinking water (and food) when he crashed, after flying for over four and a half hours and not drinking much, if any, water before that. He hated distractions in the cockpit and June 19 was a long, hot day, especially given that he flew an hour longer than I did. Only in my 50s did I understand he may not have wanted to deal with the effects of too much fluid intake. In those days, most pilots ducked into the trees or behind a van to urinate before launching on what could be a six- or seven-hour flight. We worried more about drinking too much than too little. So we sipped sparingly before and during a flight. For this reason, I came to believe dehydration and/or the sun might have impaired Dad's abilities without rendering him unconscious when he glided under me the last time. There were other medical possibilities—e.g., a TIA (transient ischemic attack, or mini stroke)—but dehydration fit the circumstances. And in recent years, experts have pointed to it as an insidious danger and the probable contributor to other comparable accidents.

Jon Krakauer's *Into Thin Air* recounts stories of experienced climbers who vanished on the slopes of Everest or who perished when they pushed on unaccountably in the face of deepening darkness and storm against all logic and reason. Grief wracked their friends and fellow climbers not only for the loss but also that no one would ever know what happened up on the mountain.

It was different for me. I had seen *exactly* what happened. I just didn't understand it. Ignoring that, however, I was steadfast that I would continue to fly and to compete in sailplanes. And the sooner the better.

PART III: FLYING WITH SUPERHEROES REDUX

CHAPTER THIRTY-THREE

Surviving the Crash Is Just the Beginning

MY FATHER'S CRASH CHANGED EVERYTHING. After the funeral, we spent months dealing with his will, insurance policies, death certificates, Social Security, lawyers, etc. Dying is easy in America. It's all the stuff that comes afterward that makes death complicated.

What I *really* wanted was the same thing I'd longed for the morning after the accident, i.e., to be back in the cockpit in a contest. So two months later, I flew to Cincinnati, picked up Diane and my mother and the LS3, and drove down to the Cordele Regional, the same way we had so many times in the past.

It wasn't the same, of course. My mother had readily agreed to go, two months after Dad's crash. But forty years later, she confessed the main reason was because she knew I needed it. When we arrived, no one questioned the wisdom of my returning to the fray, not pilots, crews, nor officials. To me, Cordele was a secure haven at a familiar venue with friends who welcomed us with warmth and compassion. Who knows what they were saying behind my back?

I hadn't flown at all since that funereal day at Deer Creek Lake. Was I doing the right thing, jumping back into the crucible of competition so soon? I wasn't afraid to fly, but how would I react when I climbed into the cockpit the first time? Should I take a check ride with someone I trusted to be sure? What if he said, "you need some more time, Chip"? Yeah, negative on that idea.

The LS3 had been in the trailer since the crash. I cringed when we pulled the wings out on the practice day. The white gel coat had a few tiny blisters where the thick felt in the padded wingtip supports had trapped moisture from the rain or dew that night at Deer Creek State Park. These flaws in our beautiful sailplane would have upset my father. Another pilot, seeing our distress, went to work with a mild abrasive to polish them out.

"Good as new!" he smiled, gesturing at the glider and—coincidentally—at me. I reached over and stroked the surgically smooth surface of the wing. Firm and unblemished, the feel of it was as much a part of me as my own hands were.

We assembled the glider, scrutinized everything, and pushed it up to the takeoff line. I hadn't been conscious of being nervous. Now, as I strapped in, I wasn't sure what to expect. I'd been on autopilot, reacting, playing a role. I needed back in the air again because that's what we men do.

I'd seldom flown a glider when my father wasn't around, and never in a stressful situation like this. I imagined everyone's eyes were on me. And yet, despite anxiety and a *soupçon* of trepidation, excitement filled me. I was on stage, poised to prove I could bounce back, with the thrill of doing it on my own.

I smiled over at Diane when she leveled the wings and gave her a thumbs up. The line boss gave the go-ahead signal. The towplane's power came on with the tuned snarl of a powerful engine and prop. The familiar tug of acceleration reeled us down the runway.

Suddenly, things were happening too fast. I was slightly behind the curve. My hand twitched on the stick when I brought the flaps down and we bobbed up as the glider lifted. For an instant, I wondered, "Oh s**t; was this a mistake?"

Then I stopped thinking and muscle memory took over. Off tow, in my first thermal with the LS3 responding to my touch smoothly and hearing a chorus on the radio of "welcome back, Jake Baker" from other pilots, I knew I was in the right place. This was where I was the best I could be.

* * *

I flew well, placing second and fifth, then winning the third day convincingly in the 15 Meter Class. At the pilots' meeting the next day, the Standard Class winner gave his speech first. It was unremarkable save for his opening line: "I'd like to dedicate this to three guys who aren't with us anymore."

Damn! I didn't see that one coming. My father, of course, was one of those guys. Two other popular Cordele pilots had also died that summer, one from heart problems on the ground at Springfield and the other in a mysterious accident in an ASW 20 at a contest out West. [It was a bad year for the ASW 20.]

When it was my turn, I blanked. This "three guys gone" tribute had rattled me. Despite being in the business world for five years, I was still not the adept public speaker my father had been. I had a rehearsed speech. Yet the situation cried out for something momentous, something insightful and eloquent and inspiring, something appropriate to the occasion.

I couldn't do it. After taking a deep breath, I was lucky to stumble through my scripted speech about another ordinary soaring day, albeit one when I had been fastest. I couldn't have extemporized a dedication to fallen comrades if my life had depended on it.

My mother had a different reaction. Upon hearing the tribute, she darted from the meeting in tears. I watched as a diminutive woman with a long blonde braid stood and rushed after her. I recognized the widow of a Southeastern pilot who had died in a crash the year before. She was visiting friends at the contest.

It was ludicrous I'd ever uttered that inane line about the most dangerous part of soaring being the drive to and from the airport. This contest was teeming with survivors of pilots who would have been far better off driving than flying!

* * *

The final day of Cordele 1980 was a turning point in my competitive career and, arguably, my life. Near the top of the score sheet, I gambled on a late start as thermal strength surged, betting the storms that threatened each day would again hold off, allowing me to smoke the course and take the lead.

It was a bad bet. Late in the flight, I needed only to photograph the last turn, and then go home. Ahead of me, parked over that turnpoint to the south, was a large thunderstorm, the ominous layers of dark cloud boiling over themselves, dropping rain, and with occasional flickers of air-to-ground lightning, spreading out to shadow the countryside for miles. Perhaps ten minutes too late, I watched the last competitor to escape the rain at the turnpoint roll into my thermal below, make a few turns, then head north on the way to the finish. He said later he knew what was going through my mind. I'm not so sure he could.

As the power of the storm subsided, I glided in under light rain and landed there. I didn't have enough altitude to escape to the sunlight. I was the only one among the leaders not to finish that day. Slumped in the driver's seat, my drive back to Cordele in the drizzle, knowing the contest and nightmarish season were over, was gloomy and dispiriting for me, my mother, and Diane. They knew better than anyone what this contest had meant. And they could tell how much my last-day tumble hurt.

I had never reacted well to setbacks in my flying. Had I made it worse this time by subconsciously drafting a melodramatic "B" movie script—i.e., "Surviving Son of Downed Pilot Dedicates Next Win to Late Father!"—and been crushed when I couldn't deliver? Who knows how our minds work? But with the season over, I had some unfinished business. I didn't know something elemental had changed.

CHAPTER THIRTY-FOUR

Mountain Madness

"*E*VERYTHING CAME TOO EASILY TO HIM,*" the confession by Robert Redford's character in the movie, *The Way We Were*[22], describes my early experiences in competition. A win in my first contest. Storming from behind to snatch runner up in my first regional contest flying a high-performance sailplane. Second place on Day One at my coming out party at the Nationals and holding on for seventh overall. And so on.

The exchanges with my father about getting on the U.S. Team no longer seemed outrageous. SSA office staff held a betting pool for the 1980 Nationals at Springfield and a young staffer there wrote me, in a condolence card after the crash, that she had picked my name to take it all. On the day my father died, I was "going for it," not merely to place, but to win the contest.

Yet I was also going for the win later that summer at the Cordele Regional when I blew it on the last day. I couldn't put that behind me. It reminded me too much of my blunder at Ionia in 1977. I had failed—publicly. Now I couldn't rest until I had reestablished my identity as a contender. The best place for that, I reasoned, was at the Nationals.

What the hell could I have been thinking? The 1981 15 Meter Nationals were at Minden, Nevada—one of the world's most awesome but intimidating places to fly gliders. Monster weather. High deserts. Higher altitudes. Harsh mountains. Vast uninhabited panoramas with few places to land. Specialized skills and local knowledge required—none of which I possessed. "Hubris" doesn't come close. Dad and I had seldom ventured beyond the flatlands of the East. Flying Minden would be like a Central Park walker tackling Mount Everest. But Minden is where the big guys would fight it out. So that's where I wanted to be.

Our family made it through our first winter holidays without Dad. Over the following months, we made elaborate preparations for a grand adventure. A week before the contest, my mother, Mark, Diane, and I set off in a used mini motorhome and headed west with the LS3 in tow. To make the full practice period meant driving non-stop for three days.

Deep into the second night, near the end of my four-hour shift, I couldn't

---

[22] *The Way We Were,* Directed by Sydney Pollack, screenplay by Arthur Laurens. Columbia Pictures, 1973. Film.

Motorhome and LS3 trailer on the road, 1981.

keep my eyes open or the trailer straight. Admitting defeat, I veered off on a random exit on Interstate 80 west of Laramie, Wyoming in the inky darkness: no gas stations, fast-food, motels, or streetlights. It was eerie as we crept down the exit ramp, across the deserted crossroad, and part way up the entrance ramp. Rolling across what we had learned were cattle guards—horizontal grids of pipes set above shallow pits in the road—the clanking sound seemed louder than usual. But I was beyond caring.

"Mark," I called over my shoulder as I eased to a stop and switched on the interior lights, "Your turn to drive. I've had it." My brother groaned and rose from the couch behind the driver's seat, shook his head to gather himself, and swapped places with me. Then:

"I need to wake up," he muttered, hopping out into the darkness.

I was already half asleep on the couch when I heard him open the driver's door: "The trailer wheel is gone."

That woke me up. "You mean we have a flat tire," I corrected him.

"No, the wheel is *gone*," he insisted, as I climbed out to see for myself.

We stood there, speechless, staring dully at the almost unrecognizable left trailer wheel. I had blown a tire. Oblivious, I had kept driving and ground the rubber tire off, then rolled the steel rim down until it was hardly bigger than the brake drum tucked inside it. Who knows how many miles I had driven on it?

Mark and I looked at each other, then went to work, jacking up the trailer and mounting the spare. We plodded back to the van and flung open the rear door. My mother and Diane jumped, startled and wide eyed in the interior lights. One was cradling our unloaded pistol. The other balanced the box of ammunition in her palm. We might have been the only human beings within 20 miles, but they were ready to back us up.

"Mama," I laughed, "What did you intend to do if someone broke in: *throw the gun at him?*"

The next morning at a Salt Lake City junkyard, recalling the specs from the day my father had picked up the trailer on the Philadelphia docks, we found a replacement wheel and tire and were on our way.

* * *

West Coast pilots dominated the entry list. I knew most by name but had met only the handful who ventured East to fly our contests. They welcomed us with enthusiasm when we rolled onto Minden's Douglas County Airport. Among those expressing condolences were several young pilots I'd flown against who confided they had always worried a little about their fathers' flying. Was this true, or had my father's accident kindled new anxieties?

As expected, flying in the West was unlike anything I had encountered. The weather was superb: cool nights; hot, dry days; brilliant sunshine; strong soaring conditions; and wind—always wind—including the occasional dust storm. After three days of practice, I was

On the grid in Minden with Diane, 1981.

psyched! I had adjusted smoothly and kept up with the gaggles.

That was reassuring. In the three years we had owned the LS3, the wings had "cured," distorting the airfoil and making the ship less competitive at high speed. So that winter, in my mother's garage, I had meticulously sanded and smoothed the wings. Ironically, if my father had been alive, he would never have gone along. Taking sandpaper to our beautiful sailplane? Aieeeee! But it worked. My LS3 was again fully equal to anything else flying there, at all speeds.

I had also researched Minden, reading up on prior contests and chatting with a veteran national champion about his experiences. I accumulated notes on landable areas (e.g., which dry lakebeds were actually dry), reliable lift and sink spots, and areas to avoid (e.g., because of sink or anti-social ranchers or Native American reservations with restricted access). I was ready!

The winning speeds astonished me, 93 mph on Day One, reflecting the outrageous cruise speeds—up to 100 knots or more—with occasional pauses to be slammed aloft in thermals bursting out of the mountains and erupting over the high desert at ten knots (1,000 feet a minute) and more. We would tuck in to ride these as high as the FAA's legal ceiling of 18,000 feet, then push the glider to run faster than I had ever cruised on the way to the next thermal.

Like most, I stopped measuring how much water we poured into the LS3's ballast tanks. For the first time, we just filled them to capacity to boost cruising speed. In the days before compulsory weighing, I was likely 100 pounds over the maximum allowable weight of half a ton and wished for more.

Task distances were formidable, averaging 300 miles. All but one exceeded anything I had flown, demanding five-plus hours a day in the cockpit over nine days, exacerbated by dry desert air, high altitudes, and late-night retrieves. I had never flown at this level of physical intensity.

The arena was daunting: mountains, desert, sagebrush, and mile upon mile of desolation, devoid of people, with few roads and disturbingly bereft of places to land. The Minden valley was 5,000 feet above sea level, and we spent most of our time above 10,000 feet, wearing an oxygen mask, also new for me.

It was exhilarating but intimidating. Day One set the pattern.

Journal Entry: June 30, 1981 (Minden, Nevada)

Nevada desert, 1981. Landable, but not without damaging the glider.

Everything is bigger and badder in Nevada. I don't look down much. From high altitude, the desert is less threatening, but I know that landing out among those innocuous-looking sagebrush would trash the glider.

With strong climbs and fast inter-thermal speeds, I am having a great run, 86 mph average up to the turnpoint 146 miles northeast of Minden to Mill City, and part way back. Alone most of the time, I spot only a few competitors. I don't know it then, but programming in a fast final glide to the finish would have put me in the top five. I am encouraged and a little cocky.

"I can fly with these guys."

Hubris again. As I near the last mountain before Minden, a massive Western thunderstorm sits squarely athwart the course line. It tops anything I've ever seen, the somber iron gray battlements vaulting up into the stratosphere and blotting out a massive swath of the sky with swirls of darkness and splashes of lightning flickering down to the ground illuminating the curtains of rain ahead.

I zig one way to go around it while the leading pilots zag the other way. Bad decision. In the enormous storm's shadow, it is ominously calm. Gone are the thermals, turbulence, and explosive energy over the desert. The air is glassy smooth. I'm in trouble. Gliding lower, I open the valves to dump the ballast, water spewing from the tanks, descending inexorably into a valley about 20 miles from the finish line. I have little hope of finishing.

There's a green field ahead with a glider already in it. In desperation, I use my last few hundred feet before entering a landing pattern to slide over the windward side of a small rocky hill. The little piece of ridge is facing into the wind at an angle. My last hope is air flowing up and over it will be enough to sustain my LS3.

This pitiful bump is nothing like a classic ridge—i.e., a steep, high, consistent ridgeline that runs for miles perpendicular to the prevailing winds. But it is enough to arrest my descent, so I begin tacking back and forth less than a mile at a time in the trickle of air blowing up its slope.

Back and forth, back and forth. Each pass requires less than a minute, at the end of which I turn away from the slope and head back in the opposite direction. Like a great white shark that must swim constantly to keep water moving over its gills to breathe, I can't stop in the feeble updraft. I must always move forward to keep air flowing over the wings.

I'm grateful to be airborne, but I'm ready to explode from stress! The LS3 is coasting along at under 60 knots, my wingtip all but scraping the rocks, never more than 800 feet above the valley and often below that, looking *up* at the rocky crest. I have almost no experience on a ridge, and none in survival conditions like this. I'm stuck, going nowhere, the clock ticking. My mouth and lips are painfully dry, but I don't dare stretch over my shoulder to search for the water bottle stashed there. At least I'm still airborne.

Minutes tick by as I tack back and forth. There's a hard lump in my parachute jammed into my lower back muscles. I shift in the cockpit, watching the airspeed every second to avoid getting too slow (and stalling) or too fast (and losing precious altitude). Forget speed; I just want to get home. I've played the waiting game before, but this is worse. I'm going nowhere.

My only hope is the small gusts coming up the slope, tiny shreds of thermals. Twice I try a circle but they're too small to make more than half a turn. The third time, in desperation, I work up the nerve to turn back into the hill to complete a circle in the little gust close to the rocks—and the wind unexpectedly pushes me back into the spillover behind the crest.

Oh, f**k! Sinking, heart thudding in my chest, I slalom around the end of the hill to get back in front of it again, part way down the slope. To my relief, the weak flow of wind dribbling up the rocks is still working. I'm climbing again, back and forth, back and forth, surfing up the rocky slope. It's a slow, painful process to climb up even with it. At last, pulse subsiding, I'm back where I started—and still trapped.

I've been at this for an hour. Now there are two gliders in the field below, one of whom, I learn later, is George Moffat. That may well be where I will have to land, but something is driving me. I don't want to give up. Back and forth, sliding past the rocky crest, the clock continues to tick.

Then, out of nowhere, another sailplane appears just above. He makes a few passes, then levels his wings in decisive fashion and turns south. I watch him glide toward a finger of ridge extending from the mountains. Is he giving up, or trying something else? What does he know that I don't? When I reverse course after my next beat, he has vanished! Where the hell did he go?

Clutching at any possibility, I gather what hope and courage remain, abandon my hill, and glide toward where I last saw him. If this doesn't work, if he's led me into a trap, I'll have to land. But that seems certain, anyway.

At the edge of the foothills, I slide over the finger of ridge. Surprise! I'm going up! Not fast, but up is up—and it's steady. I glide into the gap between rocky corrugations and fly straight on, doing nothing to disturb what's happening. After the last hour, I so want to believe, but I can't yet. It's too soon.

I still can't see the glider I presume is out ahead of me, so I follow the rocky, wind-facing slope headed south, slipping deeper into the mountains, gaining altitude. As I fly farther up the ridge and into the unlandable canyon, the safety of the valley behind me is receding, now borderline unreachable if the wind quits. But I push on, scarcely able to believe, almost giggling in relief, creeping along at 60 knots, climbing above the rugged slope.

I continue to ascend as I fly up the shoulder of the mountain. I can't keep going this way forever. I'm flying deeper into the mountains, and the only landable terrain is behind me. Finally, I'm high enough above the ridgeline to the west to make a run for it. I take a deep breath and turn right 90 degrees into the wind, aiming at the crest ahead and below. The thunderstorm has dissipated, so the air is smooth. I'm gliding west across unlandable rocks. As I approach the ridge guarding the Minden valley, I hit sink on the lee side as the wind spills over. For a moment, I'm not sure I'll clear the ridge. All I can see is a crash-only clearing, pockmarked with stumps.

I suffer the anxiety for less than a minute, not knowing for sure if I'll make it. Then, in seconds, I squeak over the edge and into the main valley. To the south is the Minden airport! I'm giddy with emotion. From zero hope to this!

Minutes later, throat still dry, I radio a scratchy "Juliet Bravo, one mile" with studied casualness. What I *really* want to say is "f**kin' A—I'm BACK!" I am so exhausted from tension, my head resting on the headrest when I roll to a stop, Mark has to help pull me up from the cockpit after six hours and fifteen minutes. I have bruises on my shoulders from straining against the shoulder straps. It has taken me two hours to come the last 20 miles.

I should be elated. I've finished when 25% of the field landed out, most of them in the same treacherous miles where I scrambled so hard to stay alive. Instead, I'm embarrassed to learn I'm 46th, last place, slowest for the day. My 52 mph would be a good speed back East, but it's absurd compared to the winner's 93 mph. I've never been this far down the scoresheet before.

In the morning pilots' meeting, the Contest Manager awarded me a stick of deodorant for "rock polishing under stress." I wasn't sure if this signaled admiration for my persistence or gentle kidding for creeping in so late and thoroughly thrashed out. No matter. It was to be my only "honor" of the contest.

More than 40 years later, I contacted Bob Nye, the pilot who appeared suddenly late in the day and led me into the mountains. The ridge we used to get home is well known by local pilots to produce lift in the right conditions to glide back to Minden. It was another example of critical local knowledge at work.

Day Two was a repeat: moments of curated virtuosity awash in mediocrity.

Journal Entry: July 1, 1981 (Gabbs, Nevada)

The high desert is restless, moaning in the night with a dry, husky wind. There is no moon. The only light is from millions of stars brilliant in the black dome of the sky suspended above us, with the glow of a 24-hour mountain-top mining operation a few miles away sullying the darkness.

Four of us are sitting on the ground in a circle at a primitive airstrip in Gabbs, Nevada. When the sun slipped behind the mountains and the temperature dropped, I'd dug my landout jacket from the cockpit. Our gliders are vague shapes in the dark near the runways bulldozed into the soft earth.

There's little noise: no cars, no animals, no voices, nothing except the wind. It's subsided, but it hasn't gone away. The wind never goes away. It's as if we are in a separate universe, that if we don't show up in the morning, no one will know what happened. Anything could be lurking out there in the darkness and we wouldn't know until it came for us.

That afternoon, I had been inordinately pleased with myself for looping far off course to avoid a storm, reminiscent of all the times I had done similar things in Cordele. I was gleeful to pivot high above Basalt, a desolate inter-section 100 miles southeast of Minden, for my turnpoint photo. I could see 21 competitors forced down there, close to one third of the fleet, shoe-horned into the scrub surrounding the tiny dirt airstrip. I had listened with growing excitement on the radio as Karl Striedieck talked each successive plane down on final, allowing the expanding crowd of pilots to wheel it out of the way to make room for the next glider close behind. Just as on Day One, I said to myself, "I can fly with these guys!" And, again, I was wrong.

Turning north, I was slow going up the second leg to Gabbs. I wasn't able to upshift into aggressive mode. By the time I arrived at the Gabbs turnpoint, I couldn't get high enough in the late afternoon to risk heading out across the desert and mountains the last 100 miles to Minden. Shortly after I landed, three other pilots descended to join me: George Moffat; Las Horvath (who had won the first day at Bryan back in 1976, when I had placed second); and another adept Western pilot I had followed for years.

I'm gratified to be chatting with three giants in the soaring world. Hours into the wait, well after dark, we watch what we speculate are headlights trail down the mountain far to the south. They stabilize and turn up the valley floor straight at us, shimmering, growing brighter for almost half an hour.

Then the first trailer appears in the darkness and turns into the airport. We derig the LS3 by headlights and begin the three-hour drive across the mountains to Minden to arrive long after midnight.

The next morning, we learned 12 pilots had finished the task with a winning speed in excess of 80 mph. The four of us at Gabbs were the closest non-finishers, but that meant little. After two days, I was tired, sleep deprived, and discouraged. I had moved up one place to 45th. To paraphrase Dorothy in *The Wizard of Oz*, "I had a feeling we weren't in Ohio anymore."

Most of the contest was a depressing variation on this theme. The single exception was the incredible Day Four, which went down in soaring history.

Journal Entry: July 3, 1981 (Minden, Nevada)

Task setting is contingent on weather, but it's more aggressive at a nationals. Still, there's an excited babble of incredulity at the pilots' meeting when, seizing upon an unusually strong forecast, the CD announces the longest task ever called in the U.S., maybe in the world: a long, flat, skinny triangle up and down the Sierra Nevada Mountains totaling 455 miles, twice as far as I have ever flown.

Just before launch, a race official hurries down the line warning each pilot. There's a major hang-gliding championship launching 300 hang gliders off the White Mountains at Bishop, California. That's 15 miles north of our first turnpoint at Big Pine in the Owens Valley, at the northern tip of Death Valley National Park. We'll be passing through their area twice, headed south on the way down and then north on the way back. Are you kidding me?

We're headed south high and fast, paralleling the Sierras in the shadow of Yosemite past Mono Lake. Mount Whitney is visible beyond. Closing on the 13,000-to-14,000-feet summits of the White Mountains, I spot pinpricks of color—like little bits of iridescent confetti—in a sparkling amorphous cloud that extends from below the jagged peaks to the 18,000 feet legal ceiling.

Drawing closer, this swirling sprinkle of colors resolves—like a Pointillist painting—into individual hang gliders in their brilliant hues, winding around in slow motion. Sixty-two sailplanes slice through this dispersed cloud of glitter at 100+ knots like a laser show. Then, after photographing the turn, we reverse course like errant missiles and head north, slashing back through it minutes later at even higher speeds.

I haul back on the stick, entering a monster thermal. Like coming off an explosive springboard, the LS3 arcs up, soaring 500 feet in a few seconds, the equivalent of a 40-story building, the G-force pressing my body into the reclining cockpit. Nose high, I see nothing but sky and hang gliders and sailplanes in the pullup until the speed bleeds off and I level out and turn in tightly. Hang glider pilots with oxygen bottles strapped to their struts wave as we track outside their circle at three times their speed. Even with our closing velocity of nearly 250 knots between northbound and southbound sailplanes and the insect-like clutter of metal-tubing-and-fabric hang gliders wafting about, no one gets hurt or even frighteningly close. It is a complex, breathtaking display of airmanship with hundreds of moving parts. I suspect if anyone from the FAA had been along to witness it, they would have wept—then returned to Washington to crank out more regulations.

Northbound, we fling ourselves along the Whites, cruising at 100 to 120 knots and pausing only for 10- to 15-knot thermals (climbing 1,000 to 1,500 feet per minute—without an engine!). It's an otherworldly sensation, the LS3 laid over on one wing in a steep bank with the force of almost two Gs pressing my entire body down into the cockpit[23], listening to the audio vario wail a keening note I've never heard sustained, and watching the needle on the altimeter wrap around faster than the second hand of a watch. And all around, harsh, fractured mountain peaks below us recede as we climb away. Over the years, I had read, with some disbelief, about days like this. Only knowing 60+ other pilots are doing exactly what I am doing—or better—keeps me from drifting off into euphoria. That and my oxygen mask, which I've been wearing since I climbed through 10,000 feet hours earlier.

The Sierras are off my left wing, harboring the forbidding peaks and unlandable treescapes of Yosemite National Park and half a dozen national forests. Barreling past Minden, the deep Lake Tahoe basin scooped out of the mountains, and then Reno, I coast out over the second turn at Flanigan, an abandoned town in the alkali flats in the back of beyond. Conditions moderate as I get my photos. I retrace my steps, headed south on the last 80-mile leg. I set up my long final glide to get down below 10,000 feet before my oxygen bottle is empty. It's anticlimactic; I've known for hours we're going to finish. My 77 mph over the 455 miles is good for 14th and moves me up a few places in the cumulative standings.

---

[23] While noticeable, this is modest compared with the five, seven, or even more Gs experienced by fighter pilots.

After landing, I swap stories with the 56 animated, laughing, and disbeliev-ing pilots who finished this breathtaking task. It finally registers. We have made history. Basking in the reflected glow of the brotherhood of pilots who completed this mission, I am part of this elite community again. For a few hours, I relax and celebrate. I can play at this level! I haven't over-reached beyond my abilities.

The truth is, I *had* overreached. When the lift was strong and I could stay high, it clicked. But the stress of struggling anytime I was low over unlandable moon-scape was debilitating. My self-assurance and lofty expectations were evaporat-ing. I was often out of touch with the weather, or the right strategy, or what the competition were doing. I was in over my head. I had worked my way up to 25th place, but that was to be the high point. On the sixth day of flogging myself, over the mountain at the Schurz turnpoint, I came to a bad end.

Journal Entry: July 6, 1981 (Schurz, Nevada)

Now what? It's taken me a long time, working very rough thermals and bits of ridge lift to climb up above the windward side of Black Mountain just beyond Schurz, the second turn. I plan to use this springboard to push out over the empty landscape toward the final turn at Bridgeport.

But the incessant turbulence and the constant wrenching of the glider up and down have taken their toll. This time, unlike my encounter with a storm in Bryan five years earlier, the rough gusts *are* trying to roll me and push the nose up and down as I fight it with the controls. I'm also unnerved by the terrain on the way to Bridgeport, which appears to comprise 50 miles of desolation and mountains, devoid of any sign of civilization, even dirt roads. If I land out there, with no telephone, will anyone hear my radio call? How long will it take to find me, much less retrieve me if I go down 20 or 30 miles from the nearest dirt track? My crew would have to borrow someone's four-wheel-drive truck. How long will my survival kit and drinking water last?

The end comes sooner than I expect. Emotionally and physically drained, rattled and defeated, I capitulate. I turn my back on the last turnpoint and use the altitude I had wrung so painfully from Black Mountain to retreat in its lee to the turnpoint at Schurz.

It's ironic that, having abandoned the fight in order to be cautious, I am hammered by violent downdrafts and the mean, boiling gusts of a rotor as the air rolls over itself and the bottom drops out of this patch of sky in massive sink. Plunging dangerously on my approach into the rough airstrip there, I fight savage turbulence and the worst crosswind I have ever experienced, using the rudder to crab the glider into the wind at an angle. As I approach the dirt strip at high airspeed, I kick it straight in the last seconds before touching down to prevent a brutal ground loop. I am fortunate to get the glider down and stopped with no damage. A fellow pilot who also manages to land there is diplomatically incredulous that, after I successfully climbed up where I had been, I hadn't pressed on.

F**k! Once again, I had choked, the same way I had at Bryan. Shame wells up inside me. I had sworn I would never succumb to anything like this again. Yet here I am. And it's not over yet.

Our grand adventure in Minden was therapeutic in one sense. It affirmed our lives would go forward even without my father. We avidly absorbed everything there was to enjoy there: the harsh but pure climate, the open skies and vast emptiness of the high desert, the backdrop of the mountains, the spectacular Lake Tahoe basin, even the long recoveries from remote landouts.

Mark had to fly home early for business, so we drove him to Reno on the rest day. In a scene I could never have scripted, we pulled my wide-eyed, straight-arrow, Southern Baptist mother into a casino. For fun, we showed her how the 25-cent slot machines worked. As we walked on, we realized she wasn't with us. Mesmerized, she had opened her purse and was pumping in her own quarters!

Earlier that day, Karl Striedieck—the U.S. dealer for Alexander Schleicher GmbH, the German maker of the ASW 20—convened a meeting to discuss the recent spate of crashes, including my father's. I learned little from those who knew the glider better. It was an uneasy reminder there were things we might never understand about Dad's death.

* * *

I had imagined Minden would mark my triumphant return following the unspeakable tragedy of my father's crash. Instead, day after day, my confidence and sense of belonging to that exclusive club of top challengers crumbled in the incessant wind as my name skidded down the scoresheet.

I landed out the last four days. Each morning after, I was more discomforted sitting in the pilots' meeting. I had lost that "winner's attitude" needed to succeed. Hell, the last few days, I was embarrassed just to be on the launch grid. I didn't belong there. It was as if I were once again a kid flying my little 1-26 against the *real* pilots at the Chester regional in 1970. I could imagine the top guys shaking their heads and asking behind my back, "What is *he* doing here?"

My only comfort was I kept flying, giving it my best. But if a positive attitude is necessary for success, a negative attitude guarantees failure. Near the end, I just hoped to avoid finishing at the bottom (I ended 49th of 65). At other contests, we would linger after the awards breakfast to chat, knowing we wouldn't see most folks for a year. This time, I couldn't wait to get on the road to Ohio.

LS3 in a field on last day at Minden, 1981. Trailer turned 90 degrees for loading.

The endless drive to Cincinnati degenerated into a forced march. Hours into it, our air conditioner blew up. That didn't matter in the high terrain of Wyoming. But on Day Two, we crawled across the low plains of Nebraska and Iowa in merciless sun, with 100°+F heat and high humidity, towels spread over the seats to absorb sweat, washcloths soaked in ice water around our necks, and Diane lying in back stricken by food poisoning. Disheartened, all I had to look forward to was the hope of expunging the entire experience from my memory.

Minden wasn't just disappointing. It was soul-crushing. The national contest I had hoped would lift me above the turmoil of the past year was, instead, humbling, dispiriting, and humiliating. In less than two weeks, Minden unraveled almost everything I had struggled to surmount and to become as a pilot—and to some extent as a person—in the 16 years since I had first soloed.

CHAPTER THIRTY-FIVE

First Responder

MINDEN'S DISASTER HAD ONE BENEFIT. It rekindled Mark's enthusiasm for soaring. He was now flying the new ASW 20 our partnership had bought with the insurance proceeds from the crash.

Our father's death had drawn us closer. We were never far apart, but we would catch up on holidays and other family reunions—and then not communicate for months. Now, having lost the father who had helped keep our family glued together for so many years, our relationship changed. Flying was one manifestation. After Minden, I continued to visit Cincinnati that summer so he and I could practice together. That's when, 15 months after my father's crash, I suffered another transformative event.

Journal Entry: September 12, 1981 (Caesar Creek Soaring Club, Ohio)

The gliders are back in the trailers after flying. We are swapping stories with other pilots on a pleasant, late summer Saturday afternoon. Mark is facing the approach end of the pattern, so he sees it first over my shoulder.

"Look out! Look out!" he shouts, his arm shooting up to point. We whirl around just in time to witness a nightmare.

Out of control! CCSC's heavy, all-metal Schweizer 2-32 glider—a type well known for its high stall speed and unforgiving spin entry—is nose down, rotating and falling, spinning in its characteristically near-vertical attitude. This is not a flying sailplane. It is a heavy object with long wings plunging straight down, spinning on its axis, as if someone had held it by its tail before dropping it, making little noise, only the air whispering along the airframe. Screams in the cockpit are trapped by the bubble canopy over the two seats.

The tragedy is maddening. Low in the pattern, a CCSC pilot giving a ride had almost certainly tried to skid the glider around in a shallow turn without adequate airspeed, feeding in rudder in a hopeless, uncoordinated attempt to avoid making a visually disconcerting-but-safer steep turn.

When the wing quit flying and the glider stalled, the 2-32 snapped into a spin, the lower wing pitching down sharply and the nose falling through. I'd seen this once before—a year earlier at Deer Creek State Park. Unlike with my father's crash, however, there was no apparent attempt to recover from the spin. Only a skillful pilot with experience and quick, counterintuitive reflexes could have saved it by pushing the stick forward to unstall the wings rather than instinctively pulling back, trying in vain to raise the nose.

It hits the ground 100 yards away with a BANG, like two cars colliding at an intersection. In a glider crash, though, there's no screech of tires. No explosion or flame or blaring horn as a body slumps against the steering wheel. No smell of burned rubber or gasoline or hot metal. No plume of smoke. Only the impact noise—then bystanders shouting and running.

Once again, I am one of the first on the scene. F**k! This is even more gruesome than my father's crash. I'm not queasy—I've seen it before—but the brief sense of helplessness is familiar. The vertical impact has destroyed the front section of the glider, compressing the forward fuselage and cockpit like a soda can. The front-seat pilot—a CCSC member I know from the old days—never regains consciousness. Seeing him reminds me—as I had learned at Dad's crash—human bodies can continue to make slight, involuntary movements during the short interval of unconsciousness before clinical death.

And then, the moment passes. We know what to do. Call 9-1-1. Send someone out to the road to help guide the ambulance into the hidden gravel drive. Tend to the passenger who, astonishingly, survives, although he will retain no memory of the event. Mark and I assist but we disappear before the rescue teams converge. I can't endure the aftermath of another crash.

I walk into my mother's house that night, dreading what I have to say. For the second time in 15 months, I need to unload, to share a horrific tale with someone to ease the pain welling up inside. In as gentle a way as I can, I relate what happened. As feared, she breaks down, confessing tearfully she knows the deceased pilot's wife and children. I learn later that Diane used to play with one of their daughters when our families were at the airport.

I try to sleep, but it's as if I am back in that Springfield hotel room, wracked by disturbing emotions and physical reactions. I lie awake, thrashing restlessly for hours, tortured by the nightmarish image of the pilot's brutalized body. Not even the most gruesome carnage depicted in the movies has prepared me for the way the crash fractured and rearranged it so grotesquely.

I banish that vision from my mind. Why torture myself with it? Then, in minutes, sometimes seconds, once again I am staring at the same vivid, grisly image of the pilot's broken corpse. My abdomen contracts painfully, drawing me into a near fetal position. Now I'm angry. This is stupid. It's f***king pathetic! What the hell is going on? I didn't even know this guy that well. It goes on for hours. At last, not long before dawn, as on the night my father died, I finally drift off and sleep fitfully.

The next day, I meet Mark at the gliderport. We strap on parachutes, and I make a flight with him in a two-seater to review spin recoveries. I don't want to deliver more sad news to my mother someday.

I hadn't known the deceased pilot well. So why had his death had a more visceral, corporeal effect on me than my father's? Years later, a psychologist friend opined that my reaction to this second crash could have been a delayed reaction to my father's death, a trigger that released emotions I had bottled up inside me then. I was unconvinced. It sounded like facile, psychological mumbo jumbo. I had dealt with my father's death just fine. This incident was an entirely different, unrelated episode.

Later—much later—I conceded she might be onto something.

CHAPTER THIRTY-SIX

Personal Best

W HY THE RUSH TO GET MARRIED? True, Kathy and I had already been together four years when she joined me the night of my father's crash. And, yes, during the following year, she did everything I could have asked to help me through that dark time. Most importantly, I was in love with her. And told her so often. And I envisioned our getting married someday.

"Someday" was the problem. I was the classic commitment-phobe, still unsure what I wanted. I needed her in my life. But after five years together, I still couldn't give her what she needed: a genuine commitment. I kept putting her off because I didn't want to discuss, really discuss, the serious decisions I needed to make. Cluelessly, I thought things were fine.

"Let's talk about it later."

Despairing more than I knew, Kathy saw no sign I would ever change. When I returned from Minden, she flew down from Boston after a TWA trip, as she had so many times over four years. She was dubious about the beard I'd grown in the Nevada desert and even more so about the Jeep CJ-7 that had replaced the scandalously unreliable BMW 320i she had talked me into three years before (there was a soft ripping sound as her pencil skirt split up the side when she climbed into the Jeep).

We caught up over dinner at a lovely restaurant. That night, she was unusually affectionate. So I was stunned at LaGuardia Airport the next day when, as she said goodbye, she told me it was for the last time. A year earlier, she had said the same thing there. I had talked her out of it then, as—emulating my father—I had often "reasoned" with the women in my life. This time, choking back tears, she was adamant. It was for the best, she said.

I've always questioned how her experiencing the immediacy of my father's accident might have affected her willingness to spend the rest of her life with me, knowing my commitment to flying. As a flight attendant, she flew every week. But she had remained dubious about my soaring. It had been frustrating trying to convince her it was safe—and damned near impossible after the crash.

Like many men, I realized only after I lost a true love how much she had meant. And of course there was the rejection, which we men seldom handle well. I was reeling, unable to sleep, eat, or function normally. I had experienced breakups before, but nothing like this. Kathy was the woman I had thought I would marry and with whom I would spend the rest of my life.

There's no optimal time for shocks like this, but from my anguished perspective, it was particularly devastating coming at the end of the soaring season, my traditional escape. It happened a month after my crushing failure at the Minden Nationals and a month before the fatal crash at our gliderport.

People say, "bad things come in threes." I call BS on that. In my experience, bad things more often come in fours and fives and sixes. Regardless, the summer of 1981 was an epically disastrous trifecta for me.

Once again, I turned to exercise as a coping mechanism. I hadn't run a marathon in two years, but I plunged into intense training, losing myself in the grueling miles and the attenuation of the pain in my heart they provided. I worked out mechanically, grimly logging up to 20 miles a day, five and six days a week.

Marathon training appealed because I could control it. And it offered a goal, the realization of which could restore my confidence. Mark had moved back to Richmond. So on the last Friday in October, I flew in for the 1981 Richmond Newspapers Marathon. I was on a mission to finish in 3 hours and 30 minutes—an 8-minute-per-mile pace, 15 minutes faster than my personal record (PR) two years earlier. I knew it was ambitious. But that's what I wanted, something to set me apart. A 3:30 wouldn't distinguish me among faster marathoners (the traditional bar for male marathoners is sub-3-hours). But it would satisfy my need to prove something, not just to myself, but to the woman who had left me.

On Saturday, we strolled around Richmond's picturesque Fan District in beautiful autumn weather. That night, I couldn't sleep, thinking of the race, Kathy, and how long it would be before I would feel normal. I gave up and lay there listening to rain until the alarm went off in the dark and people stirred.

Journal Entry: October 25, 1981 (Richmond, Virginia)

Overnight, the rain turned heavy and the temperature dropped to the low 40s F. I've run in rain many times, just never for 26 miles or for the most important race of my life. When the gun goes off, I'm wearing a light running jacket over a thin singlet and shorts. I warm up quickly. When I reach Janet, Mark's fiancée, at six miles, I toss the sodden jacket to her.

I'm not running for fun. Throughout the dismal morning, the "mission" is paramount. The only thing on my mind is sticking to my pace chart—to the second. Janet pops up here and there, smiling, cheerful and supportive. But no high-fives or grins from me. I am a humorless, focused running machine. The rain cycles between light and heavy, but never stops. It doesn't seem to discourage spectators, yet their cheering is not what is driving me.

After crossing the James River, I arrive at "The Hill," a long, awkwardly located—at mile 20—climb on everyone's mind. A mile later, at the top, I'm shocked to still feel strong. I had a big slowdown programmed into my pace chart at 20, where I expected to "hit the wall." So I toss the chart and run based on how my body feels. In these days before GPS watches, it's a mile or two before I realize I've actually sped up.

For months, I have driven myself relentlessly toward an objective, intent on proving myself to the woman with whom I had most wanted to share it. But as I speed through a park with a mile to go, pushing my body to its limits, my eyes begin to tear. Minutes from obliterating my target time, despair sweeps over me when I realize I have run this race—the race of my life—for the wrong reasons and for the wrong person. I accept Kathy is not in my life anymore and won't be waiting at the finish line to congratulate and hug me.

In fact, *no one* is waiting at the finish! Janet is still tending to Mark and a friend, who are running well behind me. In that pre-mobile-phone era, she arrives at the finish almost five minutes early for my targeted 3:30. But I'm even earlier. She settles in to wait but I'm already in the finish chute, exhausted and soaking wet, chilling dangerously in the mid-40s drizzle.

This should be one of the greatest moments of my life. I demolished my goal with a 3:25! Overshadowing that is emotional letdown and physical distress. As my core temperature and blood pressure plummet, I begin to shake. Someone rushes over to drape me with a heavy wool blanket and steers me to a bank of gas-fired industrial space heaters set up in a parking garage sheltered from the rain. For nearly an hour, I stand, then squat, then kneel in front of one, clutching the blanket flapping in the hot draft, shivering, brief waves of warmth penetrating unevenly through the soaked fabric of my clothing, and trying not to collapse. At last, my anxious group find me.

The Richmond Marathon remains my lifetime best. I'm still proud of training for and executing my "perfect" race. But as I will say about several other analogous experiences in life, I wish I'd been smart enough to enjoy it more. Then, a few weeks later, as I regained some perspective, I met the woman who would help me grow beyond the limitations that had hobbled me in the past.

CHAPTER THIRTY-SEVEN

"The One"

I FINALLY UNDERSTOOD WHAT ALL THE FUSS WAS ABOUT. For months, a guy in my office would not shut up about his best friend: "Tanya did this..." and "Tanya said that..." When we met at a Halloween party in Manhattan, it made sense. I was still emerging from the breakup with Kathy. But this woman would have floored me, anyway.

Tanya Lenkow was elegant, dark-haired, and exquisitely dressed in a classic orange Thierry Mugler dress with padded shoulders, tapering to a snug fit from the waist down. Her dark-eyed, exotic beauty and enigmatic smile spoke of her Eastern European origins. At age seven, she and her stepfather had hidden in the trunk of a car driven over the border from their home in Communist Bulgaria into Yugoslavia. The next night, they slipped into Austria the same way. Her mother, a Bulgarian translator already in Sweden, defected to join them on the way to Germany and then to the U.S. Tanya was one of the most intriguing women I had ever met. I assumed she was out of my league.

We encountered each other over the next few months at parties and Manhattan dance clubs with our mutual friend. We were opposites in so many ways. An introverted English major working in the publishing world, she loved literary fiction and New York culture, especially opera. I had become more outgoing, could talk about myself forever (still true), favored rock music and bestselling spy novels, and admitted to guilty pleasures such as television's *Charlie's Angels* and *Star Wars* movies. She smoked socially but adhered to a strict daily regimen at an exercise studio. I abhorred smoking and was a runner.

But something magical flowered in early 1982 when the three of us donned formalwear for a debutante ball at the Plaza Hotel in New York City. It was an excuse to gawk at privileged young women of society, eat mediocre food, drink cheap champagne, and dance. As the evening flowed, Tanya and I talked uninterrupted for hours, then ended up in her tiny studio apartment in the East 50s.

The next day, I was so depressed I was ill (the champagne hangover may have played a role). I had met the woman of my dreams. But in the cold, gray light of a dreary February day in New York, the prospects of a future together seemed as outrageous as any fantasy I had ever entertained.

To my immense joy, I was wrong. Within weeks, we were inseparable. We sampled neighborhood restaurants, went dancing every weekend, and had passionate discussions about everything that interested one or the other of us. She gave up smoking and started running. I began perusing *The New Yorker* and stopped complaining about movies with subtitles. Lust quickly evolved into infatuation and, almost as fast, blossomed into love. After scant months of this whirlwind relationship, wondering if I were on the rebound (definitely) or crazy (perhaps), I flew her to Cincinnati for two big tests.

The first test was introducing her to my mother. That was easy. She met us at the door: "Oh, she's so pretty!" Tanya's face lit up. I hadn't realized she was nervous. Fortunately, they bonded instantly, and on a much deeper basis.

The second test was less definitive. I drove her up to the Caesar Creek Soaring Club for her first glider ride. This is where my father and I had shared so much, where I still based my sailplane, and where I had begun to disappear every weekend to practice for the 1982 nationals.

The ideal way to introduce someone to soaring is on a cool, crisp, sunny day with lots of scenery: mountains, fall colors, etc. Take a few turns in a gentle thermal to climb up high, then tour the countryside in smooth glides pointing out the sights, including beautiful sailplanes swooping and turning close by.

Our first flight was anything but that: a hazy, warmer-than-usual spring day with endless circling in weak thermals at low altitude over a featureless landscape, with the sky a woozy, indistinct gray all around. We were the only ones in the air. It wasn't long before Tanya, trying to hold on for my sake, confessed she was feeling ill.

This wasn't my first time around the pattern, so to speak. One college girlfriend had fared better on a sweltering summer day, but another had gotten airsick on a perfect spring day after worrying herself into a frenzy of pre-launch anxiety. Kathy, a flight attendant, had no problems regardless of how I tossed the glider around. These four women with disparate reactions had one thing in common: *none* had any interest in flying apart from my obsession with it.

Regardless, I wasn't in love with Tanya because of her potential as a pilot. What really mattered would be her first experience crewing for me at the Nationals a few weeks later. From my self-absorbed perspective, I thought that outcome could determine our future together. Having this gorgeous woman by my side made me feel whole. But in a selfish and narrow-minded way, I could not envision life with someone who couldn't support me in soaring the way my mother had supported my father. I still needed someone to be there for me in this sport I had been pursuing for 17 years.

CHAPTER THIRTY-EIGHT

Meditations

I F ANYTHING, I FELT EVEN *MORE* PRESSURE at the 15 Meter Nationals in Elmira, New York, in 1982, than I had at Minden the year before. My humiliation there still stung, and I needed to believe I was a contender. Outwardly, I projected confidence. Inside, however, I was desperate to prove Minden had been a horrible aberration, a mismatch between my East Coast skills and Western geography. Conveniently, I overlooked the challenging terrain at Elmira, comprising hills and ridges in the Finger Lakes Region of upstate New York that could be almost as daunting as the mountains and high deserts of Minden. At least there were more places to land.

Journal Entry: June 30, 1982 (Elmira, New York)

On Day One, a squall line is bearing down on the Harris Hill airport perched above the city of Elmira. Some of us are already high and impatient to get out before the deluge obscures the ground. Go, go, go! We dive through the start gate, punch through the rain, and escape into the sunlight. Saved!

No. To our horror, we glide out into a sunny but absolutely dead sky. With rain blocking a retreat behind us, four sailplanes descend into the same plowed field, one after the other, some still spewing water ballast as we plow to an abrupt halt in the soft dirt.

F**k! In helpless fury, I pound my fist into the side of the cockpit, then sit, with an empty stare, stunned and disbelieving. Less than an hour after kick-off, I have blown the contest I have been planning for a year, ever since the debacle in Minden. As we stand in the field, the farmer arrives. I struggle to remain polite—this isn't his fault—while I recite my standard speech about the national contest and our launch from Harris Hill. Many residents know of it because of its rich history. I gesture vaguely in the direction of the Hill.

"It's not very far, I think."

"Yup," he responds laconically and points at a light-colored spot on a hill across the valley. "In fact, you can see it from here."

I'm almost physically ill. Brought to ground on Day One and I'm not even out of sight of the freakin' airport. No matter how bad things seem, they can always get worse. The deep rumble of thunder coming up the valley catches us by surprise. That squall line we escaped is now overrunning us with a wall of water. In minutes, the sun disappears, the sky darkens, the wind rises, and the temperature drops.

"Guys, we've got a different problem. I'm gonna climb in my glider to hold it down." This is a major league thunderstorm.

The four of us rush back to our gliders and climb in, pulling down the canopies. There's no time to turn the ships or stake down the upwind wingtips. The fierce storm hammers us hard. The rain lashing the field turns it into a sloppy, muddy stew. The airplane rocks and shudders in the gusts as I hold the control surfaces against the stops, hoping the wind will push the glider down and not get under the wing and blow it over. I squirm into and secure the seat belt and shoulder harness in case it does.

At last, the storm passes. As the light drizzle subsides, we open the canopies and step gingerly down into what has become a quagmire. Our crews arrived during the storm. Now the four tow vehicles and trailers are parked on the road at the end of the field, crews huddled inside. Members of the local volunteer fire department are also standing by.

The gliders are axle deep in mud. With no tractor to pull them out, we disassemble each glider, then awkwardly carry each wing and drag each fuselage to the edge of the field and into its trailer. Including the horizontal tail, that's four round trips for each sailplane through the steamy air and muck-filled furrows. When it's over, I can't even see my shoes; they're lumps of mud. My shoulders have dark bruises from planting the heavy LS3 wing spars on them and marching out. We are all sweaty, exhausted, and muddy.

Things can always get worse. The remnants of the storm dissipate, the sun reappears, and the day cooks off again. As we stow the last glider in its trailer, I peer up at what is now a nice soaring sky. On the short drive back to Harris Hill, incredulous, we listen to radio reports of late starters making progress around the course. My world is ending. I sit in the van with my head down and eyes closed, thinking I should just check out of the motel and return to Ohio. Fortunately (selfishly), too few pilots fly minimum distance. It's a no-contest day. We'll begin anew tomorrow. I still feel stupid. But on this rare occasion, I have been given a second chance.

When the contest resumed, I started strong with two top-ten finishes in a row. This was more like it! I was lying fifth overall and pleased with myself when Tanya arrived from New York. Her delayed arrival gave me time to reassure my mother that having my new girlfriend at the contest—something I had done only once before, with Kathy in Cordele—would not be a distraction.

Having Tanya there wasn't a problem, but the weather after she arrived was. It forced us to fly lower over the hilly terrain. That pushed me inexorably down the scoresheet until, mid-contest, for a dismal third time in my soaring career, I teetered on the edge again.

Journal Entry: July 7, 1982 (Elmira, New York)

The already marginal day is deteriorating and I'm only halfway around the course. I'm thermaling at 800 feet with another glider circling just above. We're in survival mode, sustaining altitude, too low to search for another thermal. We're not sinking, but as the wind drifts us toward a line of rising hills, our ground clearance is shrinking. Intellectually, I know if I can't climb out, I can land in an inviting field below. Emotionally, however, the urgency is growing. This thermal will never go up. I must *do* something!

Above me, the other glider continues to circle. He *must* be in lift. I'll never climb out of here! Round and round we go, not gaining a foot. As our terrain clearance dwindles, I talk to myself to remain logical as the pressure rises. But it doesn't work. Once again, emotional distress overpowers my rational self. I simply give up. Impulsively, just as on those miserable days in Bryan and Minden, I abandon the fight, pull the dive brakes out, and dive into an inviting plowed field below. The instant the glider schusses to a halt in the soft earth, I know I've made a massive mistake. WTF is going on? This is the third time I've choked. I'm flooded by a nearly unbearable sense of failure.

In contrast, Tanya is bubbly when my crew arrive. This is her first retrieve, and it's an exciting adventure! [Her attitude will "evolve" over many future landouts!]. Doesn't she realize she's not allowed to have fun if I'm not?

This time, I think we can roll rather than carrying the heavy LS3 out of the field. As we get ready to walk out to it, I point to her flip-flop sandals:

"Your running shoes will probably work better in the dirt."

"No, I'll be fine," Tanya counters, firmly.

I disagree, but she pushes back. I pause to consider whether it's worth risking our relationship or her enthusiasm for crewing. Then I concede. We have barely begun to roll the glider when Tanya's flip-flop catches in the dirt and gives up, the strap popping through the sole and dangling on her foot. We all stop. It's quiet. No one says anything. As Diane and my mother exchange furtive glances, Tanya yanks off the offending sandals, tosses them in the cockpit, and continues in her bare feet.

I tried to persuade myself I'd done the smart thing by abandoning the low save. Back at Harris Hill, I even discussed it with the other pilot, who had capped my pathetic flameout by patiently climbing away and going on a few more miles. When he saw me snap out of the thermal, nose over, and land, he worried I'd had a problem. A cerebral type from a research environment, he encouraged me to be honest with myself.

"Chip, you have some history. It's possible that's still having an effect on your flying." He paused while choosing his words with care. "Maybe you should consider if fear could be playing a role."

Instinctively, my face tightened as I opened my mouth to cut him off. I wasn't troubled that he knew about my father's crash. I suspect everyone did. But I was in no mood to discuss this.

"I hear what you're saying. But that was several years ago." We stood there, silent. I looked down, unable to hold his gaze, and continued in a milder tone: "Anything is possible, but I think I'm beyond that now."

Who wants to admit being afraid? Sure, if a grizzly bear is charging you or the IRS decides you're a tax cheat or your spouse hires an expensive divorce attorney, only a fool wouldn't cringe. But circling at low altitude? I had never been relaxed there, but I had always managed it. I was forced to admit something fundamental was broken. Anxiety had once again quashed rational thought, which I had always believed was my greatest strength.

Tanya enjoyed her first contest. She leaped into the role so effortlessly that Diane admitted feeling threatened. She had been crewing for me for 15 years and now this attractive young woman, who clearly meant something to me, was taking her place. I should have been delighted I had finally found someone who could be my partner in soaring. But that was offset by my final place slipping to a disappointing, albeit not-humiliating 15th. When the contest mercifully ended, I wasn't sure I would ever recover the skills and ease I had once enjoyed.

* * *

I blamed my setbacks at Minden and Elmira on being ill-prepared for the terrain at these venues. However, upon further reflection, I conceded my personal breakdowns were due at least as much to my increased nervousness and reduced ability to think clearly when I was flying at low altitude or in other stressful situations. With my father gone, I had no one to discuss this with. Few pilots at my club had significant competitive experience.

So at the end of each local flight, I forced myself to circle at low altitude over the airport. At first, it was difficult and visually alarming to watch the ground spin around below me, knowing I was seconds away from disaster. Sometimes when circling low, it seems you are close to impacting the ground, with trees and fences passing under the wing in alarming proximity.

Over time, it became easier. There was no sudden realization, no moment when I could announce "I'm cured," no stirring music from a movie soundtrack as the hero conquers his fear and rescues the heroine. I still wasn't happy at low altitudes. I never had been. But I could feel the improvement as I became less susceptible to panic and impulsive behavior.

I was tested a few months later flying at a regional contest in Ionia, Michigan, to prepare for the Nationals there the following year.

Journal Entry: September 3, 1982 (Ionia, Michigan)

I've been in the cockpit for over five hours, pushing hard but flying alone most of the time on a blue day. Gliding into the wind with the sun in my eyes, I know the end of the flight is near. It's been smooth since the last thermal miles back. I'm down to 1,200 feet. Time to pick out a landing spot.

Then, a gift! I feel a surge where, by all rights, there shouldn't be a thermal at this hour. It's weak, but I roll up the LS3 firmly but gently on a wingtip and I *know*, with innate certainty, that it's going up all the way around, a real thermal! This is it—my last chance. I need at least 500 feet to get up to final glide altitude. I crank up in the soft, smooth, weak, steady evening lift and make the call: I need climb rate more than I need cruise speed. So out goes the ballast. With water vaporizing from the wings and the audio vario singing softly like a lullaby, my fingers fervid and delicate on the controls, I milk this dying flower of a thermal circle by circle like it is my last chance in the world, pleading, begging, whispering, "Don't stop, please!"

Not knowing is the worst. The thermal could quit anytime. I climb in this weak updraft, still drifting back in the headwind. When I started, I was 500 feet short. Now 350 feet. Then I need just 200 feet more. Finally, with a sigh of the variometer audio tone, the climb rate settles to zero just as my calculator says I have exactly enough altitude to finish. Ten miles out at 1,700 feet. Into wind. No safety margin. I feel like my old self. Go for it!

The odd-shaped field I had picked out earlier as a landmark to help guide me in is glimmering ahead under a thin coverlet of soft haze. Barely visible beyond it is the smudge that should be the airport. It's gonna be close. I hate marginal final glides. And yet, there's something perversely alluring about them, like a dangerous drug. I would never take this risk at home flying for fun. But this isn't for fun. It's a competition. It's okay to take chances.

The air is smooth: no sink, no lift, no disturbances. I know the last few miles before Ionia are strewn with landable fields. I stare at the east-west runway, foreshortened by altitude, high on the canopy, growing closer. Gliding down through 500 feet, I should be in a landing pattern, but I'm still on glide path.

"Juliet Bravo, one mile. Straight in, very low."

"Juliet Bravo, winds are 10 knots out of the west. Preferred landing is runway two-eight."

The sunlit LS3 materializes from the haze, stretching for the finish line, the wings rock steady, parallel to the horizon, the fuselage at a constant angle with no wasted motion to disturb the airflow. One of Charlie Spratt's sharp-eyed spotters with binoculars shouts out,

"There he is, just to the right of the trees. Wow, he's low!"

I know I can reach the last field before the runway. But it's full of high corn. What to do? Pull the dive brakes and set it down before that, or go for it? It's not really a decision.

As I slide down through 200 feet, the cornfield looms ahead. That could damage the glider, even trigger a ground loop. Fighting an impulse to play it safe by landing short of the corn, I glide on, still sinking. I'm past the point of no return. Then I clear the corn by less than a wingspan and straighten out over the centerline of the paved runway. The LS3 settles down into ground effect, the cushiony layer of air compressed by the wings that helps buoy an aircraft when it's very close to the ground, ten feet above the tarmac.

I must cross the finish line halfway down the runway, flying or rolling. I let the glider float along, bleeding off airspeed. The gate crew interrupt loudly on the radio to remind me my wheel is still up. When I hear Charlie Spratt's familiar "Mark...Juliet Bravo, good finish," I snap the gear and flaps down, and, seconds later, grease the wheel onto the runway with a light touch. Wanting to savor the victory, I let it roll, coasting to a stop where my mother awaits, relieved but all smiles.

I'm back! Relief and elation flood me as I grin widely. There's no feeling like pushing a marginal final glide, knowing most pilots would not have gambled, and making it in the last seconds! After a string of embarrassing misfires, cold reasoning has prevailed over nervous panic. That old fear of choking under pressure is gone. I can't wait to redeem myself here next year.

But I *had* celebrated too soon. The following spring at the rain-shortened Nationals at the same airport in Ionia, I solidified my status as a mid-pack contender with an underwhelming 16th place finish.

After Minden and Elmira, I had consoled myself, blaming my poor showings on the terrain at those venues. But back on my home turf in Ionia, I had to face the truth. At age 32, I had peaked. My best years were behind me. And that quote I'd lifted from *On the Waterfront* six years ago was no longer amusing.

"I coulda been a contender. I coulda been somebody, instead of a bum, which is what I am."[24]

Was Minden the turning point, the debacle that arrested my progress and threatened to seal my fate for the future? Or to be more accurate, was it the first sign that something had changed because of my father's crash?

I'm not sure it mattered. As a young pilot, I achieved success and showed even greater promise for the future. When I review those results, I see a pilot who, on his good days, was flying head-to-head against the country's best.

Yet for three years, I had failed to reestablish that status. And that meant more to me than I had realized. In the decade before my father's crash, my contest successes had boosted my self-assurance and ease with whom I was. As I slid down the scoresheets, the reverse proved true.

In the "silver lining" category, there was one happy outcome from the 1983 Ionia Nationals. I met the pilot who was to help me get my soaring career turned around and moving in the right direction again—and to become my best friend.

---

[24] *On the Waterfront*, ibid.

CHAPTER THIRTY-NINE

X-ray Tango

MY FATHER HAD BEEN GONE THREE YEARS. Yet I continued to commute to Cincinnati from New Jersey to fly. Did that make sense? Not according to Robert Robertson.

I recalled seeing Robert ("Robbie" to most, but he preferred the formal form) at the 1982 Elmira Nationals in XT (X-ray Tango), his new 15 Meter Ventus sailplane, but we first met at the Ionia Nationals a year later. Robert was a quirky, likeable, good-looking 40-year-old Englishman, with an infectious grin and a Type-A personality. Except in the cockpit, he was always accompanied by Ciara Gowrie (pronounced "Shara"), his loud, territorial German shepherd.

Midway through the contest, he needed a crew for a few days. He seemed to bring out the maternal instincts in women so several alerted him my sister was arriving mid-contest. My mother and Tanya had me covered, so Robert hustled over, introduced himself with a smile, and begged for Diane's help.

When she arrived, she was unhappy to learn I had casually loaned her to an unknown pilot, like a spare battery or lug wrench. It didn't help that Tanya was doing such a fantastic job as my crew. But Diane took a liking to Robert (and Ciara). We started hanging out after the flying. By the time the contest was over, he had persuaded me to move my glider to Wurtsboro, New York, 60 miles northwest of New York City on the edge of the Catskill Mountains.

Shifting my gliding home base to Wurtsboro after 18 years in Cincinnati was a *big* deal. But I was excited. Commuting from the East Coast wasn't practical long term. And this was a chance to have a regular flying partner again.

Robert was smart, articulate, nine years older, divorced, and over-the-top besotted with soaring. He was beginning to show well at the national level in what became a sprint to the top. A former amateur race car builder/driver in Europe with skill, passion, and a fiercely competitive core, he took to sailplanes with the same energy and obsession, flying whenever possible. He put 250 hours on his Ventus the first year he owned it, roughly four times my annual average. When not flying, he invested hundreds of hours improving the glider.

Like me, he was mechanically inclined. He once confessed his most enjoyable job had been tending to the machinery in his family's U.K. factory, producing Robertson's jams and marmalades before they sold the business. After emigrating to America in the 1970s, he bought some land at the northern edge of ritzy Greenwich, Connecticut. Guided by a do-it-yourself homebuilding book and with help from friends in construction, he built his home himself.

He leveraged that into a career building and renovating houses. Managing his investment portfolio brought in some income, so he became an early member of what we refer to today as the gig economy, working when he needed to or felt like it. This allowed him to ski for a month in St. Anton, Austria, each winter and fly soaring contests in the U.S. in the spring, summer, and fall.

He usually dressed like he had been on a job site or working on his glider. He didn't endear himself to the Greenwich gentry as a tradesman in the ratty Chevrolet van he used for business and soaring. But he didn't much care.

Robert Robertson finishing task, New Castle, Virginia, 1982. (photos from his estate)

He was not above making concessions, though. Not long after he started seeing a young woman, he stopped by the local Porsche dealer to investigate upgrading his ride. He left angrily when they sized him up as unworthy of the marque. We laughed out loud. Robert could have driven their cars far more competently than the sales reps and written a check for any vehicle on the lot.

He had received an upper-class boarding-school-to-European-university education and spoke German, French, and Spanish. Yet he displayed few of the pretensions we Americans might expect. His Greenwich home juxtaposed handmade cabinetry, heirloom furniture, oriental carpets, and fine silver and china, with barnwood siding, unscreened windows, and half-finished rooms. The moderate climate didn't mandate air conditioning, but I never grew accustomed to the fly strips hanging up in the corners.

At Wurtsboro, I was soon in the cockpit every soarable weekend. Robert and I encouraged (some might say enabled) each other, as my father and I had. The difference was that Wurtsboro pilots Robert, George Moffat, and Doug Jacobs were much better than my father. Soaring is like most sports. If you want to improve, play with people better than you.

In a brief time, Doug Jacobs had risen to the top in the U.S. Two years later,

Doug Jacobs
National 15-Meter Class Champion

Doug Jacobs after his first National Championship. Soaring, January 1983. Used with permission.

he would become a world champion himself, spread-eagling the international field in the mountains 40 miles northeast of Rome. But Doug earned my respect before I ever met him, not only for his flying skills and courage, which were prodigious, but for his act a few weeks after my father crashed.

A relative newcomer, he was near the top ten late in the Standard Class Nationals when he witnessed a competitor crash in a field below him. Doug unhesitatingly landed to help, forfeiting the chance to finish high in his first big U.S. contest. No matter, he was on the way up and won his first nationals two years later at the same site, Elmira, at the contest where I encountered Robert.

One pleasure of hanging around with Robert was getting to know George and Suzanne Moffat. George had recognized Robert's talent early on and mentored him. Tanya and I often shared dinner with the three of them after flying at Wurtsboro and at contests. This gave us insight into another dimension to this extraordinary couple, a dimension not directly associated with soaring.

One evening found us discussing poetry at the Moffats' home. I knew teaching English wasn't just a day job George suffered to pay the bills for sailing and soaring. But literature had never come up in conversation. That night, I mentioned falling in thrall with Dylan Thomas's work when I first read it, especially the well-known poem "Do Not Go Gentle Into That Good Night."

George hesitated. Could he have been debating whether to inform me, since I seemed to be clueless, that Thomas wrote this poem as an anguished reaction to his father's imminent death? He pulled an album from their LP collection and queued it up on the turntable. I'd never heard the voice before, but it was so remarkable and commanding as it intoned *"rage, rage, against the dying of the light,"*[25] I knew at once it was the poet himself reading his iconic poem.

Later, I listened to George reading to his high school English students from countercultural poet Richard Brautigan's "Horse Child Breakfast." This occurs early in *The Sunship Game*[26], *the* definitive film on competitive soaring, shot in cinéma vérité style at the U.S. Nationals in Marfa, Texas in 1969, shortly after the poem was published. The brief ode to an enigmatic blonde intimated of a more complex, more romantic personality than the impassive, highly analytical front George maintained in our world. The final line, *"what you're doing to me, I want done forever"*[27] was ironic given what happened to each of us later.

I could imagine George quoting to Suzanne (even though she wasn't a blonde), her gazing up at him with the adoring eyes and beatific smile we often saw. As Suzanne and Tanya were both beautiful, intelligent, educated, self-reliant women, I imagined a certain kinship with George. All I had to do was win a few nationals and maybe a world championship, and he and I could be peers!

In the spring, he would be at Wurtsboro on weekends to assess small enhancements he had made to his glider for the upcoming season. I was also tuning my LS3. We compared different thermaling flap settings and speeds. We also glided together to compare straight-line performance. I would fly lead, with XX positioning himself less than a wingspan to one side, a twitch of the wrist away from touching wings. George would direct me to fly at different airspeeds for two minutes while he assessed if our relative performance had changed.

"Okay, Jake Baker, increase to 80 knots."

"Roger, eight-zero knots."

I wanted to pinch myself. In what other sport would a guy like me be flying one-on-one with the man who had won two world championships?

Our little Wurtsboro competition coterie would set off cross-country whenever we could remain aloft, even if thermals barely existed, adapting our daily tasks to avoid unnecessary landouts. I used this opportunity to try different

---

[25] Thomas, Dylan, *Collected Poems 1934-1953* (Great Britain: Phoenix, 1998)

[26] *The Sunship Game,* directed by Robert Drew, Drew Associates, 1970. Film. Digitally remastered, rereleased in 2010 https://drewassociates.com/films/the-sun-ship-game/

[27] Brautigan, Richard. "Horse Child Breakfast." *The Pill vs. the Springhill Mine Disaster,* (San Francisco: Four Seasons Foundation, 1968) Available at http://www.brautigan.net/pill.html

tactics and strategies against some of the best pilots in the world—with no points at stake. This, coupled with knowing I was a member of an elite group, gave me the confidence to push ahead aggressively as I had in the past.

To my dismay, this didn't translate into higher contest placings. My fall from the pantheon of serious contenders was never more glaring than one night after Robert had been reading back issues of *Soaring* magazine. He had seen my name in multiple contest results from the pre-crash era.

"You were really good," he said, trying to help.

Harsh. That's like a woman saying, "You used to be good in bed."

Robert knew my flying better than most, so his candid assessment was disheartening. When we met, I had arguably been the better contest pilot. In a few years, he had vaulted past me (and many others) on his way up.

But he was correct. In the nine years after entering my first regional contest flying competitive equipment, I had won eight SSA medallions, awarded to the top pilots in each regional and national class. My tally in the five years since my father crashed? Zero. What was I doing wrong?

During any soaring flight, expert pilots make decisions constantly. So which of mine were faulty? Sometimes it's obvious, e.g., starting too early or too late. Other times, a pilot returns from a satisfying flight, only to discover others have rocketed around the course in what they describe as an entirely different sky. It's like walking out of an appalling movie, then learning the same film is on everyone else's shortlist for the Oscars. What did they see that you missed?

* * *

That first summer, Robert became more than a flying buddy. On weathered-out weekends, Tanya and I would stay over in his guest room. Not unexpectedly, we discussed soaring, *endlessly* according to Tanya, who listened to us over breakfast, lunch, dinner, around the fireplace, and all times in between. My experiences fascinated him. He wanted to absorb it all.

At first, he was circumspect in guarding his personal life. He was English, after all. But as we shared flying, casual weekends, ski trips, camping/windsurfing weekends with girlfriends, and confidences, our trust in each other and our friendship deepened. We discussed books, movies, and music; our careers; our families; our love lives; and our frustrations and challenges.

He was an unconventional spirit with a good bit of pranksterish boy in him, too, once he got to know you. We had similarly dry and offbeat senses of humor and delighted in poking fun at various figures in soaring. One frequent target of Robert's more acerbic comments was "The Woman to Whom I Was Unfortunately Once Married." This caustic bitterness was not out of character. Robert was likable and generous. However, he was also a man of entrenched sensitivities, hair-trigger reactions, and deep-seated grudges.

The same fire that drove him competitively sometimes flickered to life in more mundane situations—usually involving some figure of authority—exacerbated by his sharp wit. Tanya and I laughed as he recounted his confrontation with a security officer at LaGuardia Airport a few years earlier. Robert was carrying a bag containing his backpack parachute to try on in the sailplane he planned to order from the dealer in Atlanta.

"Sir, you can't take that on the plane with you."

"I most certainly can. And I shall."

"No, sir, you can't."

"Why not?"

"For security reasons, sir."

"It's not a weapon. It's not a threat to anyone. You can search me. I'm not carrying anything dangerous."

"We understand, sir. But it's against our policy."

"Where? Show me the policy. Right. You can't. Because it's not in there, is it?" *[He may have been right; current TSA regulations allow parachutes in carry-on baggage and it's hard to believe things are more relaxed since 9/11.]*

"Sir, you can take it with you, but you'll have to check it."

"Absolutely not. I'm not taking a chance you'll lose it. Or damage it. I insist on bringing it with me. There's nothing in your policy that says I can't."

"Sir, we'll give you a tag for it to go into checked baggage. We won't lose it."

"You can't guarantee that. And it's worth over $1,000, so you won't replace it if you lose it, will you?"

This was pre 9/11, so with the clock ticking down to departure time, the airline capitulated, and Robert boarded the plane in triumph. The compromise involved a flight attendant stowing his parachute in a cabin luggage bin.

Robert had other scrapes with authority figures, including beach attendants; ski lift operators; police officers; doctors; lawyers; civil servants; Greenwich's old-money guardians of the gentility; and even a few soaring pilots. But most people got on with him well—if he respected them and/or they respected him.

We learned more about his family—his mother had passed, but we met his father when he visited—and his past, including the open-wheel racing car crash that hospitalized him and brought that chapter of his life to a close. When he tried soaring in the U.K. and discovered he could continue to fly long after he would lose the razor-sharp reflexes needed to race cars, he went all in.

Robert knew my father's story, although they had never met. We talked about the dangers and the chance, however remote, that we could die in a glider crash. We both dismissed that possibility. I learned later he had discussed it with his German girlfriend, Ilsa, with the same reassurances, viz., such catastrophes only befell pilots who didn't have our experience, our skills, our attitudes—in short, pilots who lacked *the right stuff*.

Tanya and I had gone with him to see the much-ballyhooed movie based on Tom Wolfe's book of the same name.

"What did you think?" I asked as we exited the theater.

"I was disappointed. The flying scenes were kind of cheesy."

Tanya tried to shift the subject. "Sam Shepard looked pretty good."

I offered a male perspective. "He ought to; he's shacking up with Jessica Lange."

"Oh, please," she responded, rolling her eyes and sighing.

"It was a long movie. Much too long. And there wasn't enough flying," Robert complained.

I agreed. "Yeah, and the flying scenes were pretty amateurish. I was surprised after all the hype."

Robert concluded our recap with: "One thing is true, though: Chuck Yeager really did have *the right stuff*."

So did we, we believed.

* * *

Robert was an exacting craftsman in metal, wood, and composites. Before soaring, he had built his own racing car. After constructing all the kitchen cabinetry for the house he built, he began taking commissions for custom mahogany furniture.

He delighted in modifying his racing machines to extract the last fraction of performance. In the winter of 1985, we moved my LS3 wings into his workshop and I commuted there several nights a week and weekends. With his help on the spray gun shooting polyester gel coat, I brought my LS3 airfoil back into shape again while teaching him a few tricks for making good sailplanes even better. But unlike those who are happiest in the workshop, for Robert this was only a means to an end. His first love was flying.

At the 1985 15 Meter Nationals in Cordele, Georgia, XT continued his climb toward the top. Frustrated, I had my second-worst contest, finishing 42nd of 61.

Robert soon tackled more advanced performance-enhancing projects on his glider. He was a perfectionist. Many pilots admired his upgrades. Few knew he often went through half a dozen or more iterations before he was satisfied.

In Europe to ski, he stopped by the German factory that had built his Ventus and struck up a friendship with Klaus Holighaus, the owner, designer/builder, and extraordinary pilot. In 1986, Klaus shipped the parts to upgrade XT to the latest version. One afternoon, I received an unusual telephone call from Robert.

"I'm installing the new winglets [the now ubiquitous turned up wingtips]. And I cut slightly too much off the ends of the wingtips."

"What's slightly too much?"

"6 mm. I measured wrong."

"Per wing, or total?"

"Total, each wing is short by half that."

"That's a quarter inch…hang on…like four hundredths of one percent. Say, 3 or 4 points over a long contest. That's not much. What are you going to do?"

"What would *you* do?"

"Do you want to know what *I* would do—or what I think *you* should do?"

"What *you* would do."

"I'd find a way to make it right. But that's just me. It's probably more work than it's worth."

"That's what I thought you'd say. I better get back in the shop."

Robert and I both had dreams of winning a place on the U.S. Team and qualifying for the world championships. Mine seemed out of reach. His seemed to be materializing when he capped a breakthrough season by winning the 1986 U.S. 15 Meter National Championship trophy in August in Uvalde, Texas.

Tanya and I were excited. We knew how much this meant to him. The dazed pride as he spoke when I rang him the morning after the contest was inspiring. Maybe my time would come.

CHAPTER FORTY

Dark Days

"**W**HAT IS THE MAN *THINKING?*" I recall mumbling, shaking my head and staring at the phone after hanging up that gray, gusty Sunday morning on August 24, 1986. We had given Robert a week to recover after he and his crew, Rod Read, returned from Texas, before inviting him over for dinner to celebrate his big win. We hadn't seen him in a month. That morning, he rang to beg off.

"Chip," he chirped brightly, "I'm going flying!"

Rushing up to Wurtsboro a few days after two weeks of all-out flying in the debilitating heat of Southwest Texas and a 24-hour non-stop return drive suggested Noël Coward's line about only mad dogs and Englishmen going out in the midday sun. But Robert's penchant for flying was irrepressible. Possessed of the furious energy of a man 20 years younger, he always gave 100%. Soaring had become his passion later in life, and he burned even more intensely for it.

We were disappointed, but we would get around to it soon. That afternoon, I studied occasional breaks of sun in the blustery sky. Before dinner, Tanya entered the bedroom as I walked out of the shower. She looked so serious.

"Chip, sit down."

I resisted. "What is it?"

"Please, sit down." I had never heard her use this tender, nervous, but insistent voice before. Over the next 25 years, I heard her use it just twice more. I wonder if we all have a voice that we find—and use—only in certain situations. She touched my arm gently, looking into my eyes. Something was different.

"What's going on?" I responded, growing impatient.

"Please, just sit down." Again, that voice.

She had me concerned, but not alarmed. I let her guide me to the bed and settled on it, impatient. "Just tell me what's wrong."

A few seconds later, I knew. A Wurtsboro friend had called with the concussive news that a few hours earlier, Robert had died in a freak glider accident.

I sat there, unmoving. I knew better than to ask, "Are you sure?" Yet it didn't seem possible. Robert was only 44. It was six years after my father's death. I'd had the pleasure of his company for only three years.

I had been numb ever since, going through the motions in a kind of trance. Robert was more than a soaring buddy. He was my closest friend. His death shook me almost as much as my father's had. Except at age 35, I was better able to respond now.

Robert between good friends Klaus Holighaus (l) and Eric Mozer (r) on the podium at Uvalde, 1986. Inside of ten years, two of these three pilots would die in gliding accidents. (photo credit: Mick Kilbourne)

I could have mouthed the same weary clichés about Robert going out the right way—with his boots on. I heard it so many times in subsequent days from our friends. But that schmaltzy last scene from the "B" movie in my head had evolved from corny to tiresome to dispiriting.

The flight that killed Robert was neither for fun *nor* practice. Karl Striedieck was planning to replace his venerable ASW 20 with either an LS6 (the successor to the LS3) or a Ventus. He had flown against both, but it's difficult to draw conclusions in a contest when you don't know how heavy each one is, where the CG is, etc. The answer was a direct, head-to-head comparison flight under controlled conditions to compare the gliders, not the pilots. Karl had borrowed Doug Jacobs' LS6 to fly against Robert in his Ventus.

They were thwarted at Wurtsboro. The commercial gliding operation on the edge of the mountains had shut down. Ceiling and visibility were acceptable, a reported 4,000 feet broken cloud layer. But there was a 15-knot crosswind gusting to 30 knots across the primary runway. Robert and Karl believed they could have towed up behind one of Wurtsboro's powerful L-19 towplanes from a seldom-used grass cross runway oriented into the wind. *[Years later, I concurred, after launching from the same runway in even worse conditions.]* But the airport owners judged it too strong to operate safely, as was their right.

Aviation safety experts speak of the *accident chain*, the sequence of events leading to disaster. If the pilot can break only one link of the chain, the accident won't occur. One can argue that the first link in the chain was Robert and Karl deciding to proceed with their plans despite the marginal weather. The second link was when the two of them, not predisposed to being told "no," drove 12 miles downwind from Wurtsboro to Randall Airport at Middletown, New York. This smaller-scale glider setup had also shuttered operations. But their runway was "only" 60 degrees off the wind line vs. 90 degrees at Wurtsboro. More important, Randall was out in the flats, far enough downstream of the mountains to escape the violent turbulence that could spill over the hills and pound us at low altitude when we launched from Wurtsboro.

The third link in the chain was Middletown's towplane not being as powerful as Wurtsboro's: not unsafe, just less margin for error given the heavy gliders. Middletown agreed to tow the two visiting U.S. champions, but only after an owner there—who knew them both well—launched first to evaluate the conditions. That owner, an experienced, long-time soaring pilot/towpilot and future national champion and U.S. Team member, briefed the towpilot extensively. Airspeed was the primary criterion. The owner instructed him to delay climbing out until he achieved it. The only obstacle were high-voltage power lines 1½ miles beyond the departure end of the runway. If the towplane's power was borderline, they could fly along at low altitude, gaining airspeed until approaching the wires before climbing. This risk-mitigation strategy wasn't unsafe, *per se,* but there was less margin for error.

The first launch—of the owner's unballasted glider—was uneventful. The owner released from the tow, thermaled up, and radioed the go-ahead.

Robert and Karl had ballasted their gliders up to their maximum allowable gross weights for the test flight, making the Ventus 400 pounds heavier than the ASW 20 that had just launched. This was the fourth link in the chain. Again, not unsafe; just less margin for error.

The next launch, with Robert, went hideously wrong. The towplane was slow to get the heavily laden Ventus up to flying speed. They never achieved sufficient takeoff velocity. Based on eyewitness accounts, XT, weighing over 1,100 lbs., finally lifted off *after* the towplane broke ground (the reverse of the normal sequence) and staggered up less than a wingspan off the ground before leveling out in ground effect. But that's as high as it could climb at the slow airspeed. I don't know when Robert realized it was too late to abort the tow and land on the runway, but foregoing this choice was the fifth link in the accident chain.

The two aircraft passed the departure end of the runway. Instead of staying low to gain airspeed, the towplane began to climb away. It's unclear whether the pilot was trying to claw his way above treetop height or had reverted to normal towing procedure. The towrope—anchored by the struggling glider bobbing behind—pulled the towplane's tail down, causing it to slow even more. The higher the towplane staggered, the steeper the angle was on the towrope. As this angle steepened, the towplane's airspeed deteriorated further. This was a dangerous feedback loop. Somewhere in here is the sixth link. By then, the tow was beyond the runway. Aborting it would have committed Robert to setting down in high corn—at maximum takeoff weight. He would have survived, but the landing gear might not have.

The terrified towpilot, at full power, but near stall speed, was about to release the towrope and dive to regain speed when the sailplane abruptly destabilized and turned nose up, out of control. It climbed steeply like a kite, soaring past the towplane hanging on the prop with the engine revving futilely.[28]

No one knows whether Robert released the towrope as the glider slowed in the climb, or the automatic tow release disengaged on its own. But in an instant, the tension on the towrope relaxed, freeing the towplane. The shaken towpilot pushed forward to recover safe airspeed and returned to land.

Not so for the glider. One pilot on the ground at the launch described seeing the top of the sailplane from behind as it soared up steeply, then slowed dramatically as if it were "hung up on the wall like a picture." Robert used the remaining velocity to push over, rotating into a steep nose-down attitude, like a diver coming off a diving board in a lazy jackknife. He regained flying speed as he plummeted and began to pull out. Tragically, there wasn't enough altitude. Partway through that terrifying plunge and recovery from the dive, the ground rushed up and met the falling sailplane in a field of standing corn. The high rate of descent and flattish impact angle were similar to my father's crash in PG.

Robert hadn't weighed enough to reach the factory's new maximum allowable gross weight, even with full ballast tanks. So in Texas, he had lashed two fabric bags of lead shot to the Ventus spars with a stout nylon towing strap. He knew the danger. We had discussed how my father had been hit in the back of

---

[28] There is debate about what caused this abrupt "kiting" maneuver. one theory is that the Ventus tail stalled and dropped, precipitating the nose-up, out-of-control climb.

the skull by a battery pack that came loose in his crash. But Robert assured me the nylon strap was strong enough. This was the last link (or first, chronologically speaking) in the accident chain.

Robert was correct; the strap didn't break. But one of the fabric shot bags did. It split open, instantly dispersing a cloud of lead shot (after the crash, the cockpit was incongruously littered with small lead pellets). That released the tension on the strap and allowed the other shot bag to slither out in the fraction of a second after impact and slam into Robert's skull.

I drove to Middletown the day after the accident, interviewed some of the parties, spoke with the FAA investigators, and helped carry the wreckage out of the field and into the trailer. This time, unlike with my father's crash, I didn't have to speculate about the glider's center of gravity. I had XT's paperwork showing the calculations to raise the approved gross weight and bring the CG to the aft limit allowed by Klaus Holighaus, who had flown with him a few weeks earlier at the Nationals. The rumors that had begun to emerge (and would persist for years) that Robert had lusted after a national championship to the extent he had exceeded the safe limits of his glider appeared to be unfounded.

* * *

Robert's elderly father, Donald, was too frail and discouraged to make the journey to the U.S. from his cottage in a small village in Scotland. He requested only that his son be cremated. Within days, an older couple, close friends of his, arrived on the Concorde to act on his behalf. Robert's agitated girlfriend, Ilsa, also arrived about the same time, in tears, from Germany. She settled into the bedroom she had shared with Robert, with the staid British couple fearful she was moving in for the long haul.

A few days later, we drove up to the funeral home in upstate New York where Robert's body lay. There Ilsa, distraught and determined, caused a scene. As they prepared to load Robert's body into the hearse to transport it to the crematorium, she insisted, with Teutonic obstinacy, she must say goodbye.

"Chip, I want to see him one more time. Ask the man to let us see him."

"Ilsa, you don't want that. I've done it. Trust me, it's a terrible last memory."

This was a simple cremation with no viewing, so the funeral home had done nothing to prepare Robert's remains. Twice before, I had seen how a horrific glider crash can rearrange the human body in gruesome fashion. Ilsa didn't want to see Robert this way. She just didn't know it.

"Please, Chip, I need to see him. Ask the man, please."

The funeral director frowned at me behind Ilsa's back and shook his head vigorously. But though we tried to dissuade her from gazing one last time at the man she knew only when he was alive and breathing, she refused to cooperate.

I gave up. I gave up not because I was wrong, but because I knew her stubbornness would prevail over logic. I escorted her back into the dark garage, trailing the irritated undertaker. This cremation was a low-budget affair: no embalming fees; no high-priced casket; no funeral home rentals, flowers, and other accoutrements. And now this pushy German woman was making a fuss.

He looked over and shrugged as if to say: "Okay, this is what the lady wants." Then he reached down, yanked the zipper of the stiff, black plastic body bag a few feet and brusquely pulled the edges apart to reveal Robert's head and neck.

I flinched at the grotesque expression frozen on my friend's face the instant before his glider had smashed into the earth, eyes wide and mouth open, lips curled back in an agonized scream that evoked an Edvard Munch painting. Ilsa crumpled, sagging against me in a helpless wail of anguish as I propped her up.

"Thanks for a great last memory," I grumbled to myself. "I told you so."

I half carried her back outside, mumbling reassurances while she wept until we were squinting in the harsh light of the August sun. With one hand, I reached into my pocket and donned my aviator-style sunglasses, then helped her into the car, ignoring the solitary tear trailing down my cheek.

At the crematorium, we sat for a long time outside on the lawn, most of the time separating ourselves. I said a prayer for my friend, who was a non-believer. At last, they delivered Robert's ashes to us and we returned to his house.

Donald had given us discretion over the disposition of the ashes so long as it was appropriate to Robert's love of soaring. We planned a memorial service at Robert's house a few days later and put the word out. We weren't sure how to deal with his ashes until that day came, when we received help from a surprising quarter, one of Hollywood's leading men.

CHAPTER FORTY-ONE

Superman

MANY OF CHRISTOPHER REEVE'S FANS knew he could fly for real. It was no secret the late "Superman" actor was a licensed pilot. But how many would have bet their lives—as I reluctantly did—that he could command a complex aircraft under stress with the same aplomb he demonstrated hanging from wires on a green screen stage?

Robert met Chris Reeve through gliding when the little-known actor was in the U.K. shooting the first *Superman* films. Back in the U.S., where Chris owned a glider, Robert would sometimes lead him around on cross-country flights.

Kathy and I had seen Chris once on Broadway, in Lanford Williams' *Fifth of July* (*not* my favorite play). But he had remained a mythical figure until he showed up early for the memorial service at Robert's house. We all pretended it was no big deal for one of the world's most famous actors to help carry benches into the backyard. It was Chris's idea to have a more participative service based on one he had orchestrated for his grandmother.

Perhaps 75 of us gathered that evening, perched on chairs and benches in a circle on the grass behind the house. Many were from soaring. News of Robert's death had raced through our community within hours in those pre-Internet days. The open question: "When will the service be?" We finally picked Monday, just over a week after the crash. But there were two people we hadn't been able to reach. I knew George and Suzanne Moffat took their sailboat on a long cruise every summer. So they could have been anywhere up and down the East Coast. Sitting in Robert's kitchen that afternoon a few hours before the service, I idly dialed their home for what seemed like the 100th time. And then, after so many unanswered calls, I was speaking to George. They had just walked in the door.

I hadn't rehearsed what to say. So for the second time in my life, I searched for the right words to deliver the most terrible news. I imagine pastors, military unit leaders, and others more familiar with horrific outcomes are better at it. In any case, George was unflappable. There was a pause, and his voice dipped with, "Oh," but it didn't waver. We discussed what we knew and the arrangements for the service that night, and he promised they would attend. Suzanne told me later it was a huge shock, but he hid it well.

As the warm September sun inched closer to the tree line, we spoke one at a time relating a special memory. Many involved humor—Robert had delighted in breaking the unwritten rules of staid society—and we laughed together in therapeutic relief after a week of grieving. The common thread we shared was expressing the joy Robert had brought into our lives and our deep sadness at his unexpected passing. Chris added his perspective. Besides gliding with Robert, the two had occasionally shared skiing and summer weekends.

A year earlier, Tanya and I had chuckled when Robert, with his European university education but little knowledge of popular culture, related how he and Ilsa had spent a weekend with Chris and his family on Martha's Vineyard. He had never heard of, much less recognized, Grammy- and Academy Award-winning singer Carly Simon at dinner. Ilsa had laughed along with us as we shook our heads at Robert's rustic ignorance of popular music.

Robert and Chris were both talented, ambitious, and self-confident, yet untaken by their accomplishments. In person, Chris seemed quiet and self-assured. Watching him chatting casually with Robert's friends, it was easy to forget we had once snickered at his suspect piloting skills.

Afterward, a few of us sat down to discuss Robert's ashes. The individuals in this group were not timid or reserved. We all had ideas—and opinions. With little delay, someone proposed spreading them over the "Big Ridge" in the Appalachian Mountains where Robert, Karl Striedieck, and two others had earlier that year established a new world record for distance around a triangular course of almost 850 miles. We nodded and mouthed our agreement as we looked around at each other. This would be an epic, symbolic tribute to our larger-than-life friend. Karl spoke up to offer his Cessna 180 for the ashes drop.

Our enthusiasm cooled at the prospect of the eight-hour round trip via car. Chris had been listening. At this point, he volunteered to fly down the next morning from his summer home in Williamstown, Massachusetts, meet us at Westchester County (New York) Airport, ferry us to the ridge, then drop us off on his way back.

We hesitated. This was a very generous offer given the cost to operate Chris's twin-engine, pressurized Beechcraft Baron 58P. I surveyed the pilots to see how everyone else was reacting. I looked to be the only one with reservations. The idea took on life straight away. Like the engineers and NASA officials in the below-freezing hours before the Challenger space shuttle explosion six months earlier, we all fell into line:

"Great idea."

"Sounds good."

"Yeah, that'll work."

"Good mission."

Most of them had to work the next day. I did not. I was unemployed, the tiny company I had joined a year earlier having run into difficulty, causing us to part ways. Moreover, there was a sense of obligation to be on that plane. At the request of his father's friends from Scotland, I had begun to inventory the assets in Robert's estate, which were scattered around the U.S., Europe, and the Cayman Islands—with no will. I had accompanied them to meet one of several lawyers in Robert's Rolodex (*not* the right lawyer, I learned later).

I suspect each of us viewed this trip as a grand gesture larger than ourselves. Robert wasn't just another pilot come to a bad end. He was a fallen hero. And we were caught up in planning a fitting tribute. Funerals are for the living, and this idea gave all of us a much-needed boost. It was, indeed, a mission. And I, more than most because of the turmoil in my own life, needed to be part of it.

Journal Entry: September 2, 1986 (White Plains, New York)

I'm belted into the co-pilot's seat, but I might as well be on United Airlines because I'm strictly a passenger. The pilot in the seat to my left, sitting tall and upright with an aviation headset, his hands firmly on the controls of the twin-engine Beech Baron cruising at 200 knots (230 mph), is Chris Reeve. As with other decisions made a few drinks into the night, I'm reconsidering this one in the light of day.

It's a little late for that. I stare at the complex array of gauges, instruments, and electronics stretching from Chris's side of the cockpit across the instrument panel to mine. As with street signs in a foreign language, I understand conceptually what these are without knowing precisely what they all mean.

Like many of his cinematic alter egos, Chris Reeve's face is calm and unruffled, reflecting none of the worries of those of us who have entrusted him with our lives. The thrum of the turbocharged engines is a muted roar, vibrating the aircraft beneath us like a heavy but responsive ocean-going vessel, reacting to every subtle change in the airflow and the controls.

I peer through the side window at the sprawling landscape of clouds passing thousands of feet below like rippled white sand at low tide on a Caribbean beach. The sky is vibrantly blue. Despite the chill outside, the morning sun is warm on the painted aluminum fuselage and wings, the edges of which glint like fine steel blades when the light reflects off them just so.

Our moods are more reflective of what's concealed *below* the cloud deck, i.e., dreary, drizzling rain. We had lifted off from Westchester County Airport less than an hour earlier and ascended into the overcast, which had obscured the earth ever since. By now, I suspect we've passed over the Delaware Water Gap and are crossing one mountain ridge after another in a series of parallel formations in Eastern Pennsylvania, like a seagull gliding over rows of breakers in the surf on the way into the beach. I know the terrain hidden beneath the deceptively benign surface of the clouds is rough and mountainous, cloaked in forests, and pockmarked by occasional strip mines and quarries.

Chris interrupts my reverie and hands me a cryptic aeronautical chart. Speaking loudly over the engine noise, he describes his intended landing: an ILS (instrument landing system) approach for runway 24 at University Park Airport just outside State College, Pennsylvania.

"What do you think?" he finishes politely, sliding the headphone off his right ear for my response and looking directly at me, as I turn toward him.

For a few seconds, I'm stumped. What do *I* think? Superman is driving a turbocharged Baron in IMC conditions (instrument meteorological conditions) and asking me what *I* think? Then I force a rueful grin.

"Chris, I'm a glider pilot. You're on your own," raising my voice over the engines and handing the chart back to him. I assume he's being polite. I hope he's not relying on us for help.

He blinks and pauses, digesting what I said. Then he turns back to the flying. At Westchester County Airport, he had seemed reassuringly capable dealing with the tower and the New York Air Traffic Control Center when we took off and climbed up into the low cloud deck before breaking out into the sun.

We glider pilots normally navigate with Sectional Charts, similar to road maps, but with data on airports, airspace, obstacles (e.g., high towers), and ground features that are identifiable from the air. In contrast, the IFR (instrument flight rules) approach plate Chris handed me comprises symbols and radio navigation data. It might as well be computer code to a non-IFR-rated pilot like me.

Instrument flying involves navigating without seeing the ground *and* keeping the aircraft upright and at the correct speed and course without reference to the horizon. Few non-pilots are aware of how little time it takes for an untrained and/or ill-equipped pilot caught inside a cloud to become unable to tell whether they are in a turn or flying straight or even which side is up as they lose control and plunge hopelessly, with the aircraft breaking up in flight or crashing into the ground. This demanding skill requires specialized training, equipment, certification—and frequent practice.

To reach our destination near State College, Chris must rely on the instruments in the cockpit until the last minutes of the flight. If he does everything by the book, the airplane will remain upright as we descend through the clouds and emerge into the clear above the minimum descent altitude. Only then will he have visual references—i.e., the ground and the horizon—for the final touchdown.

I don't know how many hours Chris has, or how they compare to the several thousand I've accumulated over 20 years. But it's irrelevant; none of mine are in power planes or IMC conditions.

My unease springs from a story many of us heard about a reality television show a few years ago called *Celebrity Daredevils.* The producers wanted Chris to conclude his segment by flying his sailplane in a fast, high-speed, ground-level pass right in front of the cameras followed by a steep climbing turn back up to altitude.

As we heard the story, with the cameras rolling, Chris pushed the nose over and dove steeply, leveling out a few feet above the runway at over 100 knots. The high-pitched whistle of the glider whipping by so closely, dipping the right wing in the seconds before it slashed overhead like a blade, frightened the host, Bert Convy, of game show fame. Our storyteller had implied Chris had let things get away from him. Maybe he was having fun. At the last second, a wide-eyed Convy threw himself flat on the runway as the wing of Chris's glider sliced over the unflinching cameraman.[29]

We threw back our heads and howled in raucous laughter: Hollywood hotshot gets in over his head trying something we pilots pull off without breaking a sweat.

Chris's middling flying skills seemed to be confirmed a few years later when I learned Robert led him out on cross-country flights from time to time. I asked what kind of pilot the real-life Superman was.

"He does okay," Robert had offered carefully.

"Okay?" I had snorted. "What the hell kind of answer is that?"

I had expected "he's a good pilot," or maybe "he's safe but doesn't know

---

[29] When last I checked, this was viewable at https://youtu.be/xUz9ed1IGo8 (accessed 16 Sep 2021; the last segment beginning at 1:32:00)

much about soaring." But "okay" was the sort of non-answer I used to get when inquiring about a proposed blind date in college. The only thing Robert needed to say to finish it off was, "He has a good personality."

Now, Robert's "okay" is all I can think about. I've put my life in the hands of an okay pilot.

Another reminder, as if I needed one, is the contest number on Chris's sailplane. "WK" was a legacy of its well-regarded former owner, Woodson K. Woods (father of Chris Woods, against whom I had flown at Springfield). It would normally translate to "Whiskey Kilo" in aviation parlance. But Superman has taken to referring to himself as "White Knuckles" in self-deprecating fashion. Other pilots gleefully emulate this behind his back in a not-so-subtle commentary on his skills.

None of this is a ringing endorsement for someone upon whom I am totally reliant for my safety. But that's no surprise.

The combination of "celebrity" and "pilot" can be problematic, especially flying complex planes like the Baron. Some wealthy individuals, with large egos and limited time, skip the traditional process of gradually advancing in aviation through more challenging and expensive aircraft.

Not surprisingly, this has led to tragic accidents involving privileged personalities who treated aviation the way some of them treated lesser mortals— with arrogance and casual disregard for the rules that apply to everyone else—and who drove their big-ticket airplanes into the ground with fatal consequences. One famous example was the crash of New York Yankees catcher Thurman Munson, said to be a competent pilot but who had been flying for just a year, who died in his $1.2 million Cessna Citation jet after misjudging a landing approach in 1979.

Both my father and I had experience as flight instructors, trying to teach soaring to those more accustomed to giving orders than taking advice. Today, however, unlike their trusting but unwitting passengers, I knew exactly what I was getting into. Our dreary aerial funeral procession over rural Pennsylvania with a Hollywood movie star is unparalleled. Yet there is unease, not anticipation or drama, despite his presence.

For much of the past 20 years, I've reassured my non-flying friends and family that, for the properly trained pilot flying within his or her abilities, "the most dangerous part of soaring is driving to and from the airport." So why am I on a mission to bury another of the finest pilots I have known?

I twist around in my seat and catch Ilsa's eye. She's huddled in the row behind me, cradling the urn with Robert's cremated remains in her arms like a frightened child clutching a favorite toy. She raises her head and smiles back wanly.

The engine noise drops as Chris eases back the throttles to begin our descent. My stress level escalates in inverse proportion to altitude. It is a spectacularly useless time to question whether our pilot knows what he is doing.

I don't bother checking to see how the other passengers behind me are faring. Most know less than I do. Ilsa isn't a pilot. Robert had cared for her a great deal and wanted a relationship with someone with whom he could share flying. He had envied the ones I have with Tanya and George Moffat has with Suzanne. But Ilsa is a free spirit, unfettered by conventions of deadlines and schedules. Robert had worried that would complicate her performance as his crew at stressful contests and diminish his concentration.

Robert's favorite crew, Rod Read, sitting right behind me, knows the most about Chris's flying. He works at the FBO (fixed-base operator) at Westchester County Airport, where Chris has his maintenance work done. But when I'd asked him about Chris's piloting creds the previous night, he had looked evasive and offered a similar non-answer:

"I only see him when he flies the Baron into Westchester. But he seems to do okay." Another ringing endorsement. At least Rod is along for the ride.

The other two friends on board know even less. None of us has the information about our pilot we should have had before embarking on an IFR flight into mountainous terrain. But it doesn't matter now. Either Chris knows what he is doing—or we will soon be reunited with our dead friend.

Sunlight illuminates the cockpit. The snowy crenellations and masses of cottony cloud appear to speed up, then flit by dangerously fast as we descend. The soft, vaporous layer changes colors from pure white as subtle grays, then darker shadows gradually appear in an oddly menacing fashion. Losing altitude, we plow into one swirling peak after another before merging with our shadow. Then we slip into the gray like a submarine easing below the surface of an oily, disquieting sea. Daylight dims, the horizon vanishes, and in seconds we are wholly without a visual reference. We could be creeping slowly on a highway in heavy, impenetrable fog on a nightmare drive, not knowing what might appear a second or two ahead. Except we are rocketing along at 170 knots, close to 200 mph.

Chris's plan calls for descending on a southwest heading toward University

Park Airport. Our path will bring us down the valley between two parallel ridges that overlook State College, home of Penn State University. The steep crests on either side of us are forested and rocky. If all goes well, we will let down neatly between them into the valley where the airport lies. If we veer off course, we risk colliding with one of the unyielding slopes with little chance of survival.

Onward we fly in the gray fog, the engines droning loudly as I watch the altimeter unwind. I'm not sure of the altitude of the nearby peaks, but I imagine we are approaching their level. I'm glad there isn't much turbulence. Then we hit light rain. Lovely.

My eyes are unblinking as I stare ahead through the water droplets scattering and streaking up the windshield. I'm half waiting for something frightening to appear ahead, too close to pull up or turn away. Even at part throttle, engine noise suppresses most communications in the cockpit. No one says anything. We just share occasional furtive glances. Surely, we'll break through this cloud layer soon.

I recall a scene in the recent movie *Sweet Dreams.* An airplane is carrying Patsy Cline and her fearful group through a violent storm. For long moments, their anxiety rises. Then, they burst out of the clouds into the clear with relief! An instant later, in a horrible shock, the plane flies straight into the vertical face of a cliff and explodes in a fireball. That was Hollywood's version. The actual crash occurred in a forest and there was no explosion. But the scene was shockingly effective when Tanya and I viewed the movie in the theater.

"Is that how it will be for us?" I muse melodramatically. We wouldn't even have time to reflect on our fate before lapsing into unconsciousness and death in a desultory conflagration of torn metal, smoking engines, shattered bones, and smoldering flesh. For some reason, this eases my anxiety. Nothing I can do will make any difference.

Motors whine and mechanisms thump in the plane as Chris lowers the flaps and undercarriage. He's configuring the Baron for landing. The sounds of the air and vibrations change. He is focused on flying the airplane, communicating with air traffic control, and adjusting the engine and flight controls. I imagine his forehead creased with anxiety. Is he sweating in the cockpit, his hands wet as his nervousness rises? I'm afraid to look. What could I do if he were in trouble? Say something? Pray?

But his face betrays neither stress nor doubt, only a calm intensity that I hope reflects his justifiable confidence. The minutes tick off. The altimeter continues to unwind with no sign of the ground increasingly near.

Then, the opaque mist begins to shred. I strain against the belts to see. Seconds later, the dark ground resolves roughly 1,000 feet below us as we drop into the clear beneath a gray overcast. Off our right and left wings are the two ridges I had worried about. Straight ahead of us, in light rain to the southwest, is runway 24. We are wings level and on glide path!

Chris's touch on the controls is solid as we continue to descend, shrinking the distance to the airport. The approaching farms appear to flash by faster. But it's just an illusion as we draw lower and closer. Slowing, the Baron floats over the threshold of the runway. Chris reduces power to both engines and eases back firmly on the control wheel to bring the nose up to flare. We settle onto the macadam in a soft touchdown. As the tires grab at the wet pavement, he pulls back the throttles and applies the wheel brakes. We feel the tug as the heavy aircraft slows, never veering from our course along the runway centerline. Perfect landing!

I suppress an undignified urge to cheer. I can't decide whether I am more surprised or impressed. Obeying radioed instructions only he can hear, Chris taxis down the runway to a paved apron. I recognize the plane parked there: the single-engine, high-wing Cessna 180 owned by Karl Striedieck. He and perennial contest start gate maestro Charlie Spratt are standing under the Cessna's wing. A week earlier, Karl had been waiting to launch right after Robert. He had watched as Robert's Ventus kited up out of control, then nosed over and plummeted into the ground.

Chris swings the Baron in next to the Cessna, pivoting on one wheel. Then he brakes and shuts down. The silence is thick after the flight. We climb down, met by Karl and Charlie. Were this another occasion, there would be a boisterous exchange of greetings and flying banter. Not this time.

Ex-fighter-pilot Karl Striedieck, seldom betraying emotion, takes command of our subdued ranks and briefs us on the mission in a clipped, military mode. The weather is marginal, but the controllers have granted his request for a Special VFR clearance. We will be legal so long as we remain clear of any clouds. The plan calls for launching both airplanes. Chris will form up on Karl's lead. We will fly straight over to the mountain still visible under the gray. Then we will turn parallel with it and run along the spine, spreading the ashes of our departed friend. Chris will fly his Baron offset to one side of Karl's Cessna to allow all who are here today to bear witness.

University Park Airport, State College, Pennsylvania, 1986. Karl Striedieck and Chris Reeve discussing the ashes drop. From left: Charlie Spratt, Karl, Donald Robertson's emissary from Scotland (hidden), Rod Read (back to camera), Chris, Ilsa, and friend.

The big concern is airspeed. Karl will slow to 80 knots for the drop run. Any faster and ashes could blow back into the cockpit, depressing and messy. But Chris must match that. Karl concludes his briefing, then turns to Chris.

"Your Baron should be okay at that airspeed."

Question? Reassurance? Or declaration? We all turn to the movie star standing taller than any of us. Suddenly the center of attention, he reflects for a moment, mentally reviewing the Baron's operating limits. It's heavier than the Cessna. Its twin engines make it more powerful but also more complex and difficult to control at lower airspeeds. I don't know if 80 knots is too slow for Chris to fly formation with the ridgeline only a few hundred feet below us and an indistinct horizon. The margin of error will be small, with zero chance to practice. Still, for a good pilot.... No one says anything. This is between the two men. Then Chris's eyes meet Karl's and hold them steady, his face serious but calm:

"No, that's too slow for me. You go ahead."

Superman has spoken, based on his assessment of the risks. No apology. No defensiveness. He knows his limits and will invite no one to talk him into trying something with which he isn't 100% confident. I believe then, as I will 36 years later, it is a gutsy call, one that separates Chris from the narcissistic, insecure movie stars with outsized egos we read about in the tabloids.

We stand there, Robert's closest friends, gathered for a burial service overseen by Karl Striedieck, a legend in soaring. Chris might be an A-list celebrity among the Hollywood glitterati. But here on a lonely ramp under a glowering overcast in Pennsylvania as the soft mist penetrates our clothing, he is just a pilot. And he's being evaluated by each of us as we watch the interaction between the two men, both at the apex of their worlds. The pressure to fly the rest of us up to the ridge must weigh deeply on Chris. There are no raised eyebrows or frowns or other visible reactions, although his pronouncement catches us unaware. In retrospect, though, it shouldn't have.

Setting aside my anxiety over his flying, my impressions of Chris at Robert's memorial service last night and this morning had been favorable. He is physically imposing, yet modest; understated without being tentative or apologetic. At age 33, he epitomizes the expression "quiet confidence." He has made his decision based on his head, not on emotion or peer pressure or ego. Chris has played Superman in many scenes involving camera angles, special effects, stuntmen, fake violence—and retakes. But this scene is real life. He would have to get it right the first time. And that's too risky.

It's quiet. The rest of us are spectators. Then Karl graciously accedes. He already witnessed one fatal accident. No need for another.

Sans the Baron, the available seats are the three in Karl's smaller Cessna. Ilsa takes one. I don't hesitate when Rod Read offers me another. I climb in after her in the back row. I hold the box with the urn containing Robert's ashes while she buckles up. It's incongruously heavy. The sensation of the contents as they shift is more like sand than feathery ashes. I am unaware then that "ashes" is a misnomer. In reality, they comprise the gravelly, ground-up bone left after cremation.

Someone helps Donald Robertson's emissary from Scotland haul himself up into the right front seat and buckles him in. Everyone backs away and Karl calls out, "Clear!" When he cranks the engine, it fires and settles into a smooth idle. The Cessna pivots and the wingtip sweeps around the impassive faces of those still standing. There are no smiles or cheery waves.

After a brief hold on the taxiway to check the engine, Karl proceeds to the runway and advances the throttle to take off. I have flown against him and shared thermals in our gliders. But this is the first time I have sat in the same cockpit with the man most American soaring pilots would place at the pinnacle of their list of those with *the right stuff*.

The Cessna is lighter and more responsive than the Baron as we break ground. It takes only a few minutes to climb up to the ridge looming over State College. In contrast to my earlier concerns about Chris's pilotage, I am as relaxed with Karl at the controls as I would be in my living room.

The overcast still hovers threateningly only a few hundred feet above the peaks. When we arrive at the ridgeline, Karl banks sharply to turn parallel with the spine. As the trees pass beneath us, Ilsa unbuckles her seat belt, leans forward, and thrusts her arms awkwardly through the side window. As Karl instructed, she positions the urn away from the fuselage and holds it there, aimed backward. She opens the cap in stages, letting the slipstream suck the ashes out rather than shaking them loose in an explosion. As another pilot had warned the night before, there's an occasional disconcerting "SPAT" as a bone fragment strikes the tail.

After she settles back in her seat, Karl rolls into a tight 180-degree turn and makes another pass back along the ridge. Reflexively, we all look down. There's no smoky contrail of ashes, of course, but we take a moment for reflection or prayer. By the end, we are bouncing in and out of the overcast, squeezed between it and the unforgiving ridgeline below.

For our final farewell, I wish I could report the sun broke through the overcast or we spotted a hawk circling right over the drop zone or some other portent. But it might as well have been sand streaming from the urn. Chris made a good call. It would have been a stressful formation flight, Chris's chase airplane uncomfortably near its published stall speed with restricted maneuverability, visibility, and safety margin.

After returning from ashes drop, last goodbyes at Karl's Cessna 180.

Our return to the airport is quicker. We do not linger after Karl taxies back and shuts down. Between American ex-military demeanor on one side and British civilian reserve on the other, this is not a crowd with an excess of sentimentality. We exchange last words as Chris comforts Ilsa, then clamber back into Chris's Baron. We lift off and climb smoothly into the overcast that had seemed so sinister an hour earlier.

High above, breaking out again in the sun on the flight back to Westchester County Airport, we settle back in our seats, weary but more relaxed this time. The mood perks up, the warm light in the cockpit signaling our dispositions. Smiling over his shoulder, Chris hands us a cocktail napkin printed with "Reeve Air" a friend had made up. We chuckle in relief over being in an airplane piloted by a Hollywood idol. None of us were looking forward to this task, but it has provided some closure, whatever that means.

I never saw Chris again. We spoke on the telephone a few times because he, alone among Robert's friends, owned a house large enough to accept some of the bigger items we removed from Robert's house. At Donald Robertson's request, I had agreed to serve as an administrator of Robert's estate.

Donald Robertson didn't ask for much from his son's personal effects, only a scrapbook from Robert's auto racing days. As for the furniture, oriental rugs, family silver and china, workshop tools, soaring equipment, and memorabilia, he asked me to parcel them out to his friends. That proved awkward. In a further complication, I discovered irregularities with the estate's lawyer and had to take action against him. I took perverse satisfaction in it not just because he was unethical, but because it made me feel useful.

We sold the house and liquidated Robert's securities, then dispatched the funds to Scotland. Not long after, Donald asked for input on making a substantial donation in his son's memory. Robert's ultimate goal had been a spot on the U.S. Team flying in the World Gliding Championships representing his adoptive country. Our discussion led to the Robert L. Robertson Trust, administered by the SSA, which provides income to support the Team. Knowing how underfunded the SSA often seemed to be, I reached out to Richard Hall, father of competitor Tigger Hall, for help drafting an ironclad trust agreement.

A month later, Tanya and I were in the U.K. for our honeymoon. Donald and the couple who had represented him in the crash's aftermath met us at the train station late at night in Dundee, Scotland, and brought us to the small hotel in the town of Edzel, where they had retired to live on a golf course. We had lunch the next day and then it was back on the train for an overnight ride to London. The weather was gloomy, but the mood was much brighter than it had been just a month earlier.

Months later, the three of them flew over to the U.S. We had a nice dinner with Doug Jacobs and a few of Robert's friends. As the evening drew to a close, I mentioned privately to Donald I was contemplating flying again after my enforced layoff. Only a short time after losing his son in a crash, Donald surprised me by insisting I should do what makes me happy and not obsess over the risks.

It was a variation on "life is short; enjoy it." Nine years later, I recalled that wisdom. I had lost touch with Chris Reeve and didn't know whether he ever flew his sailplane again. In June 1995, I was sitting in the clubhouse on a no-fly day at a contest near Harrisburg, Pennsylvania, not far from where he'd ferried us that day. Rain was drumming loudly on the roof. My eyes froze on a small story buried in the back of the local sports section. In disbelief, I read it a second time after checking the date of the newspaper to be sure.

Chris's horse had refused a jump in a competition and thrown him over headfirst, his hands tangled in the reins. In the fall, he broke his neck, paralyzing him and leaving him unable to breathe on his own.

What a tragedy! So much life, such a powerful character—in every sense of the words—in such an unassuming, thoughtful, and vibrant man. I regretted doubting his abilities as a pilot. Later I learned Chris had logged some 2,500 hours when he carried us to the ridge and done extensive training to get his commercial, flight instructor, and instrument ratings and check out in increasingly complex airplanes. As he proved in the gray skies over Pennsylvania, he was a competent, confident, and humble aviator.

How would such a man cope with his devastating injury? Impressively well, to read of his nine-plus-year journey after the accident. Most pilots there were unsentimental about the news, even the few who had been in attendance that day to see Chris prove what kind of person he was. Accidents happen. Life goes on. I understood by then most pilots do not wish to, cannot *allow* themselves to dwell on death, much less what might happen to their mortal selves while flying. To do so would be tantamount to admitting it could happen to them.

It was different for me. Over time, I reassessed the risks and consequences of accidents. I had seen the outcomes of momentary lapses in concentration or errors in judgment. I knew at a more visceral level how vulnerable we pilots were to such mistakes. Yet I don't recall pondering whether flying was too dangerous. For over 20 years, it had been the focus of my existence, anchoring everything I did. Of course I would continue to fly. Without soaring, who was I?

CHAPTER FORTY-TWO

Catalysts

W EDDING BELLS AT LAST—at age 35! But it almost didn't happen. In 1984, Tanya and I shocked our friends when we broke up after two years together. To be correct, she broke up with me. And again, just as with Kathy a few years earlier, I was shocked and devastated when the woman I'd thought was my soulmate walked out of my life.

Going through the motions of a normal life, I flew up to Boston on business not long after. Desperate for a distraction, I was browsing the inflight magazine. I don't usually read pop-psychology articles, but this one—about emotional intimacy (yawn)—caught my eye, probably with a sub-head like "do your relationships keep crashing and burning?" If I recall correctly, I scored a perfect zero on the included quiz! Well, I might have received one point for "Do you share what's most important in your life with your partner?" After all, I talked about soaring all the time!

The article was electrifying. I haven't always been the most introspective guy. But in a flash of insight, I realized this was the same problem I'd had with Kathy, i.e., my inability to commit or share my true feelings and, not incidentally, share what was important to her, as well.

Armed with a diagnosis, I could fix this. I could change. That didn't happen overnight, of course, but I gradually came to see the world from a different perspective. The challenge was showing Tanya I had evolved, rather than just telling her. That was difficult since she had broken off our relationship.

It was a long, depressing summer. I worked on recovering from the breakup; dealt with unrelated health issues; and faced a career-threatening conflict at the company where I had thrived for eight years. Single again, I tried to lose myself in relationships with several women. That was easier because of the burgeoning personal ads phenomenon in New York City publications. I discovered there were many other lonely single people out there, including (improbably) a principal actress in a top-10 television show, a dancer/singer/actress in a hit

Broadway musical, a beautiful flight attendant (they still drew me), and a long list of "normal" women looking for love in the Big Apple. I might be damaged goods. But there were a lot of jerks out there and being a nice guy was (finally) a plus.

Then, in storybook fashion, Tanya and I reconciled after a summer apart. Less than a year later, I scored a better job in a new company. She and I had been together for more than three years. Certain she was the woman with whom I wanted to spend the rest of my life, I finally "popped the question."

We coasted along, not setting a wedding date. A year later, my new job blew up in my face, and for the first time in my Harvard Business School-based career, I was on unemployment. What a comedown! Intellectually, I knew I shouldn't feel like a failure, but it was hard not to. I needed a job to mend my ego. As important: I needed health insurance.

Tanya was a copy editor at Condé Nast's *Vanity Fair*, the latest in a string of well-known magazines she had served (including *Rolling Stone, New York, Interview,* and *GQ*). At Condé Nast, she had great medical benefits, as would her husband were she to marry. How convenient! We were engaged. All we needed was a piece of paper to close the deal.

She telephoned me she saw a gap in her work schedule before the July 4th weekend. I rushed over to her office. Then we rode the subway down to the New York City Municipal Building on her lunch hour and made our dreams come true. My family were upset they hadn't been able to attend the 60-second civil ceremony, so we promised them a formal church wedding. Sadly, Robert crashed before we could do that.

Our second ceremony was in the chapel across First Avenue from the United Nations. We had ended up there after a long search for a church where a non-practicing Southern Baptist and an agnostic could feel comfortable. The pastor was a woman who—in Tanya's words—was the first intelligent person she had met who was openly religious (not counting me, of course). When Tanya was growing up in Communist Bulgaria, religion had been for old people.

As I sat at the small, elegant reception dinner, surrounded by family and friends, my joy over celebrating marriage to Tanya was mixed with melancholy over several pivotal people in my life not being there. Dad had been gone for over six years. Robert's death 30 days earlier was rawer.

I wondered how my Southern Baptist father would have reacted. Years earlier, the revelation that my girlfriend Kathy was Catholic had startled him.

Marriage to an agnostic would have been massively more disturbing[30]. Would he have tried to dissuade me? Or, since I was 35, would he have gone along quietly?

Tanya's mother, author, Tanya, author's mother at wedding, 1986, Church Center for the United Nations, New York City. (photo from Bearden family)

Unemployment grounded me temporarily. Flying had been integral to my identity for many years. The fear of someday losing it had always been existentially disturbing.

But marrying the woman I loved was uplifting. We were partners during the tough times. We had bought an old stone house in the wooded hills of New Jersey before the money stopped and I launched a whirlwind of do-it-yourself projects while I searched for the next career opportunity.

My first attempt was a disastrous venture with what turned out to be unethical partners. I leveraged my new cynicism into advisory gigs, checking out small mergers and acquisitions for my previous employer who had, themselves, been acquired. That led to a full-time job in the New York office of a London merchant bank managing a U.S. investment portfolio.

I threw myself into this high-powered, well-paying career as I never had before. For one of the few times in my life, I *lived* for my work. I clawed my way back to a sound footing financially and emotionally. In two years, I rebuilt our finances and, as important, restored my self-confidence.

Then, overnight, our Swiss parent company floundered and filed for

---

[30] Tanya later decided she wanted faith in her life and converted to Catholicism after we began attending the church where our daughters were in parochial school.

receivership. After helping unwind our U.S. portfolio, I returned to solo consulting, this time for a company we had invested in.

With my weekends open again, Tanya entered us in 5K and 10K races all over Northern New Jersey and in New York City. She had become an avid runner. We ran together occasionally in Manhattan, but I let days and even weeks go by with no exercise except for these races.

I wasn't sure why my fascination with running had cooled. Knowing my fitness had declined was disconcerting. I still considered myself to be a marathoner the way a parishioner who hasn't been to mass for years might view themselves as a lapsed Catholic instead of as an agnostic. I still believed as strongly as I ever had. I just didn't practice regularly.

My thoughts turned to flying. The LS3 hadn't been out of the trailer in five years. Was it flyable? The answer was yes, though it took a month to deal with all the mechanical and paperwork issues.

But was *I* flyable? I hadn't been in the cockpit during that time. I wasn't overly anxious when I climbed into the front seat of a two-seater with an instructor to find out. But I was happy when everything still felt right.

I was more tense before my first flight in the LS3, just as I had been the first time I flew after Dad's crash. And as in 1980, there was an awkward moment as we lifted off when things felt stiff and mechanical. Even after that passed, it took longer to feel "normal" again. But I spent the summer practicing in the Catskill Mountains in upstate New York, where I had flown so often with XT and XX.

As summer ended, Tanya and I packed our van and headed to Virginia with the LS3 for a big regional contest there. I was excited, albeit nervous, to be jumping back into the competitive fray again. I was trying to be levelheaded—this was an experiment, not a commitment. Yet I knew much was riding on this contest.

CHAPTER FORTY-THREE

Welcome Back

N EW CASTLE INTERNATIONAL is a small grass airfield near the hamlet of New Castle, Virginia, in the Blue Ridge Mountains. The crowd there are renowned for their generosity. The facility is idyllic. But the area has earned a reputation for being one of the most technical gliding sites in the U.S., offering a variety of thermals, wing-thrashing rides along windy ridge lines, and smooth high-altitude wave flying amidst mountainous terrain surrounded by forests and dotted by rural areas and limited landing options.

The terrain at New Castle is more forbidding than Elmira's, and the weather is as uncertain. Following a cold front with wind blowing against the mountains, however, it offers world-class soaring, allowing pilots to blast along the ridges at high speeds, pausing to gain altitude in thermals to jump from one ridge to another. In 1983, I flew a 469-mile ridge task there, surpassing the 455-mile thermal task at Minden two years prior. Later, pilots at New Castle raised the record for the longest competition task to over 1,000 km (622 miles).

New Castle attracts top pilots from the East Coast, but it is not for the faint of heart. There have been crashes and injuries. Some competitors have left, shaken, never to return. It might not be the ideal site for a comeback after a five-year hiatus, but I felt confident in my ability to fly there safely after having done so before.

It was an eight-hour drive from New Jersey. We didn't know what to expect when we motored in slowly with the trailer on the practice day and stopped near the main hangar. We recognized many, but not all, of the contest numbers we saw, and even a few faces. How many would recognize us, though?

As we climbed out of the van on stiff legs, local pilot and old competitor Dave Cole came striding over eagerly, calling out to greet us with a wide grin and outstretched hand. At that moment, I knew, with a peace that had eluded me for five years, that once more I belonged to this exclusive club.

Journal Entry: September 14, 1991 (New Castle, Virginia)

Dave and I stand together on the edge of the lush grass, about two-thirds of the way down the runway. We flew against each other many times, at

Cordele and New Castle, so we're reminiscing. Hearing the distinctive high-pitch drone of a small engine wound up under stress, we pause our conversation and turn to see a motorglider lifting off after a long ground run. We watch as he climbs out slowly over the remaining grass runway that sweeps down a gentle slope toward town to the north. The lightweight, retractable engine installed in the sailplane is for self-launching and occasional saves.

Dave is the first to realize something is wrong. He has launched from this runway hundreds of times and knows the hazards that lie in wait when the winds gust over the hills guarding each end. He tenses up, balls his fists, and leans forward, shouting:

"Oh, no! No, Alan!"

The pilot has chosen to self-launch. As I heard it later, to qualify for the 15 Meter Class here, he removed the small wingtip extensions that would have provided additional lift on takeoff. It's hot—close to 90°F—so the little engine is down on power. I also heard he had not pushed his glider all the way back to the south end of the runway to take advantage of its full length.

As the aircraft fights to climb, the wind spilling down the back side of the ridge is like a fishing net cast over the airport. We watch in perverse fascination as the motorglider levels out less than 100 feet high. Then, struggling in the invisible downdraft, it descends inexorably, engine wailing, aimed straight at the web of high-voltage power lines looming ahead. It's too low to turn in either direction. The pilot's only hope is to clear the wires.

I'm unable to look away, hoping this will be one of those tales that leave us shaking our heads in disbelief. From our vantage point—a bit more than a quarter mile behind the glider—it looks like he may squeak over the wires in a memorable close call. Once past that terrifying obstacle, he can drone across the tiny town and its smattering of single-story buildings and emergency landing spots with the engine screaming like a moped driven at full tilt by a manic teenager. I'm sure that's the uppermost thought in the pilot's mind, even as an icy dread fills him.

As the glider reaches the power lines strung between the tall steel towers, it appears to stop in midair. *So* close to clearing, the main wheel snags the top cable. The wire stretches and tightens as the aircraft decelerates dramatically, like a Navy fighter jet arrested by its tailhook on an aircraft carrier. Deprived of the lifting force under the wings, it tumbles forward, the tail pitching up. Then, released from the wire, it plunges straight down, propelled by gravity and the spinning prop. The pilot sees the ground rushing up before the impact throws him violently into the shoulder harness and the cockpit disintegrates around his body.

It's uncanny the way people sense something going wrong. They can be out on the airport all day with planes taking off and landing, only peripherally attentive. Then something triggers a heightened state of awareness, the way we can distinguish our names spoken softly over a cacophony of voices in a crowded room. Most had watched the crash sequence. Now many react, leaping into their cars and racing across the creek to the highway to the field half a mile away where the glider lies broken.

I reflexively step toward our van to follow, to offer help, to be part of the rescue party. We are men of action. Then I stop. There's nothing I can do there. And I can't face another of what I judge, correctly, to be a fatal accident. I'm stunned. I cannot freakin' believe it! Fifteen minutes into our first contest in six years and Tanya and I just witnessed another crash. Our eyes meet and we exchange a look that speaks volumes as I contemplate the thought of turning around and returning home.

Many questions popped into my mind as the crowd headed for the crash site. The obvious one: was this an omen we could ignore only at our peril? This was the third fatal crash I'd witnessed (and my fourth such crash site) but it was Tanya's first. She hadn't joined me in that cornfield in Middletown, New York, where Robert crashed five years earlier in 1986, or at the Caesar Creek gliderport where the club member spun in five years before, or at Deer Creek State Park where my father died one year before that. But I suspect she was uneasy that something like this could happen to me.

We did not leave. I don't recall if we even discussed it. There was a lot unsaid that day. I had just turned 40. I'd spent half a decade rebuilding my finances and establishing my life with another person. I wanted back into soaring. I hardly needed a reminder of its risks.

At the pilots' meeting the next morning, a well-meaning counselor—the wife of a local pilot—tried to facilitate a group therapy session for us to share our feelings about the accident. Her effort fizzled out in awkward silence. Most racing pilots aren't comfortable *thinking* about death, much less talking about it. Few would have voiced what was on many minds, viz., anger. This was no "wrong place at the wrong time" tragedy. The pilot was said to have made several bad calls (the accident chain, again) before he rolled.

When launching began, I leaped into the fray with the same enthusiasm, desire, and trepidation as in my first contest 23 years earlier. This is what Dad would have wanted. In his 20 years in soaring, he had known only one pilot who died in a sailplane. For him, the most dangerous part of soaring *was* driving to and from the airport. He wasn't lying. He just didn't have enough data.

I had plenty of data: seven fatal crashes by then. Yet I believe choosing to stay and fly was right, though I admit revisiting that decision hours later.

Journal Entry: September 15, 1991 (New Castle, Virginia)

After launching, I orbit in a high thermal over the gliderport, listening as the early starters encounter trouble flying into an unexpectedly weak airmass. The radio is full of landout reports. Does it make sense for me to try this?

Some pilots are still flying, so I go through the start gate after most have departed and fly alone, airport-hopping along the first leg, never beyond gliding range of a runway. Then the airports end. To continue means flying into a less hospitable area where others have been forced down.

In the old days, I wouldn't have hesitated. There are occasional fields. I haven't landed out in over five years but it's a risk of competition *[at this writing, I've landed out 100+ times—I don't even keep count anymore]*. As I top out, unsure, I realize my future in soaring could turn on this decision.

This time, I hesitate but don't choke. F**k it! I push on—and am surprised to be more relaxed after the decision. Soon, however, I'm scrambling on a long glide 90 degrees off course to distant clouds, evoking memories of my Cordele days. It works! I climb up into final glide range, then sweep in for a late, redline pass over the finish line. Several pilots rush over to ask if I have flown the course. It's wonderful to bask again in the aura of respect accorded one of the community of soaring pilots. I'm back in the game!

Plunged into soaring after five years off, I was as excited as ever.

The LS3 was 13 years old, so in early 1992, I sold it and took delivery of a new Schleicher ASW 24. I transferred over the same N707JB registration and JB contest number I'd been flying for over 20 years on the Libelle and the LS3. I was returning to the Standard Class, where I had competed in our Libelle. The ASW 24 was the least-popular and highest-priced of four competing models— with no performance advantage. I chose it for its unique, award-winning safety cockpit, designed—like modern automobiles—with crush zones to absorb crash energy progressively. Designer Gerhard Waibel received a prestigious technical award for this, which prompted all manufacturers to focus more on survivability. Before this, sailplanes could endure punishing turbulence and air loads at high speeds and G loadings. But crashworthiness was an afterthought.

Author in ASW 24 zooming up after finishing (dumping water ballast)...

...and landing (note extended dive brakes).

(photos at Elmira, New York, 2015, by Guerry Howard)

My new mission: outfit my ASW 24 as a "safety glider." I said it was for my family. But I couldn't deny it would also address my concerns. I had the factory install a set of curved steel bars to protect the pilot if the sailplane rolls through a wire fence. I wasn't worried about fences. I hoped the bars—which resemble a roll cage—might guide a power line or telephone wire up and over my head if I struck one when landing. Two pilots I knew had narrowly escaped after wire strikes and another died when a wire decapitated him. I also installed an improved seat belt/harness system from automobile racing; a crash-activated emergency locator transmitter (ELT); a flip-down rearview mirror to eliminate blind spots; an onboard drinking water supply; and an inflight urinary disposal system. I did everything I could to avoid and survive a worst-case situation.

At a later New Castle contest, I hiked up the mountainside to help retrieve a glider that had crashed in the trees. On the same day, another pilot I knew zoomed up steeply a few hundred feet after finishing, hit turbulence, and stalled. As horrified bystanders at the airport watched, he spun straight down right in front of them. By a miracle, tree branches absorbed most of the energy of the falling sailplane. It came to rest suspended vertically with the nose only inches above a flat rock, allowing the shaken pilot to open the canopy and step neatly onto the ground, as if he had planned it!

ASW 24 canopy wire deflector bars (left, photo by Bozena Michalowski). Cockpit view (r) with Cordele airport visible to right of instrument panel.

That was my second contest where two serious crashes occurred on the same day. My first year with the ASW 24, the wind died at the end of a long ridge task and forced all but one of us down in hasty field landings. One pilot stalled and spun in with moderate damage and minor injuries. The other was lucky to survive when he caught a wire with his wingtip on a low turn into a field, cartwheeled into the ground in a violent crash, and spent months in a hospital.

During my honeymoon year with the ASW 24 in 1992, flying was once again the center of my world. The first flight was like a magical encounter with a stunning woman who completes you. As with the LS3 in 1978, I knew as soon as we lifted off, she was "the one." A year earlier, simply getting back in the cockpit had been huge. But this was a fresh start.

That year, I flew two ten-day nationals and four seven-day regionals, more than I ever had before (or have since).

The next year marked another major turning point in my comeback when I did something I'd never done before—and would have sworn I never would.

Journal Entry: July 5, 1993 (Fairfield, Pennsylvania)

The day here at the Regional contest is a lost cause, but the CD keeps hoping it will improve. Not only is there little lift, but the visibility is the worst I've ever experienced. We can see other sailplanes only when they are in the same thermal with us. Multiple times we climb slowly, then attempt to cross the mountain separating us from the sunlight in the next valley. But finding no lift on the way, we turn back, broadcasting our position and course hoping not to collide with outbound gliders in the haze.

Late in the day, on my last launch, I commit, turning my back on the airport and gliding across the mountain past the point of no return. I drop into the next valley and out in the sunlight, hoping to find workable thermals. It's a longshot but no one else has even left the airport so there's a chance to do something "heroic." Instead, I'm trapped there for an hour, thermaling mostly below 1,000 feet the entire time. At least there are good landing fields in all directions, which I survey while circling.

My hopes are declining with the sun. The feeble thermals are less buoyant. I'm preparing to land, in an abbreviated pattern at 350 feet, when I hit a little bump. I know I can roll level and land in almost any direction. So, wondering if I'm crazy, I continue the turn. It's a thermal, going up slowly all the way around! I take it to the top, at 1,200 feet, before it expires. Shortly after, however, the thermals cease and I'm forced to land anyway.

I've never thermaled that low before (or since). For a relatively short flight on a no-contest day, this experience was a turning point in my comeback from the crippling anxieties I had flown with since my father's crash.

I felt focused, with soaring being at the forefront of my attention. I regained the rhythm of flying, where it became second nature and instinctive, allowing me to concentrate on making constantly optimized decisions. I was flying more like my old self than I had in a long time. The dream of winning a nationals, or at least a daily task, once again seemed achievable, and with it, the chance to reclaim the sense of validation that I had been seeking since my father's crash had upended my life.

CHAPTER FORTY-FOUR

Trials & Tribulations

L IFE WAS GOOD AGAIN. It was so good, it couldn't last. A competing company acquired my consulting client and stopped paying my monthly retainer despite a written contract. They basically said, "sue us." Like a fool, I did, allowing my ego and outrage to override common sense. It was a classic American story: I was in the right, but the other party had more money. After a year of expensive litigation, I felt fortunate for a settlement that paid my legal bills with nothing to show for massive stress and little income.

I needed to put that behind because life had gotten more complicated. Early in 1994, Tanya gave birth to our twin girls after a three-year struggle to have children, involving countless doctors, medications, and procedures. Josephine (Josie) and Christina (Tina) were an incredible gift. I just wished the black clouds of litigation and unemployment hadn't been hanging over my head.

Author and wife, with Tina and Josie, a few months after birth 1994. (photo by Ivanka Lenkow)

Parenthood at age 42 was life changing. It proved rewarding in ways I had never imagined. Tanya was the driving force behind this, for which I will always be grateful. When she went back to work after a three-month maternity leave, I "temporarily" took over the care of our daughters while I searched for a job. Apart from a well-paying six-month gig with a small mergers and acquisitions firm, I was to be the stay-at-home parent for most of the girls' first five years.

At first, I continued to fly, though my earnings were erratic. I rationalized I needed the emotional support and self-esteem flying provided. And the ASW 24 agreed with me. In the first four years, I added a couple of regional first place medallions and two more for second place, the first since before Dad's crash.

Then, at a local contest near our home, the bullet I had been dodging for a quarter of a century caught up with me.

Journal Entry: April 24, 1994 (Blairstown, New Jersey)

It is a cold, gusty, all-around-dodgy day. If not for the contest, I wouldn't even have gone to the gliderport. Now I'm in trouble, coasting back and forth over a low ridge, losing altitude with each pass. That's not sustainable.

There's an old saying about outlanding: "land in dirt, don't get hurt." Retrieves from plowed fields can be laborious, but their exposed surfaces hold few surprises because years of cultivation have removed most hazards. Pastures may look seductively smooth and offer drive-in access for the crew. That's tempting, since Tanya will arrive with our 15-week-old girls. There are reasons, though, pastures don't have crops. They're often untillable, full of rocks, stumps, chuckholes, and rough ground concealed in the grass.

The grassy field I'm surveying already has a glider resting in it. That's no guarantee of a safe landing (as my father discovered in his Diamant), but it's promising. The pilot doesn't answer my radio calls, so I execute a textbook approach, slow the airplane on final, and let the tire settle onto the ground in the grass near him.

KABAM-BAM!

The double-shot noise is astonishingly loud. The impact shudders through the cockpit. We come to a stop in less distance than usual. The fuselage seems lower in the mid-calf-height grass. The other pilot comes running over to welcome me, smiling. Before I climb out, I look up, a more serious expression on my face, and ask,

"Have a look at the wheel; I think I hit something."

He peers under the belly in the grass, then grimaces. "Oh, no!"

The main wheel had slammed into a large, half-buried rock hidden in the grass at 45 knots. Every piece in the ingenious steel landing gear mechanism instantly bent or failed—as designed—to absorb the energy of the impact. Luckily, the undamaged wheel and tire jammed up against the bottom of the fuselage and kept it off the ground, protecting me from injury when, an instant after that, I hit a second rock that creased the belly.

For over 25 years, I had accepted the dangers of landing off the airport. Do it enough times and eventually something bad will happen. A few weeks later, after an expensive insurance claim, the glider was like new again.

* * *

Our friends with small children told us it would be impossible to attend soaring contests the first few years with our new family. Obviously, they weren't as dedicated as we were.

I didn't want to give up flying again, even for a few years. I was *too close* to recovering the form that had fulfilled me years earlier. But, as we had heard, bringing the girls to contests was challenging, especially in our tent. Sometimes my mother and stepfather would meet us at contests with their big motorhome to assist and provide a base of operations.

My mother had learned to cope with independent living—and dating. She met her second husband at their church. They married seven years after my dad's crash. Foster Castleman was an ex-professional baseball player with a World Series ring to his credit. He was a wonderful addition to our family and my mother's loving partner for over 33 years before his death a few years ago.

At other times, Tanya's mother accompanied us. She had traveled with us often before the girls were born and we were very compatible. With or without assists from grandparents, however, we couldn't deny the logistics were more complex with the twins. There was more to plan, more to carry, more to do— and more that could go wrong.

On our first airport camping expedition when they were three months old, a pilot friend in the tent next to ours commented the morning after the girls had woken up screaming at 2:00 AM:

"It sounded like the wolves had gotten to them."

We were lucky the gathering was informal. If this had happened at a contest, we might have had fellow pilots complaining about not being able to sleep.

We rolled into the 1995 Elmira Regional after 10:00 PM and found the camping area. Tanya had her hands full appeasing our 19-month-old daughters in the van. Leaving the headlights on, I labored to set up our large tent alone. Then I plodded to and from the van to transfer luggage, portable cribs, and other child-care and camping gear. Once or twice, I may have wistfully remarked how nice it would be to share this experience with her.

It was a muggy August night, and the twins were unhappy. The van windows were open so as I trudged back and forth, Tanya and I amicably discussed the weather; the relaxed drive from New Jersey; humanity's pursuit of truth; and prospects for peace in the Middle East—typical married couple stuff. We may have raised our voices a few times to make sure we communicated over the girls' loud complaints or to demonstrate our conviction.

Just before midnight, everyone was in the tent and quieted. Packing, driving up from New Jersey in a frenzy, and setting up camp had exhausted me. Just before I zipped up the tent door, I switched off the flashlight for a last look in the moonlight. Then I saw it: another tent only yards from ours. I had missed it when driving in. I groaned as I remembered everything the two of us had said.

The next morning, embarrassed, I apologized profusely to the couple in it.

"It's okay, Chip. Our children are grown now, but we went through the same things." By nightfall, however, they had moved their tent. And word had spread. There was an unofficial DMZ around the Bearden tent. At least we had privacy, although not as much as we needed later that night, when Josie delightedly snatched the keys from my hands and set off the car alarm.

Many at this contest still tease the girls about the Doppler effect. One afternoon, Tanya hurried the van up the access road atop Harris Hill toward the entrance. The van windows were open, and the girls were wailing in a loud, high-pitched, cacophonous scream, said to be audible before the van came into view. As they passed a group standing on the steps of the National Soaring Museum, the pitch of the screams dropped, like the whistle of a train hurtling by.

This contest is also where I built the "world's largest playpen." Tanya had despaired over never having a moment to herself. This was bad for her and didn't augur well for my chances of getting her to future contests. So I set up a cheap ten feet-by-ten feet outdoor dining canopy with four poles, a center pole, and a sunshade. Then I wrapped orange plastic construction fencing around the outside of the poles, staked down the bottom edges, and overlapped the ends into a makeshift gate. Tanya could drop the girls into the outdoor playpen for an hour while she decompressed or napped.

Male pilots thought it was genius. Wives were aghast: "You have them penned up like animals!" Maybe so, but it worked.

Some questioned if we were pushing too hard to bring the family to contests. Perhaps. But I needed to fly. And I did not view going it alone as an alternative. I needed my crew there to support me the way it had always been in our family.

Regional contest at Fairfield, Pennsylvania when the girls were 2 ½ years old. (photo from Mid-Atlantic Soaring Association archives)

Flying was still expensive. I had co-founded a partnership in New York with an ex-Goldman Sachs investment banker to raise private equity funds for small businesses. Within months, we closed our first deal, for Kiwi International Airlines. But it was a cruel tease. The deal collapsed part way through the funding in 1996 when the ValuJet crash in the Everglades raised questions about low-fare airlines. We spent the next several years chasing a second deal, in vain.

We had little income except for Tanya's work. Finally, I parked my five-year-old ASW 24 and put soaring on hold for the second time while I looked for a real job. As before, Tanya's salary, help from my family, and credit card loans were all that kept us going. Tanya became expert at transferring credit card balances from one introductory six-month, no-interest credit card offer to another.

For the first time, I had a priority higher than my own, i.e., being the primary caregiver. I was working long unpaid hours from home and juggling meetings in New York. But the girls came first. I changed diapers, fed them, managed nap schedules, and kept them happy when they were awake. I read books to them and helped them learn colors. I watched countless episodes of *Teletubbies*, *Barney & Friends*, and *Arthur*. I took pride in my role. I knew I was making a difference that could impact their lives forever. I haven't always been the most enlightened man, but I think I have more understanding and empathy for mothers—especially working mothers—than do many of my gender.

After the first few years, I shuttled them to and from pre-school, playdates, and birthday parties. One afternoon, we arrived at a gymnastics studio for a birthday party. The moms and I watched as instructors led the children through exercise games. Then Tina appeared, looking up at me in tears.

"Dada...." she sniffled, clutching the yellow barrette that had slipped from her curls. I reached into my "Mr. Mom" bag for the hairbrush, ran it through her hair a few strokes, gathered and pulled it back, then clipped the barrette in place. Beaming, she scampered off to rejoin her friends. After I tucked the brush away, several mothers stared at me dumbfounded, mouths open and eyes wide.

"Hey, this stuff isn't difficult!" I laughed at their disbelieving faces, secretly delighted that I was doing something these women didn't think I could do.

I believe these years are one reason I have a special relationship with my daughters to this day. I wish I'd been smart enough to enjoy them more. I was obsessed, instead, over failing—as a father, as a husband, as a provider, and, in dark hours, as a man. This was not the traditional role of my father's generation.

I was glad I didn't have to explain to Dad the mess I'd made of my life. I suspect I would have heard from him often, though whether with a disapproving "I told you so," or to grill me, or to offer support, I'm not sure. Given his poor childhood, his struggle to claw his way up into the middle class, and his obsessive accountant's mindset, it's fair to say I was living one of his personal nightmares: jobless, heavy financial obligations, uneven employment history, and our young family totally dependent on my wife's income.

CHAPTER FORTY-FIVE

Running Away Again

I NEEDED A WIN. I needed a win like a man lost in the desert needs water. I was underemployed, in my mid-40s, unable to connect with a conventional job, cash flow negative, and deep in debt for the second time in less than ten years. I had twin girls. Flying was once more on hold. I knew we were more fortunate than many (no matter how bad things seem, they can always get worse), but my stress was off the charts. When I sat around feeling sorry for myself, which was most of the time, I was frantic for something positive to help get my life back on track or to buffer the sense that I had failed.

Being a full-time father helped. But it was a challenge to soldier on despite all the problems. A fog of depression had settled over my life, with a deep, creeping melancholia that threatened to consume me. Although I wasn't considering suicide, I came to understand better how someone overwhelmed by hopelessness and sadness might. People later said I appeared optimistic. But I think they were lying. They had probably all wanted to say, "Snap out of it, you jerk!"

It was Tanya who opened the door. A year after our daughters were born, she announced, at age 38, she wished to run her first marathon. I helped her train for the 1995 New York City Marathon, which she completed handily. When she signed up again the following year, I was once again running more consistently as I had 15 years before—with one difference.

Running for me had always been solitary, even when logging 50 miles a week for my first marathons. I'd had little interest in finding and scheduling compatible training partners and being forced into pacing a little too fast or too slow. Then Tanya joined a local running club and dragged me along on her group runs. We drove over to her mother's house on Saturday evenings with our toddlers for dinner and stayed over. Up before dawn, we met a group who ran together each Sunday at 7:00 AM in a neighboring town. After indulging in a guilt-free long run, we returned a few hours later to find Tanya's mother playing delightedly with her giggling granddaughters.

Running with this group helped me right myself in the sea of problems that had washed over and threatened to drown me. When I stopped flying, I had lost touch with my soaring friends. Few of them were reaching out. To be fair, neither was I. It was depressing to be around soaring when I wasn't flying. But it was mutual. I'd seen it before. When you're unable to fly—for whatever reason—

pilots often are uneasy around you. You are a living reminder their involvement in flying could end unexpectedly. Flying may be all you have in common. So, as with married couples sitting down awkwardly with a newly widowed friend, they're not sure what to say.

In my long-run group, there was a spirit of camaraderie. We were of disparate ages, abilities, experience, and ambitions, but we shared a commitment to showing up every Sunday. Like my soaring friends, we took pride in regarding ourselves as exceptional, and that sanctioned unusual forthrightness.

As Tanya trained for her second marathon, I loped along in her group at an easy pace. The weekly long run—anywhere from, say, eight to over 20 miles—is the foundation of distance training. Two simple rules govern the pace:

Rule #1: If you can't maintain a conversation, you're running too fast.

Rule #2: If you're not sweating, you're not running fast enough.

This spans a wide range. I looked forward to these long runs as therapy. We talked non-stop for hours about everything: running, of course, but also movies, books, careers, family problems, relationships, politics, jokes, sex, health, or whatever. We had our own "what happens in Vegas, stays in Vegas" code. When the workout was over, so was the chatter—and any sense of judgment. I never discussed soaring, though. It hadn't become any easier to explain. And talking about it reminded me I was out of the game.

Distance running was healthy and didn't cost much. I rediscovered the sense of purpose, accomplishment, and respect I was missing elsewhere in my life. An odd turn in the fall of 1996 set me in my new direction.

Journal Entry: October 6, 1996 (New York, New York)

We have driven into Manhattan early on the first Sunday in October so Tanya can do her last 20-mile, Central Park training run hosted by the New York Road Runners (NYRRC had dropped "Club" from their name when the New York Marathon morphed into a business).

The weather is perfect, cool, crisp, and sunny. As planned, I quit after three loops (15 miles) with Tanya and friends and grab water and a banana. But I am vaguely disgruntled at my sudden spectator status. I still feel strong. On impulse, I jump in solo and finish the last five-mile loop, tired but not exhausted. It is the first time I have been to 20 miles in 15 years.

When I find my companions, one of them—a veteran of many marathons, including Boston—appraises me suspiciously.

"What kind of runner does 20 miles *for fun?* What are you training for?"

"Nothing," I laugh. "I just felt good."

I wasn't lying. But something clicked: "I can still do this!" Contemplating a marathon after a 15-year lapse was invigorating. I would have a purpose. I could prove something to myself and earn the respect of my new friends by completing one of the most fundamental challenges of distance running.

The Philadelphia Marathon was the final East Coast marathon on the calendar, only six weeks away. Experienced marathoners know the race is half over at 20, where most amateurs "hit the wall" as the miles deplete their bodies of stored energy. It normally takes at least 13 weeks to build the mileage base to prepare for this. So I put together a modified training plan based on the long runs I had been doing with Tanya and her group and the time I had remaining before the race.

In late November, we drove down to Philly for the recently resuscitated marathon there. The next day, I ran 26.2 miles. It gratified me when our running group professed amazement at my time (3:46), which was significantly better than they expected based on our much slower training pace.

There were so many things wrong with my life. What kept me going was the support from my running group and the fulfillment I received from running marathons. Running once again became significant in my life, like it had been 15 years earlier, because it was something I could control. Everything else except for being a father was at the mercy of others, such as my business partner, clients, potential employers, and creditors. I was putting a lot of effort into my career, first in my partnership and later in a job search. But success is not always proportionate with the level of effort. Hard work might be a pre-requisite, but it is not a guarantee.

Running offered a more direct connection between effort and outcome, but with the uncertainty that made it more enthralling. I knew I wouldn't be winning any awards for speed, but I rediscovered the joy of discipline and training schedules, and the challenge of racing. I approached running the same way I did soaring, with a day-by-day training plan and mile-by-mile pace charts for each race's elevation profile. I studied race nutrition and optimized my gear, even using a kitchen scale to weigh my shoes and custom insoles.

When my soaring friend, Erik Mann, joined us one Sunday morning for a long run, my running buddies pestered him:

"Is Chip as obsessive about flying as he is about running?"

Erik laughed out loud. To him, "obsessive" was part of my personality. I doubt he knew the extent to which running was standing in for soaring.

My dream to top the list at the U.S. National Soaring Championships was on hold. Now I had a different ambition. I had listened as the better runners in our group talked casually about running the Boston Marathon. I coveted the deference shown to veterans of this prestigious race.

Boston holds the prestige of being the oldest annual marathon in the world. But the captivating allure for amateurs like us—and the challenge—is simply gaining entry. Boston, unlike almost every other marathon, is not "open." It has qualifying standards. I had a vague notion that a "BQ" (Boston Qualifier) was under three hours. It was—for men under 30. But the standard varied by age and gender. So at 47, my BQ standard was 3:25—the same time I had run back in 1981 at Richmond. True, I was 30 years old then. But if I had done it once....

Initially, as with my very first marathon attempt in New York in 1978, I kept my goal a secret—even after I began chasing it. In late 1998, at the Steamtown Marathon in Scranton, Pennsylvania, I pushed a little harder in the early downhill miles. Predictably, I hit the wall hard and struggled to finish. But my 3:37 brought me within 12 minutes of a BQ. That was a lot of time to improve, but it didn't seem impossible. The quest was on!

A year later, I had cut my time to 3:30. That wasn't bad for a 48-year-old, but it was still five minutes away from a BQ. I couldn't escape the effects of age, and soon I was running a little slower each year. Offsetting that, I was "aging up" into a new Boston age bracket every five years. My BQ became a moving target, always three to five minutes away, like a carrot dangled on a string just out of reach. As the significance of my attempts grew, I viewed gaining entry to the Holy Grail of marathons with the same gravity as I did winning at national soaring contests.

I had grown up in the shadow of my successful, handsome, athletic father. Through my second chapter of marathon running after a 15-year hiatus and battling the fear of failure in my career, I found solace in my achievements and a quiet sense of pride. Professionally, it was a different story. I was still without a job and our financial situation had deteriorated such that Tanya had gingerly raised the subject of selling the ASW 24 to pay down some of our debts. I conceded she might be right. We couldn't go on like this much longer.

CHAPTER FORTY-SIX

Once More to the Lake[31]

J UST BEFORE CLOSING OUT THE TWENTIETH CENTURY, my family celebrated Thanksgiving in Cincinnati. We were grateful for so much. The six cousins were playing happily together (Mark, Diane, and I each have two children, all within a few years). And the big news: I was working again! Thanks to an introduction by soaring friend Erik Mann, I had landed a temporary gig with Mindtree, a venture-backed software services startup he helped launch. I hoped it would transition into a full-time job, my ninth career in 25 years. That says less about my career planning than it does about my adaptability to change.

The Friday after Thanksgiving, I tossed a bucket of cold water on things. "I'd like to drive up to Deer Creek State Park again. Anyone else interested?"

There was an awkward pause. It had been 19 years since the accident and seven years since my visit. My brother confessed he had driven over the year after the crash. No one else seemed to have considered doing so.

My father's crash had been one of my life's defining moments. Even after so long, I couldn't let it go. Dad's death had affected my siblings at least as much. Yet they seemed to have been more successful moving on. We had shared much that day. Yet there were differences.

I had not stood in their shoes. Mark had gotten the news while waiting eagerly by the telephone with no warning, as if struck by a sniper's bullet. He had relayed the horrific report to our equally unsuspecting sister and mother. The blow softened little by his being there in person.

But none of them had been in the cockpit with me to see Dad fly that day, as he brought all his best qualities as a soaring pilot to the fore. They hadn't watched the unknown glider float serenely under me near the end of the flight, nor had they seen the crash that altered our lives. They hadn't approached the cockpit and been staggered by seeing him lying lifeless in the broken airplane. We had shared much, but not everything.

---

[31] With apologies to E. B. White for his short story.

Journal Entry: November 26, 1999 (Deer Creek State Park, Ohio)

To no one's great surprise, my mother declines. So Tanya, Mark, Diane, Diane's husband David, and I embark on the journey, driving 1½ hours across empty farmland under a cold, metallic gray sky in late November. It's subdued in the car. I recall the nervousness from my 1992 trip, not sure what to expect. I sit up and check their faces, wondering what is on their minds.

As before, we find no evidence of the events of June 19, 1980. More years have passed. Given the disagreeable weather, there's little enthusiasm for the quasi-archeological exploration needed to dig down through 20 sedimentary strata of decayed leaves and fallen trees to uncover whatever fragments of shattered glider might remain. We wander aimlessly for a while, then drive to the Park Office and ask the staff to retrieve the photos again.

I have a secret fear someone might have tossed or misplaced a handful of Polaroid prints stuffed into a file for an incident that predated most of the rangers. But the staff produce them straight away. I study them closely, as do my brother and sister, who are seeing them for the first time. Later, sheepish but chuckling, Diane confesses,

"It took everything I had not to just scoop them up and run!"

It was quiet on the ride back to my mother's house. Hours later—after she and my stepfather retired for the night—the rest of us gathered eagerly in a circle on the floor and talked back and forth, animated and thoughtful. I dug out some items buried in the closet, including a large photo of my father a friend had framed [see photo on the back cover of this book]. We compared memories of the crash. It was the first time in over a decade we had discussed it constructively. I suppose we all had guarded our hurts—and the way we dealt with them.

There was no epiphany, but each of us gleaned details. I wasn't aware Diane had heard our Code Four, "on final glide to land out" radio calls, or my last unanswered attempts to contact Papa Golf after I saw the unknown glider go down. And they learned more about what the crash scene had been like for me.

These oddly comforting details helped fill the gaps in what initially was a patchy, incomplete memory for me and one that, over time, eroded to become even more so. And while my siblings and I shared reminiscences and minor revelations, Tanya and Diane's husband added texture and tone to a bleak narrative they had first heard over a decade before.

CHAPTER FORTY-SEVEN

Third Time Around

I HAD BEEN CHASING A JOB FOR SO LONG, when I finally connected, I half feared the company would rescind the offer after I told everyone.

Based on my three-month subcontract with Mindtree, they had invited me to join full time. As the rest of the world celebrated the passing of the millennium, our family rejoiced at my becoming—at age 48—a full-time employee with a steady paycheck. The job was helping business users define what they needed from Web sites and software systems so our technical experts could design and build them. It leveraged my 25 multi-disciplinary years in the business world. As my career flourished, I once again dug myself out of a deep financial hole. As the rising tide of personal debt receded, I wanted it all: family, career, running, *and* soaring.

Early in my flying, just getting in the air was enough. As time went on, competing against other pilots became the main attraction. Flying locally for fun was still enjoyable and allowed me to clear my head. Making practice cross-country flights, particularly in the company of accomplished pilots, appealed. I still relished the moments of wonder, mastery, and beauty that flying offered. But competition was the driving force behind my passion for flying.

When I couldn't fly, marathon running had stood in for it—especially my pursuit of a Boston Qualifier time. But nothing ever quite replaced it.

Now I wanted back in. After getting a check out from Erik Mann (flight instructor, good friend, and colleague) and practicing up again in the summer of 2000, I drove to Dansville, New York, with my family for their Regional in late August. This was my second comeback contest after a long layoff, hopefully without the traumatic crash scene at New Castle nine years before.

"Jake Baker, good to have you back!"

I *loved* hearing that again. At the contest, we reconnected with people we hadn't seen in three or four years. I flew well, gaining confidence and moving up, until—on the last day—I put it all together the way I once had.

Journal Entry: August 26, 2000 (Dansville, New York)

After a perfect start, I push hard going down the valley southeast to the turn just short of Elmira. On the return leg, I bounce a gaggle and jump to a better-looking cloud beyond them that rewards me with a fast climb. Then I stay ahead of the pack, working a long final glide under a line of dappled cu.

I'm 12 or 13 miles out. A highly respected 15 Meter pilot pulls up on my left wing. With no warning, he pushes over in a dive and floors it, the sailplane leaping forward in full, high-speed "finish line" mode, dropping away from me as he pulls ahead. All the way up the valley, we have been romping home, zooming under each cloud to gain altitude without circling. It's too early for this exuberant display of "warp speed." I can't see the airport yet.

"What the hell is he doing?" It looks like he's diving for the finish line. Then the light bulb goes on. "No way. He wouldn't." I almost laugh out loud.

He would. Just ahead, the valley we're in empties into a deeper (by 1,400 feet) valley that leads to the Dansville airport ten miles beyond. In amused disbelief, I realize he intends to make a high-speed pass over a hilltop just before that drop off, then zoom up and glide home. I let my airspeed build to 120 knots, losing altitude fast, aiming at the pasture on the hill just ahead.

"Three-four (his contest number), Juliet Bravo is at your four o'clock."

Off his right wing and slightly behind, I level out less than 50 feet above the pasture. Shaking my head over how outrageously immature this is, we smoke past a farm building fractions of a second apart, the treetops a blur at near redline speed. This is our private indulgence; no one is watching. At the far end of the field, we pull back steeply, using that crazy airspeed to loft ourselves up to normal final glide altitude as the valley drops away. With Dansville in sight, ten miles ahead, the glide computer says "go." Five minutes later, we flash across the finish line not quite as fast, pull up not quite as steeply, and land in trail, not quite as close together. We're both laughing as we bump to a stop. It wasn't the most efficient way to come home. He admits he did it just for fun. That's okay; so did I. It's been a while.

Our six-year-old daughters can finally appreciate the contests they have attended since they were babies are not mere camping trips but are also glider races where their father competes. When it turns out I have won the day, I enliven my winner's speech, concluding with:

"And I'd like to thank [pilot X, the leader] for *finally* allowing me to answer in the affirmative when asked, as I am every day, 'Dada, did you win?'"

CHAPTER FORTY-EIGHT

The Big Slump

I T'S UNFAIR! Investment advisors caution that if it seems too good to be true, it probably is. So why, when I apply the same reasoning to life, am I accused of being pessimistic?

In my mid-50s, life was good. The new job was great. The girls were flourishing in primary school. Tanya had exited her beloved *Vanity Fair* in New York and began working at the library in the next town in a new sort of dream job. She could pick up the girls after school five minutes away, return to the library for homework and reading, and then shuttle them to skating, piano, violin, etc.

I was back in the flying game. My erstwhile dream of breaking through again seemed more real when I placed sixth at a murky, weak-weather 2003 Sports Class Nationals in Elmira. That boosted me one small step above the seventh place I had earned in my first-ever nationals at Bryan, Ohio, 27 years earlier. This 2003 contest was less consequential—it was smaller than my first nationals in 1976—but it meant at least as much. Back then, I was an eager rookie with nothing to prove. More than a quarter of a century later, I was an aging, humbled veteran with everything to prove.

In Texas, on the way to Standard Class Nationals in Hobbs, New Mexico, 2007.

To ease the chore of traveling to faraway soaring contests, I bought a three-year-old commercial, full-size Chevrolet van on eBay and had it shipped up from Texas. I stripped the interior and fitted it out with a large window, carpeting, upholstered walls and ceiling, reading lights, an audio/video system, two rows of reclining seats, and a full-width bench seat in the third row where I could lie down and nap. Thus equipped, our family traveled to contests each summer in New York, Ohio, Texas, and New Mexico. Long drives were less stressful when the girls could read, listen to music, watch videos, and nap.

Tenting at Standard Class Nationals, Hobbs, New Mexico, 2004 (the girls were 10).

* * *

I was closing in on a Boston Qualifier time, only three minutes away. I ran at least one and up to four marathons a year. Flying was still central in my life, but I spent far more time training for marathons. Juggling these was challenging. Each weekend in the spring and summer, I tried to fly on the better weather day and run long on the "off" day. A few times, desperate for a workout and a flight, I rose especially early and did both, but that was too stressful.

Chasing a BQ spanned thirteen serious attempts over nine years, plus a handful of less intense "fun" marathons with friends and family and "comeback" marathons while recovering from injuries. Pushing myself so hard in training meant that I was always one workout away from injury.

More than once, I overdid it and injuries forced me to lay off from running. The low point was a 20-mile training run five weeks before the Philly Marathon in 2004. I finished the run despite a growing pain in my heel. Within hours, it was so swollen and painful, I couldn't even walk without limping, much less run. The diagnosis: a small tear in my Achilles tendon. Disaster! I was panicky and depressed, curt, short-tempered, retreating inside myself.

Obsessed with a BQ and not wanting to lose my streak of nine Philly Marathons, I cross-trained with fervor, riding a stationary bike for an hour on weeknights. On weekends, I did my "long run" in the deep end of the swimming pool, running in place with a flotation vest for up to three hours, dodging kids jump-ing off the diving board. I swallowed anti-inflammatories and hid an ice pack under the desk at the client while icing my ankle. I ducked into the client's fire stairs to stretch my Achilles. I found it difficult to think of anything else except my recovery. I didn't know if I could even run, much less have a shot at a BQ.

I was nervous as I drove down to Philly for the race. Yet my body rose to the occasion, and I finished only three minutes off my goal. I was overjoyed!

It's ironic that my marvelous recovery before Philly 2004 gave me a false sense of invulnerability and led me to believe I could push my body to its limits, with few consequences. My running friends warned me against my obsessive training regimen, which inflicted a virtual encyclopedia of overuse injuries to my hips, legs, ankles, feet, and knees. While I never missed big races, I turned in some sub-par performances while recovering from injuries. Yet I persisted, still believing I would prevail, shrugging off aches and pains as a wily politician ignores allegations of corruption.

* * *

I was right. Life *was* too good to be true. In the spring of 2005, things took a turn for the worse. A painful lower back forced me to slow down. By fall, my marathon time had dropped by 15 minutes. I found myself running alone, unable to keep pace with my training group of nearly a decade.

There are worse problems in life, but this one deeply disturbed me. Almost missing the Philadelphia Marathon the previous year had forced me to accept I was defining my self-worth to an uncomfortable degree through marathons. Coming so dramatically and mysteriously, this slowdown was more distressing than my overtraining injuries or the inevitable decline due to aging.

In October 2005, my doctor ran a battery of tests. I grumbled when his office called to insist I come in to review the results. Why not a quick telephone dis-cussion? The CT image of my lower spine revealed one disk half as thick as the others. Not bulging or ruptured; just thinner, likely the result of 30 years of running and desk jobs hammering it down.

"What's that mean?" I asked, with studied calm. I was too young and healthy for back problems, right?

"Nothing serious, now. You might need surgery later in life," he reassured me, "But that's not what I'm concerned about. Your liver enzymes are high."

"What's *that* mean?" I asked, my eyes narrowing and voice rising [what were liver enzymes, anyway?]

He responded awkwardly. "I'm not sure. I'd like to run some more tests." Visions of liver transplants came to mind. But there was more!

"Your CPK level is high," he said, staring down at his notes, avoiding looking directly at me.

"What's *that* mean?" I shot back, more sharply this time, sitting up straight.

Worry creasing his forehead, he explained. Elevated levels of the creatine phosphokinase enzyme in the blood could signal heart muscle damage, i.e., a heart attack. Again, more tests.

"Heart attack?" I thought. "No freakin' way! I'm a marathon runner."

Unbelievably, he wasn't finished! This might have been a comedy routine if it hadn't been so worrisome. The next bombshell: "Your testosterone level is high. It's well above the range for a man your age."

Whew! Finally, some good news. He-he-he.

No smile from the doctor. Apparently not.

"What's *that* mean?" I asked, shellshocked and exhausted. The answer: he needed to examine my testicles. Fine.

A few minutes later: "You have a cyst."

I paused and looked directly at him. "How do you know it's a cyst?"

There was an awkward silence. "Actually, I don't," the doctor confessed.

I continued to stare straight at him: "What else could it be?" ignoring the trial lawyer's practice of only asking questions to which one already knows the answers.

"Well—it *could* be cancer." No cause for alarm, though. More tests.

So there it was. Minutes earlier I had walked in, a healthy 54-year-old man with a backache and a slow marathon time. Now I faced three potentially life-threatening diseases, and—if I lived long enough—back surgery!

As a flying buddy later commented: "Forget the tests, Chip. You should have driven yourself straight to the mortician!"

Lightheaded and queasy, I stumbled out to my car and drove back to my office (wearing my seat belt; I wasn't yet suicidal). I thought I managed the news rather well. But my friend Erik remarked later my face betrayed some concern.

Half an hour on the Internet (the source of all knowledge) strongly suggested what retesting confirmed a week later: the cause of the high liver enzymes and CPK levels was a 20+ mile run the day before the original blood test. *[The medical literature documents this but many doctors are unaware of it.]*

That night I stopped by an imaging clinic for an ultrasound scan of the "cyst." As we were finishing, the sonographer—sensing my anxiety—smiled:

"I'm not supposed to say anything directly to you," she said, "But you have nothing to worry about."

That left the flattened disk, bone spurs, and calcium deposits. I searched for a doctor who would do surgery on my spine. It promised a full recovery, though not without risk. A close running friend stared at me in disbelief:

"Wait a minute, Chip, you tell me you can run, work, play with your daughters, work around the house, fly your glider, and have sex. And the *only* reason you're thinking of having major surgery on your spine is that your marathon time is 15 minutes slower? Are you out of your f**king mind?"

Fair enough. Death wasn't imminent, but neither was a return to my former running form. I went through all five stages of grief: denial, anger, bargaining, depression, and—at last—acceptance. Twice I had survived forced absences from soaring. I had given up marathons for 15 years. So I would get through this. I had accomplished much. I had a beautiful family with a loving wife and two wonderful daughters. Life wasn't perfect, but it was pretty damned good.

So, I mentally acquiesced to running for fitness, if at all. It was similar to how I had earlier come to terms with being a competent but unexceptional soaring pilot years earlier. It had taken me a long time to learn to accept what life offered, but with maturity, I had become more accommodating. I still held onto my dreams, but I recognized some of them might be unattainable.

I wouldn't understand for over a year that those dreams still had some life left in them.

CHAPTER FORTY-NINE

Last Time to the Lake

T WENTY-FIVE YEARS after Joe Bearden's fatal crash, I returned to Caesar Creek Soaring Club, in June 2005, for the Standard Class Nationals. Unlike in 1980, CCSC could accommodate the smaller field of 23 gliders (part of a declining trend in soaring worldwide) with their grass runway.

While I was there, I also celebrated the 40th anniversary of my first flying lesson. Separately, it startled me to learn Deer Creek Lake had morphed into an official turnpoint. At times in the contest, we passed over the ground where my father had died. On one task, I stared down at the crash site as I circled in a thermal directly overhead. I hadn't realized this would affect me after a quarter of a century. Yet seeing the site from above still made me uneasy. I probably watched too many episodes of the original *The Twilight Zone* as a kid.

Then, late in the contest, this resonance with the past took an ominous turn.

Journal Entry: June 17, 2005 (Waynesville, Ohio)

I've been low and slow all day. That's bad news on a big, 228-mile, bowtie-shaped four-turnpoint task in Southwestern Ohio. Each time I hit a decent thermal and climb up, I exhale in relief: "Okay, let's make up some time!" Then I glide for miles, until I am forced to take a weak thermal to stay aloft.

I'm headed southeast on the second leg toward Pickaway County Airport when I sense something is wrong. On my GPS map, I should see the Columbus controlled airspace off my left wing. But there's nothing, even when zooming out. It's just missing. Then a horrific realization of what I've done sweeps over me as I reach up and touch the card slot on the navigation device.

It's empty. S**t! I forgot to replace the memory card this morning. It's the card that holds the boundaries of the FAA's do-not-enter controlled airspace. There's a lot of that around the big commercial airports at Cincinnati, Dayton, and—of course—Columbus. Fighting a rising tide of panic, I check landmarks. I'm okay so far. If I'd gone any further east of course, that might not be true. The bigger problem is the next leg. I have to thread the needle between airspace surrounding Dayton and Wright-Patt AFB to the north and

Cincinnati airspace to the south.

It's worse than I thought. Damn! Traveling west on the long third leg, there are some stunning clouds just north of course. The problem is they're sitting right up against—or even within—the restricted airspace surrounding Wright-Patterson Air Force Base and Dayton. In the old days, I would have just eyeballed it and kept a lookout for other aircraft. But it's too risky now. There's no physical boundary; the FAA didn't go around painting big red warning lines on the ground. But my GPS knows, and my flight log will expose any infringement, even by a few feet. And the penalty is crippling.

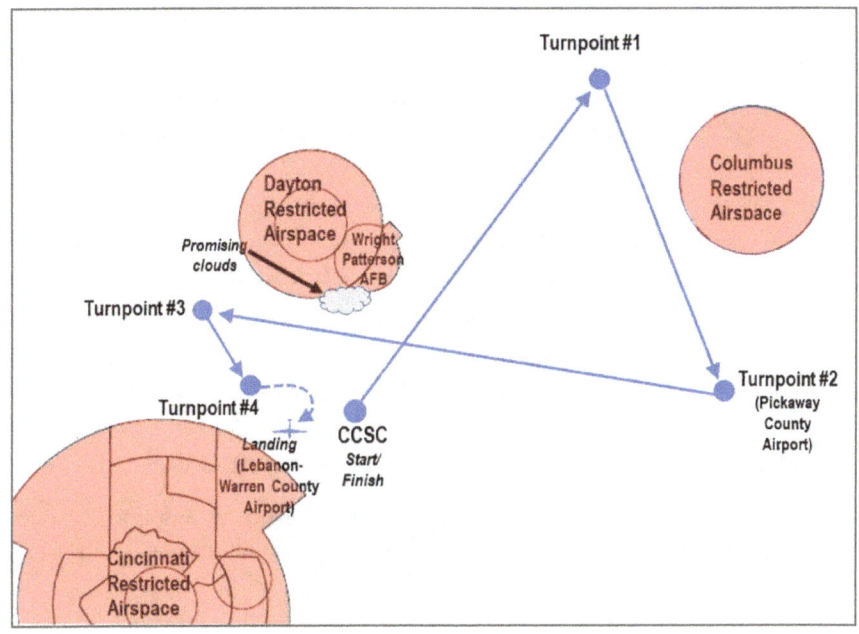

Task on 17 Jun 2005, Standard Class Nationals, Caesar Creek Soaring Club. Pilots'
kit map originally from Worldwide Turnpoint Exchange.

Tortured, I gaze at an almost certain thermal a few miles off my right wing. Then, still raging over my stupid error, I plow on west for the third turnpoint. There I turn south on the shortest leg of the bowtie to the final turn and then head for the finish 16 miles away. The air is smooth. The weak evening thermals are dying. It is a race against the sun as it sinks toward the horizon, and I am losing. The computer says I'm below final glide to the finish. It is close to 8:00 PM, an hour before sunset near the edge of the Eastern Time Zone. I'm the last guy aloft. Every other competitor has finished or reported in. I can see the Caesar Creek gliderport, not much over five miles away, beckoning to me in the evening sunlight. It's so close. But I'm so low.

The early evening air is still. Reluctant to land off the airport a few miles short of CCSC, I turn back and land eight miles from the finish line at the Lebanon-Warren County Airport. I know it well. It was the first turnpoint on that fateful Day Three of the 1980 Nationals at Springfield. I got a close-up view then and nearly had to land. I climb out of the cockpit tired, hot, head down, and feeling an acute sense of failure. I thought I was going to finish.

A mobile telephone call is my first update to my family in over an hour. My last low-altitude radio transmission didn't go through. My long-suffering mother has been waiting anxiously. When Mark arrives to retrieve me, he confides she was close to tears during the last hour. The situation is reminiscent of my father's crash, a national contest hosted by our club two days before the same date 25 years ago, with Pickaway County as a turnpoint. Guilt combines with depression over the landout. It's a long night.

Tanya and our daughters flew out to join me for the last few days of the contest after the school year concluded. When the contest was over, with another unimpressive showing for me, we piled into our van, hitched on the trailer, and headed for New Jersey. I had one stop to make.

Journal Entry: June 24, 2005 (Deer Creek State Park, Ohio)

No one at the Deer Creek State Park office knows anything about the crash 25 years earlier. They recall hearing about it, but they can't find the Polaroid photos I've seen twice before. We hang around waiting for the chief ranger, off duty that day, to return their calls. He's the only one who's been around long enough who might know where to look.

It's hot and humid. There's nothing to entertain our 11-year-old girls. I can't blame them for their lack of enthusiasm for tramping through tall grass and thorn bushes and listening to my stories about a grandfather they never met (my stepfather is the only grandfather they know). Tanya is trying to be supportive, but she's losing patience, too.

Once more, I am alone at Deer Creek State Park, trapped in my past, seeking "closure." Some episodes in life are metaphorical unraveled threads fraying in our subconsciousness, that we must clip or tuck away to resolve. Most people do so and move on. But for whatever reason, I never have.

After lunch, I give up. The chief ranger still hasn't telephoned. I don't know if the photos still exist or when I'll be back, but it's not happening today. As we merge onto I-71, the family can sense my dejection. I'm slumped in the driver's seat, withdrawn. The mood is gloomy. A few miles on, not quite an hour after we depart, my mobile phone rings.

"We finally reached our boss and we've got your photos! He knew exactly where they were!"

The head ranger had been on the scene the day my father crashed. Doubling back will delay our arrival in New Jersey until the wee hours of the morning. Tanya can read my face. We make a U-turn at the next exit.

Time has faded the Polaroid prints, but to my surprise, they are in excellent condition. While Tanya entertains our daughters, I set up my scanner in a conference room and scan each photo into my laptop PC, making backups. I keep the graphic photographs away from Josie and Tina. [Until they read a draft of this book, they had never seen them.]

Crash site, view from front & right rear. In latter, "PG" visible on left side (on vertical fin, lying flat). (photos by Bruce E. Morgan, Deer Creek State Park, Ohio)

As I place the photos in the scanner, I scrutinize them closely. Since then, I've examined them again several times using Photoshop to enhance the images and reveal details. And I learn—almost nothing. In only one photo is Joe Bearden's body visible. Other than to confirm my father lying dead in the cockpit didn't look remotely like him when he was alive, none of the images tells me much I don't already know.

The only revelation is the devastation to the aircraft. It was worse, much worse than I remembered.

CHAPTER FIFTY

Farewell to Boston

I HAD CLOSED THE BOOK on Deer Creek State Park. Now it was time to let go of the Boston Marathon. I had chased that dream for nine years. My performance was declining, and I couldn't figure out why.

What I wanted most was relief from lower back pain. So, in the spring of 2006, I scheduled a visit with a specialist, Dr. Thomas Agesen, to show him my spinal CT images. I feared his advice would echo what I'd heard so many times from doctors—i.e., "if it hurts when you run, then stop running."

The Sunday before the appointment, I surprised my old running crew for the first time in months. I didn't mention this could be our last run together. That seemed melodramatic. Maybe I should have explained. After welcoming me warmly, they loped out of sight within half a mile. I never saw them again.

My CT images didn't discourage Dr. Agesen. He thought calcium deposits might be impinging on a nerve. A former All-American soccer player at Penn State, he was eager to find a solution. When an anti-inflammatory injection had no effect, he sent me to a physical therapist. After a few months of working with her, my decline began to reverse.

When I started running seriously back in the 1970s, I put in a lot of effort to achieve my goals. I spent months planning, training, making sacrifices, dealing with pain, and tracking my progress. The end goal was always a big race, where I either succeeded or failed.

Injuries involve a different kind of goal. There's not always a "big day." It's more of a journey. I've spent countless hours running in place in the deep end of a pool, on a stationary bike, or on an elliptical trainer, without knowing how long it would take for me to recover, or even *if* I would recover. Unless I had a marathon approaching, my focus was more on making progress.

Recovering from illness is similar. A common cold may only take a week or two. Other illnesses can take longer. Some of my recoveries have taken two years. Sometimes I haven't known if I would ever get back to normal. A few times, I haven't. Much of the healing process is out of my control. Even with modern medicine, my body heals when it wants to. I've learned to be patient, to stick to my plan even when it seems hopeless, which has often been the case.

Regardless of whether it's an injury or illness, I can't always chase the recovery. I need to keep going, persevere, and wait for the recovery to come to me.

This was one of those times. I didn't know when or if I would ever return to normal. But when we left for Texas to fly the Nationals in early August, I was pain free and slowly getting faster.

* * *

Uvalde, Texas, is the birthplace of Academy-Award-Winning actor Matthew McConaughey *[and the site of a tragic mass school shooting in 2022]*. The draw for me, however, was the 2006 Standard Class Nationals. We drove 2,000 miles to this small town on the edge of the Texas hill country.

Uvalde is renowned for hosting multiple world and U.S. national championships in superb soaring conditions. The weather on the ground, however, is insufferable, often over 100°F and humid. It's worse than Cordele, albeit without the gnats. It's so unbearable, I made an exception to our 25-year routine and booked a hotel room with a swimming pool instead of camping. I was a hero in the eyes of my family!

The reward was nine (out of ten) exceptional soaring days. It was the first time since Minden, 25 years earlier, I could look ahead at incredible streets of high, redolent cumulus clouds and know simply by pulling up and slowing in the thermals, then pushing over to 80 to 100 knots between them, I could close the last 50 miles into the finish without making a single circle.

We flew long tasks at high speeds, and I finished the contest with no landouts and another solid, albeit unimpressive, result.

* * *

I returned to New Jersey after having not exercised for two weeks, owing to the dangerously elevated temperatures and humidity. A client, a senior executive at Avis Budget Group—sponsor of the New York City Marathon—offered me a bib number for that highly sought-after race. It tempted me. I hadn't run New York since 1979. But if marathon training had provoked my back pain and slowdown, how smart would it be to do it again?

Being smart about marathons has never been my *forte*. The lure of New York triumphed over common sense. I ramped up my training without injury and finished the race in early November in a so-so 3:54. That was better. But Boston still seemed out of reach even though, having turned 55, my BQ was now 3:45.

The Philadelphia Marathon was in two weeks. I'd never run back-to-back marathons so soon, even when healthy. And I wasn't sure I was healthy; I'd been in recovery mode for months and running New York hadn't helped. Philly on two weeks' rest would be crazier than New York had been.

Then Laura, a friend who had spectated at New York, emailed:

"I looked for you up and down First Ave and was so sorry to miss you—so imagine my surprise to see what an amazing finish!!! You have been way too modest about your preparedness. What a killer comeback! So what will it take to get you to Philly to pace me in two weeks!?!"

"I'll just hold you back," I warned. Her flattery was a nice sales job, but there's no way I could maintain her target pace, which was five minutes faster than anything I'd done since before my slowdown. But it would be terrific to keep my streak alive at Philly (11 in a row) and have company in the early miles. So, without telling our running friends, I drove down alone and entered the 2006 Philadelphia Marathon the day before the race.

Journal Entry: November 19, 2006 (Philadelphia Marathon)

I have a long relationship with the Philly Marathon, reconnecting with it each year. The course is urban, with a few hills. The late November weather, barren trees, and gray skies often evoke that Simon and Garfunkel song from my high school days, "A Hazy Shade of Winter." The race has grown exponentially since I first ran it ten years ago, but it's still a part of me.

Laura and I miss each other at the start (I'm not sure what part of "I'll meet you five yards behind the starting line on the left curb" was confusing), but from the gun, I run as if I am on a genuine BQ attempt (i.e., 8:35 per mile). I don't feel strong in the first half, but I maintain a slightly faster pace, anyway. I'm encouraged as we move through downtown Philly, then up the steepest hill into Fairmount Park at ten miles, and back down to the Schuylkill River again. Mile by mile, I build a 45-second cushion on top of the 59-second margin Boston customarily allows. *[in those days, for my 3:45 target, Boston accepted times up to 3:45:59]*

Philly and I may be old friends, but she is mercurial, sometimes delighting me, at other times disappointing and even jilting me. I seldom know which it will be early in the race. This is my 13th serious BQ attempt—my ninth at Philly—and I've been on pace at this point for most if not all of them. So I am coy with my emotions. I've been this far too many times.

I reach the halfway point, musing to myself—is this real? As we re-cross the Schuylkill River by Boathouse Row and climb up from the basin through the crowds massed at the Art Museum start/finish line at 13 miles, I have a 100+ second buffer that will allow me to run an 8:44 pace for the remaining 12 miles. But from experience, I know I will almost certainly hit the wall somewhere between 18 and 20, slow at least one minute per mile, and lose that cushion in no time. I almost always do.

Those last 12 miles comprise six miles up Kelly Drive along the Schuylkill River, a U-turn in the town of Manayunk at 20, then returning those same six miles down Kelly Drive. As I run up the river, the world outside seems to recede, leaving me with the steady cadence of my breathing, the sound of my feet on the pavement, cheers and encouragement from spotty knots of spectators, and the unfeeling numbers on the faces of my digital watches.

I'm checking my pace chart at each mile marker and modulating my effort using my heart rate monitor. It warns me real time if I've slowed from lack of concentration or speeded up from overexuberance. My pace *is* slowing, first to 8:40, then to 8:45 per mile. I'm losing my hard-won cushion. But I'm also drawing closer to the finish. So, my "worst case" pace is rising slowly as I make the turn. On the way back, I pass the 22-mile marker, marveling that I haven't hit the wall yet but convinced it's around the next curve.

It's like being in my sailplane on a marginal final glide, monitoring the altitude needed to glide home. Each uphill (i.e., patch of sink) costs me a few seconds (i.e., feet). Conversely, each downhill (bit of lift) rewards me with a few additional seconds (feet). At every point as I coast up and down on the slightly rolling hills, I'm projecting ahead to the finish to see how many seconds (feet) I'll have left when I arrive. My safety margin is bleeding away. Like being on final glide, the question is whether I'll run out of clock (altitude) before I run out of distance.

Something otherworldly is at work. For only the third time in my marathoning, I feel detached from my body instead of being relentlessly reminded how much it hurts. I am focusing on posture and keeping efficient arm swing. When my cadence drops, I shorten my stride and spin my legs faster. At 23, I let my hopes soar before reining them in. I need to average 8:56 to the finish, and my last mile was 8:41. But I'm still too far out if I crash now.

I slow a few seconds in mile 24. Is this the beginning of the end? I only need to average 8:59 for the last two miles, but I physically won't be able to hold on if I hit the wall now. After all this time, will I miss it by only seconds?

Then, out of nowhere, I'm overtaking a runner from my Sunday morning group, cramped up, hobbling painfully, struggling to finish. I know running with someone the last few miles will boost my pace!

"Mike, I need two more miles at nine-minute pace to get in, please!" I plead. But his legs have locked up. So he gives me an encouraging shout as I go by and continues plodding. The excitement of seeing him gives me a lift, and I complete mile 25 a little faster. Now I only need to average 9:10 for the last 1.22 miles. That's when I let my guard down. For an instant, I allow myself to believe this long-sought goal is finally within my grasp.

No! I'm so close, but If I crash now, I'll still fall short. Yet I can't help myself. As the last mile unreels, the dream I have chased for nine years is literally within sight as the back face of the Philadelphia Art Museum emerges around a bend in the river.

I could still lose it to a devastating leg cramp. Or a collision. Or a stumble and fall. All have threatened during the last miles. But with less than a mile to go, hope swells again and I can no longer restrain it. I could be only minutes from completing my quest. A wave of emotion sweeps over me as it did a quarter of a century ago at the Richmond Marathon in 1981 when I realized I was going to crush my target time—and the woman with whom I most wanted to share it wouldn't be waiting for me at the finish. There's a deep stab of regret no one is waiting for me at the finish this year, either.

I push down Kelly Drive along the snow fencing approaching the 26-mile marker where I have finished painfully so many times. The noisy crowds swell as I pull even with the Art Museum and enter the adrenaline zone of cheering, public address announcers, blaring music, course workers, screaming spectators, banners, and masses of runners. I'm two minutes away from living a dream I have chased for nearly ten years before relinquishing it as unreachable. In a perverse way, I'm *still* harboring anxieties over not being an athlete, fearful any athletic goal within my reach must not be that difficult. It's like that old Groucho Marx quip about not wanting to belong to any club that would have him as a member.

There's no pain as I open up over the final two tenths of a mile, astonished I still can and trying not to stumble as I peek at my watches. Despite my obsessive projections over the last hour, I have an irrational fear that I've miscalculated and will fall short by a few seconds.

The course deposits us at the bottom of a slight rise only 50 yards before the finish line at the foot of the Art Museum steps, where "Rocky" raised his arms in triumph. The numerals incrementing silently on the big digital clock above the electronic timing mats are the only thing that matters.

I lean in and push off on my final strides. I know my race will be over in seconds. But though I long to watch that Boston Qualifier time come up, I also want to make the moment last, to capture it, to preserve it so I can relive it again. There are only so many first times in life.

I turn it on in the last 50 yards, sprinting past runners and across the finish line, my pulse hammering, my breath searing painfully in my lungs, stabbing at the buttons on my race watches. I stagger to a stop, gasping, barely able to stand, and stare at the digits, disbelieving. 3:44:48, 12 seconds under my qualifying time! I won't even need the added 59 seconds (or worry the policy will change, as it did a few years later). I'm giddy but wobbling, hacking, coughing, hands to knees, oblivious. I read the time aloud. I *must* be sure.

I make a small bow as a volunteer blesses me by looping a ribboned finisher's medal around my neck. Another gently drapes a metallic Mylar "heat sheet" over my trembling body to ward off the chill. Snugging the heat sheet around me, I stumble to the curb and sit down heavily, stiffening up rapidly as volunteers assist the hundreds of other finishers crossing the line.

I am overwhelmed by a mix of emotions, tears in my eyes, my facial muscles twitching. I lower my head in exhaustion as I'm carried away by a transcendent reverence for this fragile, luminous, perfect moment. I want, I *need* to treasure it, worship it, lest I ruin it by saying or doing the wrong thing. What should you feel, what should you think when you fear you'll never experience such pure, undiluted joy again?

I want to hold on to this perfect moment forever, to remember it like a cherished ticket stub or the flower I wore in my lapel at my wedding. I want to bottle up these emotions like spirits, so I can uncork and imbibe them when I need to revisit this moment.

With the enormity of what has occurred, I'm still holding back. Something could go wrong. The timing system might not record my finish. It happens.

Despite this, I want to celebrate with wild abandon, to howl, laugh, weep, dance, and high-five those around me. I want to rejoice. I'm Rocky! I'm Superman! I'm a mess of contradictory sensations.

One of those sensations was loneliness. There was no one there to share the moment. Neither my wife nor my daughters were in Philly, echoing my experience of finishing my PR race at Richmond 25 years earlier. My running friends were still on the course or already finished and dispersed. On one of the most extraordinary days of my life, at the pinnacle of my improbable 29-year running journey, I sat on the curb ignored by tens of thousands of people, none of whom knew a thing about me or my struggle, with tears of happiness and isolation pooling in the corners of my eyes.

I used my hands to push off and stagger up—fending off worried inquiries from young volunteers unused to seeing a gray-haired man my age (55) so alarmingly depleted ("Are you okay, sir?"). I retrieved my bag, struggled into my sweats, and found my mobile phone. My first call was to Tanya, with a friend in New York that day.

"Hey, it's me. I had a good race. I finally did it! I qualified!"

[long pause] "Really?"

That was underwhelming. I'm not sure she believed me after the years of setbacks. The next call was to a friend in our office, a Boston veteran.

"Joe, it's Chip. I'm gonna need a hotel recommendation in Boston in April."

This was more like it! Hearing Joe and his wife shrieking in the background was huge. Then the sweetest responses of all: my 12-year-old daughters were wildly excited. When I arrived home that afternoon, they had dragged their grandmother to the local supermarket to get a congratulatory cake for me. They might not grasp the full context yet, but they knew how happy their father was.

That night, I could hear the drums beating. A group email hit the ether from my running club with a lengthy list of members who had finished Philly—with my name missing. Only Laura had known I was running, and no one had thought to check. When I emailed to correct the record, the response was quick.

"Extra, extra, some more amazing news from Philly. Chip Bearden snuck into Philly at the last minute without telling anyone and just two weeks after New York he ran his first BQ after 9 long years of trying. He needed a 3:45 and ran a 3:44:48. Great job, Chip, I'm so happy for you!"

The congratulations started pouring in and didn't stop for over 24 hours.

"I am ecstatic and so happy for you! I was just saying to H___ this morning that I thought you did a great job in NY. I was wondering if you were going to sneak into Philly. This is great, I think you get the performance of the year, certainly the 'most persistent' runner award."

"You were on my mind all day. I didn't know you were running Philly, but I did know that no one seemed to know where you were. You must be a

quick healer. To have raced a BQ two weeks after New York is a great ac-complishment."

"H___ and I do really know what yesterday meant to you. We were scream-ing and jumping up and down with joy last nite upon reading the news."

"Congratulations to Chip on earning his first Boston Qualifier, two weeks after running New York and nine years after embarking on his pursuit of the Boston Grail. I have given Chip a lot of crap over the years, almost all of it deserved, but know this about Chip: He has run many marathons, suf-fered through many more injuries and put in even more effort while trying to qualify for Boston. Crazy as some of us may have thought he has been, no one has earned his BQ more. And I can't imagine anyone has felt more gratified in earning a spot in Boston."

These are only a self-indulgent sample. I could fill up an entire chapter, maybe even another small book. When I dug them out to write this, I sat there re-reading them and reliving that night 15 years earlier, replaying the sense of validation and suffused with the same vivid sensations. I can't recall a time when I felt more at peace with who I was and my place in the world than when I was receiving so many congratulatory messages.

The profound effect qualifying for Boston had on how I viewed myself wasn't entirely healthy. I shouldn't have relied on external validation so much for my self-esteem. But overnight, like a supporting player who breaks through with the winning score, I felt like a star, receiving accolades from friends, even from non-runners who knew Boston was so significant. After my father's accident in 1980, my motivation had been to achieve something great at the national level. However, my moment of triumph came not at the U.S. National Soaring Cham-pionships, but at the prestigious Boston Marathon. Twenty-eight years after completing my first marathon in New York City with the music from *Rocky* blaring over the loudspeakers, I had my personal Rocky moment.

The cruel irony was this coincided with the end of another chapter in life. A few weeks later, I learned my marriage of 20 years was headed for divorce.

CHAPTER FIFTY-ONE

The Most Dangerous Part of Marriage

I FELL IN LOVE WITH TANYA soon after our first night together in early 1982. It was a fairy tale: ordinary guy wins hand of beautiful princess.

We went through a lot together. She supported me unconditionally during tough times, emotionally, physically, and financially, for almost 25 years. We weren't a perfect match. Some of our differences were appealingly complementary. Others were grating. To outsiders, we often appeared to be the ideal couple. The reality, as with most romantic relationships, was complicated.

Relying on each other as we faced tough times seemed to bring us closer. Though each of us was unhappy with aspects of our marriage, I credulously assumed our journey together and our love for each other would prevail. The truth jolted, bewildered, and depressed me.

No matter how bad things seem, they can always get worse. Weeks later, Tanya's mother died in an automobile accident. We were away with our daughters and their synchronized skating team at a big tournament. Tanya took a telephone call at dinner as we watched the girls celebrating their birthday with their teammates at the other end of a long table. I knew something wasn't right.

She ended the call, hesitated, and turned to me. "My mother is gone."

It was "the voice," the same one she had used to inform me of Robert's death 21 years earlier. She used it again the next morning when we delivered the news to our devastated daughters. They lost a grandmother who had been like another parent. Tanya and I lost someone we loved and trusted who had been a stabilizing force in our union.

Predictably, I took the collapse of our marriage as a personal failure. I was numb and raw. This was another of the many challenges I had faced over the years, including breakups, my erratic soaring and running, business failures and unemployment, financial crises, full-time parenthood, and the inability to support my family. My emotions were attenuated. I was idling along in a dark equilibrium with neither the highs nor the lows nudging me far off center. I was better off than many people, but that didn't offset the sense of loss.

Though soaring had often been an escape, I was fortunate it was not available during those weathered-out winter months in early 2007. Some of life's most severe stresses do not mix well with activities requiring total concentration—such as neurosurgery, bomb disposal, and flying. I came through it, leaning on trusted friends in running and flying, my family, and my faith. But it took longer than I wanted.

Soaring, of course, was implicated. Anyone who has tried to balance a relationship with another all-consuming passion knows the frustrations. In the early years, we both enjoyed weekend flying expeditions to the Catskills airport at Wurtsboro with Robert and contests with the exceptional people we met there. Over time, however, my relentless focus on flying fueled resentment that I structured so much of our lives around what *I* wanted to do.

After the twins were born, Tanya stopped going to the airport with me on weekends, though we still attended soaring contests as a family. As our daughters grew older, they looked forward to reuniting with their soaring friends, whether at small grass gliderports such as Caesar Creek and New Castle; local airports at places such as Uvalde, Elmira, and Sugarbush, Vermont; or vast, decommissioned World War II airbases like Hobbs, New Mexico.

These sites offered a lot for kids on roller blades and bicycles to explore and none of the usual urban hazards (crime, traffic, drugs). Ten-year-old Josie wrote a short piece discussing her adventures at the New Castle Regional that *Soaring* magazine published, endearing typos and all (appended to this book). There were complications: one Hobbs Nationals involved rattlesnakes, scorpions, tarantulas, a rope swing over swampy water, and excitement over their being filmed for a television commercial promoting a local casino. Much of the time, though, we could turn the girls loose at these places and they were delighted to run all day with the pack of airport kids.

Yet Tanya increasingly questioned my reluctance to give up a major soaring contest in favor of a winter ski trip or a summer beach vacation. My growing obsession with qualifying for Boston added to the mix. The irony was running, unlike soaring, wasn't just "my" sport. Tanya had run five marathons herself.

It frustrated me she didn't seem to appreciate the difference between the many things we shared I *liked* to do—e.g., skiing, traveling, attending movies and Broadway shows and concerts, beach outings—and the few things I was *driven* to do, specifically soaring and marathon running. This was exacerbated by a growing awareness my soaring life will one day end, like a woman in her late 30s who frets uneasily over her remaining childbearing years.

Airline pilots must retire at age 65. Glider pilots can legally fly so long as, in their judgment, they are not medically unfit. A few, for example, Karl Striedieck, continue to compete well into their 80s. But there are limits, and some encounter them earlier in life. Eyesight degrades. Reflexes slow. The capacity to process information and multi-task under stress declines. "Situational awareness" is the ability to remain cognizant of what is going on around you, no matter what task you are performing. When that is gone, so is the ability to fly safely, at least in the high-stress crucible of competitive soaring. I don't know how many more years I might have left to fly competitively. There is one incontrovertible truth: if we live long enough, someday age will ground us all and our contesting will come to a permanent end.

So, like a professional athlete with a finite number of productive years, I selfishly envisioned each of Tanya's requests to swap a summer soaring competition for a more leisurely non-flying vacation with a reflexive sense of deprivation. In my narrow view, that would be a year of major contest experience lost forever, my finite series of annual tourneys reduced irreversibly by one.

I didn't have the same concerns about running. Runners in good health can keep going almost indefinitely, albeit at a slower pace. But I was defensive when Tanya complained about my relentless pursuit of a BQ:

"Why can't you enjoy running without beating yourself up trying to get marginally better?" she asked one night, shaking her head with an explosive sigh. To her, this seemed the same obsessive-compulsive behavior as for flying:

"Why can't you just fly for fun?"

Our lack of understanding vexed both of us. Was this a *"Men Are from Mars, Women Are from Venus"* thing? No, I've run with female marathoners and competed with female pilots who are as committed as I am, if not more so. Tanya and I were just different souls. I tried to explain:

"I don't think you understand. Chasing ambitious goals *makes* it fun for me. It's the same with flying *and* running. Without goals, it's just not as exciting."

More accurately, without goals—chasing them and occasionally achieving them—I didn't get the same sense of validation and self-esteem.

Did soaring cause our divorce? No, but both soaring and marathoning—i.e., the aspects of my personality that resonated so powerfully with them—no doubt contributed. I don't have insight into other pilots' marriages. But soaring is a small community, and I've wondered if it's coincidental that several pilots in this book also experienced divorces about the same time, including George Moffat, Doug Jacobs, Karl Striedieck, and Chris Woods. It prompted me to quip, "The most dangerous part of marriage is driving to and from the airport."

CHAPTER FIFTY-TWO

The Last Hurrah

A FTER ALMOST TEN YEARS of pounding on the door, I was in the exalted Boston Marathon. Here I would collect the unassailable athletic credential that would endure for the rest of my days, i.e., a Boston Marathon finisher's medal.

But would there even be a race this year? The previous night, 50 mph winds from a Nor'easter moving along the coast threatened to knock us down as we crossed the exposed plaza on the way to the pre-race pasta dinner in downtown Boston. It was snowing out west in Hopkinton (the start), already awash in rain. The organizers would make the final call in the early hours based on whether they could clear the historic 26.2-mile course of fallen trees and power lines *and* keep it safe from storm hazards in the morning. After 5 AM, the word went out: proceed as planned. Knowing thousands of runners would have run unofficially even if organizers canceled the race was doubtless a factor in the decision.

I had another question: could Boston live up to the hype? During my nine years of BQ attempts, friends had reassured me that Boston is "not that big a deal" and "just another marathon." After I qualified, they sang a different tune:

"Chip, you can't believe it. There's nothing like it! The Athletes' Village, the crowds, it's like the Olympics!"

My response: "Were you lying to me then or are you lying to me now?" I'd learn the answer for myself in the morning.

My family had missed my BQ. They weren't missing Boston, however, even though Patriot's Day, Monday, is a school day in New Jersey. I had run big-city marathons, so the spectacle impressed but did not intimidate me. I was now a member of the elite, albeit an elite comprising 20,000 other runners.

There was one pleasant surprise. At pre-race pasta dinners, there's always one bozo at each table who "casually" drops how many famous marathons they've run or their PR or some other boastworthy factoid. But here, at the most hallowed marathon apart from the Olympics, there was none of that. All of us, regardless of experience and ability, had qualified the same way: by meeting a standard. None of us needed to prove anything. We were peers. I could understand when athletes testify that marching in the Olympic Games opening ceremony with so many athletes gathered from around the world is itself a thrill.

Nothing could detract, not my looming divorce or the Nor'easter. Like many other experiences, my first Boston Marathon is a collection of memory snippets. Shivering in the starting corral in chilly rain blowing horizontally. Flowing down the first-mile hill with thousands of runners. Passing through the Wellesley College "scream tunnel" of female voices audible more than half a mile away. Jogging slowly up the Newton (Heartbreak) Hills with thousands of spectators waving signs and shouting encouragement. And turning the corner onto Boylston Street with the blue finish banner ahead in the noise of the crowds. Having that Boston Marathon finisher's medal hung around my neck was worth every painful mile I'd logged and disappointment I'd endured for nine years.

Awful weather. Slow time. Indescribable experience. Boston Marathon 2007, with finisher's medal peeking out of my jacket, Tina, and Josie. (photo by Tanya Lenkow)

* * *

Not long after, I drove out alone to fly the 2007 Standard Class Nationals in Hobbs. I had only flown a few contest days *sans* crew and never for a ten-day nationals. This brought back memories of losing my coach and biggest advocate when my father crashed in 1980. Could soaring ever be the same?

During the three-day drive to New Mexico, I had time to reflect on my new life. There were distractions—satellite radio, audio books, MP3s, and my mobile phone. But I couldn't ignore the challenge I faced. When younger, I was preoccupied with whether the woman in my life could play the same role in my soaring that my mother had played in my father's. How myopic! Now, even if I met someone in my later years with a spark of romantic attraction—a big "if" the older I got—soaring might be outside the scope of that relationship.

There was one compensation for traveling alone. Life was less complicated. Gasoline stops were ten minutes, not half an hour. Food could be quick pauses for snack foods or Subway or pizza, not hour-long, sit-down meals with lengthy debate over menus and gift shop visits. Overnight layovers were simple: pull off in an Interstate highway rest area and park with the 18-wheelers.

I was sleeping in my van—dubbed the Motel Chevrolet—every night. Tanya and I had done that for years in an earlier van before having children pushed us into a tent. Days at Hobbs were hot, but evenings cooled down in the wind that scoured the huge ramp like an onshore breeze, sweeping away airborne bugs. Even more delightful was the low humidity.

The Motel Chevrolet. It's free! The problem is noise if parked next to an idling big rig.

Sleeping in the van was restorative. No longer were late night thunderstorms a threat. In the past, I'd had to dash out of our tent and reposition the van to block the wind, then return inside and stand with my back against the tent fabric, holding it up, hoping water wouldn't end up under the tent to leak through the floor. In the van, however, such storms were soothing white noise, the rain drumming pleasantly on the metal roof, the outside world far away.

Camping at the airport has always made for a more elemental experience. My contests are like vacations for other people. The difference is that soaring is all-consuming and compelling. I don't think about my real-world obligations at a contest. It's not just that I temporarily escape the real world. It's more that the real world is *suspended*. The downside is that unlike traditional vacationers who return from their time off energized, I arrive back at my desk mentally and physically drained from too many hours on the grid and in the cockpit in hot weather and too many exhausting highway miles on the homeward drive. It's always been this way. Now, operating solo, I feared it would be even more so.

Hobbs 2007 was a respectable debut for my new crewless status. I completed every task, so didn't need a retrieve. I tried not to let the lack of a crew influence the way I flew, but I was probably holding back, anyway. Then, the morning after the contest, I almost lost consciousness.

Journal Entry: July 7, 2007 (Hobbs, New Mexico)

Most mornings here, I've been running a 4+ mile loop around the airport. On my day of departure, I finish later than usual, when it's much hotter. Afterward, I'm wiped out, sprawled in the back of my van. A friend stops to check.

"Are you alright?"

I lift my head and deflect his concern. "Just tired. I'll be okay after a shower."

He looks doubtful. "Are you sure? You don't look good."

"People have been telling me I look like I'm dying when I run since 1977. I'll be fine after a shower," I reassure him. My face tightens; it's an effort.

Half an hour later, after showering, I'm lying back, resting in the van again, not feeling much better. Another friend, tipped off by the first pilot that I might be in trouble, stops by to invite me to breakfast.

When I stand to walk over to his motorhome, my blood pressure drops. I lower my head to look down and my vision tunnels in and goes black. I reach out with my arms for balance and manage to stay on my feet as my blood pressure stabilizes. Something is very wrong. I extend my arms and shuffle carefully to my friend's motorhome, then lean against it gratefully. I extend our chat for a few minutes just to make certain things are back to normal. I don't want him to know what happened.

For a pilot, an incident like this can mean the end of flying. But I'm due in Colorado Springs to stay with Bif and Ceil Huss that night, so I hook up the trailer, switch on the air conditioning, and head north, trying not to worry.

It is a ten-hour drive. I still have a flat of 20-ounce Gatorade bottles left over from the contest, so I keep an open bottle next to me the entire trip, drinking often and tossing the empties in the back of the van. When I arrive at Bif's and Ceil's house, I feel normal. Better than that, I feel great!

The next morning when I clean out the empty bottles, I calculate I drank well over a gallon of Gatorade and only stopped once to pee. Without knowing, I had become severely dehydrated in Hobbs that morning.

How could this happen to someone who is arguably a poster child against de-hydration? During the contest, I had drunk water constantly. But when the contest was over, I let down my guard. It was a useful reminder. Even today, if I don't pay attention to fluid intake, I can get lightheaded when I stand suddenly.

Visiting with Bif and Ceil Huss was great. Tanya and I had gotten to know them on the contest circuit, in part because their two daughters enjoyed spending time with our two. Bif is an ex-Navy F-14 carrier pilot, air combat instructor, and Navy Fighter Weapons School (Top Gun) Adversary graduate who was rising in the competitive soaring ranks. Bif would, in the years to come, win several national championships and be named to the U.S. Team.

The next morning, I stashed the glider/trailer at his glider club and headed to Denver to pick up Tanya and the girls flying in from New Jersey. My grand plan called for three weeks of tent camping from the van in a big loop of Colorado, Utah, and Arizona. I was hoping it would be a wonderful, carefully choreographed, unforgettable family adventure, the "last hurrah" before we split.

It was unforgettable, alright—just not the way I had envisioned. My daughters were seasoned travelers, now, and no longer awed by flying commercially. They would have preferred to join their classmates on a summer road trip led by their science teacher, which was happening at the same time over much of the same route. And Tanya was unhappy to be taking so much time away from her library job.

As we departed the Denver airport, the constant bickering was getting on my nerves. I had to restrain myself from shouting, "Don't you understand? This is our last family vacation and you're ruining it!" We hadn't told the girls about the pending divorce.

The key to winning them over was not about telling them how great it would be, but by showing them. We adopted a relaxed, loosely scheduled travel style, seldom driving more than a few hours a day. We often eschewed Interstate highways and favored local roads where the pace was slower and the scenery better. When we saw something interesting, we stopped to check it out. If we wanted to extend a stay, we did. If bored, we moved on.

I had created a tentative itinerary using guidebooks and suggestions from flying buddies. I entered it on an early GPS navigation system, adding or removing stops, then clicking "optimize the route" to learn what came next.

We visited nine national parks plus assorted state parks and private campgrounds. On a long hike in Arches National Park (my favorite, for its shimmering dry August heat and dearth of stereotypical American tourists), I was tricked out in sun protective shirt, cargo shorts, sun hat, sunglasses, sunscreen, and enough water to take us through almost any contingency. As 13-year-old Josie and I surmounted finback rock formations with steep drop-offs on both sides of the narrow primitive trail, she reached up for my hand for reassurance. It's the last time I remember either of them doing anything like that.

One week in, just as it seemed we had turned the corner, our little family threatened to self-destruct. After exciting stops in Leadville and Aspen, Colorado, a marvelous three days in Moab, Utah, and a 100-mile detour just to take a 25-minute car ferry ride across Lake Powell, we were driving south toward Bryce Canyon on Utah Route 12 above Capitol Reef National Park. The van was sweeping in and out of the clouds at 9,000 feet, exploding from the shredded mist to breathtaking views of the vast empty mountains, plateaus, and canyons of the Grand Staircase-Escalante National Monument glinting in the late afternoon sunlight. Speeding along that high and so close to cloudbase, the view was almost like flying.

Yet the mood in the van was sour, filled with whining, petty arguments, and fights. No one was looking outside. We could have been inching along the Cross Bronx Expressway at rush hour, abutted by grim urban housing projects, concrete retaining walls, and stripped hulks of abandoned cars.

I had hoped this trip would be something we could all remember fondly in the coming years. How naïve of me! Why would we be any different from other families ripped apart by divorce, reducing them to bitter parents swapping time with their sullen kids every other week and on holidays? Hell, we couldn't even get along on a *vacation*.

As I thought about the end of my 21-year marriage and the breakup of our family, depression swept over me. My shoulders slumped and my hands tightened on the steering wheel as I bit back what I wanted to say ("This is what you've been asking for: a *non-flying* vacation—and no one is happy!"). Instead, I braked hard and pulled off the deserted highway, shut down the engine, and stumbled across the road into the rock field toward the lip of the escarpment.

I needed to step back (emotionally, that is; I wasn't planning to jump). Like so much of my adult life, this trip had become all about what *I* wanted. Following my father's lead, I had tried to orchestrate my family's reactions and emotions—and it wasn't working. The sense of loneliness, failure, and permanent loss was almost unbearable. With everyone in the van staring at me from across the road, I took deep breaths and let them out slowly, summoning a relaxation response. Then I stood up straight, returned, and climbed into the driver's seat.

"This isn't working out like I hoped," I sighed, swiveling in the seat so I could speak to all three of them. "I've tried, I really have. But you all seem more interested in fighting each other than in enjoying some of the most amazing sights we're ever likely to see." Helpless before the implosion of the family I had taken for granted for so long, I swept my arm around at the vista before us. "I never had this chance when I was growing up. Maybe I made a mistake not letting you go on that school trip with your friends. But it's too late for that now."

"I can't go on like this." I paused to let the weight of those words sink in and to let them wonder just how depressed I was. "It's just too depressing to listen to you try to hurt each other over and over and over again. So here's the deal: I will take you three to the closest major airport and put you on a plane and you can all fly home. I don't care what it costs. I'm going to finish this trip because I've been planning it for a month and there are some fantastic places coming up, places I've wanted to see most of my life. So make up your minds. I'm not starting the van until you decide. We can sit here all night."

No one wanted to speak first. Josie once told me she didn't like it when I threatened, because I always did what I said I would do. I suspect they were all wondering what it would be like to sleep in the van on a highway in the middle of nowhere. Did that help seal the deal? Who knows? But we altered course. It wasn't perfect afterward, but behaviors changed.

We seldom booked ahead. We would arrive before noon and request a tent camping site, not one of the wildly popular RV sites. It worked at every national park, even at the peak of summer vacation season. Freed from the tyranny of a schedule, we continued to add and remove stops from our itinerary.

I didn't abandon all attempts to script our activities. In Bryce Canyon National Park, I waited until we were halfway around what I knew was a 9-mile hiking loop before revealing my intentions (*not* popular with the girls). At Zion National Park, we rode our bicycles up the canyon and coasted back down to our campsite along a stream (better received).

We camped on Lake Powell's sandy beach at the Glen Canyon Dam. At the Grand Canyon, we tagged the North Rim and left to avoid the crowds. We struggled up ladders in ancient cliff dwellings in Mesa Verde National Park.

In need of an overnight stop, we impulsively pulled into Durango, Colorado. The local Chamber of Commerce (our first stop in any new town) excitedly informed us the La Plata County Fair was in full swing. It was an eye-opening concoction of pies, quilts, a talent competition, a tractor pull, and shampooed farm animals. This was a side of America our girls had never imagined.

The next morning, we awoke to a chuffing sound and the cacophonous shriek of a steam whistle. It seemed headed straight for us! Had we accidentally camped on the railroad right of way in the dark? I leaped out of my sleeping bag and unzipped the tent in time to watch a narrow-gauge steam locomotive and tender hauling several passenger cars chugging right through our campground 30 feet away, billowing thick smoke.

As we were packing up, one girl, excited, pointed up at a Schweizer two-place training glider on tow about 1,500 feet above us. For an instant, I considered checking out the local glider operation. But this wasn't that kind of trip. Except for this fleeting moment, I scarcely noticed the outstanding soaring weather that prevailed everywhere we went.

We paralleled the railroad up the Million Dollar Highway to Ouray, Colorado, where we soaked in three progressively hotter natural springs. We arose early the next morning and hiked up to an abandoned silver mine at 10,000 feet, cautiously negotiating switchbacks and precipitous drop-offs on the trail.

The steep, shifting slopes in Great Sand Dunes National Park were a challenge. From over 700 feet atop the highest dune, we watched a fearsome afternoon display of lightning flicker out of purple thunderheads glowering over the mountains. On the last day, we rafted down the white-water rapids of the Arkansas River, the girls shrieking as we paddled furiously to help our guide avoid huge rocks in the torrent of icy, cascading water.

We closed the loop in Colorado Springs and spent the night with Bif and Ceil Huss again. I thought Tanya and I did an admirable job of projecting marital *bonhomie*, but our hosts told me later they could tell something was wrong.

The next morning, after surviving a destructive Rocky Mountain hailstorm, we hauled the ASW 24 trailer out of the soggy grass where it had settled for three weeks. Turning our backs on the mountains, we set off downhill. Our grand adventure was coming to an end. Once again, we were in drive-all-day mode, descending into the steamy lower elevations of the Great Plains. But one more surprise awaited. Late the first afternoon, Tanya was researching budget motels in Kansas when one girl spoke up.

"Dada, do you think we could find a campground and stay in the tent one more time?"

I blinked to clear my eyes as they threatened to flood. I wanted to stop, turn around, and hug my daughters fiercely with gratitude and joy. I realized my gamble—when I insisted on making the Western trip as a family rather than packing the girls off with their friends, teacher, and chaperones—had paid off.

At the campground the next morning we encountered an astonishing coincidence. My glider trailer attracts attention everywhere, but this was different. The Polish-born owner, a machinist who retired after years of working in Detroit auto manufacturing, had been on his country's gliding squad as a youth. The Poles were a gliding superpower in the 1960s. He was fascinated by my ASW 24. It was his first sailplane sighting since leaving his home country 40 years earlier, seeking freedom in America. His face lit up when I was able to recall the names of two Polish world champions from that era (Edward Makula and Jan Wroblewski) and their state-of-the-art gliders (the Zefir and Foka series). I pulled the fuselage out and he sat in the cockpit, reverently gazing at how much had changed.

After we returned home, one girl told me she was glad we had made our family trip. After comparing notes with her friends, she realized we had seen and done so much more in the same national parks than the group, partly because of the near impossibility of shepherding 20 adolescents up narrow trails with sheer drop-offs without unreasonable risk.

Sometimes it's better to be lucky than good.

Our deceptively "normal" family at Independence Pass, Colorado, July 2007.

CHAPTER FIFTY-THREE

Best Day Ever—and the Worst

S OMETHING IS WRONG. Not "wrong" wrong. It's just that the numbers I'm seeing don't make sense.

Journal Entry: November 18, 2007 (Philadelphia Marathon)

At my 12th Philadelphia Marathon, I'm running easily. Too easily. The first three miles went by fast, yet my heart rate monitor says I'm less stressed than normal. Still, I'm nervous. Savvy marathon runners know it's difficult to run too slowly in the early miles. You can almost always make it up in the last six miles if you're feeling good. But go out too fast, and you'll crash and slow horribly, losing all the time gained in the early miles plus some.

I've wondered how I could top last year's BQ. Would I ever again be motivated as I had been? Could I feel the same thrill of success? This year, again thanks to my Avis Budget friend, I ran the New York Marathon two weeks before, just as I did in 2006. Tanya and the girls missed my BQ last year, so they've vowed to be here this year. But as my rare perfect race unfolds, they're not at any of their usual cheering spots. Where the hell are they?

I can't explain my early pace. True, I ran and hiked at high altitude out west, but that was three months ago. Perhaps running New York two weeks before is the secret to success. I let the heart rate monitor guide me, embracing the faster-than-expected miles while dreading the inevitable slowdown.

All the way up the river to the familiar 20-mile turnaround and returning the same way, excitement is offset by anger and resentment. I qualified for Boston alone last year and I can do it again, with or without my family! But I wish my daughters could see me. At 56, I won't be able to run like this forever. I'm sure they'll be at the finish. But I so wish they could see their father running strongly on the course and remember me this way.

I'm having an unbelievable day. At this rate, I'll be five minutes faster than my breakthrough BQ last year, a stunning improvement after nine years of chipping away at the old mark 30 seconds at a time. I'm spotting runners ahead of me and reeling them in one by one, a new sensation that feeds on itself. Miles go by and I'm not slowing. Soon, the 25-mile marker is just ahead. But just as in 2006, it looks like there won't be anyone around to celebrate. My face is more anguished and grim than usual. How could they do this to me? I can't freakin' believe it!

Then I hear shouting. I swivel, surprised, and spot the twins sprinting out to join me for the final push to the finish. My heart soars! What a rush! I am cruising with power in the last mile of one of my best-ever marathons with my 13-year-old daughters—now cross-country and track athletes—loafing along on either side. They are wide-eyed, enchanted by the growing throngs of screaming spectators, laughing in astonishment at the spectacle and noise they have never experienced before, and cheering me.

"Dada, you're running really fast!" Yet it feels so easy now.

Life doesn't get much better than this. My spiraling euphoria rivals the emotional peak that qualifying for Boston provided 12 months earlier. As we approach the crowd control fences at 26, the girls peel off with big smiles, headed for the finish area a quarter mile away. I put everything I have into kicking in the last few hundred yards, running harder than I have in years, feeling nothing except the rapture of a perfect day and an epic triumph over all the failures and losses and disappointments and insecurities that have ever plagued my life. A father could replay these glorious memories a thousand times and never grow tired of them.

Tanya and I signed a contract for a nearby house in the same school district for the three of them. If this puzzled the girls, they kept quiet. After their 14th birthday, in early 2008, we called a family meeting. Popular literature and trusted friends had assured us our children had seen the split looming.

"Relax, Chip, the only surprise to them will be why it took you two so long."

As with meteorologists and economists, so much for expert advice. Tanya and I had apparently nurtured them to feel so loved and secure, it never occurred to them their parents might be separating. Once again, I listened as Tanya leaned toward the girls, looked into their eyes, and used "the voice," the same tender-but-firm intonation I heard when she broke the news of Robert's death 22 years earlier and again for her mother's demise the year before.

It was a horrific shock to both. We could have said one of us was dying. Their bodies sagged. One girl's face crumbled. It shattered. Only for a second, then she gathered herself. But that glimpse into her soul, into the total despair washing over her, will haunt me forever. It was one of the worst moments of my life, not for the collapse of my marriage—that was old news—but because I failed to protect my daughters from this pain. One sister unthinkingly asked if we would still live in the same house together. The other lashed out, eyes narrowing,

"Of course we won't be living together! They're getting divorced!"

They had seen too many school friends hurt by acrimonious splits, awkward joint custodies, and parental relocations to other cities. But we reassured them of our love for them. We promised we wouldn't let this tear our family apart. They responded, and by the end of the session were making jokes, smiling:

"Does this mean we'll get two sets of presents at Christmas?"

Somehow, we adjusted. Tanya and I arrived at an amicable settlement and spent far less money on a do-it-yourself divorce (guided by a mutual friend-cum-family lawyer) than most families drop at Disney World. Today, we're still a family, albeit a non-traditional one. And we've remained friends. We love our daughters. We also respect the 25 years we spent with each other and the feelings we once had. Fifteen years after separating, we're still sharing experiences, including holidays and family reunions (where Tanya is welcomed warmly).

It's been a decade since my mostly divorced friends warned me it was naïve to think I could stay on amicable terms with my ex. One of them later joked I had become a poster child for divorce (an honor I politely declined).

A few years ago, I was late arriving at the workshop of my friend Hank Nixon, while refinishing my ASW 24. I had stopped to check on Tanya's house and the girls' cat during bitter winter weather while the three of them were away. I waited for the inevitable eye roll and sardonic comment. Hank surprised me by opining that despite getting divorced, the two of us appeared to have remained committed to watching out for each other "till death do us part."

I hadn't thought of it that way, but it makes sense. After we separated, I struggled with the idea I had failed. Tens of millions of American couples may not have idyllic marriages, either. Hell, they might even be miserable, bound by inertia, mutual loss of hope, and economic necessity. But they're still married.

I was angry then, and probably still am at some level. But anger was mixed with regret for my role. I went through dark times encumbered by a deep sense of loss. Life was busy: work, flying, running, my daughters, and medical challenges. Like so many newly divorced men, I was desperate to replace my failed relationship with another, to soothe my heart and male ego. But that passed.

Did the four of us come through one of a family's most devastating shocks without acute damage? I hope so, but I've been wrong so many times.

CHAPTER FIFTY-FOUR

Georgia on My Mind

C ORDELE SEEMED EVEN MORE oppressively hot and humid in 2008 than it had been during my first trip 37 years earlier. Blame global warming. Equally likely was my decreasing tolerance for such weather. It was still a gnat-infested, small-town gasoline stop on Interstate 75. Crisp County Airport smelled the same, with the hot, acrid, malodorous aroma of pesticides and herbicides applied by local crop-dusting planes. The biggest changes I saw were a Walmart and a Home Depot.

I had never arrived at a major contest with zero time. The spring weather in New Jersey had been appalling, and the 2008 Standard Class Nationals came early, in mid-May, to avoid the summer thunderstorms for which Cordele is so justly renowned. A short practice flight there was my first of the year.

Cordele is where I broke through as a competitive pilot in 1971, vaulting into second place on the final day of the Regional. It's where I won my first regional, in 1977, redeeming myself for my debacle in Ionia. It's also where my trajectory turned down in 1980 when I fell off a podium finish on the final day to conclude a season blackened by my father's crash. The landscape I traversed those three decisive days was, fittingly, precisely the same terrain along I-75, where the contest tasked us on a vastly different Day Three in 2008.

Journal Entry: May 17, 2008 (Cordele, Georgia)

We're broiling, caught between the pitiless, blinding sun above and waves of heat shimmering from the runway. Perspiration is bubbling out of our reddened skin and oozing into our clothing, dissolving multiple layers of sunblock and insect repellant. The thick South Georgia heat and humidity would be insufferable even without the maddening clouds of gnats buzzing in and around our ears, eyes, noses, and mouths.

We wait, exerting as little effort as possible. Not long after sunrise, when it was cooler, we had assembled and staged the gliders on the grid. Now heat waves are reflecting off the runway. Most pilots and crews are taking a break, some in air-conditioned motorhomes and others on the grid, sprawled in narrow slices of shade under wings, chatting, fanning at gnats.

Several "sniffer" pilots are struggling in weak thermals below tow-release altitude under an ill-formed cloud deck. The rest of us all have the same question: are we wasting our time? They won't launch everyone until the sniffers report sustainable lift. No sense throwing a bunch of gliders into an empty sky, then watching them glide down and land, littering the runway with fiberglass, then retrieving and slotting them back into the launch grid.

The presence of 28 gliders in the Nationals and 22 more in a concurrent Regional is a big crowd. No one wants myriad relights and the collision risk of 50 gliders circling low together. If we wait much longer, though, we won't have time to launch the fleet and fly a short task before the day shuts off.

Launch grid at the Cordele Standard Class Nationals, 2008.

Glancing up at the sky and then down at his watch, the CD orders the launch. That will take an hour, so he's gambling the weather will improve. The tow-planes are relentless, landing, taxiing into position ahead of the next glider, then powering away as soon as they get the "go" signal for another loud, four-minute climb to 2,000 feet, followed by a kamikaze-like descent.

Now, as the remaining clouds burn off and the sky blues out, we're all circling low, desperate to remain aloft without colliding, sharing a few over-crowded thermals ("furballs"). Earlier this morning, every pilot had gone by the playbook and loaded water ballast. Who knows, the day *might* improve.

But before launching, we face reality and open the dump valves, the water splashing noisily, sheeting, spreading under each sailplane in a steaming puddle as it evaporates. This is not a day to be heavy.

We're aloft, now, in survival mode, hanging on grimly. The CD is soliciting input over the radio from his advisors. I've spent close to 20 minutes in my first thermal climbing up, then circling at the top slightly above 3,000 feet simply to stay airborne. It would be madness to send us on a task.

Forty years ago, a CD wouldn't have hesitated. This is the Nationals! To hell with mass landouts. The terrain is benign (lots of empty fields and a not-insignificant number of small airports). However, today's CDs know the sailplanes are more refined and less robust. Landing out is not undertaken as lightly. Many pilots, like me, are here *sans* crew. A modern CD would invite criticism for opening the task without a reasonable chance of completions.

Pre-start thermal; 22 gliders, almost half of the fleet. (photo by Baude Litt)

To our disappointment, frustration, and relief, the CD radios he intends to cancel the day. We could have left the gliders in the trailers this morning and saved a lot of effort. But wait! His airborne advisors push back. Conditions are improving slowly so they recommend he open the short backup task. Their unspoken logic: with the threat of a rain-shortened contest looming, even a short task is better than none. We need four days with scorable results[32] to make things official and can't afford to waste one.

Competitors maneuvering over the ex-World War II training airbase are reporting gradually rising thermal tops and strengths. The CD shifts gears and assigns the 80 mile "dump" task straight down I-75 south to Tifton, and return. I've flown this task so many times I know it by heart. He roll calls each pilot, asking us to acknowledge the new task while we enter it in our GPS navigation computers. This might be the most dangerous five minutes of the day as 50 pilots go heads down, peering at little TV screens and tapping keys while circling closely in crowded thermals.

With no fanfare, he declares the task open. Like parting the doors of a crowded subway car, this triggers a torrent of pilots exiting the five-mile-radius start cylinder that has replaced the start line with the advent of GPS. No one wants to play "start gate roulette" trying to be the last one to leave. I've dropped below 3,000 feet and am not thrilled to be starting that low. In sixth place, I don't want a "dice roll" day where missing one thermal might mean landing out. But the race is on! I give up trying to regain the few hundred feet I lost and float slowly out of the start cylinder around 3:00 PM.

I'm nervous on the slow, eight-mile glide to the first gaggle, but the thermal is still working when I arrive, just above tow release altitude. The next thermal is 12 miles farther on. This time I slide in only 1,500 feet above the Georgia terrain. The thermal is working, but I'm not happy. There's no room for poor decisions or bad luck. Missing a thermal could mean landing out.

Thank goodness for markers. The task has squeezed the fleet into a 40-mile-long corridor a few miles wide along I-75 between 1,000 and 3,000 feet. As we approach Tifton, we're meeting earlier starters headed for home. Every second counts. On a five-hour task, losing a few minutes struggling back up from a low point may not hurt much. But with a likely elapsed time of 90 minutes today, losing the same few minutes could be more costly.

I make a strategic mistake going into the turnpoint. Instead of staying with

---

[32] At this time, 25% of the competitors (i.e., 7 in this nationals) must score at least 60 miles for a day to be official. Sometimes only one or two more pilots are needed to reach 25%, rendering it a "no contest" day, often to the frustration of the more successful pilots. This rule prevents (i) scoring a day when most or all pilots simply take a tow and glide as far as they can before landing; and (ii) situations where one or a few pilots are able to find lift that no one else does and post impressive distances, deemed too luck-prone for fairness.

the gaggles, I get ambitious and angle further west to a big plume of black smoke. A farmer is burning the stubble in a field to get it ready for planting. This environmentally questionable practice can reward the pilot with a rocket ship ride atop the conflagration—*if* the timing is right. But I'm late and this thermal is past its prime. So I angle back toward the turn. Pilots who started after me are catching up. Gloom.

I climb in a good thermal near the turn until it tops out, letting the wind drift me south. I could tag the front side of the one-mile radius turn cylinder and head north for home. Instead, I glide all the way to the back edge of it to get the extra distance. I'm hoping my higher speed on those miles will improve my overall average. Then I turn into the wind for the return leg.

My late start, deviation to the field fire, and decision to tag the back side of the turn cylinder mean I'm trailing most pilots. There are fewer markers in the blue ahead and I'm flying mostly alone. The short day is weakening. It's only 40 miles north, but I can't get high enough for final glide. Four times I drive down to 1,500 feet above the ground before hitting a thermal. I'm scant minutes from landing, scanning for fields.

This is the way I used to fly: pushing aggressively for the stronger thermal I want, taking only enough weak lift when low to allow me to climb up part way and push on. Post-crash, though, my default strategy in dicey situations has been survival. I'd rather finish slow than not finish at all.

Three times I catch a save, climb for a few minutes in the weak lift, then push on. The fourth time, nerves raw, I finally get what I want—my "go home" thermal. As I climb up to final glide altitude, I can hear and see others thrashing around below me as the day weakens, desperately trying to stay airborne. When the results are in, over a third of the 28 Nationals pilots will have landed out, most here in the last 15 miles.

On final glide, I'm relieved to approach the airport and radio the mandatory, "Juliet Bravo, four miles," then push over to burn off my safety altitude. It's been a lot of work for such a short flight. I enter the finish cylinder above the hard deck and descend into the oppressive lower layer of heat and humidity, relieved to be back. I climb out, sweating again, and submit my GPS flight log, hoping for a decent speed. My computer estimates it at 49 mph.

I clean the insects off the ASW 24 and put it in the trailer. Years earlier, I built special equipment that allows me to assemble and disassemble it alone. Except in high-wind situations, the only time I need help is if I land out. On that subject, Erik Mann stops by to say our friend Bif Huss landed a few miles short. None of us has a crew, so we're in a mutual-assistance pact.

Bif's 4WD Ford pickup truck makes the retrieve from far out in an enormous red dirt plowed field in South Georgia straightforward. When we arrive back at the airport, though, we are sweat-streaked and grimy. We stop at the scorer's trailer so Bif can turn in his GPS flight record. It looks deserted. Most folks have already left for dinner.

I scan the preliminary daily score sheet taped up outside. WTF? I'm showing as a zero. No flight! This resurfaces memories of Ionia 30 years ago. There's another explanation just as disastrous. Two days before, my GPS logger had refused to disgorge my flight record. Erik had salvaged the corrupted data from the memory, which I emailed to a technical expert in Vermont who is familiar with the bug in the code. He repaired the file so the contest could score it. Was this a repeat? My anxiety is peaking as I climb the steps to the air-conditioned trailer.

With Erik Mann (c) and Bif Huss (r), Cordele Nationals 2008.

The scorer reassures me: "There's no problem with your file, Chip. We just can't find it. We need to upload it again."

I try to relax, but my body is tense. I hope I have flown well. But I am prepared for another corrupted file or a disappointing speed. Early in my soaring career, I was often pleasantly surprised by my score. Post-crash, more often the reverse has been true; I've been shocked and dismayed by how poorly I've flown compared to the brilliant performances of top pilots. The memory card is in my pocket. The scorer uploads my GPS file to the scoring computer. That's further than I got two days ago, anyway.

"Please, please let the file be okay!" I murmur to myself. I have a dark fear the earlier problem with my GPS logger was a warning it is going bad.

The scorer uploads my file to the scoring system. That's promising. Then he brings up the scoring table. After a brief pause, he spins around in his chair with a broad smile on his face and thrusts his hand out.

"You won the day."

I don't know that anything has ever shocked me in such an epic way. It's a struggle to keep my composure. I want to believe him. I know he wouldn't joke about it. But how cruel would it be, after waiting *so* long for this—over 30 years—to discover my flight wouldn't count for some arcane reason? In the obscure world of contest scoring, there are many such reasons.

"There must be a problem. Check out the flight," I joke, half serious.

The scorer understands my unease, although there's no way he can appreciate the depth or import of it. Step by step, he verifies I have a valid start (check). I entered the 1 mile-radius turnpoint cylinder (check). I have a valid finish (check). I did not intrude on any restricted airspace (check). The encrypted security of the computerized file is intact (check). Everyone else has reported in, so mine is the last flight to be scored (check).

I exhale, trying not to be obvious. For a brief interlude, for the time that will elapse before we fly the next task, I am Number One, the best Standard Class pilot in the country.

It had been 32 years since my debut at the National Soaring Championships in Bryan, Ohio, in 1976, where I snatched second place on opening day with so much promise. That promise flowered—and then died. Since 1980, I had mostly gone backwards, with disappointing, sometimes embarrassing performances.

For top pilots, a daily win at a national contest is a non-event. Many take multiple days. A few—e.g., George Moffat and Doug Jacobs—have stunningly won nearly every day at major races, dominating the field. The scorer's team congratulated me. But they couldn't understand the true significance of the day.

Back at the truck, Erik and Bif were lounging impatiently to go to dinner, their faces questioning. I wasn't sure what to say. This was unfamiliar territory.

"I won the day," was my plain, unadorned, almost uneasy answer.

I could see the startled expressions on their faces. The three of us were at a comparable level then. I wondered if it was like learning the next-door neighbor has won $10 million in the lottery. The neighbors are happy for him. But behind every pair of eyes lingers a troubling question:

"Why not me? Why couldn't this happen to me?"[33]

We celebrated over dinner. Erik had come close himself in third place. Bif would rebound two days later with his first, far more decisive daily win.

My success in Cordele after persevering for so many years paralleled the way I finally nailed my Boston Qualifier marathon time after a long pursuit. There was one difference. On the streets of Philadelphia, I had watched my BQ coming all the way around the course. It was never certain, but I had tracked my progress every mile for close to four hours, assessing, projecting, then resolving into a triumphant last mile and a glorious, victorious sprint across the finish line to cheering crowds, arms raised in triumph!

In contrast, my Cordele win 18 months later was just another contest flight. The first intimation I had achieved a lifelong ambition came hours after I landed. There was no anticipation, no buildup, no cresting of the wave. Perhaps that is why it evoked a less mystical reaction. But it didn't go unnoticed.

The next morning, I awoke to find a cryptic email: "Welcome to the club."

These words meant so much! I had met Rick Walters, many-time national champion from the West Coast, in 1992 when I returned to soaring. I was impressed not only with his formidable flying skills, but with the man himself. Even with his imposing physical stature (he was taller than I am, so we had exchanged tips for squeezing into small sailplane cockpits) and top competitive record, he was well-liked and revered by all those who knew him.

Like Dad, Rick seemed able to relate to everyone, regardless of their position in the competitive hierarchy. My sister Diane crewed for him several times, so Rick was more aware of our family's soaring history than most. His generosity in sending that message, knowing what it would mean, made a real impression.

[Years later, Rick and I had exchanged thoughts on the ASW 24 (he had borrowed one for the Nationals and asked for my insights, though he had already figured out the conventional wisdom about the ASW 24 was off). I was looking forward to catching up at the Nationals in 2015, which he encouraged me to enter. We hadn't seen each other in five years. A few weeks before, Diane emailed with the staggering news that Rick had died in a bicycling accident in the hills above his home in Minden, Nevada. The outpouring of grief from the soaring world echoed my deep sense of loss. Almost 15 years have elapsed, but I still recall his simple, thoughtful gesture. Requiescat in pace, 3R.]

---

[33] Both have gone on to further success. Thanks, P3 and H7, for your friendship over the years.

I had given winner's speeches but never on the national stage. I wanted to get it right. This wasn't just another day. I was realistic; this might be my only chance—ever.

When the organizers called my name, I strode to the front of the large room and turned to face the crowd. Part of me wanted to be matter of fact, to be dispassionate, and to hold back how much this meant, how long I had waited for it, and how many times I had been jilted over the years. But like an ebullient new father who bounces around the hospital handing out cigars to everyone he encounters to celebrate the birth of his first child, another part of me wanted to share my joy that day with everyone who would listen. So although, to my knowledge, there's only one photograph of me that morning, I suspect I was only partially successful in controlling the smile that threatened to erupt as I began to talk.

From fellow pilot John Bojack's flattering report on the contest on the Soaring Society of America Web site (www.ssa.org)[34]:

"The highlight of the meeting today was Chip Bearden's winner's speech, he having won the day yesterday. Many commented it was one of the best winner's speeches they'd ever had the privilege to hear. This was Chip's first win at a Nationals and he was obviously gratified. To paraphrase his talk...he took an informal poll of the pilots with reference to years of experience and number of national contests flown in relationship to how many had ever won a day at the Nationals. Very skillfully delivered, Chip eloquently made it known that he was one of the most experienced contesters in the room, and that he had one of the longest histories of anybody present of flying in Nationals. That this was his first ever daily win was offered as a tribute that if willing to persist and to try long and hard enough, anyone could win a day at the Nationals. Bravo, Chip. It was great to have heard your speech and I only wish every contest pilot could have been there to hear it also."

I could have said so many other things, including regretting not being able to share it with those who could appreciate it most. That included my father, but also my family. Winning a day at the U.S. Nationals and qualifying for the Boston Marathon 18 months earlier were two of the greatest moments of my life. Yet neither Tanya nor my daughters (still in school in May this year) were there. Mark and Diane were working. My mother and stepfather had stopped

---

34https://www.ssa.org/ContestResults.asp?contestId=289&ContestDetailId=3531&Contest-
Name=Standard+Class+Nationals (accessed 3 Oct 2020)

crewing in their 80s when driving their RV had become difficult.

There is no prize money in soaring, but contest organizers often award small prizes to daily winners. By chance, my prize that day was a woman's handbag. *What?* I've received hats, T-shirts, and bottles of wine. But a purse? Maybe a local retail store was a sponsor. As I was walking out, another pilot joked I now had something to give Tanya when I went home.

I paused, then shot back: "That's ironic since we're getting divorced."

There was total silence, then shocked reaction from pilots within earshot. I had told only a few close friends.

At Springfield in 1980, as I closed the canopy on the takeoff line, my sister Diane wished me good luck before running my wingtip. Her concerns were over how well I would place that day, not about safety. Until then, our lives had been untouched by the dangers in our sport.

In later years, it was often my mother, then Tanya, and later still, my daughters standing as I closed the canopy with a grin and a "See you back here!" They always smiled and waved. Were they, like me, caught up in the competition and unconcerned about the hazards? Or were they forcing their smiles to hide their anxiety, knowing that once in a while, things go wrong?

It was worth it: 43 years of struggle before the big reward! Unbelievably, this is the author's only photo of this day. Cordele 2008 (photo by Erik Mann)

From Cora Bennett, widow of 1920s Naval Aviator and Medal of Honor re-cipient Floyd Bennett, in the commotion of Lindbergh's Atlantic crossing:

"[F]or every young man whose eyes are fixed on some far limit of space which is the goal of his ambition, there is a girl who must stand on the ground and wait while he soars into unfathomable space where she can never follow him. Sometimes he does not come back—and she must wait on and on forever."[35]

It seemed unfair that those closest to me who had lived with unease that they might have to "wait on and on forever" weren't there to share this occasion.

For one ephemeral moment that morning—through skill, luck, and sheer perseverance over 17 national contests spanning 32 years—I was at the pinna-cle. I paused after my speech, not knowing if I would ever experience this again, warmed by applause from acquaintances; from new competitors who only knew my name; from those I had flown against for years, including a few from the 1970s who had known my father; and from friends like Erik Mann—who has done so much for me personally and professionally—who knew my story well.

Such joy should be unmitigated. Indeed, there was a flush of pride and inner peace about living a dream I had nourished for so long, as when I qualified for Boston. When I stepped outside after the pilots' meeting, the humid air blan-keting the airport filled my nose with an aroma I could instantly associate with my effort: the sweat and blood and aviation fuel; the fear, the adrenaline, and the exhaustion; and the pesticides and herbicides that had soaked into the ground over the years. And that morning, I could smell the exhilaration of my achievement that wiped clean the lingering odor of my earlier failures.

Yet, through my sense of elation and fulfillment, I couldn't deny—a few days before my 57th birthday and working my way through an amicable divorce—that I felt more alone than I had in decades. Unlike those bits of video shown at the conclusion of so many televised sporting events, at Cordele that day there was no one I loved and who loved me back to grasp my arm, lean into me, and gaze up adoringly, happy and proud of the man I was and what I had accomplished.

---

[35] With its archaic implication that the ambitious pilot is always male: Booth, Ann. "Shall I Marry an Aviator? An Interview with Mrs. Floyd Bennett," *Good Housekeeping*, v89 #2, August 1929

CHAPTER FIFTY-FIVE

Change of Life

I F I WERE A PROFESSIONAL ATHLETE, investigators from the World Anti-Doping Agency would have been calling for an investigation, knocking at my door requesting blood and urine samples. After Cordele, my times in 5K races dropped to levels I hadn't run in 15 years, and kept improving throughout the summer, finally reaching a 7:15 pace 5K. This compares with my typical eight-minute pace. Friends started joking about performance-enhancing drugs. I couldn't explain it. But I was enjoying it, including two BQs.

The rest of my life was equally charmed. Josie and Tina were perfect daughters, happy, loving, outgoing, and involved at a high level in music, sports, and academics. My career was thriving at Mindtree, which verged on being my longest-term employer. In soaring, I was coming off a daily win at the Nationals. And I was turning back the clock physically. What could possibly go wrong?

I didn't have to wait long to find out. After my 13th Philly Marathon in November, my marvelous resurgence reversed. A year later, when I turned 59, my running had degraded, once again, to an alarming degree.

* * *

Marathons weren't on my mind driving out to the 2010 Standard Class Nationals in Hobbs. After three years being one of "The Young and the Crewless" (to paraphrase America's highest-rated soap opera), I was excited to have a crew, albeit an ambivalent one. Sixteen-year-old Tina had accepted my last-minute invitation. I hoped it would be good for both of us.

The 2,000-mile trip was not without challenges. The first day, Tina retreated to the van's third-row seat with a book and iPod. I could barely see her in the rearview mirror. She might as well have been riding in the glider trailer. On the second day, she moved up to the navigator's seat as we rolled through Tennessee. After we splurged on dinner in Texarkana, the van quit in the parking lot—at 10:00 PM on Friday night. We had the rig towed to a Chevy dealer and slept in it overnight. The sweltering heat forced us to lower the windows, fortunately without attracting the ravenous mosquitos we feared.

The next morning, the dealer had us on our way. Hours later, we blew a trailer tire in Abilene and rushed to Walmart for new tires minutes before they closed. The last hour on the two-lane highway was in torrential rain, the night sky lit up with a massive display of lightning and thunder. We drove onto the airport outside Hobbs at midnight with a sigh of relief. Our problems were over!

Not really. That storm portended rain—relentless, flooded-streets rain—in New Mexico. I used the downtime to teach Tina how to drive the van on the mammoth concrete ramp (500 x 7600 feet) at the old Army Air Forces B-17 training base. She had never driven a car, but after two days, she could reverse a full-size van into a narrow parking slot, with or without a 30-foot trailer!

Tina at the wheel on one of the many rain days at Hobbs, 2010.

Two landouts at Hobbs, 2010, under deceptively good skies. In the right photo, four gliders went into the same field when the thermals died.

The rain paused enough to fly four of ten days, so I volunteered Tina to run wingtips during launching. Her confidence and popularity with pilots soared after her first blazingly fast, flawless wing run. A year later, she leveraged that into a winning college admissions essay (appended to this book). There were too few miles and scorable days for an official contest. Yet, it was a priceless life experience. As Tina joined garrulous pilots and crews for dinner, chatted on the grid, ran wingtips, and hunted for drivers to help retrieve me, she grew up before my eyes. She returned to New Jersey more relaxed, confident, and mature.

* * *

Back home, my running continued to decline. Two doctors dismissed it. One, my primary care doc—a friend and marathoner—smiled indulgently:

"Chip, there is *nothing* wrong with you. You're just getting older."

I wasn't buying it: "Doctor [X], you don't lose 90 seconds a mile in a few months because of age."

I was right. The third doctor—Dr. Agesen, the specialist who had read my spinal CT four years earlier—had a hunch. When he and his colleagues failed to find anything, he ordered a blood test before more invasive tests. He didn't need an office visit to deliver the news:

"You have Lyme disease."

"Are you sure?"

"O-o-o-h, yes. The test isn't always definitive, but you lit up just about every reactive band. You've got it. We need to get you on antibiotics—today—and you need to see an infectious disease specialist right away."

Tick-borne Lyme was rampant in our area, but I had none of the classic symptoms (e.g., tick bite, bullseye rash, fever, joint pain). Within hours, I was on a massive dose of doxycycline. Looking back at my slowdown, I probably had it for a while, allowing the bacterium to burrow in deeply.

The infectious disease specialist assured me 30 days of antibiotics had cured me. Months later, still languishing, I found a second specialist by cross-referencing a list of New Jersey's Best Doctors against finishers at New Jersey distance races. I wanted to run Boston in a few months and needed someone with running creds to tell me what I *could* do, not what I *shouldn't* do.

The Lyme infection was still active, so my new doctor, Dr. Max DeShaw, prescribed antibiotic cocktails and other drugs. I was grateful for support from family, friends, and employer, including the manager who elbowed me gently in client meetings when I threatened to nod off from fatigue and drugs. I grounded myself from soaring. I could have flown safely but not competed the way I wanted. I had no idea it would be three years to get back in the cockpit.

As a runner, Dr. DeShaw shared my concern about my slowdown. He sent me to my cardiologist to rule out heart problems. This was frightening as a pilot. I underwent (for fans of *Grey's Anatomy)* a stress test, echocardiogram, nuclear stress test, and stress echocardiogram. All good, but the cardiologist wanted *one more test* to be certain.

A cardiac catheterization involves inserting a narrow catheter into the femoral artery in the groin, snaking it up into the chest and injecting contrast dye to track blood flow through arteries and heart using x-rays. I wasn't anxious about the test—I'd had something similar years before—but he insisted on it *before* any more strenuous runs. The Boston Marathon was in less than a week.

We hurriedly scheduled the test for Friday, three days before the race on Monday. I assured the cardiologist this would provide the requisite "48 hours before resuming normal activities." He didn't think that was funny.

"I can't recommend you run a marathon three days after a cardiac catheterization," he frowned as we prepped.

I wasn't asking for his approval. I suspected there wasn't a heart expert in the country who would provide that. I could picture his medical malpractice insurance carrier shuddering. But I feared (correctly) this would be my last chance to run Boston. And the Boston Athletic Association had turned down my request for a medical deferment.

So I countered: "Look, Doctor, I'm a consultant. So let's play a game. I know you can't recommend I run. And if you find something wrong with my heart, then of course I won't. I'm not stupid [I was wounded he didn't nod to acknowledge my admirable restraint]. But if this test checks out and I tell you I'm going to run anyway, are there things you can do *today* to reduce the risks for me on Monday?"

He paused, then looked up and smiled with a faraway look in his eyes. I had removed him from the liability loop, allowing him to focus on a fascinating medical question.

"Yes, actually there are!" he exclaimed with surprising enthusiasm. "I can use a 5 French catheter instead of a 6 French to go into your artery. It should be large enough. And I won't use a collagen plug in the puncture site. It might get dislodged. I'll tell the nurse to get a good clot there before we let you go."

Then, with a stern look, he looked back down at me and caught himself: "But I can't recommend it."

* * *

The procedure was uneventful. With a marathon in three days, I declined the customary sedation, not wanting more drugs in my system. I was on the table when he told me I had no significant blockage. That was doctor-speak.

"Help me out, Doctor. What does 'significant' mean? 20%? 30%? 40%?"

He laughed. "Actually, I don't see *any* blockage. Everything's clear. Forget that baby aspirin we told you to take every day. You don't need it."

The staff gave me gauze and a transparent plastic patch for the wound in my groin so any bleeding would be obvious. As I lay waiting for the clot to firm up, every staffer in the Cardiac Care Unit pleaded with me not to run, some close to tears. Only one sympathetic nurse broke ranks, reassuring me quietly:

"There's almost no chance it will start bleeding. But if it does, push your thumb down hard on the femoral artery and lie down. At the Boston Marathon, the EMTs will be there immediately, and you'll be okay." At my request, he used a black Sharpie pen to make an X on the skin over my femoral artery ("Push here to save your life"). Just in case.

My family were a tougher sell. Tanya rolled her eyes and threw up her hands. This was another of my self-indulgent obsessions. I could bleed to death! My 17-year-old daughters were more sympathetic but afraid something terrible could happen. I didn't want to stress them. Then I had a brilliant idea! I promised I would hit the ground at once if I started bleeding, whether at the starting line or at mile 26 with the finish in sight. And I would text them at every mile, with 26 texts queued up in advance on my BlackBerry (e.g., "OK at 18").

I concluded by asking them to trust me to be smart and careful, *just as I trusted them when they went out at night*. Friends scolded me later for what they viewed as an underhanded trick, but it got my daughters on board.

Journal Entry: April 18, 2011 (Boston Marathon)

On Patriot's Day (Monday), sixty-five hours after the procedure, I'm in my starting corral for my last Boston Marathon, getting strange looks as I peer into my shorts at the plastic patch over the puncture site. I start at an easy pace. Hours later, the race has degenerated into one of my most agonizing running experiences. I still have Lyme. Later, a doctor informs me the catheterization procedure itself exacted a toll. By the time I stagger to the summit of the Newton Hills at 21, I am so spent and in such pain, I can jog awkwardly only when going downhill. With the finish line crowd screaming, I summon a pathetic trot the last few steps. As I go hands to knees, coughing and wheezing, a course worker drapes the coveted third Boston Marathon medal around my neck. When I sag against a light pole, a worried attendant asks if I'd like to step into the medical tent.

"I would love to!" I have no pride left. Chilled and exhausted, I am desperate to lie down and collapse.

She holds a pen poised over a clipboard: "Any current medical conditions?"

I hesitate. But, hey, what can they do to me now? "Well, I have Lyme disease [pausing]. And I had a cardiac catheterization three days ago."

I might as well have said I'm having a heart attack. Her jaw drops, her eyes round, she stops scribbling, and she hurries off to get help. Lots of help.

They whisk me onto a gurney and into the tent. I'm a VIP! Medical staff crowd around two deep, eager to learn how (or maybe if) I have survived. I'm checking for news cameras. There is some jostling among the top doctors over who's in charge. I'm one of a few cases worthy of their skills. That resolved, the big dog shakes his head gravely, inspecting the rapidly healing wound in my groin. He questions me as I lie there, still breathing hard.

"When did you have the procedure? And why?"

"Did your doctor approve of your running the race today?"

"Are you aware the puncture could have opened up and bled profusely?"

"Are you a freakin' idiot?" [I'm joking, but that's his subtext.]

I lie there, chastened and defensive. Satisfied he has lectured me enough (not that I plan to do it again), the doctor concedes I appear to have gotten away with it. They just don't have any data on the safety of what I did.

"It would make a fascinating study," he smiles at me, the stern scowl gone. "But I don't think we're going to get many test subjects to volunteer for it."

When it's clear I am not in danger, the disappointed crowd disperses. A young nurse standing next to me checks to make sure no one is in earshot.

"I'm a runner and I would have done the same thing!" she whispers, smiling at our secret.

Fellow runners criticized my actions as reckless. I agreed there were risks. Life is full of risks. But, as in my flying, I believe I took precautions to mitigate them.

The nightmare continued that summer fighting Lyme disease. It took nearly nine months to bring it under control, including eight weeks of twice-daily intravenous infusions of antibiotics—at home—through a semi-permanent line in my arm. The infusions became so routine that I might have gotten a little cocky.

Faced with an early meeting with a client near Wall Street in New York, I decided to multitask by infusing on the bus. No big deal. Seated in the back, I connected the fist-size pressurized plastic ball of antibiotic solution to the IV line, then stuffed it up my jacket sleeve. The infusion only took 30 minutes, but the bus was full by then, so I rode downtown on the subway, then stopped a block from the client. I disconnected the deflated ball and let the IV line dangle while I reached for syringes and alcohol wipes to flush the line before wrapping it around my arm again. I had picked a deserted street café because bringing out syringes on the streets of Manhattan can attract the wrong crowd.

When I looked down to grab the line: "Holy crap—I'M BLEEDING OUT!"

The normally clear plastic line was dark red, sprinkling blood on my trousers as it swung back and forth! By mistake, I had unscrewed the check valve, leaving an open line into my vein. I frantically found and replaced the valve, flushed the line, and mopped up what I could. Chastened, I shuffled through building security holding my jacket in front of me, then sponged the blood off my clothes in the men's room. I was more careful after that.

Running was painful due to lower back pain that forced me to stop every half mile. I also struggled with shortness of breath. Frustrated and depressed, I continued to hobble along at a walking pace. In 2011, I shocked many by skipping what would have been my 16th consecutive Philly Marathon. "The Streak" was over. I feared gutting out another marathon would set back my recovery, as had occurred after my Philly 2010 and Boston 2011 races.

My emotional return to marathoning came a year later in 2012—at Philly—and was even sweeter for passing up the year before. Unfortunately, my joy was short-lived as I suffered a slowdown following my first flu shot in 20 years. It could have been a rare side effect or just an allergic reaction.

The fun didn't stop, however. Not long after that slowdown, I developed deep venous thromboses (blood clots) in my lower right leg and a pulmonary embolism (clot) in my left lung, thus proving my point that bad things come in fours and fives and sixes! There was no explanation for these life-threatening clots, so I dosed up on anticoagulants and—with my doctors' okay—kept running. In eight months, I was off the meds and the clots have never recurred.

But I also never recovered my old speed, either, though I've continued to run the Philly Marathon, even with laughable times (one to two hours slower). I wanted to prove I could still do it, and that kept me going through some of my most excruciating, painful, and slowest races. I didn't know then, but if I had quit, I would have missed some uplifting marathons.

The impact on my soaring was more severe. I lost almost four flying seasons. It wasn't until the fall of 2014 that I jumped back into my ASW 24 at age 63, thanks to the encouragement of Erik Mann. Without his support, I might not have had the confidence to resume flying after a third long-term layoff. And I would have missed some joyous moments in *that* part of my life.

CHAPTER FIFTY-SIX

Gone West

B AD THINGS HAPPEN. We don't like to talk about them. They're rare. But glider pilots die in accidents, just like race car drivers and moun-taineers. Fatal accidents are embedded in the shared fabric of the social bond of aviation. We take secret pride in engaging in what we perceive as a dangerous activity (even though we know the danger is overblown). We thrill in managing risks from which mere mortals shrink. And when things go wrong with one of our number, we console each other with our favorite platitude:

"That's the way he would have wanted to go, with his boots on."

I heard that so often in the months after my father's crash. And after Robert's death. Hell, I said it myself. It even popped up in Dad's *In Memoriam*. It's a cliché, but it has the right sound. The idea appeals and comforts not only from the reassurance the person was in a happy place (well, until the last seconds, anyway), but also because of the idealistic notions many pilots cling to about a noble end, the way certain bold seafarers have perished on their voyages.

Aviation has so many analogies to the sea. The romance of the unknown. Expeditions of discovery and hazard. Rituals. Stories passed down over the ages. Tales of quest, exploration, heroism, survival, and wartime. Larger-than-life figures. Mystical conceptions of birth, life, death, failure, and redemption.

And there are the dangers. In seafaring, these no longer include sea monsters and dragons, but other perils continue to claim lives, including storms, running aground, rogue waves, equipment failures, and modern pirates.

Aviation—from its beginning, thousands of years after maritime pioneers first ventured out on the water—has always involved danger. There's even a parallel vocabulary: nautical euphemisms such as "in Davy Jones's Locker" have their aeronautical counterparts in "buying the farm" and "gone west." Mariners have burials at sea. Aviators have the "missing man" formation, which honors a fallen pilot by vacating a slot in a pre-arranged flyover.[36]

Man's relationship with a cruel-but-compelling sea has been the subject of myriad remarkable books, from fiction such as Homer's *The Odyssey* and Hemingway's *The Old Man and the Sea* to fact-based works such as *The Perfect*

---

[36] In 2012, U.S. Navy F/A-18 jets performed this aerial salute for astronaut Neil Armstrong over the village in Cincinnati where my parents had bought their dream home almost 35 years earlier. It can also be seen in the movie *Top Gun: Maverick* at Iceman's funeral.

Storm by Sebastian Junger.

The literature of flying is no less rich, despite being thousands of years younger. One masterwork is Antoine de Saint-Exupéry's poetic novel *Night Flight*, meditations on the meaning of life during long airmail flights at the controls of an early flying machine. Non-fiction classics include *West with the Night* by early aviatrix Beryl Markham and *Fate Is the Hunter*, Ernest K. Gann's eloquent and engrossing memoir about the initial expansion of the U.S. airline industry. No list would be complete without *The Right Stuff*, Tom Wolfe's New Journalism reportage of American test pilots and Mercury astronauts, warriors at the dawn of the space age admired by their peers and adored by the public for their apparent indifference to the horrific risks they took.

Some of the most lyrical testimonies came from Charles Lindbergh, who ignored the many who had perished vying to be the first man to fly solo across the Atlantic Ocean.

> *"If one took no chances, one would not fly at all. Safety lies in the judgment of the chances one takes. That judgment, in turn, must rest upon one's outlook on life. Any coward can sit in his home and criticize a pilot for flying into a mountain in fog. But I would rather, by far, die on a mountainside than in bed... What kind of man would live where there is no daring? And is life so dear that we should blame men for dying in adventure? Is there a better way to die?"*[37]

Lindbergh's views on how aviation distinguishes pilots reflect my lofty pretension that soaring is the thing that distinguishes me from other people. As he referred to residents of Manhattan while preparing for his historic flight:

> *"[M]illions of people...each one surrounded by a little aura of his problems and his thoughts, hardly conscious of earth's expanse beyond."*[38]

That sounds condescending. No one is "little." We are all special. But I can't argue that soaring—and rising to its challenges—has made me *feel* special. It is what most defined my adulthood, and it is still a driver of my self-image today.

Because aviation attracts many for whom risk is invigorating, eulogies for fallen pilots can lean toward the melodramatic, as when author Pat Conroy honored his father, decorated Marine Corps pilot Colonel Donald Conroy, the model for the protagonist of the novel and film, *The Great Santini*:

> *"There should be no sorrow at this funeral because The Great Santini lived*

---

[37] Lindbergh, Charles A., journal entry, 26 August 1938, from *The Wartime Journals of Charlies A. Lindbergh* (New York: Harcourt, 1970)

[38] Lindbergh, Charles A. *The Spirit of St. Louis* (New York: Charles Scribner's Sons, 1953)

life at full throttle, moved always in the fast lanes, gunned every engine,
teetered on every edge, seized every moment and shook it like a terrier
shaking a rat. He did not know what moderation was or where you'd go to
look for it."[39]

Last scene of a movie: fade to black as the deceased pilot's comrades fly off
into the sunset, the music crescendos, and the credits roll. It's a tired script. But
put it up on the big screen with a stirring soundtrack, and a majority of the
aviating tough guys in the audience will grow uncomfortably misty-eyed.

We're all going to die. When pilots think about it—which isn't often—many
imagine that when, far into the future, it is their time, it would be *so* much better
if they could go out the right way, with style, heroically. Dying while serving
one's country in a fighter jet, or in a medivac helicopter extracting a victim, or
in a fire bomber penetrating a forest fire is infinitely more appealing than slipping away into dementia, succumbing to illness in a stained nursing home bed,
or being crushed on the way home from the supermarket by an 18-wheel truck
carrying a load of scrap metal. Regrettably, gliding offers few opportunities for
heroism. The "missions" are for fun, not for saving lives or defending freedom.

Heroic or not, many aviators share one anxiety about death. A pilot's exit
must never be the shameful result of their own fumbling error. Objectively, this
is irrational. Once a pilot has "gone west," what does it matter to them if their
demise tarnished their reputation or image? Aviation psychologists determined
in the 1970s—i.e., when I was coming up the competitive ladder—that how a
pilot perceives others view him could be one of their most powerful behavioral
traits. Sometimes saving face was more important to them than safety.

America's first astronaut, Alan Shepard, exemplified this, strapped into the
Mercury space capsule waiting for launch, when he blurted over an open mic:

"Dear Lord, please don't let me fuck up,"[40] reflecting many pilots' fear not
so much of dying, but that their own humiliating error might be their undoing.

---

[39] https://www.usna63.org/tradition/history/Eulogy_Conroy.html
[40] Wolfe, ibid.

CHAPTER FIFTY-SEVEN

Close Encounters

THE CLOSEST I HAVE COME TO DYING IN A GLIDER involved near-mid-air collisions. Most risks of modern soaring are within our control. We should be safe if we're competent, alert, and careful; follow the rules; and don't make big mistakes when taking off, landing, circling at low altitude, transiting rough terrain, flying in rough weather, selecting fields, and caring for our equipment. Most soaring accidents result from avoidable human error.

Mid-air collisions are the exception. They're the Ebola of aviation: a rare but often lethal risk, not only for us but also for pilots and passengers aboard other aircraft. Every pilot I know has one or more near-miss stories. It's my biggest concern because I have less control over it.

Legally, gliders have the right of way over most other aircraft. Wonderful. That's like saying pedestrians have the right of way in Manhattan: legally sound but ill advised. Under the "see and avoid" doctrine underlying much of aviation, we constantly scan sectors of the sky for aircraft. That works well if we are diligent, although there's a lot of sky to scan. The biggest risk arises from what we can't scan, i.e., the sky *behind* us.

Journal Entry: August 5, 2006 (Uvalde, Texas)

Out on course at the 2006 Standard Class Nationals in Uvalde, Texas, a dozen sailplanes are stacked up in twin thermals not far apart. They're going up equally fast and mine is less crowded, so I stay put. When I top out, I alter course slightly to check out the other thermal. It's no better, so I complete a circle, then push over to cruising speed headed for the next turn.

At dinner, one of the leading pilots, very controlled, pulls me aside to ask,

"Juliet Bravo, did you see me?" referring to the twin thermals.

My eyes harden and I stand straighter. What happened? I knew I could be in his blind spot when I merged into the thermal ahead of and below him. That's why I hadn't pulled up right in front of him to slow. I had kept my speed, staying ahead and below as I made a single circuit before leaving. I choose my words with care, conscious that I might have screwed up.

"Yes, I remember the two thermals together. I saw you there when I came into yours. Was there a problem?"

His *real* question: was I watching when we almost collided? I knew we were in each other's blind spots, but *he* did not. We both decided it was time to leave at the same instant. As he pushed over to pick up speed, my tail appeared a few feet in front, nose down and accelerating! Shocked, he said he could have reached out and touched my rudder with his hand! He was too close to maneuver under or over me. As a high-time fighter pilot, he instantly assessed that our speeds and acceleration were close to identical. He held his course—and breath—as our paths gradually diverged.

A few years later, I used this as an illustration for a safety talk in a room full of experienced pilots at a national contest. I replayed our GPS flight tracks (with the contest numbers disguised) on a big screen using software that displayed our paths in 3D, like a video game. There was a collective intake of breath and nervous laughter as our two little glider icons—with real people in them—merged into one, bloomed, then separated. If he had sliced off my horizontal tail, rendering the glider uncontrollable, I would have had enough altitude to jettison the canopy, release the harness, exit the glider, and use the parachute. But that would have pushed my soaring into a whole new risk category. It was as close as I've ever come to colliding with another aircraft.

I assumed the blame for sliding into his blind spot. But to many, this was just one of those things that happen when two aircraft, by chance, occupy the same tiny piece of sky at the same moment.

A year later, it happened again. This time it was with a power plane. Powered aircraft are the wild card. They move faster and aren't watching out for us.

Journal Entry: June 30, 2007 (Sussex, New Jersey)

Late in the afternoon, I'm headed southwest on final glide to our airport at Blairstown, New Jersey. The sun is reflecting off the canopy in the haze. The GPS flight computer says I have just enough altitude to glide straight in.

It's a practice flight and I don't feel like taking chances. So when I fly through a weak thermal, I pull up gently to make an exploratory circle. I'd rather make a few extra turns in weak lift here than be a mile short with the stress and risk of a last-minute landout.

There's no warning. The sound comes out of nowhere, engine/prop noise rising loudly to a snarl. My head snaps over, alarmed. It's close, *really* close! F**k, it's *behind* me! *["we've traced the call, it's coming from* inside *the house!"⁴¹]* Now the noise is SO close. In an instantaneous jolt, a low-wing, single-engine power plane overtakes and bursts by me savagely from behind, less than 100 yards off my right side, his wing down hard, banking sharply to avoid running over me! He is precisely at my altitude—yet I can see the stains on the belly of his plane clearly as he breaks hard right. The noise rises in seconds, peaks as he whips past, then drops off just as quickly. He recovers and straightens out, and I watch as he disappears in the distance—straight on course for Blairstown. I hardly have time to flinch.

Fate had brought us within a blink of a violent encounter. We were at the same altitude headed for the same airport, his airplane closing from behind, almost 100 knots faster. We both had the sun in our eyes. If I hadn't pulled up and turned slightly, my long, thin wings glinting white in the haze like a warning flash, we would probably have collided. This time, bailing out would have been less viable even if I had survived the high-speed collision. We didn't look each other up to compare notes after we arrived back at Blairstown.

Most mid-airs occur in clear weather within five miles of an airport, and involve pilots who *should* be able to see each other but involve crossing or overtaking flight, often a faster aircraft coming up on a slower one—just like this.

These two incidents occurred 15 years ago. Today's technology could help avoid, though not eliminate them. Most competition sailplanes carry electronic FLARM devices that alert pilots if they are on a collision course with similarly equipped aircraft. That could have alerted us to the near miss in Uvalde.

Powered aircraft use radar transponders and other equipment with the air traffic control system to avoid collisions. A small number of gliders are so equipped, though it might not have helped me avoid the New Jersey near miss.

"See and avoid" is still the primary defense. The Big Sky Theory of aviation posits three-dimensional airspace is so large and individual aircraft are so small, they are unlikely to be in the same place at the same time. Like finding your soulmate, though, mid-air collisions may be unlikely, but they can happen.

---

⁴¹ Analogous to the classic line about a deranged killer harassing a babysitter via telephone, hiding *inside* the house where she is barricaded. Most notably from *When a Stranger Calls*, directed by Fred Walton, written by Steve Feke and Fred Walton. Columbia Pictures, 1979. Film.

CHAPTER FIFTY-EIGHT

Unforced Errors

NOT EVERY RISK IS ASSOCIATED WITH DEATH. In gliding, as in life, risks fall on a continuum. Training and local flying are less risky than flying cross country, which is less risky than competition. Minor glider damage is more likely than major damage, which is more likely than injury, which is more likely than death. Some risks even have a humorous side.

Journal Entry: May 18, 2008 (Cordele, Georgia)

It's the 2008 Cordele Nationals. I land in a pasture (proving I haven't learned my lesson). Unlike the one that claimed my landing gear, this pasture is benign. I telephone back, then settle in to read my paperback book. Everyone in the contest has landed out, so I'm not sure who will be retrieving me.

Late that afternoon, cattle returning to the barn spot a shiny new object: my ASW 24. Intensely curious, they alter course directly for it. The herd flows around the glider, surrounding it. Then they begin crowding in on all sides. It's not quite like Alfred Hitchcock's *The Birds*, but it feels menacing.

I charge one group, yelling loudly and waving my arms until they reluctantly back away. Success! Opposable thumbs and bigger brains are why we're eating nachos with guacamole while cows are still munching grass. But when I turn around, cattle are pushing in from the other side. I sprint around the wing to get ahead of them with more yelling and arm waving. The cows respond with more flanking maneuvers. It's like playing Whac-A-Mole, the perimeter shrinking with each incursion. Anxious and needing expert advice, I telephone Erik Mann (P3), waiting in another field.

JB: What do you know about cows?

P3: I'm from New Jersey, what do you think?

He suggests loud static on the radio. I already tried that. The ring of animals—each of which weighs almost three times as much as my glider—continues to tighten. Some are almost close enough now to reach the delicate control surfaces. I'm running out of ideas. There are stories of cows damaging unattended gliders.

In desperation, I pull out the 25 feet of towline I carry and begin swinging a big loop overhead like a helicopter, with loud cowboy whoops. It works! Who knows what the cows think, but they lose interest and head for the barn. It will be a funny story back at Cordele, but I'm not laughing now.

Getting low over inhospitable terrain or waiting too late to select a landing spot can bring a pilot down in a rough field (I know of many examples over the years); in the trees (half a dozen pilots I know, all of whom escaped severe injury); or in a lake or a swamp (all three pilots I know survived uninjured and with modest damage to their gliders). More common are hazards lying in wait, such as the hidden rocks that destroyed the landing gear of my ASW 24.

Experts say landing is one of the most dangerous phases of a soaring flight. There's less time to react. Higher stress makes the pilot more likely to make mistakes. And the consequences of a mistake are more severe when the aircraft is low and slow with few alternatives.

We could mitigate most of these risks if we were perfect. I'm not.

Journal Entry: July 30, 2015 (Elmira, New York)

What the hell happened to the thermals?

The farther I glide, the lower—and more unsettled—I get. I'm in the closing miles of a long task at the 2015 Standard Class Nationals in Elmira. My GPS-based glide computer is unrelenting that I've been below glide path for 40+ miles in a shallow descent into the Watkins Glen turnpoint. None of the nice-looking cumulus has worked. It's like someone flipped a switch and shut down the thermals. We've seen this on other days. But I push on. Surely, I'll find something.

I don't. Still in a dead glide, I tag the perimeter of the Watkins Glen turnpoint cylinder, then hook a sharp right and head south for the twin asphalt strips sitting on top of Harris Hill gliderport, nine miles away, like a carrier deck in the distance. I'm down to 1,200 feet above the Hill, still below glide path. Sweating now, I cross the Interstate and sail over the bump that juts into the valley across the Chemung River from Harris Hill. Less than 300 feet above the crest, the wind flowing over it boosts me up about 50 feet. That's encouraging, so I angle back on course over the valley.

"Juliet Bravo, two miles, low, straight in."

I'm falling below the crest. My blood pressure is climbing and I'm chewing my lower lip. I can abort and land at the big Elmira regional airport in the valley 800 feet below. But I won't get a speed finish unless I'm on top of the Hill. F**k, I can't *believe* I've come this far—over 50 miles on final glide—just to miss it by a hundred feet. With apologies to my ex-Navy friends—whose exposure to danger makes soaring look tame—it must be a little like nursing a damaged fighter jet back to the carrier for nearly an hour and then, in the last 30 seconds, being forced to ditch in the water.

There's one hope. With the wind at my back, the front face of Harris Hill directly ahead *should* generate lift as the wind sweeps up and over it. Gliders have been flying this ridge since the 1930s. I watch the runway disappearing as I sink inexorably below it, approaching the precipitous slope of the Hill in front of me, trees and grass and rocks and the access road that snakes along below the crest growing larger. I try not to think of the almost identical situation 20 years ago during a regional when the Hill *didn't* work—and I landed in an emergency strip at the bottom. Seconds before impacting the rocky incline, I bank hard left to turn parallel with it. If the ridge is working, if the wind is blowing up this slope, I will know right away.

YES! Unbelievable! Flying along below the hill with the crest out of sight above my right wing, the wind flowing up the slope lifts me smoothly, like an elevator, with the audio variometer singing like crazy. Hope surges! As my ASW 24 slides along the hillside parallel with the ridge at 55 knots, it doesn't take long to regain the altitude to be level with the Hill. As the gliderport comes back into view. I want to shout with glee!

Then—still gaining altitude—I'm above the crest! The exhilaration is insane! The gliderport spreads across the top of the Hill off my right wing just below me. At this contest, I can land anywhere on the airport, in any direction, and receive a finish. The stress and uncertainty are over! I just need to turn right and land straight ahead. That will put the wind at my back, but who cares?

And that's what I do: a 90-degree right turn onto a low, short final approach to land downwind. Everyone else is finishing high, then making a 180-degree turn to land into the wind (i.e., facing me) on the main runway on the left. But I just need to get it on the ground. I can land downwind on the narrow runway on the right; there's no one else there right now. But I can't overshoot. The far end has a steep drop off. Now I'm over the grassy verge of the gliderport. I've made it: I've finished! A sense of triumph infuses me.

I level the wings, extend the dive brakes, and lower the nose to descend over the soft, welcoming grass. The wind is at my back, so I need to get it on the ground. I round out and drive it gently, but firmly, onto the turf.

WHUMP!!!

F**k! It's a rude shock, but in an instant, I realize what I've done. Overworked, stressed, and thrilled to be finishing. I never mentally shift gears from final glide mode into landing mode. For the first time in 45 years, I totally forget my landing checklist. I touch down abruptly on the aircraft's belly—with the wheel still securely retracted inside the fuselage.

It's too late to pull up. I slide along in the grass, awash in a massive sense of stupidity. But it's okay. Landing *sans* wheel on this smooth turf isn't a big deal. Polish the grass stain off and worry about scratches later. Then the grass ends abruptly, and we hit the raised lip of the near end of the paved runway. Oh, s**t! The fuselage clobbers it with a muffled CRUNCH and rides up over it, now skidding along the tarmac, scrubbing off speed and gel coat. I can hear it abrading, leaving a long, perfectly centered white stripe on the asphalt. It's painful to hear. The sound—like a rasp through soft wood—provokes an almost physical illness. It doesn't last long, though. The ASW 24 decelerates fast, literally grinding to a halt.

Aviators refer to the inevitability of wheels-up landings: *"There are those who have and those who will."* It's a lot funnier when it's said about other pilots.

My transition from one cohort to the other was mortifying. *Everyone* at the airport could see my glider resting low on the pavement. I was obstructing traffic, so someone radioed helpfully, "Juliet Bravo just landed gear up! We need help moving him out of the way." Great, now everyone within 50 miles knew.

My sense of failure and embarrassment was complete, made worse by the dizzying plunge from the euphoria I had reached only seconds before. This was the first time I had broken something on a glider from pilot error. I had more empathy for my father not wanting to admit he had ground looped his Diamant 48 years earlier. For a few hours, the sense I had failed in some irrefutable, inexcusable, public way washed over every other emotion.

The damage was more serious than we thought. Slamming into the raised lip of the asphalt had cracked the belly. I was in fourth place at the U.S. Nationals, my highest ever this late in a major contest in nearly 40 years. I desperately needed to keep flying.

But I also wanted to just curl up in a ball and go to sleep, hoping it was a bad dream. It wasn't until that evening, with the wings off and the fuselage turned belly up in a hangar so competitor and good friend Hank Nixon could do a temporary repair under the lights, that I knew I would have the chance to redeem myself the next day by flying, rather than watching forlornly from the ground.

Pilots stopped by to watch Hank work his magic. Many commiserated, admitting they had done the same thing. A few conceded privately they had done it twice! That was little comfort. I had made a stupid, public mistake in the high-stress environment where I had always taken pride in coolly acquitting myself.

Emergency repair from gear-up landing. Fuselage upside down: landing gear and gear doors to the right; teardrop-shaped damaged area in middle.

There was an ugly scar on the ASW 24's belly the next day, but it was flyable. I held on to finish fourth, another step up the ladder after years of lackluster results. By the following season, I had put it behind me. I would never forget my gear-up landing. But it was one lapse in 50 years. We all make mistakes.

My next major mistake, one year later, was more egregious and costly. It involved the other statistically "most dangerous" mode of flight: takeoff.

It was Day One of the 2016 Standard Class Nationals in Nephi, Utah. Those of us in the first rows on the grid were launching downwind. The organizers predicted the 10- to 12-knot tailwind would soon swing around to become a headwind for most of the field. I had launched downwind before, though never at altitude or in hot temperatures. As the slack came out of the rope, I glanced sideways to see my wing runner was the youngest (by a lot!) volunteer boy, not my brother. Mark had driven out to the contest with me, reliving our journey to Minden 35 years earlier. But he wasn't wearing running shoes that day.

Journal Entry: June 21, 2016 (Nephi, Utah)

The towpilot locks his brakes and opens the throttle, then releases. The rope stretches, then yanks the glider forward like a rubber band. The explosion of acceleration jerks the ASW 24's wingtip out of the small hands of the inexperienced young boy running the wingtip. Startled, he tries to hang on to it, a serious rookie mistake. That slews me off to the right as I start to roll. Then he gives up and drops it. The wingtip, heavy from water sloshing down on that side, hits the ground with a bang—and drags.

There's a procedure I've used several times in 40 years. Release, brake to a stop, then wait to be wheeled back into line. No thinking. No exceptions. It's almost impossible to get a ballasted wing up after it goes down.

Instead of releasing, I hang on with full left stick and left rudder, hoping to level the wings and straighten out my track. The heavy right wing stays down, the wingtip skid grinding away noisily. We're gaining speed. The edge of the runway is approaching. The wing *has* to come up, damnit!

We're accelerating slower than usual because of the high altitude and temperature. My track is diverging further and further from the towplane's, like a water skier skimming out to one side of the wake. Any second now, it's gotta come up. There are no people or vehicles in the way. But now the wingtip drops off the runway into the gravel along the edge.

It is *way* past time to release—when, at last, the right wing bounces up! Yes! With wings level, I lift off, then rudder back in behind the towplane as he also breaks ground. I exhale in relief. Never again! As we climb, I hear another pilot towing out behind me warn there's a dust devil approaching the departure path. With no delay, the imperious voice of the official responds:

"Continue the launch." No questions. No hesitation. He's the man in charge and won't brook any interference with his neat, precision (well, except for my wing runner) launch operation. All eyes are watching as the next pilot to be towed out nearly loses it in the violent turbulence a few hundred feet above the ground, screeching over the radio to complain. Good, my off-runway excursion will be old news.

But it wasn't old news. In fact, I was on the freakin' front page. As my right wingtip came up, I never saw, heard, or felt the impact as it clobbered a runway landing light, breaking it off at the base and putting a fist-sized fracture in the wing's leading edge, then gouging the lower surface of the wing and aileron.

Ignorant of this, I finished the arduous task, pleased when so many had landed out. Before I could exit the cockpit, one of the organizers—with the grim countenance of a mob enforcer—slid to a halt in his car, leaped out, and began snapping away rudely at the wing with his camera. Now I know what it's like when loathsome paparazzi ambush a Hollywood starlet stepping out on her porch in a robe. I restrained my impulse to jerk the camera out of his hands and smash it on the tarmac.

Despite this fellow's clumsy eagerness to document the damage, I didn't judge it as serious. Two repair experts concurred the next morning after reviewing my photos: "Tape over the holes and fly it," advised the dealer.

But—surprise—the organizers, fearful of liability, demanded I repair the wing before they would tow me. Reasoning with them was a waste of time.

So, once again, I received expert help from another pilot/competitor during a furious repair session. [Thanks, York Zentner. You saved our entire massive effort to drive out to Utah.] This repair was too complex for overnight, and we worked through the next day. But the weather relegated that day to no-fly status, so I was on the grid the following day without losing points.

My instinctive reaction was to justify not pulling the release. But ex-Top Gun graduate and good friend Bif Huss (who would win the contest) would have none of that. He forced me to admit hanging onto the towline would have been the wrong decision *even if I hadn't hit the runway light.*

I could have blamed the downwind launch and novice wing runner. Some of the launch crew proffered that later, reassuring me it wasn't my fault. But the damage *was* my fault for not releasing the towrope when the wing went down.

Leading edge and lower surface of wing after striking landing light.

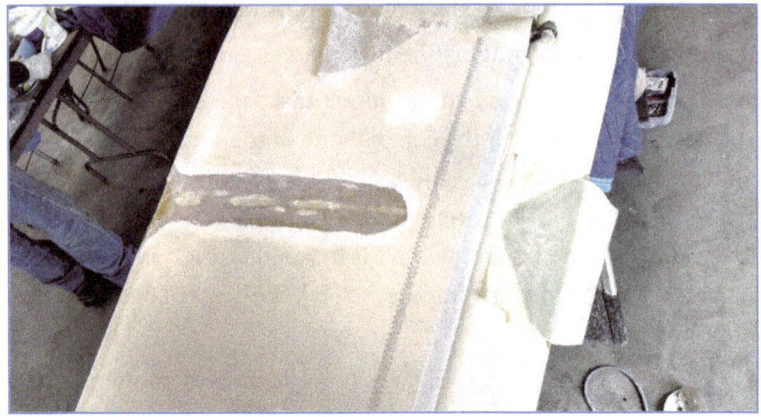

Bottom of wing after sanding to expose damage before repair. Repair to underside of aileron in progress (triangular patch, far right).

I concluded there were two reasons for my poor decision. First, I allowed pressure to maintain the launch cadence push me into doing something stupid. With over 50 gliders in three classes, the organizers had repeatedly stressed getting everyone in the air on time. That's no excuse, of course.

Second, I suspect I didn't want to "fail" in front of a big crowd of top pilots. In the back of my mind was the idea that "good pilots can fly their way out of situations like this." Of course, I failed anyway when I broke a rule.[42]

This more serious lapse in judgment was tougher to put behind me. I couldn't, in fact, until a year later, on the takeoff line at the 2017 Nationals, in Cordele, Georgia. Once again, my right wing went down as we started to roll. This couldn't be happening to me; three or four times in 50 years and now twice in 12 months? This time, however, I didn't hesitate. I released the towrope (to the relief of several onlookers who had been at Nephi) and coasted off to the side. I felt very conspicuous again. Two takeoff incidents in two years. But I was back on the line five minutes later without ever leaving the cockpit—and with no damage.

It was so simple.

---

[42] For a video peek at the Nephi launch grid, see https://youtu.be/reNYaxBV5ps by a soaring friend of mine. I believe I'm shown launching (uneventfully this time) at 2:45.

CHAPTER FIFTY-NINE

Texas Shooting Gallery

"**I**S THE SHOOTER STILL OUT THERE?" I didn't know whether to hit the deck or call 9-1-1. Sweeping my eyes around in the morning sun, I could imagine a sniper sitting up on the hill to the north.

It sounds crazy, but I didn't notice the bullet holes. One morning midway through the 2018 Standard Class Nationals in Midlothian, Texas, I had pulled the fuselage out of the trailer to assemble the ASW 24. Something wasn't right. The cockpit had tiny plastic and metal shards scattered about. At first, I felt stupid: I must have broken something putting the glider in the trailer. Damn!

But my main and backup battery switches on the instrument panel were missing, along with the fuse holders just below them. In their place was a small hole with frayed fiberglass edges. It took me a few minutes to put it all together.

Overnight, someone with a gun had stopped on the road 30 yards away and fired five times into the front of my trailer—with the glider inside! Three shots struck the aluminum trailer sidewalls, doing minor damage. One shot penetrated the fiberglass front door of the trailer and went through the right wing.

The prize for "most damage from one bullet" was the slug that tore through the left trailer side wall; then drilled through the upper and lower skins of the left wing; punched a small hole in the left front corner of the Plexiglas canopy; pierced the instrument panel cover; exploded from the instrument panel (i.e., the first hole I spotted); and blew a fist-size hole in the right side of the canopy. Seven layers, two of which—the wing skins—contained Kevlar (the stuff in bulletproof vests).

The entry holes were small and neat where the jacketed slugs penetrated the trailer and wings. The exit holes were frayed like the one in the instrument panel. Five bullets. Thirteen holes in multiple layers of the trailer and glider.

It was a lot to take in. Stunned, I drove over to contest HQ and pulled CD Mark Keene aside before the pilots' meeting. "Uh, Mark, I've got a situation."

He was alarmed and upset. Nothing like this had ever happened at the gliderport (and only once or twice elsewhere in the country over the years, we later determined). He promised to contact local law enforcement. Then:

"Chip, do you want to fly?"

"Yes. If the glider is airworthy, I'm flying." I appreciated his asking rather than assuming I wouldn't or couldn't. "But I probably won't be on the grid on time. There's just too much to do."

"Don't worry, we'll get you a tow. You focus on getting the glider and yourself ready to fly." *[I thanked Mark for his rational, level-headed, and supportive attitude, more constructive than I might have encountered at other contests.]*

Several pilots quietly questioned whether I should fly, given the possibility of hidden damage. But the holes were behind the spars, not in the more critical leading edges of the wings. Peering through access ports, I verified the bullets had passed cleanly through the upper and lower skins without striking the spars, control linkages, ballast tanks, or any other critical areas. Remarkably, the bullet through the instrument panel had disintegrated switches and wiring (photo below) but left the instruments untouched. The aircraft was safe to fly. The biggest question: could I patch it up and be ready in time?

Bullet passed through trailer skin (layer 1); upper/lower wing surfaces (layers 2 & 3); punctured canopy (layer 4) and instrument pod (layer 5)—note arrow; then exited instrument panel (layer 6)—note arrow, with missing power switch and fuses; before breaking larger hole in canopy, (layer 7)—see following photo.

The sheriff's deputy arrived as the pilots' meeting began, so I ducked out to brief her. Airport shootings get top priority even in Texas! She took photos, dug two copper-jacketed 9 mm slugs out of the trailer, and promised to follow up.

Word had spread. Most knew not to pester me with questions. A gratifying number offered help. It was a race against the clock to ready the glider. I applied speed tape to the holes, giving the ASW 24 the aura of surviving aerial combat. The swath of tape on the canopy to the right of my head (see photo, with cracks extending beyond the hole) didn't impair my vision. I clipped out the shattered electrical components and twisted bare wires together to connect the primary battery (I ignored the seldom needed backup battery). I still had to assemble and equip the glider; load water ballast; pull it to the grid; return the van to the trailer and connect it in case I landed out; and input the task (which I hadn't yet seen) into the GPS navigation systems. I *really* missed having a crew.

Canopy damage, with white speed tape over the hole and cracks radiating from it.
(photo by Nirmal Mathrani)

I tried to ignore the launch while I was working. It was as if I were on autopilot, ticking off each point on my checklist (with a handful of added items in the brand-new category of "Repair Ballistic Damage"). By the time I was strapping in, everyone else had been airborne for a while. This would be the longest task of the contest at 335 miles, not the best day for a late takeoff.

"The Killing Fields": Midlothian, Texas. From here, bullet holes are difficult to spot (l)
9 mm bullet after passing through seven layers of my ASW 24 (r).

As I sat waiting for the line crew to hook me up, Mark Keene briefed me on the task. I knew he was also assuring himself I was in the right frame of mind to fly. Satisfied, he wished me luck, and the towplane powered away.

I climbed up and started right away, knowing I was behind the field. I flew aggressively, keeping a watchful eye on the primary battery voltage. If it died, I would lose most instruments, the radio, and the GPS navigation and loggers. I would be safe and able to return (I had a map). But I would be out of the contest.

As I caught stragglers, jumped gaggles, and worked my way around the course under a tricky sky—with wide bands of high cloud that threatened to shut us down—I began to relax. In the sun on the last leg with the voltage still in the safe zone, I was growing more confident about coming back from a near disaster. I felt energized, bringing to mind (figuratively) Winston Churchill's line that *"Nothing in life is so exhilarating as to be shot at without result."*[43] I even posted a decent speed. That night, I borrowed switches from a competitor (thanks, Danny Sorenson, one place ahead of me) and repaired the wiring.

The sheriff's investigator found five empty shell casings by the road. But with no fingerprints or security cameras, the only theories were (i) alcohol and guns on a Friday night in Texas, or (ii) a disgruntled local farmer with an alleged drinking history who may have resented the daily noise of our launch over his farm. The investigation died. Total cost of the insurance claim: over $9,000.

Later, I was discomfited to learn I was being referred to as "badass" by some of the younger pilots. I couldn't enjoy it. I felt like an imposter. Badass was when you were *in the aircraft* in a war zone—as several of them had been in Afghanistan. They seemed impressed I had pushed hard to fly. Did they think most pilots would have stood down? Or were they surprised a man in his late 60s persisted? I decided I didn't need to know. Being regarded this way by pilots half my age was enough.

* * *

I reflected on it all as I drove home. I had flown well, but not well enough. Once again, I had been too conservative. I had completed every task but had finished behind two pilots who each landed out once. Their cumulative scores bested mine because of their higher speeds on other days. That had been my story for years. I could blame some of my caution on not having a crew, but that was an excuse. I simply wasn't flying the way I had long ago.

---

[43] Churchill, Winston S., *The Story of the Malakand Field Force* (London: Longmans, Green and Co., 1898).

CHAPTER SIXTY

If I Had to Choose

W HICH IS MORE IMPORTANT, FLYING OR RUNNING? It's a *Sophie's Choice* question. I love both—don't make me choose! Each is part of my identity, having had enormous impact on my confidence and self-worth. Each has brought me immense satisfaction and joy. When my life has been adrift, I have clung to one sport or the other, sometimes both.

For a long time, the answer was simple. Running was a pastime, a stress reducer. It kept me healthy and enhanced my ego. Running was *fun*. Soaring, on the other hand, was a *passion,* inspiring, uplifting, fulfilling, the ultimate escape that allowed me to elude everything that bound, inhibited, constrained, or depressed me.

In soaring, I often said, even a bad contest day beat a good day almost anywhere else. In running, a bad day at a race was just a bad day.

Today, it's more complicated. My soaring friends would insist nothing compares to flying. I mostly agree. "High Flight"—the poem my brother, sister, and I read at my father's memorial service—eloquently captures flying's unique challenge, appeal, and transcendent aura. There's nothing like it. For much of my adult life, I feared that if I could no longer fly, I would be lost. Flying had changed the way I thought of myself and the way I interacted with others. When, in my prayers, I enumerated the many ways I had been blessed, flying was always near the top of the list. As the Air Force Academy cadet heroine of Kim Ponders' *The Last Blue Mile* reflects in closing:

"How lucky she was to belong to the world, to be able to fly through it."[44]

But I have also felt the same way about running. Running has sustained me when I wasn't flying, providing challenges that have obsessed and rewarded me. I wouldn't express it as lyrically as did Dr. George Sheehan, accorded cult status for his 1970s book *Running and Being*. My magical moments are infrequent, typically occurring at the emotional starts and physically depleted finishes of life-changing marathons.

But running marathons has provided the same temporary escape from the real world as soaring. Even now, slower than I've ever been, I enjoy setting goals and driving myself to the limits of physical and mental exhaustion. There aren't

---

[44] Ponders, Kimberley A., *The Last Blue Mile* (New York: Harper, 2007)

many places where I can do that at age 72. I'm more likely to hear "calm down," "slow down," "act your age," or the maddeningly common "are you okay, sir?"

In the waning miles of a marathon, I can push myself hard, putting everything I have into the effort and knowing—whether because of others urging me on, or crowd noise, or the clock counting up inexorably, and I reach deeper and discover a new tolerance for pain I didn't know I had—that life is simple and elemental. When I finish, hands to knees, lungs burning, coughing, and wobbling, I have the satisfaction of knowing I held nothing back. In the clarity of those moments, when I know I have given 100% to achieve something that would ordinarily be beyond me, running does as much for me as soaring does.

* * *

How much we enjoy a sport often turns on how proficient we are. I was never as good a runner as I am a soaring pilot. It's not for lack of trying. But experts opine that 85% of running performance depends on genetics. Success at the highest level turns on how well gifted athletes manage the other 15% through training. I'm proud of squeezing everything from my unimpressive 85% but, with apologies to my parents, I've always felt shortchanged.

Running Boston three times was satisfying. But my few other accolades as a runner have accrued not for my middling talent, but for my tenacity. There's a saying: "You must be present to win." Sometimes that's *all* you have to do—be the last one standing when the music stops. For the past half-dozen years, the Philadelphia Marathon has honored me as one of a handful of LEGacy Runners who have finished at least 15 Philly Marathons. On my way to completing 24 of the 27, I've attended press conferences and VIP dinners, met politicians, and conversed with former world #1 marathoner Bill Rodgers, winner of my first marathon (NYC 1978).

Ironically, being the last one standing has also applied to soaring where, *mirabile dictu,* I came within one slot of qualifying for the U.S. Team going to the 2018 World Gliding Championships in Poland. Multiple factors contributed to this unlikely outcome, including my respectable finishes in the smaller fields at recent Standard Class nationals and the decision by a few pilots above me to turn down spots because of the expense or having qualified for another class.

No matter, I was but one pilot away from representing my country, as my father and I had discussed 50 years ago. That idea seemed brash then. In my frustrating decline following his crash, it was embarrassing. Now, briefly, it was no more improbable than qualifying for the Boston Marathon had once been.

Winning a spot on the Team would have been an elegant way to close another loop. My 2018 ranking is likely the closest I will ever come to benefiting directly from the Robert L. Robertson Trust I helped Donald Robertson establish for the U.S. Team. I'm delighted it endures as intended, though the number of pilots who knew Robert—or are even aware of his legacy—shrinks each year.

* * *

Soaring contests and marathons both require training, preparation, special equipment, and logistical planning and support. That said, I can don my running gear and be on the roads in ten minutes, run for an hour, and be showered and ready for the real world in less time than it takes to hook up the trailer to the van, drive to the airport, and get my ASW 24 assembled and ready to fly.

Once I'm under way, running and soaring offer almost infinite possibilities. Running is obvious. But even in today's hyper-regulated world, in my sailplane, I can fly almost anywhere I wish (except major cities and airports and military facilities) without approval. I can thermal a few hundred feet over a farmer's field even though it's risky. I can push my ASW 24 up to 151 knots—or more if I'm suicidal or playing test pilot. I can fly into unlandable mountains knowing the responsibility for maintaining a glide angle back out to a safe landing area is mine alone and not that of a bureaucratic rule or "do not enter" sign.

A soaring buddy pulling up exuberantly after a high-speed, low-level pass.
(photo by Bozena Michalowski)

There are even a few contests that still offer a finish line with a 50 feet minimum height where we can make a low, high-speed pass and pull up hard in a big celebratory climb just like the old days. Soaring's freedom is the aeronautical equivalent of my high school classmate's "if it feels good, do it, and whatever turns you on."

* * *

Sharing these sports with my family is a factor in my enjoyment. I was shocked when pilots first arrived at big contests *sans* crew 30 years ago. I'd had a guaranteed family crew since 1968 and couldn't imagine flying an important contest without their support. As of 2007, however, with a few exceptions, I've been one of the growing crewless contingent. I miss the support, but also the sharing. I suppose this was inevitable. Soaring never was as family friendly as I imagined. My father *made* it so. I tried his approach—imposing my will to make soaring part of our lives. I was successful for a while, but it no doubt contributed to our divorce.

My family have been more successful sharing running. We started involving all of us from the beginning and have continued for almost 30 years. Living in New York, my daughters run local races, often with Tanya. And our family still attend most big marathons together. At Philly, the girls began jumping in late in the race to escort me in 2010, after I contracted Lyme disease. Each year after that, one or both have accompanied me for part of the race. Their biggest challenge came in 2016.

Journal Entry: November 20, 2016 (Philadelphia Marathon)

I'm in trouble. I've *been* in trouble since my lower back tightened up at ten miles. The past few years, I've had hip pain so severe in the late stages that I've had trouble finishing. This is worse. I'm listing to the left as I go by the family at 14 and turn upriver for the last six-mile out and back. Soon, I'm walking painfully more than running. And I'm stopping to stretch. A 65-year-old man dropping to the ground in the closing miles of a marathon to kneel (yoga's "child pose") is an invitation to dial 9-1-1.

"Are you okay, sir?"

At the 20-mile turnaround, my upper body is wrenched to one side. I'm ready to topple over. My face is a mask of pain. A spectator offers ibuprofen. A runner hands me a hot pack, saying I look like I need it more than she does. I thank her through clenched teeth: "You're very perceptive!"

And I'm chilled. At my dismal pace, I'm generating less body heat. I'm falling apart. For the first time in 41 marathons, I'm considering dropping out.

My worried daughters are running out to meet me. I can't straighten up when they arrive at 23 miles. Smiling and upbeat, they don't appear to be alarmed to see their father near collapse. As Tina blithely assured a worried finish line worker a few years ago, "Don't worry; he does this all the time." They assess the situation expertly—no cringing or helpless fluttering—then utter the words I shall never forget: "We'll help get you in!" A rush of gratitude and love and resolve swells within me. I *can't* stop now.

No rolling of their eyes about my absurd conduct, the state I'm in, or my pathetic pace. Just the same unequivocal support they have always given me in this sport, in the good times and in the bad times.

They tie Mylar finish line heat sheets around me to block the cold wind cutting through my clothing. They arrange themselves on either side—swapping every few minutes—and we set off walking. One supports my leftward lean. The other holds the hot pack against my lower back. Slowly, I straighten up. We take close to an hour to cover the last 3+ miles. As grim as it sounds, it's one of the high points of my running life. I'll never forget the sense of love, joy, and relief when we shuffled across the line, or how unsteady I was for hours afterward, or how grateful I still am.

Two post-marathon finishes: my daughters escorting me at Philly after near collapse in 2016, and their first marathon there in 2018. (photos by Tanya Lenkow)

Two years later, at the same race, Josie and Tina ran their first marathons. Both finished far ahead of me. But watching them fly by me on the course, then being welcomed at the finish and sharing their elation was indescribable.

These shared experiences have been so uplifting that I've worried, once again, that life is *too* good. Recently, I smiled at a quote from *Pride and Prejudice* by Jane Austen:

"I must learn to be content with being happier than I deserve."

I'm working on it. Less than a year after Philly 2018, Tina and I flew out to Seattle with Tanya to run the Tunnel Light Marathon in the mountains. The gentle downhill on an old gravel rail bed sweeps down from the Snoqualmie Pass through old-growth forests, by mountain waterfalls, and across vertiginous railroad trestles. It electrified me to learn during the race Tina had missed a BQ by only six minutes. I hit the wall at 18 and staggered in long after.

I must have looked beaten up when I exited the finish chute because someone slid a chair under me. I didn't hesitate to collapse into it. But it was worth it—the months of training, the injuries, the long flight to Seattle in a cramped seat, the pain of the last eight miles, the whole 42 years of running—when Tina leaned in with a delighted smile, still exhilarated by her 22-minute PR in only her second marathon, and whispered:

"I'm so proud of you!" For a father, it doesn't get much better than that.

Tina and author midway at 2022 Boston Marathon. (photo by Samuel Hoad)

Increasingly, I'm sharing my children's running rather than vice versa.

Josie's husband, Sam, is a rising marathoner, and she seems likely to tackle her next marathon soon. Tina has run nine of them, notching a BQ in her fourth and eclipsing not only my protracted pursuit of that goal but my all-time PR. I was thrilled, matched only by seeing her at Boston in 2022.

We were waiting at the halfway point, peering intently up course watching for her. She was running with an injured knee, so we weren't sure what to expect. There was no guarantee she'd make it this far. Then, "There she is!"

Excitement soared as she came into view and spotted us shrieking and waving at her. Her face was incandescent as she ran over to the barrier to hug me fiercely. When I glimpsed tears in her eyes, I pulled back, my voice rising:

"Are you okay? How's your knee? Are you in pain?"

"No," shaking her head at her silly father, with a watery smile, "I'm just happy!"

* * *

Soaring and running appeal for many of the same reasons. There are two irrefutable distinctions, however.

The first, of course, is risk. Both sports allow me to push myself as hard as I wish. I've made some dubious decisions running, but it's undeniable that the consequences of overextending myself in soaring are far more severe. That said, a recent study assessed marathon running to be 17 times as risky as flying on a commercial jet, though less than one tenth as risky as soaring.[45]

The second distinction is that flying demands total focus with no distractions. For most of my 3,000 hours in the air, I've not only been *able* to ignore what is happening in my life, I've been *required* to.

Running is the opposite. It's true that racing a marathon properly requires concentration. But I've averaged only one of those annually since I started running. Excluding marathons and other races, I estimate I have spent close to ten thousand hours drifting off, musing over life's problems, and clarifying my thinking while running.

Simplistically, soaring helps me temporarily ignore or even forget my problems. Running helps me deal with them. I need both.

Which is *most* important? Sorry, but my answer is a lawyerly "it depends."

---

[45] https://chessintheair.com/the-risk-of-dying-doing-what-we-love/

CHAPTER SIXTY-ONE

The Riskiest Thing I Do

WHAT COULD MY FATHER HAVE BEEN THINKING? He was a career accountant, conservative to a fault. How could he *possibly* have sent his 14-year-old son off on his first solo flight? In his view, my taking a sturdy 2-22 for a quick circuit around the landing pattern at a quiet airport was safe enough. Maybe he was right. Given the carnage on the highways during those pre-seat-belt days, gliding's risk might have been comparable to that of my driving our fragile little Volkswagen Beetle.

But that calculus changed three years later with my first contest. Did Dad fly then as I do today, knowing we had moved closer to disaster, cantilevered a little farther out over the dark, bottomless chasm than if we had continued to coast around the local airport on weekend afternoons?

I doubt it. Several years ago, my mother sold the dream house my parents had bought four decades earlier. Sorting through boxes there, I found an interview with Dad in P&G's in-house magazine in 1975. At that point, I'd been flying for ten years. He had been soaring for 15.

Do I look like pilot material? My 14th birthday, one week before my first flying lesson. (photo by Joseph N. Bearden Jr.)

"What happens if you don't find a thermal?" [asks the interviewer]

"Nothing alarming," claims Joe. *"You simply drift gently downwards, directing the glider to a smooth landing spot. You're not going to go 'whap' unless you do something wrong."*[46]

When I closed my eyes, I could see him look up and smile, and hear his

---

[46] *Moonbeams*, No. 6/June 1975, Procter & Gamble Company, Cincinnati, OH

affable, reassuring confidence. Soaring was not dangerous. You could only get hurt if you made a mistake. And the subtext: pilots like us don't make mistakes.

* * *

Some vocations circumscribe their practitioners. Consider the police officer. Or soldier. Or actor, nurse, surgeon, auto mechanic, tax attorney, Wall Street banker, plumber, or Naval aviator. Without meeting a one, we presume to know who they are, what they do, the clothes they wear, their personalities, and their socioeconomic status. The job defines the person, we say.

That's presumptuous. None of my nine careers defined me. Work was never my life. I didn't hate my job. Sometimes I even enjoyed it. I took pride in doing it well. But I labored more often to pay bills than for self-actualization. I relied on soaring and running for that.

But for a long time I did not view soaring's hazards the way police officers and soldiers might consider the well-documented perils of their occupations, i.e., with arbitrary threats over which they have only partial control. In soaring, I naively believed, managing the risk was entirely within my power. As long as I didn't make a big mistake—and I wouldn't—I'd be okay.

Now I know better. I still believe gliding at a local airport is reasonably safe, notwithstanding a recent study that concluded soaring is twice as risky as riding a motorcycle—and 200 times as dangerous as commercial aviation.[47]

But in my 58 years flying gliders, as I have evolved from a naïve 14-year-old to a more pragmatic 72, my father and Robert Robertson are just two of the twenty (20) soaring pilots I have met who died doing what they loved. The list would be substantially longer were I to include pilots I knew only by name.

My list of 20 fatal crashes—45% of which occurred during competition—might be less disturbing if the victims were hot-headed pilots vying recklessly in unregulated races. Or brash, barnstorming aeronauts from aviation's early days. Or cocky, sound-barrier-era test pilots pushing experimental aircraft to their limits. Not so. The competitions were SSA-sanctioned and conducted under tightly defined rules. And nearly all accidents involved experienced pilots flying modern equipment.

Lest anyone accuse me of overdramatizing the risks of my lifelong sport, I am well aware that the risks in soaring, even in contests, pale compared with those assumed every day by military aviators in peacetime, much less in combat. I will also stipulate most accidents I discuss were avoidable, i.e., they were

---

[47] https://chessintheair.com/the-risk-of-dying-doing-what-we-love/

the direct or indirect result of a pilot erring or making a bad decision.

But pilots, even good pilots, make mistakes. I have known pilots with skills equal to or better than mine who succumbed. We are all capable of making serious, even fatal mistakes. I have seen too many pilots die and been uncomfortably close myself a few times. So I am obliged not to shrink from the reality of my experiences.

One pilot pushed back last year when I gave a safety talk citing these statistics. He agreed 20 fatal accidents were too many, but commented it isn't a huge number spread over the 50+ years I've been flying.

"That's true," I admitted, "But in those same 50+ years, I've only known two or three people killed in automobile accidents, despite knowing at least an order of magnitude more people who travel in automobiles than fly gliders." The consequences of a momentary lapse or minor mistake can be far more severe in flying than in driving.

A British aviator captured it succinctly in the 1930s:

"Aviation in itself is not inherently dangerous. But to an even greater degree than the sea, it is terribly unforgiving of any carelessness, incapacity, or neglect."[48]

* * *

I don't understand horror movies. Why do people enjoy being scared when the hockey-mask-clad slasher pops up over the starlet's shoulder?

I'm not a daredevil or thrill seeker. I prefer challenging—not terrifying—myself. I don't drive so fast that I worry about losing control. I no longer ski into dodgy terrain for the rush of surviving the descent. And I don't do anything in a glider that puts me at significant risk.

That doesn't mean I'm always relaxed. Each time I exit a thermal and push over to cruising speed, it could be the last glide before I'm forced to land. If I'm high and moving well, it's a non-issue. But as I glide lower, my unease grows. Why haven't I hit a decent thermal? What did everyone else recognize—that I missed? Will that thermal marked by a gaggle up ahead still be working when I get there (and what will I do if it isn't)? Will the wind blowing against that ridge sustain me when I glide to it? And as the ground approaches, where the hell am I going to land?

Every sporting endeavor involves risk: the risk of losing, of not doing one's

---

[48] Attributed to Captain Alfred Gilmer Lamplugh, British Aviation Insurance Group, London. ca. early 1930s.

best, or of failing in spectacular fashion. But in soaring, as in mountain climbing, downhill skiing, and motor racing, the risks, however small—and I believe they *are* small, or I wouldn't continue to fly—also include injury or death. In the past, I often insisted to outsiders that soaring was no riskier than most things we do. But that's disingenuous. I know its hazards better than most. And confronting my anxieties is part of the appeal.

* * *

After Dad crashed, some might have expected my siblings would never want to see another glider. In fact, it was the opposite. They seemed to be drawn even deeper into this world that took the life of our father. Was it an attempt to defy our mortality? Fascination with what had turned out to be a very different sport than we had imagined? Paying homage? Or (d) all the above?

Mark had already flown local contests. Post-crash, he moved up to become an eager competitor at the regional and national levels. His fiancée/wife and our mother were supportive. But things changed after Robert's death. Whether because of family pressure or his own concerns about the now undeniable risks, Mark cut back and then stopped flying.

A few years later, Diane surprised us by resuming her flying lessons. Her biggest challenge had always been self-confidence. Dad's technique, sitting in the rear seat, was to rest his hands lightly on the student's shoulders to signal they had full control. I laughed when Diane told me whenever she was overloaded, she would bat his hands away from her shoulders and replace them with hers, forcing my father to take the controls.

Diane's uncertain confidence related only to flying, not to interacting with Dad. We still chuckle over her lengthy campaign to get her ears pierced. Finally, in eighth grade (it was a different time), she won over my mother. My father remained opposed.

"Diane, if God had intended you to have pierced ears, he would have given you holes in them."

"Dad," she popped back, "If God had intended you to fly, he would have given you wings."

She had her ears pierced the following week.

We were all proud when, without fanfare, she soloed. She's spoken about how Dad's death inspired her to take on more responsibility at age 22. Pushing herself to solo was another manifestation. Then, like Mark, she put flying away, although she continued to crew at contests with enthusiasm.

Our mother, both before and after she remarried, crewed for Mark and me many times. I'm sure she had mixed emotions, not only about visiting people and places she had known with Dad, but also about the risks, which were no longer hypothetical. But she was always upbeat and supportive.

She and I talk almost every day. During the season, she asks if I am going flying and seems excited when I tell her I am. As I've done for years, I telephone her when I land, especially after contest tasks. I also text my family. A few years ago, I asked if she worries when I leave for a big contest.

She spoke carefully. "Chip, I guess I could let myself go back to a dark place. But I just assume things will work out and you'll be okay. So, no, I don't worry."

I wondered: does she really believe that? Is this what she would *like* to believe? Does she think that's what I want to hear?

Most remarkably, beginning a few months after the crash, she managed her anxieties and found ways to enjoy contest experiences. Everything she said and did was consistent with wanting me to continue flying because she knew that's what makes me happy.

* * *

Soaring pilots are aggressive—especially competition pilots—but we're not stupid. We know the risks and try like hell to manage them. That said, we sometimes view them with a sort of academic detachment. Being brought face to face with reality affects us in different ways.

Most pilots seem not to be deterred when a comrade is killed or injured. Our first reaction is to want to know the cause. Our second, almost simultaneous reaction is "that could never happen to me."

Even when it does—i.e., when pilots survive crashes—it doesn't seem to dissuade most of them. I know half a dozen pilots who dropped out of soaring after surviving serious accidents. But that's far outweighed by the number who jumped right back in the cockpit after a crash, undeterred.

* * *

There's one way to eliminate soaring's risk entirely: stop flying. As pilots, we seldom discuss this, except in the context of getting older. Yet I know a handful who have cited it, and I suspect there are more.

Pilots drift away from soaring for many reasons: age, other interests, career and family conflicts, time, health, and money. But 30 years ago, one excellent pilot conceded to me, unapologetically, he was leaving because of the risk. He was comfortable with it himself, but his wife had recently passed away, leaving him with young children. He didn't believe it was right to expose himself to soaring's risks—however small and manageable we might think they are—when the consequences could mean orphaning his kids. This baffled me. I didn't understand then.

Decades later, another widely respected competition pilot confided to me this had been a factor in his own decision to back away from the sport when his children were younger. This time I understood very well. I wonder how many others do, at least those still involved. Pilots who call it quits at least partly on that basis are likely to cite other reasons in order to avoid being labeled as lacking dedication or courage.

*　*　*

I rarely admit it (my secret's out now!), but it should shock no one when I confess to harboring dark thoughts. The possibility of disaster is on my mind before every flying weekend and contest. I don't obsess, or I might never fly again. But I think of my daughters and reflect on how my family reacted when my father crashed. I consider the chance that something could go wrong—never viscerally before takeoff in the excitement of the mission, but in an uneasy, abstract way in the preceding days or weeks. It's not fear of flying. It's more "have I put my affairs in order to spare them sorting through a mess?" Years ago, I began leaving a letter for my daughters that reiterates how much they mean to me—just in case. I only do this for flying, not for marathons, or driving into New York City, or doing anything else with risk attached. I don't know whether that's thoughtful and considerate, or melodramatic.

One pilot joked he was never coming to another one of my contest safety talks. I had mentioned my letter, noting it includes financial accounts, passwords, etc. This pilot's spouse (sitting in the audience) perked up and later queried her husband: "Honey, where do you keep *your* letter?"

*　*　*

All this raises three uncomfortable questions:

First, why have I continued to fly after witnessing three fatal crashes, including my father's, and losing my closest friend in another? Soaring might be statistically safer than climbing Everest or driving in Formula One, but *it is the riskiest thing I do* (though some would argue running the Boston marathon with a hole in my femoral artery was right up there).

A few years after my father's crash, Ted Williams followed up his *In Memoriam* with another personal essay called *Crossing the Bar*. He described his shock when he received the news, via a telex in Chile, of my father's death. He reminisced about the good times the two of them had shared in flying and re-counted tales of other friends he had lost in aviation over the years. He analyzed a few close calls of his own. He mused about the fascination of flying:

> *"Part of its seductiveness has always been the risk, hasn't it? The possibil-ity, the chance, however slight, that the swiftest, most advanced apparatus engineered by man, riding the crest of the human wave, may falter, for whatever reason, personal or mechanical, and suffer the most devastating, irrevocable transformation in a matter of seconds, scattering itself at ran-dom across the countryside?"[49]*

Mr. Williams, who passed away a few years ago, was a Harvard-educated, long-established *Soaring* magazine contributor with a decade's worth of well-regarded articles in our journal. It frustrated him that *Soaring* declined to pub-lish this one. They said it could appear to glorify the danger and make soaring pilots seem like thrill-seeking adrenaline junkies.

I understand. I served on the SSA's Board of Directors for ten years, much of that time as Vice Chairman. Soaring is not an "extreme sport" and the SSA do not wish it to be perceived that way by our members, by the public, or espe-cially by the FAA. Of the 30,000 licensed glider pilots in this country (fewer than a third of whom are active members of the SSA), only half a dozen die each year in accidents. Still, our goal is zero fatalities, which we pursue by encourag-ing training and safety programs. That said, you don't need a Ph.D. in psychol-ogy to realize soaring fascinates some (though not all) pilots, not despite the modest risk, but precisely *because* of it.

Ted found another outlet for *Crossing the Bar* in *Gliding International*, a small magazine then from Belgium. I enjoyed it, not only because it featured my father, but also because of Ted's insight into why many of us fly.

In the 38 years since Ted's article, however, my thoughts have evolved and grown more nuanced and, some might say, more mature. I'm not alone. The machismo in the competitive arena years ago is no longer entertaining, nor is pushing the edges of the envelope indiscriminately. Ironically, it was Karl Striedieck who laughed at a seminar a few years ago that there's less testos-terone in our sport than in the old days. It could be the retirement of the ex-World War II pilots who dominated the scene when I was coming up. Or per-haps it's the rising average age in gliding. Another aviation aphorism is:

---

[49] Williams, Edward P., "Crossing the Bar," *Gliding International*, February-March 1983.

"There are old pilots and bold pilots, but no old, bold pilots."[50]

The potential consequences of flirting with marginal risks are too cataclysmic. Walking up to the brink and peering over the edge for a thrill? Maybe. Leaping into the void, hoping somehow to survive? No way.

Competitive soaring is not a deadly struggle between two conflicting philosophies of life, or between right and wrong. We do not fly sailplanes for the same reasons others make speeches, rally supporters; form alliances; mount election campaigns; conduct political intrigues; negotiate feverishly; build armies; stockpile weapons; go to war; sacrifice lives; award medals; author poems; and build monuments to glorify fallen heroes. Soaring is an obscure sport, not a cause.

Neither is it a video game, all special effects and exaggerated violence with the ability to click "Pause" or "Play Again." The risks are real. And the consequences can be devastating and permanent.

Flying is still enormous fun for me, with as much romance and seductive fascination as ever. I concede that were it somehow to become risk free, it would no longer have quite the same appeal. But years ago, I renounced my adolescent illusions about a noble demise. Likewise, any naïve notion of staring death in the face is well behind me.

There are no glorious deaths in our sport. Whether a pilot bows out going for the win in the crucible of national competition or through a senseless error on a weekend fun flight, his or her death leaves family and friends grieving.

Danger will always lurk. Risk is a part of aviation, as it is a part of life. I have abundant confidence in my abilities as a pilot. I maintain what I believe is an objective assessment of my limits. Like Superman Chris Reeve, I am possessed of an unyielding resolve never to extend myself beyond them.

My understanding of soaring's risks increased slowly and unevenly over the years as it evolved from *"the most dangerous part of soaring is driving to and from the airport"* to *"soaring is the riskiest thing I do."* For a long time, I have agreed with what world soaring champion Bruno Gantenbrink of Germany addressed in a widely hailed speech over a decade after my father's death, viz., for competitive soaring pilots, driving to and from the airport is *not* the most dangerous part of the day.[51]

---

[50] Attributed by various sources to E. Hamilton Lee, early airmail pilot who rose to become United Airlines' most senior captain when he retired.

[51] Gantenbrink, Bruno. "Safety Comes First," originally published in *Aerokurier*, February 1993, downloaded from https://www.dg-flugzeugbau.de/en/library/safety-comes-first

The second question is more pointed: would I have continued to fly if I had been more aware of soaring's risks when my daughters were young, when losing their father would have been devastating? That's a difficult question. My current understanding of soaring's hazards was not an epiphany. Rather, it was a gradual realization that occurred in recent years, partly as a result of working on this book. But I've been selfish about flying my entire adult life, so I suspect I would have flown then as I still do now. But who knows?

And the third question: how would I react as a parent if one or both daughters wanted to learn how to fly gliders? I could dodge this since neither one has ever shown interest in flying. But if a young person were interested in soaring, I would encourage the parent to discuss with the child what is involved. Soaring is not inherently dangerous, but there are risks, just as there are risks in other sports parents allow their children to participate in, for example, American football, lacrosse, ice hockey, and motocross. My daughters were deeply involved in competitive synchronized skating during their school years. One suffered a concussion in a fall on the ice while the other had her knee stitched up after being badly slashed by another skater's blade.

If a parent is considering allowing their child to fly with a soaring club or commercial operation, they should vet it. This includes looking at their safety record, written operating and training procedures, the quality of their gliders and towplanes, and, most important, the attitudes of everyone involved.

You don't have to be an expert to evaluate safety in an unfamiliar sport. Use common sense, don't be afraid to ask questions, and trust your instincts.

Journal Entry: March 15, 2009 (Lake Hopatcong, New Jersey)

It's cold (45°F), but excitement is high for our high school's newest (club) sport: rowing. One of my freshmen daughters has been working out with them in the gym and tank but today is their first ever on-the-water practice. The young coach is directing the two crews as they put their narrow four-person shells in the water, gingerly climb in, and ease away from the shore.

The parent organizers have purchased used boats, trailer, and launches, and hired a young coach. Knowing little about rowing, I've assumed our daughter is in good hands. But when I stroll over to peer at the big transport trailer, I'm shocked to see a Class 1 trailer hitch (load limit 2,000 lbs.) on the pickup truck they use. No one knows what the trailer weighs, but with the heavy plywood improvements they've added, we estimate it's at least 3,500 lbs. I suggest, diplomatically, they might want to upgrade the hitch. Their response: "Well, it's worked fine so far." Now I'm uneasy.

In perfect concert with my anxiety, shouts erupt on the shore. Someone on the water with a mobile phone reports an emergency. Parents race to the backup launch, but it refuses to start. No one thought to test run the motor. Worse, we see that in the coach's eagerness to chase her boats, she left the fire extinguisher, life jackets, exposure blankets, and paddles on the dock.

About half a mile out on the lake, the coach had shut off the outboard motor to allow shouting instructions. In the restart, flames erupted. Panicking, she leaped into the 40°F water, shrieking from the near-freezing cold. Her young assistant calmly closed the gasoline shutoff valve to extinguish the flame. But he could barely haul the flailing and now hypothermic coach back into the launch. Without paddles (and with her shivering), the two of them had to splash ashore using their hands. The two shells—crewed mostly by neophytes—returned safely thanks to a few calm and experienced rowers.

We learned the team had received little guidance about the conditions except to dress warmly and stay with the boat if it capsized. Unfortunately, most were wearing cotton sweatsuits and no hats, useless if they had gone in the water. If one shell had capsized (uncommon but possible), the time of effective mobility in 40°F water would have been 10 minutes or less. After that, the kids would have been unable to hold on to floating oars or the shell or anything else. I learned most clubs would have postponed training in these conditions.

A club email humorously described the incident as a "perfect storm" of minor glitches. Even allowing for the desire to reassure parents, this struck me as disingenuous. My request that they convene a formal safety meeting to review the incident and address deficiencies in safe practices was politely declined.

To our daughter's credit, she recognized the attitude problem and quit the team. A soaring friend also involved in rowing was shocked by the club's casual disregard for safety before and after the incident. The eager-but-undisciplined coach didn't last, and the club's season proceeded without further drama. Lax safety practices don't insure disasters. But when things go wrong, they can make the difference between a successful recovery and a tragic outcome.

There's risk in everything we do. Our task is to manage those risks intelligently. Most soaring clubs and commercial operators do that, but parents should make their own assessment.

CHAPTER SIXTY-TWO

Love Story

COMPETITIVE SOARING IS LIKE AN ILLICIT DRUG. It doesn't make my problems disappear. It just allows me to forget them for a while.

For me and many other pilots, romantic relationships often top the list of problems. The overwhelmingly male aviation world is rife with jokes comparing women unfavorably with airplanes. Whether you think these are amusing (as most men do) or childish and insulting (as I suspect most women do), they're revealing for what they say about how some male pilots are challenged (read: threatened) interacting with the women in their lives.

- Airplanes come with manuals to explain their operation.
- Airplanes don't mind if you look at other airplanes.
- Airplanes don't comment on your piloting skills.
- Airplanes don't care how many other airplanes you've flown.
- "When I'm inside my airplane, *I* am in control!"

I admit to chuckling at these (sorry) even as I know they don't reflect reality. Yes, that's hypocritical. But I've learned that similarly unflattering comparisons of men vs. aircraft exist from a female perspective:

- Airplanes don't stare at your chest when you're flying.
- An airplane is happy to be flown only by you.
- Your airplane and you always arrive at the same time.
- An airplane doesn't think it's the only airplane in the sky.
- You never have to listen to an aircraft planesplaining how to land.

To some men, flying is a demanding diversion that appeals partly because it offers a beguiling escape from interacting with women in healthy relationships. For a man threatened by strong women or reeling from a painful past or insecurities, an aircraft can seem like a welcome companion.

* * *

There have been times—most often when my personal life has been a shambles—when flying has been my refuge. My sailplane has sometimes seemed like the partner who inspires me to greatness and who is there to support me in my struggle, whether in glory or disgrace. She has accommodated my whims and forgiven my every error—while making few demands. I know this bargain is flawed and is far less rich than one involving an equal partner. But it is a bargain many of us embrace.

My sailplane has sometimes played the role of a mistress who responds— happy and uncomplaining—no matter how I look or what I am wearing or how well-spoken or funny or spontaneous or polite or insensitive or ill-mannered I am. I confess it is then, wounded by failings in my relationships, that I know with my sailplane I can be the best pilot, the best person I can be and never worry if that is enough.

Unlike with the women in my life, I never fear being rejected by my glider. I am never emotionally at risk, at the mercy of her feelings for me. In this "relationship," my attentiveness may wane temporarily or for longer periods, but I never fret that my sailplane's fondness for me has diminished. Conversely, if another pilot ogles my glider with appreciation or ill-disguised envy, I am never jealous or threatened she might leave me for him (or her).

Compared to an awkward reunion with a woman from my past, I can slip into my sailplane's cockpit after a prolonged absence and enjoy the instant rapport as she responds to me as surely as a comfortable dance partner or long-term lover. In that way, I can celebrate the same oneness with her in which I have delighted since our first flight 30+ years ago.

Compared to interacting with women, flying is just so *easy!*

Without saying a word, I am assured my sailplane knows my depth of caring for her. I can confess my innermost thoughts and desires with unreserved candor, untroubled that I might offend her or discomfort myself. Conversely, I am free to express impatience or unhappiness or anger without hurting or alienating her. No matter what I thoughtlessly do or say in the heat of a stressful flight, my glider never judges or grows angry or holds grudges. This is self-indulgent of me, but sometimes I just want to vent without repercussions.

I can cancel an important flying outing and disappoint no one but myself. If I forget a meaningful date on the calendar—for example, 25 years, the silver anniversary of my sailplane entering my life in 1992—she will not be upset or cross. Yet, disingenuously, I can lust after and even fly other sailplanes with no angst over unfaithfulness, and never fear my glider will be wounded or jealous.

To be blunt, with my glider—in contrast with the women I hold dear in my life—I am free to be unapologetically selfish. In those ungracious moments, I can focus entirely on pursuing *my* desires and *my* joy in the most shameless, narcissistic, guilt-free way.

My glider gives of herself unstintingly. So long as I do not clumsily mishandle her, exceed the limits set by her designer, or ask her to do things impossible under the laws of physics or aerodynamics, she will not complain, protest, or rebuke me. When she moans, it is not from pleasure, but from being flown excessively fast. It is then, if we venture too close to the edge, she informs me she is *in extremis*. When turbulence thrashes us violently, she makes known the pain she is under and the risk I am recklessly incurring. Even then, she will attempt to do my bidding, never questioning my skill or motives.

Whatever it might say about my willingness to share, with my glider, I always take the lead. Morbidly, were I ever to lose all hope and wish to end my life, she would unhesitatingly sacrifice herself to assist me.

We are an odd team. Because both of us are of a certain age, we are underdogs on the launch grid. Any success we enjoy is sweeter for that. Yet any failure reveals my shortcomings alone. I never lash out at her for these lapses, for I know they are mine and she gave all she had. This is not my generous spirit. Plainly said, I know her limits and am critical only of mine.

My sailplane and I have been together longer than I was married. I am fortunate to remain friends with Tanya, but our relationship is different. We are more distant, more removed from each other. Yet I am still as close to my ASW 24 as the day I first met her coming off the boat from Germany.

U.S. Air Force and Desert Storm vet Kim Ponders alludes to this in her perceptive book, *The Art of Uncontrolled Flight*:

> *"[Air Force Captain Annie Shaw] believed that the love of flying was like any other love affair, with its raw beginning, when the feel of an airplane's controls is enough to keep a pilot awake at night, and the building into routine, when a pilot learns the airplane's strengths and weaknesses, and then later still, when he begins to love them."*[52]

When my sailplane and I lift off behind the towplane and the earth falls away in those first few seconds of flight, I embrace her as a cherished partner, as if I have embarked with her on a quest for greatness. At age 72, I admit nothing has captivated and obsessed me for so long. The bargain that I and so many other male pilots have struck is imperfect. But given the ebbs and flows in my personal life, it has been good.

Of course, we can never consummate our relationship. My sailplane has a tragic flaw: she is inanimate. She is only a machine. However much she may warm to my touch on her perfect silhouette or react to my hands on her delicate-

---

[52] Ponders, Kimberley A., *The Art of Uncontrolled Flight* (New York: HarperCollins Publishers, 2005)

yet-responsive controls, or murmur to me as the air flows over her exquisite contours, she cannot talk or reciprocate or feel. She cannot celebrate or share the joy in my life, nor I in hers. She cannot counsel me when I am uncertain, reassure me when I doubt myself, or console me when I falter.

Is soaring a refuge from loneliness? Many pilots speak of flying in the same terms others reserve for falling in love, with a similar passion, obsession, ache, and even desperation. I've heard competitive female glider pilots express similar views, so I suspect this is not an exclusively male notion.

The intense flame of new love of a young man or woman swept away by passion and by the urgent desire to merge him- or herself with another person emotionally and physically cannot blaze with such luminosity forever. As time passes, it inevitably attenuates into something more modest, more comfortable, and more sustainable over a lifetime.

In contrast with this, however, the highs I experience with my sailplane are as dizzying, intoxicating, powerful, and pure as they were 30 years ago.

Sadly, so are the lows.

CHAPTER SIXTY-THREE

God

I NO LONGER MURMER A PRAYER WHEN I'M DESPERATELY LOW in my sailplane. It's not lack of faith. It just seems unlikely God would be inclined to make deals to help me score more contest points. I do, however, whisper a prayer of thanksgiving each time I'm plucked from a near-certain landing and carried aloft by a miracle thermal. I know there's a flaw in that reasoning. That's okay. I don't pretend to have it all figured out.

My quest to qualify for the Boston Marathon over nine years helped evolve the way I view individual success in the context of my faith. I wrote what I refer to as The Runner's Prayer, which I still repeat to myself before every marathon.

"Lord, thank you for this day and for the opportunity to share it with like-minded people. Please help us do our best and to be both proud of and satisfied with that. And bring us home safely to our family, friends, and loved ones at the end of the day. Amen."

It might seem ironic that my belief in God is stronger *because* of that terrible day in 1980 when my father crashed. As with anything relating to the spiritual or supernatural, no one can ever know for sure, whether fervent believer or inveterate atheist. As the cliché goes, that's why they call it faith. But I am more confident than before that a Higher Power plays a role in directing our lives.

This was a corroboration, not a battlefield conversion. I grew up in a religious household. My father dedicated himself to Christ and church and wasn't afraid to show that in his day-to-day life. I have been a Christian most of my life, though less demonstratively than my father. We three kids were exposed to as much religion as anyone outside of a seminary. We were a Christian family who took God for granted the same way we bought into the Procter & Gamble lifestyle: devotedly, obediently, and unquestioningly. When I ceased attending church regularly, it was because of expediency, not a crisis of faith.

Over time, I developed my own political and religious beliefs. My father was a staunch Republican. I consider myself socially liberal and fiscally conservative [which leaves me without a party these days]. Dad was a Southern Baptist. I am a Christian, but less concerned with dogma.

Like most believers, I had doubts. Does God exist? Does He answer prayer? Do things happen for a reason?

I believe I received a more affirmative answer to at least one of those questions during that exhilarating, demanding, and ultimately elegiac day with my father in 1980. This is a personal construct. Where I glimpsed a metaphorical fractal pattern and Guiding Hand, others might see coincidences. But I base my interpretation—and firm belief in a Higher Power—on an awareness of the implausibly correlated sequence of experiences that made our last flight unique:

- My father's uncharacteristically adept assembly of his ASW 20 that day. A non-event for most, this was an amazing, first-time accomplishment for him.

- Our unprecedented plan to fly together. Fearing he would slow us down, I agreed to it, anyway, this first (and only) time.

- His locating me seconds before my start gate run. There were several "gate" thermals with pilots climbing up before their starts, though Dad wouldn't have been able to read contest numbers without getting close. So he may have checked more than one thermal before he found me. If he hadn't arrived when he did, by even one minute, I would not have waited. And he would never have caught up.

- His following me through the start gate at high speed. This remains a fascinating mystery to this day. My marvelously overbuilt LS3 was almost impervious to flutter. Many early ASW 20s were vulnerable to it. I hit the top of the gate at redline speed or more. Yet at the first thermal down the course line, there he was. Dad must have blasted through the gate at the same altitude and velocity as I did, something he was usually unwilling to do and that put his aircraft at risk.

- All the aspects of our extraordinary flight together throughout the long day, including his ability to keep up. My father was a good follower, but I usually eased away from him in both practice and contest flights. He was particularly astute in choosing not to follow me when I was too aggressive going into the first turnpoint and nearly landed.

- The extended private run across 70 miles of Southwestern Ohio on the second leg with George Moffat, the pilot we had followed vicariously since he was breaking through 15 years earlier. The singularity of this encompasses not only the honor of flying with the champion we had cheered for so many times. More important, my father had a front-row seat as I went head-to-head with George and, on that specific day, came out on top by a tiny margin.

- Our low-altitude rendezvous at Deer Creek Lake after having separated after Pickaway County Airport, 15 miles back. Pilots had scattered, and I had not seen PG for close to half an hour. He could have followed me, though I think I would have seen him circling below in those earlier slow climbs. He appeared out of nowhere, passing under me on a heading that was over 90 degrees off course and substantially lower. Why hadn't I spotted him in my sweeps of the area looking for other gliders? Did he see me from afar or just appear there serendipitously?

- Spotting his sailplane gliding beneath me, despite assuming I was alone.

- A few circles later, glancing out from precisely the right point, enabling me to track the progression of the crash from start to finish before it disappeared behind me as I continued the turn. If his accident sequence had begun a few seconds earlier or later, I would not have been able to view it in its entirety, or even at all, and would have flown on, oblivious.

- After witnessing the crash, sacrificing my competitive position to land, even knowing I could not help the unknown pilot.

- My brother Mark impulsively driving from Dayton to Springfield in his business suit that afternoon and stationing himself by the retrieve telephone at the perfect moment to take my call.

- My girlfriend Kathy's pre-arranged flight into Ohio that night that placed her there in the hour I most needed her.

I'm not an expert on multivariate probabilities. But I believe the likelihood of these events occurring within nine hours on the same day structured around my father's death—even though some are related—transcends coincidence. This may not be the conclusive proof of a Divine Being man has sought, in vain, for thousands of years, but it's good enough for me.

I realize this sounds self-serving. It is what I *want to* believe. Those in a different place spiritually might go further and say it is what I *need* to believe.

Regardless, for me, it satisfies one of humanity's oldest yearnings. At some level, whether we embrace religion or place our trust in karma or fate or destiny, many of us wish to believe in a purpose or a pattern to life. Good shall be rewarded. Evil shall be punished. What goes around, comes around. Our joys and sorrows are not arbitrary or capricious but are part of a plan. If we are good, if we are faithful to our Higher Power or belief system, and we are in need of help, we may receive it, not randomly, but by the hand of a Supreme Being or Force.

Each night, I say a prayer thanking God for all the ways I've been blessed. I try not to obsess over things I've never had or once possessed and then lost.

I'm not uncompromising about the form my faith should take. I'm a Christian. But I've had some interesting exchanges with Muslim friends. One was amused over my surprise at his open-minded attitude:

"We all worship the same God," he smiled tolerantly.

Who am I to disagree? I'm down with saying God exists and there are many ways of worshipping Him—or Her. I don't presume to have exclusive insight.

I am also untroubled my faith may be congruent with one of man's most fundamental needs. I believe the events at the U.S. Nationals on June 19, 1980, were not random and some Higher Power was choreographing them.

My biggest question—one that will not be answered in this life—is "why?"

CHAPTER SIXTY-FOUR

Pretentious Psychobabble?

O NE ATTRIBUTE OF SUCCESS is learning from our mistakes and moving on. No regrets. No obsessive second-guessing.

I will admit this is not my forte. In the past, I've wasted too much time compelled to redeem myself. But in soaring (and running), what did I have to prove? Why was I driven to validate myself before the tribunal of public opinion? Experts say successful pilots have ample self-confidence and egos. I had the ego part nailed. Why did my assurance and self-confidence waver?

Then I stumbled across the theory of "precarious manhood" advanced by University of South Florida Professors Jennifer K. Bosson and Joseph A. Vandello.[53] As I understand it, precarious manhood is based on two notions.

- First, unlike the passage from girlhood to womanhood, a male's transition to manhood isn't primarily physical. It involves earning an elusive *social status* through displays of courage, strength, endurance, and dominance.

- Second, manhood, like other types of social status, is *"tenuous (it must be demonstrated repeatedly through [publicly verifiable] actions)."*

Under this framework, achieving manhood is neither biological nor ritualistic (e.g., the Jewish *bar mitzvah,* when a boy becomes responsible for his actions). For most of human history, rites of passage delineated the transition to manhood. Today, these have all but disappeared. I never faced violent sports; painful tribal initiations; bootcamps; or military service, much less combat. I was deemed to be a man by legislative fiat during the Vietnam era when the voting age dropped to 18 from 21 and many states' drinking ages aligned, reasoning anyone old enough to die for his country was old enough to vote and drink.

Today, manhood is not a highly evolved state men reach after completing an arduous journey. *[Skeptical women may opine that most men never reach a highly evolved state!]* Nor is it a permanent distinction, e.g., a university degree or knighthood. Manhood, like a hard-won social status or a #1 ranking in sport, is difficult to achieve but easy to lose, as when a man is defeated in sports,

---

[53] Vandello, Joseph A.; Bosson, Jennifer K.; Cohen, Dov; Burnaford, Rochelle M. and Weaver, Jonathan R., "Precarious Manhood," *Journal of Personality and Social Psychology,* v. 95, issue 6, 2008, p. 1325-1339

politics, business, or romance, or cannot provide for his family.

Men, especially pilots—like to show off. Precarious manhood could help explain what drives us to do so. It's also been linked to toxic masculinity, the cultural pressure on men to be über-aggressive even when it is self-destructive and harmful to society.

This concept could help explain much of my adult life. Many early challenges involved flying: my first solo; my first contests; my modest first victories; even my landouts. So in situations when I feared my identity as a respected soaring pilot was threatened, might I have felt anxious about my manhood?

Or, in my yearning for a unifying theory of my life, was I overreaching? I recalled a night flight 40+ years ago in TWA's First Class cabin. After the lights dimmed, I eavesdropped as a smooth-talking passenger coaxed an attractive flight attendant to allow him to read her palm.

Passenger: [very deliberate, inspecting her hand in some detail, then looking up] "I see you have some anxiety in your life."

Flight Attendant: [suspicious, leaning back slightly] "Well, sure."

Passenger: "And this line here [tracing her palm lightly with his forefinger] tells me it might have something to do with a relationship?"

Flight Attendant: [reacting to his touch and/or the idea, leaning forward a bit] "Maybe..."

Passenger: "It's someone close to you—your family? [no response] Maybe a romantic relationship."

Flight Attendant: [voice catching, eyes widening] "Yes, my boyfriend!"

Passenger: "See this line that forks into two smaller lines? You have a decision to make [she breathes in a sharp intake]. Or perhaps things are different now than they were before?"

Flight Attendant: [leaning forward eagerly, agitated] "Yes, yes, how did you know?"

This guy was good. He kept her spellbound for 20 minutes, teasing out her entire life story while convincing her that from the creases in her hand, he could read her future—or at least the next few hours with him after we landed. But the real secret to his success was *telling her things she wanted to hear.*

Was precarious manhood something *I* wanted to hear? Years ago, I might have laughed at the idea. But given the role of competitive soaring and marathon running in my self-worth, I now concede there might be something to it. With so much of my identity accruing from those activities, successes would buttress it. Failures would threaten it. It follows that one of the reasons I have continued to fly might be that I *need* it, and the continued validation of self-worth it provides.

After all, how many heroic acts are driven by fear of embarrassment or being labeled a coward? How often does bravery arise from an ignoble lust for glory? How much does the pursuit of excellence or an admirable will to win owe to the drive to dominate others? Does it really matter?

It would be dangerous to assume all men's minds work the same way. Yet I suspect many are influenced subconsciously by the forces of precarious manhood, bound to the relentless pursuit of repeated affirmations of their masculinity in business or sports or the arts or with the women in their lives.

One study focusing on pilots makes the linkage with aviation explicit:

Pilots, particularly young males, take up flying for reasons closely allied to feelings of identity and masculinity. The anxiety of guilt arising from their own shortcomings is deep-rooted and strong. For young males, proof of manhood is a more important requirement than safety.[54]

I wish I had been more aware of this earlier. I might not have been able to change the way I acted. But it could have made the second half of my life more explicable—and less stressful—as it threatened to unravel.

---

[54] Murray, Stephen R., "FACE: Fear of Loss of Face and the Five Hazardous Attitudes Concept," International Journal of Aviation Psychology, 9(4):403-11, February 1999.

CHAPTER SIXTY-FIVE

Full Circle

"IF I CAN'T WIN HERE, I CAN'T WIN ANYWHERE." I was at my old club, CCSC, for the 2019 Standard Class Nationals, 54 years after I soloed and 39 years after my father crashed. This was still "home turf" for me, but I was less cocky—and less entitled—than I had been in 1980.

The whole idea of holding a major contest in Ohio in August was questionable. The weather is closer to South Georgia than Southwest Texas: i.e., hot, humid, weak thermals, low cloudbases, poor visibility, thunderstorms, and stationary fronts. But there was no choice. Torrential spring rains had flooded the area and gliderport and forced postponement from the original date in June.

I had envisioned having to explain who I was at CCSC. Despite growing up here, I'd visited only a few times since leaving in 1983 and not at all in 14 years. But many times I introduced myself to strangers who grinned and said they remembered me from the early days. Diane drove over from her home in Oxford, Ohio, several times in another reminder of a previous life.

The clubhouse fireplace had a small brass plate with the name of the club member who spun to his death a few hundred yards away while my brother and I watched, horrified, the year after Dad crashed. Tucked away on a high shelf was the dusty perpetual trophy dating from the 1940s—with the Bendix Corporation as the sponsor[55]—for our old Wright Memorial Glider Meet. It held many illustrious names, including A.J. Smith's six times. Mine appeared five times, first in 1975 when my father and I won it as a team. I had history here.

As in 1980, I might never have a better chance to show. I was flying well. It was a small field. And I was more familiar with the contest arena than anyone.

At first, the weather surprised us, more like June than August, with two solid contest days. Then two days of rain, then another good day. We only needed one of the last three days to make it official. But the forecast was discouraging.

I was in fifth place. I'd flown well but too conservatively (shocking!). I wasn't losing sleep over it, but I knew I could improve.

Twice we'd flown west far enough to glimpse the old Richmond Municipal Airport where I learned to fly. From a distance, it looked frozen in time, the

---

[55] The original "Bendix Trophy" of aviation history was first awarded to the winner of a transcontinental air race from Burbank, California to Cleveland, Ohio, in 1931.

same as it was in 1965, like Brigadoon, the mythical village in the Scottish highlands that reappears once every 100 years for one day, perfectly preserved.

Richmond (Indiana) Municipal Airport, August 2019. Could just as well be 1965.

The next day, the weather reverted to the steamy reality of August in Ohio.

Journal Entry: August 29, 2019 (CCSC Gliderport, Waynesville, Ohio)

It's a hot, humid survival day: low cloudbases, weak lift, a short day that will start late and end early. This plays to my strengths, but the narrow altitude band is risky. We sit and swelter while the sniffer flails around. Finally, we launch late on a small polygon around CCSC with close-in turnpoints.

I have trouble climbing high enough for a start and am one of the last to leave. I'm alone the entire flight, glimpsing few other gliders ahead. Thermals are difficult to find and center, but I keep moving. I get a little low at the second turn, recover, then get even lower after a long glide into the third turnpoint. I shift into survival mode and work a desperation thermal at near-landing-pattern altitude. I don't care about climb rate. I need to stay aloft. It takes a while before I'm moving again.

I saw the leader up high a few minutes ago. The radio suggests two pilots ahead of me in the standings have landed out or failed to get away from the airport at all. The name of the game today is staying airborne.

But the poor weather is getting even softer, and I know the day will quit soon. I need to stay high—while still moving. After the fourth turnpoint, I climb, then cut across the course line to reach the only clouds in range. A few miles short of the CCSC gliderport, I circle up slowly, the audio variometer beeping reassuringly as I near the top. I have two options. The sure thing is to put down at CCSC, only five miles straight ahead. This avoids a retrieve, but I'll earn points for distance only, no speed points.

The more aggressive option is to continue past CCSC to tag the fifth turn-point, then double back for a proper speed finish. This will entail a 19-mile final glide—twelve miles out and seven miles back. It's marginal. I'm showing 500 feet over an ideal maximum-performance glide. That's *not* guaranteed. And there's no assurance there will be any more thermals in the placid, hazy, late afternoon sky.

One risk is finishing below the 700-foot hard deck of the finish cylinder, with a penalty. An even worse risk is falling short of CCSC entirely. The previous contest day, as I flew through long stretches of murderous sink, I'd watched 1,000 feet of safety altitude spin off dizzyingly in the last dozen miles of what should have been a conservative final glide. If that happens today, I'll be in a farmer's field short of the finish.

Decision time. This thermal is weakening, and the wind is drifting me in the wrong direction. CCSC is tempting me ahead in the sunlight. Most pilots in my class are landing out. I'm far enough behind the leader that even a speed score won't catapult me over him unless he lands out, and that's unlikely. I have no crew. Maybe I should do the sensible thing.

"No, damn it!" I swear. "That's been your problem for years."

Snippets of memories from my flight on that pivotal day at the 1980 Nationals in Springfield remind me of the way I used to fly: analytically, aggressively, taking intelligent risks, pushing where it made sense. Since 1980, however, too many times, my strategy has been to minimize the risks of getting low and landing out. This works well back East, where my cautious style often pays off, where scrambling to finish the task when others stumble or give up can be more important than speed. What's missing—as my results in Texas last year reminded me—is the aggressiveness I had when I was younger, *before I started flying too often like my father.*

Today it's down to one decision: turn in for the sure thing at CCSC or pass it by and go for the turnpoint at Lebanon-Warren County, accepting the risk I might not make it. I recall my commitment before this contest:

"Fly to win, even if you don't."

I know how. I've known *how* since 1980. I just suck at executing. Forty years ago, I wouldn't have hesitated. I recall Robert's comment a few years later:

"You were really good."

I *had* been good. Now I'm angry at myself for wavering. F**k it! I level the wings and set course for the turnpoint at Lebanon-Warren County Airport, watching the runway at CCSC slide by under my right wing.

As feared, at once I'm in sinking air. The variometer needles flick down for disconcertingly prolonged periods as the audio output moans. The sink isn't strong, but it persists, bleeding away my safety altitude with every mile. Flying into the wind, the distance ticks off slowly on the glide computer screen, skimming down lower all the while. My cushion over final glide has shrunk from 500 to 400 to 350 feet. A few miles later, another 150 feet evaporate. I consider turning back to CCSC, out of sight behind me but *right there* if I do a 180. There's aggressive—and then there's stupid.

This is reminiscent of Day Three at Springfield back in 1980, when Lebanon-Warren County was the upwind turnpoint. Back then, I was desperate to tag it and turn downwind for the second turn at Pickaway County, 68 miles distant. Once again, I'm frantic to tag it and head downwind, this time aiming at the finish at CCSC, less than eight miles away.

In 1980, I nearly landed doing this. Twenty-five years later, at the 2005 Nationals, I *did* land here, turning back in the early evening after being too low to glide to CCSC. I watch the runway and hangars drawing closer. Which will it be today: 1980's success, or 2005's failure?

In the long glide upwind at 60 knots, it takes forever to reach the one-mile-radius turn cylinder. The stress grows with each interval of sinking air. The GPS flight computer is counting down the distance remaining and updating the altitude margin, declining at a depressing rate. I can see scattered cu, but nothing near the course. And they've been unreliable all day. If I divert to a cloud and it doesn't work, I won't make it to CCSC. My best chance is a quick tap on the edge of the turn cylinder and a desperation glide home.

I zoom the GPS screen in all the way. As the glider icon enters the one-mile circle around the Lebanon-Warren County airport, the screen paints an "x" for a single fix inside the cylinder. I'm already pulling up smoothly into a 180-degree turn to reverse course for CCSC. My margin over a best glide path in still air has shrunk to less than 100 feet.

But this isn't still air. The direct route to CCSC is right back through the same subsiding air I traversed to get here. Sure enough, areas of sink continue to nibble away at my safety margin. Flying slower, the wind at my back, I'm coasting along, pulling up delicately in rising air too dispersed to allow circling, then pushing over again to regain speed.

Five miles out and low, I know that without lift, I will finish below the "hard deck" floor of the finish cylinder, with a penalty. In the old days, there was no hard deck. The floor of the finish gate was the ground. Falling short on a marginal final glide could bring a pilot to earth a mile or less from the airport, with the risk of a last-second off-airport landing. I'd had a few of those.

I'm lower, but I'm also drawing closer: "Juliet Bravo, four miles, low."

I fly through more sink and accelerate to get through it. Briefly, I consider my options if I'm forced down before the finish. The harvest is weeks behind schedule because of the wet spring, so the fields visible ahead, not much more than 1,000 feet below me, still have crops. Most are high corn, which will damage the glider as the ears of corn slam into the wings and tail at 45 knots, not to mention the inevitable ground loop. Two days ago, on a rain day, I scouted several fields at the base of the hill below the gliderport (on a 20-mile pre-marathon training run). But if things go wrong, I won't have much altitude to set up a landing.

I fly through a few seconds of rising air and ease back on the stick to pull up, then push over to continue. The gliderport is still high in my canopy. I'll be below the 700 feet minimum finish height for sure, but I'm more confident I can reach the airport. There's nothing more I can do.

The edge of the one-mile finish cylinder is looming. Again, I zoom in as the little glider icon draws closer. Seconds before I reach the edge, I ease back on the stick and coast up as high as I can without stalling. At minimum speed, slightly weightless, I float into the finish cylinder as if suspended by a thread, then push over to recover airspeed. It's difficult to get right. There's no tree line or fence or wire to clear, just a line on my computer screen 700 feet in the air.

Less than a minute later and disconcertingly low, I turn final in a tight pattern, drop the gear, and get the dive brakes out. As I roll to a stop, the tension of the 20-minute final glide dissipates. I'm swept up in the euphoria of a close finish. The rush never goes away! But this time I'm troubled by the threat of a penalty for finishing too low. That said, I see only one other Standard Class glider. I know other pilots had trouble. Is it possible?

It is! The current leader and I are the only two to complete the task! I accept congratulations as we tow my ASW 24 back to its trailer. It's an amazing glider, underappreciated by everyone except me and good friend Hank Nixon, who helped me refinish it in the past few winters. I'm trying to keep my emotions in check while I email my GPS flight logs to the scorer.

Minutes later, a pilot walks over, peering at his mobile phone. "Hey, Juliet Bravo, you're in second place."

On final approach after finishing, Standard Class Nationals, CCSC, 2019. (photo by Bozena Michalowski)

I'm sure the corners of my mouth twitch as I absorb this and suppress my emotions, which range from "f**kin' A!" to "what could go wrong?" I feign casual disinterest. Then, as soon as he's gone, I grab my mobile phone and pull up the real-time scores. My whole body reacts. How great would this be? Okay, first place would be better, but I can't complain about second!

I respond the same way I did in 2008 when I won the day at Cordele. I question the result. My flight has vaulted me over three of the four pilots ahead of me into second place by a narrow margin over Hank Nixon. An excellent and consistent pilot and former national champion and member of the U.S. Team, improbably Hank landed out near CCSC, dropping from second place. He needed one more climb to get home. This time, the luck fell my way.

It's too early to celebrate. Within minutes, a seven-point penalty appears next to my name for finishing below the hard deck (by 25 feet—my low-G pull up erased most of the deficit). The last pilot to score will affect the formula and he hasn't turned in his GPS trace. So I could yet drop into third place. I've been on both sides of tiny-but-crucial point spreads that swing the final result. I'll deal with it no matter the outcome. Later in the evening, what I hope is the final version chops my margin over Hank to a single point.

One point out of almost 2,700 keeps me in second place. Three feet lower, and Hank and I would be tied. Lower still and I would drop to third. After four days of flying, only one point—less than 15 seconds—separates us.

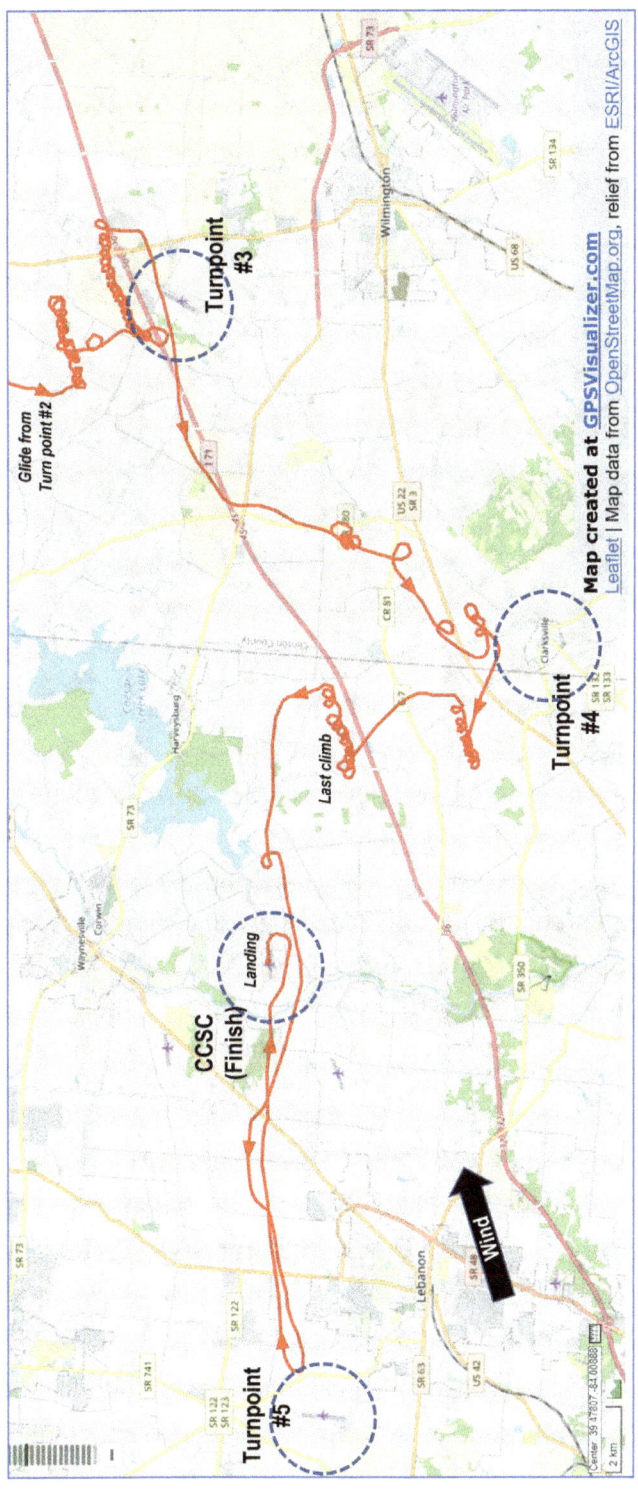

August 29, 2019, Standard Class Nationals: Last half of flight, from slow climb out at Turnpoint #3, tagging edge of Turnpoint #4, then last climb before long glide to tap Turnpoint #5 (Lebanon-Warren County Airport) and back to the finish at CCSC. (Map created at GPSVisualizer.com Leaf-let | Map data from OpenStreetMap.org, relief from ESRI/ArcGIS)

I'm already receiving congratulations. Tomorrow's forecast is worse and most seem to believe the contest is over. I can't allow myself to be swept up. Today has been a fantastic surprise. With two more days of dodgy weather, can I overtake the leader if he stumbles? Can I hang onto second?

Launch grid at CCSC, 2019 Nationals (photo by Bozena Michalowski)

The next morning, we assemble the gliders and stage them on the grid at noon. Apart from my being in second place at the U.S. Nationals for only the second time in 43 years, it's just another contest day.

A high school friend I haven't seen in 50 years stops by to visit. It's great to catch up, but I'm preoccupied. Later, she laughs and confesses she had no idea what was at stake. I guess I covered it well, or she was being kind.

The sniffer launches, struggles to stay aloft, and lands. The CD turns and scans the sky, hesitates, then raises his handheld radio and orders him to launch again. Thunderheads are building in several quadrants. With storms threatening, no one seems keen to fly. After hours of sweating in the sun in the worst humidity of the contest, the CD concedes and cancels the day. We tow the gliders back and rush to get them in the trailers just before the rain.

The next day, with the identical conditions, forecast, and threatening sky, once again the CD cancels the day and declares the contest over. It's official.

Over the years, I had become accustomed to celebrating these bright, shining moments in my life alone, as when I qualified for the Boston Marathon in 2006 and in 2008 when I won a day at the U.S. Nationals. Here, too, there was no one from my family at CCSC with whom I could share being on the podium at a national contest for the first time in over 50 years.

At the awards ceremony, I accepted applause, the official SSA silver second-place medallion, and an etched glass trophy awarded by the organizers. I had won bronze medallions at national contests but never a silver. After four-plus decades, I could kick back and enjoy the sensation.

There was an eerie symmetry. On this last day in 2019, I had finished second for the day and second overall, the same as 43 years earlier on the kickoff day of my debut national contest, in Bryan, Ohio, 140 miles to the north.

If my life were a Hollywood screenplay, the nerve-wracking final glide to CCSC that culminated in a desperation lunge into the finish cylinder would have won the day and the contest by one point. But this was reality, not a movie, and second place was enough. Things had fallen my way, with the small field and the luck factor. I had paid my dues. So I relaxed, secure I deserved it, even by a single point.

That I had prevailed with an aggressive decision on the type of iffy day for which I was known was gratifying. It gave me confidence this might mark the conclusion of one chapter of my life and the beginning of another—even at 68.

On the nine-hour-plus drive back from Ohio, for once I didn't punish myself reflying my mistakes. It had been a while since I had mulled over the things I did *right!* Ninety minutes from home, I blew a tire on the trailer and damaged the wheel. I had to change it on a narrow stretch of Interstate 78, crouched over the jack and tire tools as heavy trucks slammed by at 70 mph, rocking the trailer and the van. I couldn't have cared less!

There were no stops at Deer Creek State Park. I knew I had all the answers I was ever going to get from there. A more complete understanding of June 19, 1980, will not come until I depart this earth.

Epilogue (2020)

A S I APPROACHED THE 1980 NATIONALS, I was proud of how far I had come from an introverted 14-year-old boy. I was on my way up and leading a charmed life while doing it.

In the years following the crash, I knew nothing about "precarious manhood." Yet there was a sense of starting over, haunted not so much by goals I might never reach, but by what I had already achieved—and lost.

But I was wrong. I'm more than the sum of my contest placings and marathon times and marriage and financial assets and other entries in the "wins and losses" columns of life. I've achieved most of my big goals. One goal that came a little later than others was helping raise two incredible daughters.

Children are a reflection of their parents. Fortunately, both girls take after Tanya in appearance! I hope I've helped raise them with the right values and with high self-esteem. I'm not critical of my parents, but Josie and Tina seemed to be more confident than I was growing up. They did it all in school, are successful in their careers, and seem to enjoy life in the bargain. When I reflect on the problems some parents have, I say a prayer each night for the blessing my two have been in my life and the role they still allow me to play in theirs.

So I'm much happier with myself now, with the totality of what and who I am, than I was in my prior life. I noticed it when I returned to soaring in 2014. Even a disastrous outing like the 2016 Nephi Nationals—where I botched the takeoff on the first day and flew the wrong task the last day to plummet in the standings—wasn't debilitating. And I'm more fulfilled in contests even when I make mistakes, provided I am flying well, learning, and enjoying myself.

It's possible, like my father, I've developed an "explanatory style" that allows me to blame my errors on factors beyond my control. Or I've accepted that I'm not perfect. Or maybe my manhood is not so precarious as it once was.

I also consider what my friend Sarah Arnold, U.S. and World Gliding Champion, told me about not flying up to her standard at a national contest years ago, viz., for best results, she must stay in touch with what gives her joy and not think about contest points while flying. She admitted it's difficult [and might appear to be counterintuitive for a World Champion]. She also commented she is still working on it.

A competitor of her caliber giving me "permission" to enjoy myself even when things go wrong has helped liberate me to appreciate my contesting, and without taking the edge off my desire to excel. Does her possessing "mad skills" and a fierce desire to win unencumbered by the baggage of precarious manhood give her an advantage over male pilots? It's an interesting thesis.

Whatever the reasons, my life *is* different. There's more balance. Even after off days, I sleep better. I don't obsess about what I should have/could have done or what might have been. Likewise, the good days are more restrained. My finish at CCSC in 2019 didn't trigger the euphoric, lyrical response my first marathon or qualifying for Boston did. You could say I have more perspective.

But another reason for my more restrained reaction is that my emotions are more attenuated. The lows aren't as black, which is good. But the highs are also more subdued. Am I more mature? Or just emotionally scarred?

One upside for this "new me" is I'm not as driven to seek the approbation of others. I won't lie. I still value and enjoy their approval and acclaim (see happy photo from 2019). Who doesn't? I just don't *need* it the way I did for so long.

Standard Class Nationals 2019 (l to r) CD John Lubon, author, winner Tom Holloran, 3rd place Hank Nixon, Contest Manager Chuck Lohre. (photo from Chuck Lohre)

Of course, it's easy to say this coming off my best soaring performance ever and an encouraging marathon. "We'll check back with you next year, Chip," you might joke, challenging me. That's fair. But I know I'm happier.

* * *

Most of this book focuses on what soaring has meant to me. It's my book! Until recently, I hadn't dug deeply into what soaring meant to my father.

Joe Bearden was no larger-than-life, Hemingwayesque adventurer who operated on the edge. He was a conservative "by the book" player who lived within the lines. His was a modest success story, having pulled himself up into the middle class through hard work and devotion to his employer and God. While he enjoyed success throughout his life, he was more Everyman than exceptional: an honest, reliable, spiritual, and all-around good guy who made the most of his talents and was respected by many.

Soaring distinguished him from the masses, and he basked in that. I don't believe the risks of gliding were titillating for him. He was cautious to a fault. He spent too much time reassuring others that soaring was safe. I'm confident he genuinely believed the most dangerous part of soaring was driving to and from the airport. But I'm also sure he enjoyed being *perceived* by others as daring, and that this appealed to his ego.

He especially loved soaring contests. Competition had inspired him his entire life. I'm sure he harbored the conviction, until the end, that he would break through if only he kept at it. In his papers, I found numerous well-structured approaches to improve his soaring skills. He was like the weekend golfer who analyzes his scorecard: "If I hadn't hooked into the rough on 13, and dropped it into the water on 17, and if I'd made those easy putts on 5, 6, and 14, and if I could drive the way I did on the first few holes—well, I'd be a scratch golfer!" My father could analyze his failings in contests. He just couldn't eliminate them.

The concept of precarious manhood probably applied to him. Dad earned the elusive social status of manhood in his late teens, with the requisite public displays of courage, strength, endurance, and dominance in sports, and with the girls at his school. I'm sure soaring had the same appeal long after his days as an athlete were behind him, and in particular, as his business career stalled.

Did his desire to succeed in the cockpit prove to be his undoing? On June 19, 1980, did he somehow overreach, as Icarus hubristically flew too close to the sun? No. On that day, Dad did everything right—until the last seconds. I attribute his demise not to grasping beyond his abilities, but to falling victim to forces few of us understood very well then.

I believe Dad loved the act of flying as others love the crack of a bat as it hammers a baseball perfectly, or the thrill of a flawless golf swing off the tee, or watching a football settle into a receiver's hands after a textbook spiral. The origin of that fascination is still a mystery.

* * *

My daughter Tina was running with fellow Brooklyn Track Club members early in 2020 and related a few stories about my tumultuous running career, observing that I am still plodding away years after Lyme disease.

"Your dad sounds like a warrior," said one, less than half my age, graciously.

That's the way I'd like to be remembered, as someone who kept going despite being knocked down multiple times. I wasn't the best at anything. I wasn't always even particularly good. I certainly didn't live up to my early promise. But I never gave up. If, on my deathbed, I am assured my daughters will remember this about me as a role model, I will be able to move on in peace, knowing they understood and, perhaps, learned from me, and knew I was happy with this.

To the obvious question: yes, I have wondered whether I would have been as motivated to achieve certain goals if I hadn't been driven by my insecurities to prove myself repeatedly. I'd love to say yes. I have always held myself to lofty standards. But can we ever really know ourselves well enough to answer that?

* * *

One of the first music albums I ever bought—in vinyl LP format (I still own it!)—back in 1969, was *Bookends* by Simon & Garfunkel. The title song concludes with a sentiment many have expressed over the years: *"Preserve your memories; they're all that's left you."*[56]

I have so many wonderful memories, even more than I've documented here. There's one I've worked hard to preserve, even though my subconscious did its best to suppress it. It's the reason I sat at a small table in a Holiday Inn in Springfield, Ohio, before dawn 40+ years ago and scribbled down everything I could remember about my father's crash 12 hours earlier. It's the reason I've spent thousands of hours since then teasing out my recollections, reading and researching, talking and emailing with people, and building this story.

For all the life-changing impact June 19, 1980, had on me, the special memory I have is about flying with my father on what was, until the last tragic seconds, perhaps his finest day in the cockpit and unquestionably the greatest flight we ever shared. I'm not sure how I may feel as I approach the close of my life. But today, that's a memory I don't want to lose.

---

[56] Simon & Garfunkel, (1968) *Bookends* [vinyl album]. Capitol

IN MEMORIAM

As published in Soaring *magazine, October 1980. Used with permission.*

‖ IN MEMORIAM ‖

"... Here's a toast, to the host of the men
Who love the vastness of the sky . . ."
— Army Air Corps Song

On June 19, 1980, **Joseph N. Bearden, Jr.** of Cincinnati died in the crash of his AS-W 20 during the 15-Meter Nationals in Ohio. The accident occurred at the end of a long contest day during which Joe had been racing very fast over familiar terrain. Regardless of what the FAA may have to say, his family and friends believe that the causes of this accident will never be fully explained.

I concur with those friends of Joe who expressed the sentiment that, if he had had his druthers, this is the way Joe would have preferred to go, with his boots on. He was at the height of his business career, doing what he loved, competing in a national contest with A.J. and most of the old gang he had flown with since the days of the *Sisu*. All his family was nearby, and by a strange coincidence his son Chip was in the air close to him when he went down and was the first pilot to reach the crash site.

It is hard to sum up in a few words a person like Joe. He was the kind of man who inspired confidence, and his major responsibilities as administrator of the employee benefit programs at the Proctor & Gamble Company reflect the recognition of this trait by the business world. He was friendly, down-to-earth, intense, enthusiastic, an Alabama boy with a wide grin and a sophisticated business outlook. He devoted much energy to his family and his church. He was a good friend who was always giving support when it was needed most. A highly experienced and conservative pilot, a patient instructor, a tireless promoter of soaring in the Ohio Valley, he was never too busy to help a neophyte who was just starting.

Joe had been involved in soaring since the early 1960's and was a leading figure in the Soaring Society of Dayton and the Caesar Creek Soaring Club. He made numerous contributions to these groups as an officer and as a strong advocate of disciplined flight instruction programs. In addition to the time he put in as a regular instructor, it was characteristic of him to pass up hours of good soaring in his own sailplane to pitch in and give extra instruction to club members when the duty instructors were overloaded.

Contest flying was an important part of his life and he consistently did well, although he may have lacked that streak of recklessness needed to win a national competition. Soaring in Ohio will not be the same without him.

For his family — Thelma, Chip, Mark, and Diane — and his many friends throughout the country, I recall the words of Samuel Johnson, spoken in 1769:

"It matters not how a man dies, but how he lives".

— EDWARD PRESCOTT WILLIAMS

"In Memoriam" *author Ted Williams (l) with my father in Cincinnati, Ohio, March 1980, three months before the crash. (photo by Ted's daughter, Chantal Williams, from the estate of Joseph N. Bearden Jr.)*

RIP: SOARING PILOTS I HAVE KNOWN

1. **Doug Gaines** 1979 (41), crashed his ASW 17 on high-speed final glide during practice (FL). Possible cause: instability in modified elevator control.

2. *Joe Bearden** 1980 (53), low stall/spin at the Springfield, OH, 15 Meter Nat'ls in an ASW 20. Possible medical problem (dehydration).

3. **Mahlon Weir** 1980 (48), crashed near Hobbs, NM, in the Open Class Nat'ls in a new ASW 20. Possible medical problem.

4. *Al Levinson** 1981 (60), long-time Caesar Creek Soaring Club (OH) member. Cause: low skidding turn to base or final leading to stall/spin in a 2-32.

5. **Larry Rogers** 1984 (61), in his Ventus A. Collided with Karl Striedieck's ASW 20 entering a pre-start gaggle at 15 Meter Nat'ls, Ephrata, WA.

6. **Robert Robertson** 1986 (44), in his Ventus A. Slow, high-gross-weight tow from Middletown, NY, on a test flight.

7. *Alan Greer** 1991 (60), crashed while attempting to self-launch in Ventus CM on practice day at New Castle, VA, Region 4S contest.

8. **Bobby Bridges** 1992 (54), engine failure on takeoff at his airport in GA in new DG600 by high-time airline and experienced competition pilot.

9. **Klaus Holighaus** 1994 (54), crash in Swiss Alps by highly experienced sailplane designer/builder/competitor in his Nimbus 4. Cause: unknown.

10. **Mark Savage** 1997 (74), crash of BG-12A on tow to Ohio History of Flight Museum by experienced pilot/instructor. Cause: control system failure in an older homebuilt aircraft.

11. & 12. **Bill Ivans** 1999 (89), high-time competitor with co-pilot and FAA Administrator **Don Engen (**75, inflight breakup of Nimbus 4DM at Minden, NV. Cause: structural failure recovering from high-speed spiral dive.

13. **Clem Bowman** 1999 (52), experienced pilot on U.S. Team, crashed on takeoff of Genesis at Std. Class Nat'ls, Minden, NV. Cause: assembly error (horizontal tail not secured).

14. **Peter Masak** 2004 (46), stall/spin on ridge at 15 Meter Nat'ls, Mifflin, PA, by experienced competitor/designer/builder on U.S. Team in his Scimitar.

15. **Dick Johnson** 2008 (85), high-time, many-time nat'l champion, U.S. Team member, world record holder; inflight loss of control in his Ventus A, Midlothian, TX. Cause: possible medical problem.

16. **Chris O'Callaghan** 2010 (51), experienced competitor in Ventus 2 at 15 Meter Nat'ls, Uvalde, TX. Cause: head-on mid-air collision with another sailplane.

17. **Tim Gossfeld** 2012 (53); Ionia, MI, ASW 27, Region 6 contest, pre-start. Cause: low stall/spin in windy conditions.

18. **Joe Shepherd** 2015 (72), Moriarty, NM, experienced competitor in ASW 27, destroyed in crash. Cause: unknown; possible medical problem.

19. **Steven Coggins** 2019 (33), Uvalde, TX, JS1, crashed at the Uvalde Invitational contest, where he was flying with his father. Cause: unknown.

20. **Bill Hanson** 2019 (65), Blairstown, NY, LAK-17 FES destroyed in crash returning from a ridge flight, likely stall/spin. Cause: unknown.

*Crashes I witnessed.

NOTE: Details are based on my interpretation of accident reports and my limited knowledge of certain incidents and are subject to error. I intend no disrespect to any of these pilots.

ACKNOWLEDGEMENTS

So many people helped me bring this book to a conclusion:

- My family: my mother, Thelma; my brother, Mark; and my sister, Diane, who supported me, provided insights, and corrected my memories. My daughters, Josie and Tina, and my nieces, Melissa and Meredith Bearden, read drafts and suggested significant changes.

- My editors, Kristin Lucas—who did so much to help me reimagine the book and whose impact is embedded in nearly every page; and Jesse Coleman—who provided critical input on restructuring and style.

- Sarah Arnold, U.S. and world champion soaring pilot, a late "beta reader" who expressed enthusiasm for the book at a time when I was discouraged and thinking, (once again) of abandoning it. I will be forever grateful, Sarah.

- Erik Mann, good friend and another late "beta reader" who flattered me by confessing he had read close to 300 pages in 24 hours. True, he was a captive audience on a flight to the U.S. from Germany. But this was high praise from someone who has been rightly critical of my wordy style for years.

- My other "beta readers": Deborah Hust Allison, Martta Rose Kelly, Veronica Mager Ford, Bif Huss, and Mitch Hudson, friends from various facets of my life who made myriad helpful comments and recommendations.

- Bo Michalowski, good friend and esteemed soaring photographer, whose work I was honored to be allowed to display. Other photographers whose work I included are credited with their photos.

- Denise Layton, Executive Director of the Soaring Society of America, for allowing me to extract from *Soaring* magazine—and for asking her husband to drive with Tina to retrieve me in Hobbs in 2010.

- My high school friend, Barbara "Bobsey" Munyan Ardell, whose encouragement several years ago spurred me to carry on.

- Sharon Morrissey, an early reader whose initial enthusiasm and positive feedback helped sustain my energy at a low point in my life.

- The late Chris O'Callaghan, fellow contest pilot and writer who read an early draft of what became Part II and provided encouragement and suggestions.

- Last but certainly not least, my friend George B. Moffat Jr., "XX," twice world soaring champion, English teacher, and author, who read the same early draft of Part II and provided helpful criticism and flattering encouragement. George's legacy includes his impact on my life as a soaring pilot based on our flight together on June 19, 1980; our flying at Wurtsboro in the 1980s; and his input into what was still an article in 2006.

DEDICATION

Dedicated to the two people who have had the most influence and impact on my life over the past three decades: my twin daughters, Josephine Noel Bearden and Christina Alexiev Bearden. I have included their essays on soaring, written when they were much younger.

Josephine N. Bearden (at age nine)[57]

(with apologies to Josie, published as-is, endearing mistakes and all)

Two or three times a year I get to go to my dad's glider contests, and I love it! It's a very fun way for me and my family to spend a vacation.

On the morning of the trip we put all our things in the van, then we set off. Some of the drives were long, and some were short.

When we get there we pitch up the tent. Then we go back to the pavillion and say hello. Some of the people are new, but some we had known since I was a baby!

Later my sister and I usually make some friends. All day we laugh, play, and have fun! At night all the pilots gather in the pavillion for dinner.

The next day I usually go watch my dad take-off. Gliders can't take-off by themselves, so toe-planes take them up into the air. When all the planes are in the sky they go. The pilots all make different routes. They all come in different places too.

I think I'm lucky having a dad who flies gliders. I always love going to all the contests; it's the best place to be!

Christina A. Bearden (at age 17)[58]

I'm standing on the runway, staring out at the mirage created by the chart-topping temperatures this summer in Hobbs, New Mexico. Behind me are forty world-class gliders, worth an average $150,000. My dad has been a glider pilot for 45 years, and it's been a part of my life since I was a baby. The flying community addresses my sister and me as "the Bearden twins." If you've never seen a glider/sailplane, it's a sleek, white, fiberglass structure with a one-person cockpit and long, graceful wings. Ready for competition, gliders weigh 1,000 pounds or more even though they don't have motors. A plane tows the glider

---

[57] Josie writing about her experiences at the 2003 regional contest in New Castle, Virginia. Originally published as a sidebar to the report on the 2004 U.S. Standard Class National Soaring Championships in *Soaring* magazine, November 2004, and used with permission.

[58] Tina's college admissions Common App essay at age 17, a year after crewing for me at the 2010 Standard Class National Championships in Hobbs, New Mexico. Used with permission.

high enough where it can utilize thermals from the sun to gain elevation and glide around the course.

Although I've been a part of the flying community for years, I've never "run a wing" before. A glider only has one wheel, so the wing tip rests on the ground when it's not flying. Until the glider gets enough speed so the pilot can balance the wings with the controls, someone must run along holding a wing tip level. It's not especially easy, and it's a lot of responsibility. You can easily damage or drop the wing or, worse, steer the glider off the runway and into another plane or spectators.

It was the first day of the two-week National contest and pilots and crews were out on the line getting ready to launch. The line crew was getting complaints about their only wing runner. As I mentioned, I'm well known throughout the community. Someone asked if I'd ever run a wing before. They knew that I ran cross-country and track and needed someone who could keep up. I laughed nervously and told them I had only done it once before, for my father. My dad reassured me that I'd be fine and quickly gave me a few tips.

With the "Okay" from the operations director and pilot, I bent down to grab the wingtip and balance the wings. I needed to control my emotions. There was a lot of tension. My father's friend who used to fly jets in the Navy told us the launch line is a lot like an aircraft carrier deck with the noise and stress of launching every 60 seconds. I could not help thinking, "What if I drop the wing? Or hold it back and steer it off course?" I struggled to push them aside, but they vanished as the towplane roared and my feet started to move by instinct. I was running and the wingtip was still level in my hand in spite of the gusty desert winds. I was doing it!

Within a few seconds, just as I felt I couldn't sprint any faster, the wings balanced, and the wingtip flew out of my hand effortlessly. Relief. I slowed and jogged back down the runway to where the crew and remaining pilots waited. They gave me applause and the crew chief ran over to ask if I'd like to run for the rest of the contest. I, still in shock, laughed and politely agreed. After receiving a high five from my dad, I ran the wings of the majority of the pilots that day. Although the line crew had other wing runners, I became high in demand. I was a natural, and it was a great feeling to have a group of people who I've grown up around see me mature like this. To be able to run a wing and do it well is no small feat in the flying community.

I overcame my emotions and took on the responsibility. I cannot say this was easy, but I could not have asked for a better way to learn how to react in a situation where you are put on the spot. Although flying is mainly my dad's thing, it's a huge part of my life and has taught me life skills that I would have a hard time learning anywhere else.